TACKLING CHILD SEXUAL ABUSE

Radical approaches to prevention, protection and support

Sarah Nelson

First published in Great Britain in 2016 by

Policy Press
University of Bristol
1-9 Old Park Hill
Bristol BS2 8BB
UK
+44 (0)117 954 5940
pp-info@bristol.ac.uk
www.policypress.co.uk

North America office:
Policy Press
c/o The University of Chicago Press
1427 East 60th Street
Chicago, IL 60637, USA
t: +1 773 702 7700
f: +1 773 702 9756
sales@press.uchicago.edu
www.press.uchicago.edu

© Policy Press 2016

British Library Cataloguing in Publication Data
A catalogue record for this book is available from the British Library.

Library of Congress Cataloging-in-Publication Data
A catalog record for this book has been requested.

ISBN 978 1 44731 387 8 paperback
ISBN 978 1 44731 386 1 hardback
ISBN 978 1 44731 389 2 ePub
ISBN 978 1 44731 390 8 Mobi

Cover design by Double Dagger
Printed and bound in Great Britain by Clays Ltd, St Ives plc
Policy Press uses environmentally responsible print partners

Contents

Acknowledgements

I could never list all the people who helped and enabled me to write this book. My greatest debt is to all those sexual abuse survivors who over many years – as participants in my research, as colleagues or as friends – trusted me with their experiences and committed their ideas on what must change. They may not wish to be named but know who they are, and populate much of this book.

Over the decades I have drawn particular courage and inspiration from Norma Baldwin, Bea Campbell, Ross Cheit, Liz Davies, Marilyn Van Derbur, Emily Driver, Eileen Fairweather, Sandor Ferenczi, Lenny Harper, Judith Herman, Ann Jennings, Kathy Kerr, Jeffrey Masson, Laurie Matthew, Marjorie Orr, John Read, Florence Rush, Valerie Sinason, Rich Snowden, Roland Summit, Sara Swann, Sam Warner and Leslie Young; from Noreen Winchester and Audrey Middleton who launched this whole journey in Belfast; and from every professional – paediatricians, journalists, social workers, doctors, psychologists, psychiatrists, counsellors and others – who refused to keep quiet or abandon their commitment, in the face of vilification and damage to their own careers.

Lynn Jamieson – who has been a continuing support over many years – other directors and all staff at Edinburgh University's Centre for Research on Families and Relationships (CRFR) vitally supported and guided me through two research projects and this book. Many other people contributed to the book, through their discussions, their informed awareness, and generous sharing of ideas and experience. Extra thanks to – among others – Norma, Bea, Liz, Lynn, John and Laurie (again!), Sandra Buck, Malcolm Cowburn, Harriet Dempster, Ilene Easton, Darrell Fisher, Sandy Gulyurtlu, the late Janette de Haan, Sue Hampson, Martin Henry, Anne Houston, Norma Howes, Gordon Jack,

Alexis Jay, Ruth Lewis, Jan Moran, Annie Macdonald, Kirsteen Mackay, Jan Macleod, Carole Mallard, Joanna Moncrieff, Gill Ottley, David Pilgrim, Ethel Quayle, Jean Rafferty, Janine Rennie, Sara Rowbotham, Michael Salter, Julie Taylor, Alison Todd, Amanda Williams; and to many organisations, especially KASP, Open Secret, Say Women and the Women's Support Project, Glasgow. Any errors are mine!

I want to thank Isobel Bainton, Laura Greaves and all at Policy Press, Bristol, very much indeed for their continuing patience, wise words of advice and kindness over several years. My Edinburgh University office colleagues Richard McAllister, Stanley Raffel, Russell Keat and Roona Simpson sustained me with their humour and our lunches – while my daughter Rowan and all my personal friends put up with me far more, and for much longer, than I deserved.

Funding

I was unsalaried throughout while writing this book. Without the generosity of organisations and individuals in donating funding, it would have been impossible to carry out three years of work. Every donor trusted me to write whatever I wished. Many, many thanks to Children 1st; Rachel Chapple and the Real Stories Gallery Foundation, New York; 18 and Under; Sandra Brown and the Moira Anderson Foundation; Margaret Macintosh; NSPCC Scotland; Sue Robertson; Jan Souter; Sara Trevelyan; and every single person and organisation who contributed to my GoFundMe appeal in 2015 – an appeal organised by Professor Liz Kelly and Laura McBeth.

Introduction

It is more than 30 years since the first edition of my book, *Incest: Fact and Myth*, was published (Nelson, 1982). Since then vast numbers of books, academic research studies, media documentaries, press articles and online materials have been produced about child sexual abuse (CSA), and its effects throughout life. What can be the justification for yet another book?

First of all, the majority have been about intervention or therapy after the event, or personal perspectives on the impact of abuse, about overcoming it or failing to do so. Fewer concentrate – as this book aims to do – on primary prevention, protection and deterrence, or can visualise a society where CSA is drastically reduced. Fewer concentrate – as this book aims to do – on campaigning for change, and on proposing models for change.

Inevitable social problem or crime?

That is not to downplay the vital need for therapy and support after child sexual abuse, which still remain far too scarce or too expensive for most survivors, and indeed this book discusses those issues at several points. But CSA is a serious crime: not some unfortunate, ever-present disease from which we can only help children and adults to recover. In other serious crimes, greatest effort goes into convicting perpetrators and reducing opportunities for further crime. We do not tackle street violence by opening head injury clinics.

CSA is also a major public health issue, with serious consequences for mental and physical health. Vital advances in public health have come through prevention (such as the provision of clean water) and through eradication of serious diseases. We did not tackle diseases of poor sanitation by building

1

more fever hospitals. Placing the key emphasis on 'healing' can also lead to a comforting complacency. If children and adults can recover, perhaps CSA is not too serious? That reduces the impetus and funding for prevention and deterrence. And it clouds a harsh reality: that many courageous survivors of CSA will only ever make a partial recovery.

Much of the literature is thus heavily oriented towards a 'convalescence' model. This seeks effective ways of treating, counselling or healing child and adult survivors. The extent of this emphasis has been criticised by writers like Betty McLellan in her book *Beyond Psych-Oppression* (McLellan, 1995), and more sweepingly by the radical feminist Louise Armstrong. (Armstrong, 1990, 1994) She claimed women had been 'therapised' by a massive industry of individual healing, growth and recovery, which neutralised anger and the thirst for justice:

> In speaking out, we hoped to raise hell. Instead, we have raised for the issue a certain normalcy. We hoped to raise a passion for change. Instead, what we raised was discourse, and a sizeable problem-management industry. (Armstrong, 1990)

Retreat from progress

A key theme of this book is that we need an urgent wake-up call, against the complacent notion that we have achieved, and are achieving, continuing progress in protecting children and young people against sexual abuse. I contend that, despite child sexual abuse issues being so prominent in popular, professional and media discourse – in light, especially, of recent scandals about 'celebrity' abusers, in-care abuse and child sexual exploitation – in many ways progress in the UK has either been stationary or in retreat. Renewed public, professional and media awareness and concern about CSA is valuable and welcome. But we cannot build on these without admitting current failures, and without adopting and sustaining *different* ways of working in future.

Adult survivors still struggle to find trauma-aware services in a mental health system which remains dominated by medical models of mental illness; in a wider healthcare system which too often dismisses their chronic pain and disability as symptoms of tiresome 'heartsink patients'; and in a criminal justice system still reluctant to consider the bitter pathways which lead many abused young people into offending. While ever more sex offenders against children are being identified, there remains more hope than certainty that current sex offender programmes will prompt them to stop abusing.

As for sexually abused children, I believe their situation has barely improved in 25 years, in that most still remain undetected, unacknowledged or disbelieved.In one vivid example it was estimated in 2013 and 2014 that at least 1,400 vulnerable teenage girls were repeatedly raped, brutalised and degraded by sexual exploitation gangs in Rotherham. They had been treated by many in the police, social services and others with contempt and 'absolute disrespect', seen as consenting to their own exploitation (Williams, 2012a; Jay, 2014). Yet a full 15 years before, Sara Swann, through Barnardo's Streets and Lanes project in Bradford, had described exactly this process of grooming and abuse against very vulnerable young women. She had made absolutely clear to agencies that the young people were *victims* and indeed that there was no such thing as a child prostitute, only an abused child (Swann, 2000). So too did subsequent British legislation and guidance make these points clear. All were inexcusably ignored. It is not enough to say how shocking this has been. Supposedly caring professionals need to ask themselves at length why they ignored the suffering in front of them, and how this is going to change.

Indeed Professor Jay's powerful and distressing Rotherham Inquiry report brought to mind the remarks of the Report of the National Commission of Inquiry into the Prevention of Child Abuse back in 1997, that

> Despite a series of wideranging, well-publicised and expensive inquiries ... over the past 20 years, and despite a flow of recommendations deriving from these inquiries, the abuses that gave rise to those reports persist, largely unaffected by such efforts as have been made to prevent them. (Williams, 1997)

Effects of the backlash

Again, many professionals continue to be marginalised or frightened into keeping below the parapet by powerful backlash movements against exposure of child sexual abuse, even though it is decades since prominent child abuse cases in Rochdale, Orkney and Cleveland in the late 1980s and early 1990s. Claims for instance have been made of 'false memory syndrome', 'satanic panic' or 'parental alienation syndrome'. As the first two chapters of this book describe, theories such as these have played upon historic prejudices, about children as ready liars or fantasisers and women as malicious accusers of respected men. This has resulted in many perpetrators escaping justice, in organised abuse being downplayed or discredited, and in abusive ex-partners gaining custody of children. 'Backlash' attacks have encouraged defensive policies in child protection agencies, which often in effect better protect staff than children.

Such attacks have driven a widespread and continuing fear in schools and youth organisations against asking children whom they suspect of suffering sexual abuse if it has happened to them. This contributes to persistently very low rates of disclosure in most such settings, and is surely as senseless as it is dangerous to children. Why have suggestive signs and symptoms been written into child protection guidelines for decades if adults caring for children are too fearful to act on them?

Survivor agencies: a genuine involvement?

Another problem is that the role of most voluntary sector sexual abuse support agencies, and survivors' own support groups (so prominent in campaigning for survivors in the 1980s), has largely been channelled into therapeutic support after abuse, usually filling gaps in statutory services. They face an increasing struggle for resources, just to sustain their levels of service. With exceptions, their cutting edge role as campaigners for survivors has been diminished as a result.

In the UK since 2013, the stream of disclosures, police inquiries and the launch of official inquiries following revelations about decades of sex offending by the disc jockey and presenter

Jimmy Savile has given new force, organisation, strength and determination to survivors and their allies in the fight against sexual abuse. Thus the National Association for People Abused in Childhood, The Survivors' Trust and the White Ribbon Campaign, 'men working to end violence against women' have been prominent in media comment, and in campaigning for inquiries with a strong survivor voice.[1] Survivor movements must now be genuinely welcomed and actively involved, both in historic inquiries, and in policymaking. They should not be seen as obstructive nuisances, nor briefly consulted when this is expedient, nor feted obsequiously for their 'great courage' while in fact remaining marginalised.

Action against CSA in retreat

Moving forward, however, demands first an honest look back at what is wrong and what is not working well. Addressing child sexual abuse in children and young people has in recent years – and despite its high public profile – received lower priority for social services departments across the UK, compared with heightened emphasis on, for instance, emotional abuse and neglect. Known cases of CSA remain tiny in comparison with the prevalence revealed by adult survivors. In Scotland a group of prominent campaigners, practitioners and researchers expressed their serious worries about this with the Association of Directors of Social Work, and through the media. They reported many social workers' concerns that CSA was regarded as 'yesterday's issue' and 'bottom of our list of priorities' (Dempster et al, 2013).

New challenges

Ever-developing online technologies pose perhaps today's greatest challenges to prevention and protection, from massive increases in online images of abuse, to greater opportunities for national and international trafficking, to the wide availability to children and young people of sadistic and violent pornography.

---

[1]   www.napac.org.uk; www.thesurvivorstrust.org; www.whiteribboncampaign. co.uk

There are ever-increasing opportunities too for peer abuse and peer sexual harassment, and the production of youth-produced sexual content online, including self-generated sexual images of children under 10 years old (Office of the Children's Commissioner, 2011; Internet Watch Foundation, 2015).

Individualism and professionalisation

Another problem is that while national and local government rhetoric states that everyone must be involved in protecting children, child sexual abuse work has gradually become more rigidly professionalised. Communities, voluntary organisations and abuse survivors are told to report, rather than directly contributing their experience and wisdom to protecting children. Swathes of the population are now largely excluded from effective influence over child protection policy and practice.

Instead individualistic, case-by-case crisis management in child protection has remained. Publicised failures involving child deaths or serious abuse only appear to intensify commitment to improving a model which will always face a bottomless pit of need. These crises tend to generate exhausting structural reorganisations, rather than an examination of basic values and principles. As a result many child protection practitioners remain stressed, isolated and drowning in a sea of guidelines, regulations and procedures: at the cost of informed awareness, the use of professional skills and judgement, strong ethical direction and collaborative support.

This book offers an alternative, community prevention model which can actively involve local young people and adults and local organisations in genuine partnership with statutory agencies in preventing sexual crime.

Finally, protection and criminal justice systems remain largely based on the opposite of what we know about how real, sexually abused children think, act, feel and speak (or rather do not speak). The systems still rely heavily on the testimony of children and teenagers, who are very frequently disbelieved and re-traumatised in court, despite sincere attempts at improving court experience for vulnerable witnesses. Yet sexually abused children find it extremely hard to disclose abuse directly, or in ways considered appropriate for evidence gathering. In my own research with sexually abused young people, in a single half-hour discussion they gave 14 different reasons why they had stayed silent as children (Nelson, ed. 2008).Hence this book calls for different models of protection and detection in child sexual abuse, employing perpetrator-focused strategies, and including the Scottish 'Stop to Listen' model which gives young people time and safety for disclosure of their abuse.

Accepting problems makes us stronger

Thus if protecting young people against sexual abuse and supporting its survivors effectively is to improve, it is essential first to face up honestly to failures, stagnation, retreats and new challenges, as well as to take heart from undoubted achievements. That is why the book opens with a hard look at such problems, rather than opening with a bland and optimistic list of improvements.

This is not about being a wailing Cassandra, depressing and deterring sincere people from a subject which is already stressful and professionally isolating. It is not about undermining the palpable, reawakened desire among so many people to seek justice for historic abuses. It is certainly not about making some easy, sweeping, critique of all professionals who are involved, often tirelessly and with strong commitment, as social workers, health staff, police, teachers and others, in child protection work. My argument throughout is that it is mainly systems, very heavy bureaucratic demands and individualistic case-by-case investigation which create an almost impossible and demoralising task. Thus, changes in ways of working are likely to *increase* professional morale, and the sense of reward and efficacy.I argue that we need to harness realism to the new awareness and public concern about child sexual abuse, taking on board honestly what remains problematic, and what the barriers are.

It is about accepting that the reduction of CSA will demand continuing stamina, vigilance, commitment and progressive thinking. If we recognise this we become stronger, less easily demoralised, less deceived by persuasive backlash rhetoric, and more willing to consider the need for radical, child-centred change in ways of working.

It is important to face the reasons why it seems uniquely difficult to make continuing improvements in CSA work, why it requires such vigilance and commitment, and why we often seem to take two steps forward then two back.

Wealth, power and fear

The principal reason is that so many people at all levels of society, individually and in organised networks (often wealthy and powerful), benefit directly from it, have a considerable stake in it and sustain it with vigour. Its industries reap immense financial rewards, from sexual exploitation rings and people-trafficking, local, national and international, to the vast global trade in online child abuse images. These individuals and networks have power and resources – to keep secrets, to fight back, to intimidate and silence, and to deceive by spreading disinformation, often in the most reasonable-sounding, educated, intellectual middle class way. We need to regard them as criminals, not as interesting, challenging participants in the child abuse debate.

Against such forces, this book suggests, we can become more streetwise, less gullible, more questioning, and braver in acting with collective strength on behalf of children and stigmatised adults. Surely abused children and adults have spoken out over decades in sufficient numbers that the clichéd admonition to them to 'break the silence' should now apply to others?

In particular we need continuing courage to speak out for those whom society belittles, leaves vulnerable or casts aside. Victims of abusive networks are so often young people the rest of society has judged less worthy, less important, and less believable. Who were often left unprotected from sexual abuse when they were younger. Runaways, children and teenagers in care, drug misusers, young offenders, children with disabilities, children from minority ethnic groups, young gay men, trafficked women and children, refugees, the poorest single mothers and their children, single homeless people, teenagers with mental health problems... these have formed easy prey and 'fresh meat' to perpetrators, individually or in abuse rings. Often, too, their grooming has taken place in public view: but both public and professionals have made a judgement about who is to blame in what they see.

This book contends that the time is overdue to turn these stigmatised victims into vital and knowledgeable allies against child sexual abuse and exploitation.

Painful to confront

Another reason for continuing difficulty in sustaining progress against child sexual abuse is that in every generation, many people understandably find it very upsetting and anxiety-provoking to confront, both personally and professionally. (There's no other way for example to explain persistent resistance to routine inquiry about CSA in key professions such as mental health.) So it is crucially important to maintain, and frequently to repeat, training and awareness-raising in a wide range of professions working with abused children and adults. That training has to be reflexive, to explore supportively people's anxieties and fears, rather than sternly to instruct staff on guidelines and procedures. It must include access to survivor support agencies for the many professionals and carers who will themselves have been sexually abused.

Background, scope, principles and approach of this book

Although this is unapologetically a polemical and campaigning book, it is informed throughout by examples from research and practice, and by my experience and that of my co-contributors in working with sexual abuse survivors.

My background

My MA and PhD degrees are in social science. My own research background has involved humanistic qualitative research with marginalised or disaffected groups of people. I gained my PhD working with such groups in Belfast during the 'Troubles'. I also encountered a highly publicised case of child sexual abuse there, which led me to write an influential book, *Incest: Fact and*

Myth (Nelson, 1982, 1987). This explored the role of gendered power relations in CSA, in contrast to contemporary theories which placed the main responsibility on children, their mothers or the so-called 'dysfunctional family'.

I became a professional journalist, with the *Scotsman* newspaper then later as a freelance. I covered the Orkney case and inquiry in some depth, before returning to an academic career in 1997. Since then I have carried out a range of research, reports, evaluations and collaborative work into CSA and its effects throughout life (see About the Authors).

Co-authors

I am delighted that in Chapters Five and Six I have been able to collaborate with two people who have been a continuing inspiration to my work. Dr Liz Davies has been both an innovative social work practitioner and academic, whose bold, outspoken, proactive approach to protecting children and addressing organised abuse has given new courage to many besides myself. Professor Norma Baldwin has had a longstanding and distinguished influence on social work and child protection, especially in areas of deprivation. My writing on community protection against sexual crime would not have left the starting-blocks without her imaginative ideas and practice, especially her use of coordinated mapping exercises to demonstrate local community needs, problems and strengths. Chapter Nine on male (non-sexual) offenders was considerably informed by my research assistants on our male survivor study at Edinburgh University, Dr Ruth Lewis and Dr Sandy Gulyurtlu.

Scope, principles and approach

This book does not in any way claim to be comprehensive, but reflects my own areas of personal knowledge, research and exploration. There is already much excellent work, for example, on therapeutic support for children and adults, on children's still-unmet needs when giving evidence in adversarial court settings, on historical in-care abuse, and on the use of ever-developing online technologies and social media to promote, or prevent, abuse and exploitation. I discuss all of these at points in the book but could not hope to match existing work, even had I greater knowledge of these topics. However, the chapters are not merely random. I hope rather that they demonstrate clearly the interconnecting needs, throughout people's whole lives, of prevention, protection and support – and sadly, the interconnecting effects of the *lack* of those things.

The book aims always to be informed by the voices of survivors of child sexual abuse, with whom I have had the privilege of working in several qualitative research projects. I have been inspired by third sector organisations who support survivors, and by brave writers and professional practitioners, and I describe throughout some innovative examples of their work.

I have tried throughout to avoid academic jargon and convoluted concepts, and hope the book is therefore as useful for practitioners, policymakers and support groups as it is for academic colleagues.

This book ranges mainly over Scottish and English experience, but I hope that as far as possible, it is relevant across the UK and beyond it. This is because I tend to concentrate on the need to challenge broad principles, ethical priorities and key points of practice, rather than on the detail of different laws, guidance and professional structures across geographical borders.

Constructive proposals for change

Wherever possible criticism of current policy is followed by constructive proposals for improvement, and models of working which can be adopted or revisited. Although I challenge others to change, at times I have also challenged the assumptions of myself and others who come from a feminist tradition of analysing sexual violence. For instance Chapter Ten asks feminists to reconsider the relevance and implications of a sexual abuse history in many convicted male sex offenders.

In my positive proposals for change I know well that there will be many models of excellent practice of which I have been unaware, which have been omitted. Please, rather than be offended and complain, use the message of the book to promote the widest possible adoption of your own good practice everywhere. Because that is the spirit in which the book is written, and that is its intention. This book seeks to inspire action, rather than making the usual calls for more and more research. Such calls usually cause more frustrating delays (plus more work opportunities for academics and judges!) However, I hope the book will also encourage new research and a reassessment of current theories, especially the chapter on *physical health issues* for adult survivors, and the chapters on *male survivor offenders*. I have not been afraid to speculate in parts of this book, believing that informed speculation can be valuable and important as a spur to increasing our understanding and knowledge through being tested in research.

Because addressing child sexual abuse often moves two steps forward and two back, excellent ideas from the past are often abandoned or undeveloped. I resurrect some innovative ideas, and unashamedly reference some books and papers from the 1970s to the 1990s which have valuable but neglected insights. There are important and radical approaches from the past. Current obsessions among academics, policymakers and research funders that only the latest references have full value result in missing important insights. That is especially true in this field, with its cycles of attention and neglect.

Summary of structure and chapters

After the critiques of current policies and the backlash in Part I, Part II considers improving protection and prevention for *children and teenagers*. Part III considers improving provision and protection for *adult survivors of sexual abuse*. However, each part is relevant to the other, and prevention themes run through the whole. Thus in the mental health chapter (Part 3) the relevance of the trauma paradigm points back to the need for prevention in childhood (Part 2). The histories of survivor offenders (Part 3) point back to a similar need.

Part I: Setting the scene: some barriers to progress

Chapter One: From rediscovery to suppression? Challenges to reducing CSA

This chapter challenges any complacent assumption of continuing progress in tackling child sexual abuse. It challenges some statistics which suggest a decline in child sexual abuse since the early 1990s. It asks if it is commitment to tackle CSA which has declined, influenced by an intimidating backlash, the closure of promising investigations and ideologically motivated central and local government changes to child protection systems. This chapter sets the scene for a range of changes which, I argue, need to happen if CSA is to be reduced substantially as a serious social problem.

Chapter Two: Lies and deception in the backlash

This chapter focuses on disinformation by lobbies supporting accused adults. It examines flaws in theories such as the 'satanic panic', 'false memory syndrome' and 'parental alienation syndrome', and in attacks on named writers and practitioners. It examines why so many people among media, public, academics and other professionals readily believed these claims despite their very obvious flaws. The theories played upon what many sincere people have preferred to believe. Modern 'backlash theories' are placed in the context of a long history of similar attempts to minimise or discredit child sexual abuse. Less gullibility, and stronger critical awareness, will help to protect abused children and adults in future.

Part II: Children and young people

Chapter Three: Fact, myth and legacy in notorious child abuse cases: Orkney in context

Notorious cases influence public and professional opinion and subsequent legislation, which makes them important to analyse. This chapter examines the 'Orkney child abuse affair' to describe how children at the heart of highly publicised sex abuse cases can be marginalised during them, and through an expensive inquiry. It reassesses this case, which I covered closely while a journalist specialising in social work. The Orkney case is placed within the context of previous and subsequent inquiries about CSA. The chapter suggests some lessons about the necessity of making central to child abuse inquiries the needs of vulnerable children, including the actual children at the centre of the case.

Chapter Four: Stigmatised young people: key allies against abuse and exploitation

Prejudices against stigmatised, despised young people by many professionals, media and public have in effect led to collusion with perpetrators who target these young people for abuse and exploitation. Examples discussed include gross failures to protect victims of sexual exploitation rings, and my own research on publicly vilified, pre-teen pregnant girls. Treating them with respect, housing them more safely, recognising and addressing their past abuse, ensuring alternatives to school exclusions, harnessing their unique knowledge of abusers and their techniques, and enabling them to speak out safely will, this chapter argues, protect them better and bring to justice many hidden perpetrators.

Chapter Five: Models for ethical, effective child protection (with Liz Davies)

This chapter considers two approaches to better protect abused children, and to identify perpetrators: first, models which assist silenced children and young people to disclose abuse are described, including the 'Stop to Listen' scheme being piloted in Scotland from 2016. This offers increased (though not total) confidentiality, giving sexually abused children more control over the timing of investigation, and more support during it. The second part of the chapter gives examples of proactive, perpetrator-focused inquiry and evidence gathering. Some are new, while some are excellent examples from the past, which were discontinued.

Chapter Six: Community prevention of CSA: a model for practice (with Norma Baldwin)

Another key to reducing child sexual abuse will be the creation of genuinely informed, aware communities to protect children. This chapter considers why whole-community prevention has remained a low priority in child protection, and proposes a detailed schema for neighbourhood mapping for children's safety from sexual crime. Building on original projects from Edinburgh and Coventry, it demonstrates how young people and adults in any type of urban, rural, wealthy or disadvantaged neighbourhood can actively contribute to community mapping of risk and support points, strengths and needs. They can design community safety plans against sexual crime, in genuine partnership with statutory and voluntary agencies.

Part III: Adult survivors of child sexual abuse

Chapter Seven: Physical ill health: the serious impacts of sexual violence

This gives evidence from my own and a range of other research for an epidemic of illness, pain and disability in adult survivors. An over-emphasis on psychosomatic diagnoses has hampered open-minded search for both causes and effective treatments. I question popular theories of somatisation or needy care-seeking, presenting instead suggestive evidence that many conditions may result directly from severe, prolonged sexual violence and domestic torture. This chapter calls for physical health issues to become a priority: in work with survivors, in research, and in collaborations with international experts working against issues such as political torture. Recognition of the gravity of survivors' ill health will also raise the perceived gravity of CSA as a serious crime, and direct efforts towards more effective prevention earlier in life.

Chapter Eight: Producing radical change in mental health: implications of the trauma paradigm

Psychiatric and secure hospitals are filled with the victims of sexual crime. This constitutes in effect, within healthcare, a major obscuring of crime, for despite all the evidence for the trauma paradigm, medical models of mental illness remain dominant, fuelled by the power and influence of pharmaceutical companies. That increases survivors' distressing experiences of services. Their own expressed care needs must finally be implemented, but the *primary prevention* implications of the trauma paradigm must also be followed through. Mental health systems should actively contribute to multidisciplinary efforts to prevent child sexual abuse, and detect perpetrators: for instance through advice services by police and legal staff in every psychiatric and special hospital.

Chapter Nine: Pathways into crime after sexual abuse: the voices of male offenders

This describes growing evidence that male offenders share with female ones high rates of sexual abuse as children, and examines clues which they gave earlier in life that they were in need of help and protection. My qualitative research project explores young men's pathways into (non-sexual) offending in relation to betrayal, rage, shame, hopelessness, pleas for attention and the high risk effects of school exclusion policies. Offending can be serious, even including killings of gay men, whom they often scapegoat. Routine abuse trauma services for male offenders in prisons, probation services, youth projects and the community are needed, along with much stronger prevention strategies. Examples are given of good practice, with some encouraging outcomes.

Chapter Ten: Rethinking sex offender programmes for survivor-perpetrators

That past sexual trauma may influence many male sex offenders has been resisted by feminists, by survivors of child sexual abuse and by staff in sex offender programmes. It has been seen as an excuse for crime, and as supporting a simplistic 'cycle of abuse'. But we need to tackle the implications of the fact that many convicted sex offenders have been sexually abused, and ethically meet their rights to therapy as survivors. Feminists can accommodate this past trauma not as a simplistic cycle, but as a form of male socialisation. Prison projects suggest that addressing CSA trauma in survivor offenders can restore empathy and human connection, and motivate more effectively against future abuse, thus better protecting women and children, and helping to prevent sexual crime.

The Conclusion draws together common themes revealed in this book, and looks ahead to major challenges in the future, particularly with respect to sexual crimes against children facilitated by our constantly developing online systems and new technologies.

Final thoughts in this Introduction

Olafson, Corwin and Summit (1993, p. 19) memorably conclude that burial and re-burial of the truth about child sexual abuse has not happened:

> Because child sexual abuse is peripheral to major social interest, but because it is so central that as a society we choose to reject our knowledge of it, rather than make the changes in our thinking, our institutions and our daily lives that sustained awareness of child sexual victimisation demands.

It will need strong political will and united commitment to sustain a much higher priority for detecting, prosecuting and reducing through prevention schemes the incidence of CSA. This should not deter us. Remember there are always far more people who want to protect children than those who want to abuse them. We should use – and be heartened by – the great potential in that collective strength. Can there be a better time to work together with a new determination? We can be much encouraged by the genuine shock, sorrow and disgust among public, media and professionals at revelations of widespread historic abuse by Jimmy Savile and other celebrities and powerful people; by the bravery of their victims in speaking out; by the reopening of historic organised abuse cases; by more respectful approaches to survivors by police and prosecutors; and by a revived courage and determination among police and other professionals whose cases were once closed down, who now see new hopes for justice. We can all, collectively, work together to make sure that CSA does not ever 'disappear' again.

I do not see the point of writing another book unless its chapters can be taken up as active agents for change, and can help to make a difference. I wonder too if there is a point in reading yet another book about sexual abuse, unless it encourages readers to work for change. Or if there is a point in writing or reading yet again about all the bitter post-traumatic outcomes which so many survivors face after CSA, unless we say that this is absolutely not acceptable any longer; and that the most effective prevention and deterrence, and the best possible support, should at last become twin priorities for action.

PART I

Setting the scene:
some barriers to progress

ONE

From rediscovery to suppression? Challenges to reducing CSA

Introduction

Cause for optimism?

Surely in the UK we are now tackling child sexual abuse (CSA) more successfully, giving us all confidence for continuing progress? Consider the vast array of child protection procedures and guidelines now in place, and the almost weekly media publicity about CSA, which suggests this hidden crime is now being addressed more openly and more effectively. Consider the powerful impetus which shocking revelations of large scale, unrecognised or previously unaddressed sexual abuse against children has given to efforts against its repetition. That includes widespread revelations of sexual abuse by clergy, particularly by Catholic and Anglican priests; and growing acknowledgement of the silencing power which was held over victims and prospective whistleblowers by these religious figures, by showbusiness celebrities and by politicians.

A succession of inquiries in 2013 and 2014 followed the televised exposé in October 2012 into many hundreds of assaults over five decades by the late disc jockey and presenter Jimmy Savile, whose targets included disabled and mentally distressed young hospital patients. Few attacks had been reported, and none prosecuted (Gray and Watt, 2013). Convictions of the artist and international entertainer Rolf Harris and the broadcaster Stuart Hall for sexual offences against girls followed (BBC News, 2014a; Spillett, 2014). Longstanding abuse of boys by the late

Cyril Smith MP had apparently been concealed for decades by the authorities, while investigations were also launched into suspected child sexual abuse by several prominent former members of the British Parliament (Glennie, 2013; MacKean, 2013; BBC News, 2015c; Grierson, 2015).

Then police inquiries were belatedly reopened into in-care abuse rings where perpetrators allegedly included influential figures from politics, business and social care, for instance in North Wales and London (Dobson, 2013). Following a raft of new individual inquiries, inquiries into historical abuse were set up in both England and Wales and Scotland – though it has proved a fraught process in England, involving first the resignation of its first two nominated chairs (Chorley, 2014; Constance, 2014; STV News, 2014; BBC News, 2015d, 2015e; Davies, 2015).

Meanwhile there was widespread public and professional shock at child sexual exploitation scandals which erupted in English towns and cities including Rochdale, Rotherham and Oxford (Williams, 2012a, 2012b; Rawlinson et al, 2013; Jay, 2014; and Chapter Four). Widespread organised abuse of vulnerable young teenage and pre-teenage girls had been disturbingly ignored for many years, largely due to derogatory, contemptuous attitudes to 'difficult' young girls of a supposedly 'promiscuous' lifestyle, and to alleged fears of appearing racist against men of Pakistani heritage.

The fallout from all these abuse scandals, and the recommendations of the inquiries, are expected to improve further the protection of children from sexual assault.

Overall decline in prevalence?

Another cause for apparent optimism lies in statistics which suggest that overall, child sexual abuse has declined since the early 1990s. Some distinguished international child protection figures such as Professor David Finkelhor argue that this indicates it is being addressed more effectively. All these developments give hope that the historic movement of child sexual abuse from 'cycles of discovery' back to 'cycles of suppression' (Olafson et al, 1993) has ended at last.

... or a decline in protection?

In contrast, I believe that protection of children from sexual assault has in many ways *declined* over the past two decades. Thus, meeting current challenges will call for more than good intentions: many policies, practices and structures need radically to change. We must redesign a positive, proactive child protection policy in the interests of sexually abused children and young people (Davies and Duckett, 2008).

In these concerns I am neither dismissing improvements made, nor denying that child sexual abuse can be reduced. I strongly believe that it can be, or I would not continue to work and campaign in this field. It is also very likely that reductions of CSA have occurred in some settings (for example, in residential care) given the past three decades of modern awareness about CSA in a context of increased knowledge of children's views, and the strength and contribution of survivor organisations. However, growth in other settings is also very likely (for example, through internet and social media-related sexual crime, including peer-on-peer abuse, and child trafficking).

This chapter outlines some methodological and other flaws in research which suggests an overall decline in CSA. I argue that the backlash has had a very intimidatory effect on its exposure, and that changes in policy and practice have decreased the detection and prosecution of, and the safeguarding of children against, sexual abuse. Priority for professional investigation of CSA in child protection has seriously declined across England, Scotland and Wales in comparison with other forms of abuse and neglect. While the recent focus on addressing child sexual exploitation (CSE) more effectively in teenagers, especially from gangs and groups, is very welcome, it can make limited impact if many of those at greatest risk of CSE – children who have previously been abused, often within the home – are not protected earlier in life.

This chapter considers some impacts of the backlash, by accused adults and their supporters, against the exposure of child sexual abuse (the content of backlash theories is critically explored in Chapter Two). It is precisely since the early 1990s and the growth of this backlash that the reductions in substantiated

CSA cases have taken place. I argue that fearful, defensive policies in response to this intimidation need assertively to be reversed.

During and after the 1990s ideological influences affecting central and local government decisions have also undermined children's safety from sexual abuse. I am greatly indebted to the work of Liz Davies in highlighting this. There has been a major shift towards family support and assessment of need, rather than protection and investigation of harm; increased targeting of services, even though child sexual abuse affects all social classes and ethnic groups; and other damaging changes to protection from CSA. The chapter concludes by asking how we might genuinely prevent, detect and reduce CSA in various settings, and how we might in future more accurately measure decline, stasis or increase in this serious crime. That sets the scene for forthcoming chapters of this book.

Reassuring statistics of decline?

Statistics which suggest a decline in substantiated cases of child sexual abuse have come largely from the USA and Australia. There is no long-term study in the UK, although a few apparently encouraging surveys have been published. Nonetheless we should consider these decline statistics seriously, especially as someone of Professor Finkelhor's standing and contribution to child sexual abuse research has promoted them widely; and use them to think through what *kinds* of questions should be asked about ways of assessing the prevalence of sexual abuse.

In the USA, a National Incidence Study of Child Abuse and Neglect found that both known physical and sexual abuses of children have dropped significantly over 25 years.

Numbers of substantiated CSA victims began increasing nationally after 1977, with recognition of the issue, until 1992.[1] Between 1993 and 2005, substantiated numbers of sexually abused children dropped by 38%, while physical abuse numbers

---

[1] 'Substantiated' in US child protection terminology means that it was investigated by child welfare authorities, that it used a 'preponderance of the evidence' standard, and that the authority decided child maltreatment occurred, according to their statutory standards.

fell by 15 %. Even between 1992 and 1998, substantiated cases of CSA declined from a national estimated peak of 149,800 cases in 1992 to 103,600 cases in 1998 (Almeida et al, 2008; Finkelhor et al, 2010, 2014; National Children's Advocacy Center, 2011; Finkelhor and Jones, 2012). The authors conclude 'There is fairly consistent and convergent evidence from a variety of sources pointing to large declines in sexual abuse, from 1992 to 2010' (Finkelhor and Jones, 2012). This can only be a brief discussion of statistics gathered in these studies over the years, and more detailed, regularly updated figures can be found via the NDACAN website.[2]

Encouraging UK study?

It also seems initially encouraging that a recent NSPCC prevalence study in the UK found very low reports of child sexual abuse, at only 5% of respondents. Contact and non-contact sexual abuse by a parent or guardian was even more rarely reported, at 1.7% of cases. No past-year reports of parent/guardian-perpetrated sexual abuse were made for any age group. Only 1.5% of females aged 18–24 reported that CSA happened during their childhood (Radford et al, 2011).

Child protection statistics

Further, reduced registrations and concerns about child sexual abuse in the child protection statistics appear to suggest that the problem is declining.

For instance in Scotland (and despite continuing increases in the total numbers of children on child protection registers for any abuse, neglect or other concern), between 2007 to 2013 inclusive, the numbers of children registered for sexual abuse concerns varied between only 190 and 240. Approximately 887,400 of the Scottish population are under 16. Even in the year with the highest annual number of CSA registrations, this is only .00027 of that young population (Scottish Government, 2014).

---

[2] www.ndacan.cornell.edu

In England, figures relate to the Child Protection Register until 2010, and to child protection plans from 2010 onwards. Numbers of CSA-related cases varied, between 2010 and 2013, between 2,000 and 2,400. There are approximately 9.99 million children under 16 in England. The proportion of this young population on registers or child protection plans for sexual abuse during those years was between .00024 and .00020 (HM Government, 2014).

Both percentages and numbers of children with sexual abuse-related concerns were considerably higher in the 1990s. For example in England between 1994 and 1998, while the percentage of CSA-related registrations fell somewhat, from 26% to 21%, they were still considerably above today's figures.

So, looking at those statistics, one possible hypothesis is that since the early 1990s the authorities and society as a whole have gradually been addressing and preventing the crime of CSA more effectively. Another possible hypothesis is that between 1977 and the early 1990s, CSA was being uncovered ever more effectively; but events then happened to impede and slow down this progress in protecting children, a decline which continues.

Acknowledging likely areas of reduction

It is important to acknowledge that *preventive work in some settings* over recent decades is very likely to have reduced the incidence of child sexual abuse in those settings. This is especially true of organised, systematic or opportunistic crime by abusers who deliberately seek out paid work and volunteering with children. Through enforced background checks and use of stricter references, through restrictions on taking children away overnight and other precautions, opportunities for sexual abuse by adults have become more difficult (though far from impossible: see Robinson, 2014). These adults include teachers, care staff and youth leaders who work in authorised child and youth care settings, and institutional and residential care.

Considering Jimmy Savile for instance, it is unlikely now that a lone unrelated male – whatever his status – would be allowed to take children from care settings repeatedly to his car, caravan or dressing room. Many more institutions now have child protection procedures around unchaperoned settings. (Although this does not mean that *peer-on-peer* abuse in residential care settings has necessarily diminished, and is unlikely to do so without coherent protective planning and a keener awareness of gender issues: see Green, 2005.)

Second, acute modern fears (however disproportionate) about allowing children to play outside, or to walk unaccompanied to school, will protect some children who were previously at risk. In my own research with both women and men, adult survivors described being sexually abused while playing outside, while walking long distances alone to school, or on errands for the family: by shopkeepers, farmers, farm labourers, caravan owners, relatives, older children or others, sometimes for many years (Nelson, 2001, 2009).

Third, it is important to acknowledge that the intensive work and skills involved in monitoring known sex offenders through registration and multi-agency public protection arrangements (MAPPA) is likely to have reduced opportunities for perpetration in those offenders: even though caution is needed in that known offenders remain very much a minority of all perpetrators. The imprisonment of ever more sex offenders will reduce some risks, especially by some of the most dangerous or prolific ones: at least while they are confined. It remains difficult to assess accurately the effectiveness of sex offender programmes in reducing CSA, because recidivism rates poorly test their effectiveness. It is easy, given developing new online technologies, for perpetrators to continue committing undetected, unreported sexual crime. Issues for sex offender programmes are discussed in detail in Chapter Ten.

Problems with the figures

Do statistics of decline give grounds for optimism, or a more uncertain message? What are some of the problems they raise?

Methodological issues

Substantiated cases are a small minority: the fact that the American statistics relate either wholly or largely to *substantiated* cases of child sexual abuse must reduce much of their worth. It remains notoriously difficult legally to substantiate the majority of CSA cases. A major study by the Children's Commissioner for England (2015) estimated for example that only one in eight children who are sexually abused is identified by professionals. The majority, they found, remained unidentified, largely because protective services were geared to children self-reporting, yet children rarely do this. An analysis of more than 200 international studies of prevalence, from 1980 to 2008, with a total of nearly 10 million participants, revealed wider disparities still: prevalence figures of self-reported sexual assault (18.0% of women, 7.6% of men), 30 times higher than the prevalence rates reported by authorities (Stoltenborgh et al, 2011).

Recall surveys without confidentiality are unreliable: proponents of genuine decline point out that recall findings from adults and young people also indicate a reduction in CSA. It is true that recall findings are usually more reliable statistically than others, but methodological problems in some quoted surveys are clear.

Take the British NSPCC research findings (Radford et al, 2011) which are strikingly below the usual range of CSA prevalence findings. The reason may lie in serious methodological problems. The survey used interviews, with questionnaires, with caregivers of children under 11; with young people aged 11–17 and their caregivers; and with young adults aged 18–24. For children of 10 or under, the primary caregiver was interviewed about the child's experiences. For young people between 11 and 17, both primary caregiver and young person were interviewed consecutively, while both were at home. The caregiver had to give consent for all under-18s.

But caregivers of children under 11 might be abusive themselves; might be quite unaware their child was being abused; might be uncertain, or understandably fearful of the consequences of saying 'yes', such as having their child or a partner removed from home. Both abusive and fearful caregivers could readily deny consent for interview. Sexual abuse is particularly difficult and shameful for young people under 18 to disclose to anyone (see Chapters Four and Five), let alone to a stranger, and most particularly when their own parent or guardian is with them. These caregivers might be abusive, or they might be protected by the child from the distressing knowledge of abuse. While some young adults of 18–24 will reveal sexual abuse, they will not necessarily reveal it to a stranger in that setting; many are still not ready to reveal it till later in life, and young men in particular remain unlikely to do so (see Chapter Five).

I believe the NSPCC should seriously reconsider the reliability of this particular study, and end the considerable publicity it gives to its findings.

Similar methodological problems exist in relation to studies from the USA showing a decline in sexual abuse, which directly question young people. Two cross-sectional national telephone surveys to people's homes, using identical questions in the Juvenile Victimization Questionnaire[3] were carried out in 2003 and 2008 to assess children's exposure to abuse, violence, and crime. Participants were aged 2 to 17. Interviews were conducted with their caretakers and (older) children themselves. Sexual assault was reported significantly less often in 2008 than in 2003.

However, as Cromer and Goldsmith noted (2010), there was no way to control if an abuser was present during the telephone interview, or if the parent failed to disclose abuse of a child. Further, these national studies do not include young people in detention or in inpatient treatment, runaways, and homeless children: groups who, they pointed out, are or have already been sexually abused at far higher rates than other children.

Finkelhor and Jones (2012), discussing self-report studies by young people, are confident that 'It seems unlikely that, in the face of more public attention to sexual abuse and decreasing stigma, youth would be more reluctant to disclose in surveys.' However, there is no evidence that young people find it less of a stigma to disclose abuse than it was in the past, and disclosure rates remain very low (see Chapter Five). These problems all suggest the great importance of employing methodologies in recall studies which are not only of proven quality, but which respond closely to what we *already* know about the special difficulties young people have about revealing sexual abuse. In particular, children and young people need to be asked in reassuring, safe and truly confidential settings (see Chapter Five).

---

3 www.unh.edu/ccrc/pdf/jvq/CV55newedition04.pdf

Real decline – or shifting priorities?

Another significant problem about assuming a genuine decline in child sexual abuse is that in the UK, the fall in officially known cases and concerns has taken place side by side with a considerable growth in cases and concerns about, for instance, emotional abuse, neglect and parental substance misuse. That is suggestive not of genuine declines or increases, but rather of changed policy decisions and professional priorities, affected by political pressures. One example would be the fallout after highly publicised child deaths such as that of the neglected and severely abused toddler, 'Baby Peter' Connelly in 2007 (Haringey LSCB, 2009, 2010). Fears of another high-profile death have brought big increases in care orders in the UK involving young children where there are concerns about neglect or physical abuse (McLeod et al, 2010), with all the cost and workload implications for local authorities and their staff.

The number of children in England who were subject to a child protection plan increased by 47% between 2008 and 2012; and numbers of children on child protection registers increased in Wales (+17.5%), Scotland (+23%) and Northern Ireland (+2.7%). Yet the percentage of these related to CSA has continued to decline.

In England for example, neglect cases rose considerably from 12,500 in 2007 to 20,970 in 2014. Between 2010 and 2014 children made subject of child protection plans for emotional abuse rose from 10,800 to 15,860. But sexual abuse was not only the smallest of all categories recorded, but dropped slightly in that time from 2,300 to 2,210 (HM Government, 2014; DfE, 2014). In Scotland between 1998 and 2003, numbers of children added to the Child Protection Register through emotional abuse rose by 108% and physical neglect by 80%. For sexual abuse, numbers fell by 32% (Scottish Executive, 2004). In 2007–08, registrations for sexual abuse were down by 33% on the previous year alone. Yet registrations for emotional abuse rose 22% in the same year (Scottish Government, 2014a). Munro et al (2011), in a useful UK-wide snapshot of children who were subject to a child protection plan or on the register for the year 2010, found sexual abuse at between 6% and 9% of cases, by far the smallest category; with, for instance, emotional abuse at 28% of cases in England, and 26% in Scotland.

From 2012 in Scotland, multiple concerns could be recorded at each case conference. Most common were parental substance misuse (39%), emotional abuse (39%) and domestic abuse (37%). Sexual abuse was ninth in a list of 11 concerns, at just over 3% (Scottish Government, 2014b)

In Wales, since 2000 the percentage of registrations under categories involving sexual abuse has fallen from 14% to 7%. For the same period, however, categories involving neglect have increased from 44% in 2002 to a peak of 52% in 2006, falling to 42% in 2014. Emotional abuse has increased to 36%, more than double the rate in 2006 (Bwletin Ystadegol, 2014).

Overall, only 5% of all the children on child protection registers or subject to child protection plans in the UK were under a category that included sexual abuse on 31 March 2013 (31 July 2013 in Scotland) (HM Government, 2014; Scottish Government, 2014).

Further – and accepting that placing children on child protection registers and making child protection plans only form one way of addressing sexual abuse – such figures do not begin to reflect the most conservative estimates of CSA prevalence. Take just one city, say greater Dundee. If there are currently approximately 27,360 children under 16 and if one in ten is a present or past victim, that would equal 2,736 children. If we took the NSPCC survey's really conservative estimate of one in 20 CSA victims, the figure for sexually abused children would be 1,368 in greater Dundee alone.

Contrast with police figures

Yet in stark contrast to the very low figures in child protection statistics, police have been recording at least 85 allegations of sexual assaults against children every day, according to Freedom of Information data released in June 2015. The figures for England and Wales revealed 31,238 recorded cases of sexual offences against children in 2013/14, with the majority of victims aged between 12 and 16. A quarter of these children were under 11. This was a rise of more than one-third over the previous year's figures. In Scotland, government figures revealed that in 2013–14 there were 3,742 sexual offences against children under 18 recorded, including rape, sexual assault and grooming – a ten-year high (NSPCC, 2015).

Peter Wanless, the NSPCC chief executive, said:

> "These figures are disturbing and clearly illustrate child sexual abuse is a continuing and widespread problem that needs urgent action. But we know this is still only a fraction of the true number of victims, because some endure an agonising wait of many years before telling anyone – and others never reveal what has happened to them." (Sky News, 2015)

Particular problems in investigating and detecting intra-familial child sexual abuse have been explored in research (Horvath et al, 2014; Children's Commissioner, 2015). They include younger children not realising this was abnormal in families and that they could complain, along with children's great difficulties in disclosing The English study of Davidson et al (2012) found notably problematic issues among staff to be time constraints; lack of consultation with the children and young people; insufficient use of intermediaries to help children express themselves; and high police staff turnover in specialist units.

"It's yesterday's issue"

Suggestive evidence (which needs much wider investigation) that recent statistics indicate a switch in professional priorities, not a genuine decline in child sexual abuse, has come from the repeated experience of myself and colleagues working with child sexual abuse throughout the UK. We have been told in conferences, seminars and discussions with child protection professionals, including social workers, children's panel members and safeguarding board members that:

> "It's bottom of our list of priorities – we're told to concentrate on drugs."

"We've been told it's yesterday's issue."

"Since Baby Peter it's all physical abuse and neglect in the youngest kids, and older kids get left to look after themselves."

"If we asked the question, we'd have to do something about it."

These comments, typical of numerous others, can be dismissed as 'merely anecdotal', or they can be taken seriously and research on this situation can now be launched with practitioners and managers.

Concern about this trend was such that in 2013 Scottish specialists in CSA and child protection issues wrote to the media and met the Association of Directors of Social Work about their deep concern that 'sexual abuse is being allowed to disappear off the statutory radar' (Dempster et al, 2013). They said it had been overshadowed by a higher priority for other child maltreatment, and by the reduction in time for social workers to listen and talk to clients, on an issue that requires a slow and patient build-up of trust. They said different types of abuse 'should not be in competition with each other for resources, but approached on the basis of need'. They urged the Scottish Government and local authorities to take active steps to reverse this decline, and asked that awareness-raising, training and 'time for listening' be increased throughout the Scottish social work professions. Government should work closely with Scotland's child protection committees and voluntary sector agencies on the issue (Dempster et al, 2013).

But at the Children's Panel Members' Conference in May 2014 in Glasgow, few delegates recalled any sexual abuse-related referrals, and longstanding panel members said such referrals had considerably declined. Training in the subject is currently extremely brief. Yet in Scotland children's panels are crucial in being able to identify risks and influences of CSA, since young people are frequently coming before them with acting-out behaviours, school truancy and addictions. Senior social workers from Glasgow protested later that year that they were indeed referring many cases of suspected CSA to the children's panel reporters, but that reporters were not even putting these cases before the panels. They claimed growing use of lawyers by accused parents had intimidated reporters into only going for 'court-reliable' cases – even though they only have to prove on 'balance of probabilities' to take protective action (Say Women, 2014). These are serious concerns, which call for prompt investigation.

Effective anti-abuse work would increase known CSA cases

This is perhaps the major flaw in the optimists' position. The problem about arguing that fewer substantiated cases mean prevention must be working is that when such crimes are tackled assertively, or when victims suddenly find new confidence to disclose, reports, charges and convictions grow. The incidence of sexual abuse suddenly appears to increase – sometimes considerably. This is a feature of secretive, shameful crimes generally, that without assertive work to expose them they tend to remain largely hidden. Roland Summit (1988) evocatively describes these revelations as 'fleeting glimpses of the reality brought by each brief clearing of the fog'.

Here are a few examples.

- One sex ring was identified in South Leeds in 1984. Painstaking investigations in this one police division identified ten more rings, and more than 170 child victims. Numerous prosecutions were secured. Yet in similar socioeconomic areas of the city, nothing had been uncovered. Doctors Chris Hobbs and Jane Wynne said the key appeared to be the presence of interested, aware professionals with adequate time, enthusiasm and energy: 'It was hypothesised that other rings must exist elsewhere, but were unrecognised' (Hobbs and Wynne, 1994).

- Highly publicised cases bring a rush of victims to report. The initial revelations about Jimmy Savile's abuse did not just lead to hundreds more allegations that Savile himself had committed abuse over decades. Some support agencies recorded an eightfold increase in calls from adults, both about other historic abuse, and about *current* child abuse which they suspected (BBC News, 2014b; NAPAC, 2014).

• Police investigated sexual abuse of boys, allegedly committed during the 1970s and 1980s at the Medomsley detention centre, Co Durham, after the conviction of one prolific offender, Neville Husband. They announced in 2014 that they had uncovered an organised paedophile ring with up to 900 victims (Palmer, 2014).

• After years of official neglect of child sexual exploitation in Oxford, one police officer, Detective Inspector Simon Morton, proactively began gathering information on suspected perpetrators and on girls repeatedly going missing in the city. He set up Operation Bullfinch, considerably increased his staff and gradually gathered vital information about both perpetrators and potential victims (see Chapter Five). Only when the men were in custody did he go to the girls and 80% of them spoke to the police about their abuse. There were seven initial convictions in 2013 (Rawlinson et al, 2013).

• When in 2014 Professor Alexis Jay, after extensive study of records, calculated that at least 1,400 children had been sexually exploited in Rotherham over 16 years, it became clear these cases had been neither classified nor recorded as sexual abuse, since the stigmatised girls were viewed by most authorities as freely choosing prostitution. Thus, only now will these cases count in official records as 'substantiated' (Jay, 2014; Norfolk, 2013).

Harder-to-reach communities

Increases in known cases would be an important indicator that child sexual abuse was being addressed in communities, such as some minority ethnic communities, where research and practice experience (for example Gilligan and Akhtar, 2006; Brown et al, 2011) has found under-reporting of sexual abuse, and under-representation of sexual abuse cases, in proportion to population. Where is the evidence, by those who claim reductions in CSA, that this is changing in terms of disclosures, protection or criminal charges, despite the innovative work and campaigning of organisations such as Roshni: No More Secrets?[4]

Particular issues for some black and minority ethnic (BME) communities include strong values of obedience to paternal authority, shame and family honour, and cultural preconceptions among majority-community agencies (Stevenson, 2012).For instance in her Rotherham report, Alexis Jay highlighted that agencies there ignored sexual abuse which was taking place within Pakistani heritage communities, as well as against white girls, and had only consulted traditional male leaders in these communities (Jay, 2014). Other issues have been a lack of appropriate vocabulary, and a perception that CSA is a western problem. Gilligan and Akhtar (2006) came to similar conclusions after research with 50 Asian organisations. Their responses emphasised the 'taboo' nature of CSA; an unwillingness to believe it existed, especially within families; lack of understanding and appropriate vocabulary; and lack of accessible, culturally sensitive information in this area.

Many of these issues appeared to be still current in Javita Narang and Nauman Quereshi's (2015) Scottish research on the needs of BME communities in relation to sexual abuse, presented through a documentary. Based on interviews with adult survivors of abuse, Members of the Scottish Parliament, Police Scotland, voluntary organisations, researchers and practitioners, it found numerous barriers to the reporting of CSA, to prevention and to the care of adult survivors. Main concerns identified were:

- Cultural issues tending to the denial of CSA and the prevention of disclosure.

- Lack of research or of data collection by police and other agencies, in relation to prevalence in BME communities and the needs of BME children.

---

[4] www.roshni.org.uk

- Lack of culturally specific services, language barriers, too few translators and interpreters, and lack of information or awareness of services.

Respondents to her research called for closer partnership working between statutory and BME organisations, and the training of support people at local level. They urged research on CSA issues in minority ethnic communities, including exploration of the best ways of reaching out to particular (sometimes varied and diverse) communities. Developing 'keep safe' modules for children in schools, modules to which all communities could agree, to encourage their personal safety and enhance prevention, was seen as particularly important, particularly as parents from some BME communities will take their children out of sex education classes in schools.

Children with disabilities

Another group currently barely visible in statistics, despite the realities of sexual abuse, are disabled children and young people. Miller and Brown (2014) and Taylor et al (2014) provide wideranging and valuable reviews of their situation, of the research to date, and of recommendations to improve identification and pursuit of cases.

They find disabled children face significantly higher risk of abuse, including sexual abuse, than non-disabled children. Intervention thresholds are often higher, even though children's dependence on carers for personal assistance raises the risk of abuse. Yet comparatively few children on child protection registers or child protection plans are recorded as having an impairment.

Problems have included reluctance to believe disabled children are abused; indicators of abuse being attributed to a child's impairment; communication problems; a perception that if cases are pursued, these young people will be unreliable witnesses; and a lack of staff confidence and relevant training

The impact of the backlash

The intimidatory impact on professionals of the backlash against exposure of child sexual abuse is inadequately discussed in the US research on possible reasons for statistical decline of substantiated CSA. Finkelhor and Jones (2012) admit the difficulties in researching this factor, when such amorphous attitudes and pressures can be involved. The relevance of abusers' power to disrupt and intimidate the work of child protection agencies is even less discussed. This is surprising since sexual abuse is about inequalities of power and influence.

I argue that the experience of many practitioners working over recent decades with CSA is that the backlash has had lasting effects on many areas of their work.

Legitimate and unjustified criticism

In the UK, the legal outcome and the media coverage – largely hostile to child protection staff – of a few, highly publicised, sexual abuse cases in the late 1980s and early 1990s had disproportionate impact on child protection against child sexual abuse. This was particularly so after Rochdale (1990), Cleveland (1987–88) and Orkney (1991–92) (see Chapters Two and Three). Of course justified as well as unjustified criticisms were involved. Justified criticism especially concerned precipitate removal of children from home, even before sources of abuse had been identified; in the Cleveland case, about placing them in unsuitable hospital wards; and about the questioning of children, with insufficient safeguards against poor recording or undue pressure on the children (Butler-Sloss, 1988; Clyde, 1992).

New legislation less child-friendly

The problem here is whether attempted improvements in response to abuse allegations made it easier, or harder, to protect children from child sexual abuse. The Children Act 1989 (England & Wales) and the Children (Scotland) Act 1995 made it much more difficult to remove children from home and gave more power to parents, even harmful ones. Speight and Wynne (2000) called the (English) Children Act a charter for abusive parents, with substantial shifts in the burden of proof needed to protect children: 'Social workers feel they have to let the child be re-abused to show the judge (as enjoined by the Children Act) that they are only having recourse to legal proceedings as a last resort.'

They quoted one judge who said: 'the more serious the allegation, the less likely it is to have occurred, and hence the stronger should be the evidence before the court concludes that the allegation is established'. They responded: 'According to this logic it should be harder to protect a child who has been raped than one who has been indecently assaulted.'

Interviewing problems with ABE

The formalisation of, and regulation around, interviewing of children, in prescribed official settings through Memorandum of Good Practice interviews, can be very valuable in court if carried out sensitively after building children's confidence and trust. The ABE (Achieving Best Evidence) phased interview approach centrally includes building rapport with the child, creating a child-centred environment and providing a free narrative phase, for the child to give a non-chronological account in his or her own words.

But researchers have found that in practice many such interviews have been conducted in a flawed and unhelpful way for children. That includes the interview environment not being conducive for establishing rapport, not taking into account the child's age or trauma levels, inappropriate questioning, failure to account for confusion and memory problems, and frequent failure to build initial rapport (Westcott and Kynan, 2006; Robinson, 2008). There is also an inherent problem about the importance given to a *child's free narrative* in these interviews. This is a well-intentioned response to repeated claims that interviewers had been influencing children with suggestive questions. But sexual abuse is precisely a subject which most children feel constrained, ashamed or humiliated to talk about freely in the first place, most of all about the nature of degrading sexual acts committed on them. If they cannot be prompted by gentle yes-no questions, for example 'I wonder if perhaps this happened to you?' (without, of course, suggesting who the perpetrator was), many will not reveal much through free narrative. This problem is a classic example of defensive responses and reactions to the backlash, which do not actually fit well with children's own feelings, difficulties and reactions.

Many interviews also still place stressed children in unnatural settings, with unfamiliar people. It has left the considerable and the greatest problem, that of aggressive defence cross-examination in court, untouched. It has responded to older social assumptions about the unreliability and untruthfulness of children, and to attempts to protect *staff* from accusations of poor practice. While gaining disclosures of child sexual abuse from children can be considerably improved, there needs to be far more emphasis on gaining other sources of evidence (see Chapter Five on both issues).

Professionalisation

The effort to 'professionalise' (in the sense of limiting work to qualified professionals, rather than in the sense of improving quality of service), and to formalise in response to criticism of professionals' conduct, reduced trust in the judgement and skills of low-status staff and ordinary people. The value of disclosures children made to adults whom they trusted, in informal settings, was diminished. Voluntary sector organisations have had to fight, often unsuccessfully, for representation on child protection committees and safeguarding boards. Local communities often became virtually excluded from involvement in child protection (see Chapter Six).

A fear of losing professional control and of running into legal minefields with children's parents and others has been especially noticeable in the persistent failure of most statutory authorities to provide, enable or support refuges for runaway children under 16, even though legal provision for these was provided back in 1989 in England & Wales, and 1995 in Scotland. This constitutes in my view a shameful failure to safeguard these young people, who are still running, in their thousands every year, to the streets and to other unsafe places and people (see Chapter Four).

Closing down of successful investigations

The closing down of investigations in the 1980s and early 1990s which proved successful in identifying many perpetrators, especially the influential and wealthy, suggests that powerful people have considered such investigations and their promising techniques unacceptable, and influenced their closure or discredit. These closures would inevitably have an intimidatory effect on subsequent investigations, and even on the likelihood of these being launched. The experience also suggests that successful methods can be resurrected and updated, but also that they may risk being closed down once more unless we are extremely vigilant about this. A growing number of police and social work figures came forward in 2013–14 to talk about closed inquiries in the community or in institutions during the 1980s and 1990s. Two examples concerned Peter McKelvie and Clive Driscoll.

Peter McKelvie headed a specialist social work team, working with a police team, from 1988 to 1995, in Hereford and Worcester, dealing only with child sexual abuse. It received about 4,000 referrals, successfully convicted 38 paedophiles, closed seven boarding schools and found considerable CSA within families. The team worked proactively with communities, and gathered all possible information about suspected perpetrators and children at risk. They were strongly supported by the social services director, David Tombs. They identified a large paedophile ring including many professionals. This was felt to damage the reputation of the council, and overwhelm the child protection system, and when a new director took over, the team and McKelvie were seen as the problem. They were closed down almost overnight in 1995, and all their records were destroyed.

McKelvie's team also unearthed evidence of a ring, stretching up to the House of Commons and House of Lords, connected with the notorious paedophile Peter Righton. It was subject to renewed interest from 2014 onwards. Nothing came of the team's request for a major investigation and the large body of evidence against Righton fell into a 'black hole'. McKelvie and other concerned professionals lodged a complaint in 1994, demanded action and named MPs they believed were involved in the organised network (Watt and Wintour, 2014; personal interview, 2014).

Clive Driscoll, a former senior, and respected, Metropolitan Police officer, complained that during his 1988 inquiry into abuse in South London children's homes, he was moved from his post when he revealed plans to investigate politicians. He said after he had shared his suspicions and the names of a list of suspects at a case conference, he was taken off the investigation, while whistleblowers about the abuse feared reprisals against both themselves and their families.

> "I was unhappy with the interference of some senior officers who did not appear to have a logical connection to my investigation into child sex abuse in Lambeth … I never had a chance to investigate [named politicians] because I was moved before I could do so." (Pettifor, 2013)

Driscoll told how disciplinary proceedings were started against him after he named the politicians in a confidential meeting. He was investigated and questioned under caution by other officers. Disciplinary proceedings were dropped once he was off the case (Kuenssberg, 2014).

Closing down of ritual abuse investigations

During the later 1980s, when sexual abuse disclosures from children were being listened to more seriously than in the past, bizarre and disturbing disclosures from some seriously distressed children and adults internationally led to investigations of ritual abuse. This was a particularly sadistic organised form of sexual, physical and emotional abuse of children (and, frequently, adults). It involved rituals and belief systems which included occult religious cults. Some participants appeared to have been part of longstanding intergenerational patterns of family abuse (see Chapters Two and Three).

Following legal decisions which discredited alleged ritual abuse cases in Rochdale (1990) and Orkney (1991) the government set up an inquiry into ritual abuse, headed by Professor Jean la Fontaine (1994). This concluded that there was minimal evidence that ritual abuse existed. Only three, she decided, of 84 cases she studied were ritual (but not satanic), where self-proclaimed mystical/magical powers were used to entrap children for purposes of sexual abuse.

Despite numerous flaws, discussed in Chapter Two, in this scanty report, the government accepted its findings. From then onwards, overt inquiries and charges in relation to ritual abuse virtually ended or were overturned. This has also adversely affected investigations of organised sexual abuse in general, of which ritual abuse is one example. Thus in a major case of multi-perpetrator abuse in Ayrshire in 1990 Sheriff Neil Gow, shocked at apparent evidence of sadistic brutalities against the children, declared that there were 'sinister elements of sadism, ritualism and torture'. But Sheriff Colin Miller in 1994, in a re-hearing, later declared the evidence not proven and the children were returned home. He said that in 1990 there was a fashion to seek out sexual abuse, in particular ritual or satanic abuse: 'I am aware that nearly five years later, the climate has reversed' (McKain, 1995; Nelson, 2000).

Elaborate accounts of 'satanic abuse' as a 'moral panic' were widely circulated (see Chapter Two) to ridicule the existence of ritual abuse, and continue to this day (Aaronovitch, 2015). In this intimidatory or ridiculing climate, most voluntary sector organisations which had raised serious concerns about ritual abuse in the past now disassociated themselves from these concerns. In the early 1990s the NSPCC and Royal Society for Prevention of Cruelty to Children (RSSPCC) had expressed great concern over child abuse involving bizarre occult rituals and abusive ceremonies, including in the Orkney case (Jukes and Duce, 1990; and Chapter Three). They had publicly stated that they had encountered sex ritual abuse cases (Creighton, 1993). Yet immediately after Professor la Fontaine's report was published, Christopher Brown, Director of the NSPCC, said on BBC Radio 4: 'We have no evidence for so-called Satanism. Whether it exists or not, I don't know' (Mallard, 2008).

Liz Davies has meticulously charted the way definitions of and action against 'ritual abuse' were gradually weakened or disappeared from formal guidance. She says: "Definitions were slowly and consistently eroded between 1991 and 2013. There was also a substitution of 'belief systems' in general by 'belief in spirit possession' as situated only within 'immigrant communities'" (personal interview, 2014).

Mallard's experience

Former Metropolitan Police sergeant Carole Mallard, an experienced child protection officer, has detailed her and her managers' experience of evidence of ritual abuse being closed down and files disappearing.

Her involvement in a joint investigation with social services revealed puzzling behaviours by a mother including trance-like states, violent dreams involving blood and knives, childlike regression, terror of insects, hatred of cameras and videotaping. The woman implicated relatives in child rape and abortion; investigators taped numerous interviews, concerned that serious crimes were involved.

Mallard and her boss now found their credibility and objectivity questioned. Their report disappeared and they were told they must leave the team. But in late 1991 internal research into organised and ritualistic abuse was re-authorised. Staff were to produce guidelines on investigating ritual abuse, for officers and questionnaires on their experience of cases, so that information could be collated on a database. They supported Professor la Fontaine's research into ritual abuse by ensuring their questionnaires went to all Metropolitan Police child protection teams, were completed and passed to her. The NSPCC offered help. People increasingly rang them with information, which the team assembled on 40 cases, usually involving cruelty and torture.

But in January 1993 Mallard was told she would be returned to ordinary police duties. The team's report was locked away and never published. People who asked to see it were given different explanations of its location, or on whether or not it was completed. Only ritual killings or ritual abuses among people from distant countries were considered credible (Bowcott, 2003).

RA is only accepted if victim from a country like Africa, such as the 'Torso in the Thames case' when in

August 2001, the headless torso of a small black boy was found in the river. Genetic information suggested he came from West Africa. It has been described as a voodoo, muti or witchcraft sacrifice, a sacrificial killing and a ritual killing in the UK press. The story was not discredited, because it was seen as an 'African crime'. (Mallard, 2008)

Intimidation of health and social work

An example of failures of courage, especially at senior levels, which set a tone for the future concerned the resignation of Sue Richardson from NCH-Action for Children in 1997.

A major figure in the Cleveland child abuse controversy of 1987 in north-east England (see Chapter Two), she resigned from the NCH-Action for Children adult survivors' project in Glasgow after NCH managers forbade her from taking part in a television documentary. This programme, *Unspeakable Truths* (Channel 4, 1997), reassessed the Cleveland case. Managers had threatened to sack her for 'gross misconduct', believing that her very appearance would bring bad publicity to NCH-Action for Children by linking it with the Cleveland case. Yet at that time, NCH faced revelations that paedophiles had worked in its residential settings, revelations which were more damaging than any public identification with Ms Richardson (Nelson, 1997).

The documentary offered new evidence to support Richardson's televised claims that abused children in Cleveland had not been protected. As child abuse consultant in Cleveland in 1987, when 121 children were taken into care on suspicion of having been sexually abused after investigations including medical diagnoses, Ms Richardson was criticised in the inquiry report. She was said to have contributed to breakdowns in relationships between police and social services, but was praised for her strong commitment to protecting children (Butler-Sloss, 1988) The *Unspeakable Truths* documentary found many of these 121 children were re-referred to social services after being returned home by the courts, and that an independent medical panel subsequently found that 70–75% of the paediatricians' diagnoses of contested cases were correct. Further details which put Cleveland in a different light are discussed in Chapter Three.

In November 1997, *after* this publicised reassessment, a tenth anniversary conference of the Cleveland abuse crisis was held in Newcastle. It was unusual as controversial figures were invited to speak: Dr Marietta Higgs, Dr Geoffrey Wyatt, Sue Richardson, Heather Bacon, Marjorie Dunn, Dr Jane Wynne. It was also unusual because survivors and community groups were given a platform. Yet amid allegations of an official boycott, not a single serving health professional attended, nor any senior social services managers, in contrast to the major 'Cleveland: 10 Years On' conference in Newcastle in April that year. Then, speakers were judges, QCs, professors and eminent psychiatrists. No survivor or community group was thought fit to be invited to share the platform. It seems officials working with children at risk preferred safe topics, and lacked the courage to be seen with controversial people and issues.

Yet speakers at the boycotted conference offered some damning statistics on the reduction of protection for children following the Cleveland crisis, and professionals' reaction to the waves of criticism. It would have been important for health and social service professionals to hear these figures. The paediatrician Dr Wynne said that between 1986 and 1988 children aged three to six formed the largest category of children referred for suspected sexual abuse. But this group had now almost disappeared from referrals. The child psychologist Heather Bacon told delegates that in 1987 32% of her referrals came from concerns over medical signs: the 1997 figure was nil. In that decade referrals through known abuse of an older sibling dropped from 29% to nil. (Rosella Roars Associates, 1997).

'We mustn't have another Orkney/Cleveland' has been a mantra since for many agencies in child protection. I and others have heard it from professionals at all levels, and continue regularly to do so. It especially influences reluctance to ask children if they have been sexually abused, if they suspect this has taken place. The damning report on repeated failures to protect sadistically abused children in Western Isles (Eilean Siar) in 2005 despite more than 100 case conferences on the girls involved, suggested that the post-Orkney Children (Scotland) Act 1995, and the aftermath of Orkney, contributed to reluctance to remove the children from home (SWIA, 2005; and Chapter Three).

Fear of parents, fear of being accused of over-reaction, and fear of being sued can paralyse and intimidate, making systems timid, more concerned about keeping staff out of trouble than about exposing risks to children. Professionals from the past are speaking out now, but senior staff in all statutory and voluntary agencies need to find equal courage (Nelson, 1998a, 2000).

Physical evidence of CSA weakened

The aftermath of the Cleveland case also damaged and intimidated the paediatric profession's confidence and ability to draw conclusions on physical evidence of child sexual abuse. Because physical evidence is especially important in cases involving very young, non-verbal and pre-verbal children, this further restricted protection available to society's most vulnerable young children.

Although in fact the Cleveland Inquiry declared the controversial RAD (reflex anal dilatation) as a sign that remained 'abnormal and suspicious' (Butler-Sloss, 1988, p. 193) and although (as above) an expert panel vindicated at least 75% of Drs. Higgs and Wyatt's diagnoses, they were both removed from child protection work, Higgs for several years and Wyatt permanently. Hostile media and public reaction created a negative and suspicious atmosphere for child protection paediatricians to work in.

Since the publication of a paper on a rarely explored topic (Hobbs and Wynne, 1986) which gave evidence for the frequency of buggery in childhood – a paper which created a professional furore – and since the Cleveland case and inquiry, remarkably little peer-reviewed research on anal abuse of children, or indeed major conferences on the subject, can be found. Further, in relation to child abuse cases generally, and amid much publicity, some of the most eminent and respected child protection paediatricians in Britain such as Dr Roy Meadow and Dr David Southall were struck off by the General Medical Council for 'serious professional misconduct'. They either had to wait years for legal vindication and reinstatement, or were brought before the GMC and savagely denounced by a judge, in the case of the respected paediatrician Dr Camille de San Lazaro (Dyer, 2006; BBC News, 2006b; Gornall, 2007; Matthews et al, 2009; Campbell, 2010).

The fact that these were so senior and so respected in their profession sent a particularly alarming message to other paediatricians, raising strong fears in the profession that paediatricians would now avoid child protection work, or that it would take '30 years' to remove public suspicions against them (Laville, 2004).

Ideological changes at policy level

As well as backlash pressures, ideologically influenced policy changes at central and local government level under both Conservative and New Labour governments from the 1990s onwards reduced the identification and prosecution of child sexual abuse. This has particularly affected England and Wales. Dr Liz Davies has charted and analysed these changes in depth). In brief, she has highlighted:

1. The landmark *Messages from research* (Bullock et al, 1995), as a watershed in the development of policy and practice in child protection and child welfare. It was the rationale for work to be re-focused from 'children at risk' to 'children in need' with assessment and treatment of families' needs, rather than harms. Yet children in need are often also children at risk! Too many children, it was thought, were being unfairly drawn, over-zealously, into the child protection 'net'. Support for families was more appealing. Narrowing down the state response, social workers became commissioners of services. But as a result, identification of really dangerous situations was lost, and in reality, services like health visitors and school nurses, vital for early intervention, were being cut. Careful risk assessments over a period of time (vital for the detection of child sexual abuse, in particular) were reduced in the interests of cost-cutting.

2. The structure of Children's Services was altered to fit with policy changes. Child protection specialist teams, which had

often been co-located with the specialist police teams, were abandoned and replaced by Child in Need social work teams. There was also a sudden decline in specialist child protection social workers who had been trained to work jointly with police, with a loss of focus on perpetrators. As joint working in child protection became an outdated concept, so did joint training. This also undermined the ability to collate data which revealed abuse by gangs and groups involved in child sexual exploitation. Moves towards deregulation included abolition of the Child Protection Register in England and a drastic reduction in statutory guidance there.

3. Davies and Duckett explain the process of what they see as a dangerous decline in protection of children from harm in England and Wales:

> *Working Together* [HM Government, 2013] removed the term *joint investigation* altogether, referring to investigation as solely a police activity associated with criminal proceedings … there is now a gap in processes whereby social workers focus on the assessment of the child's needs and police focus on investigation of crime. The joint investigation of *significant harm* has been lost from policy and practice guidance. The vulnerable child was generally referred to Children's Services and defined as a child in need (s17 CA 1989 – which is to promote the welfare of the child and provide relevant services) rather than a child in need of protection and consequently no multi-agency protection plan was in place.
>
> Social work child protection teams became child in need teams and assessment of the child's needs became the dominant mode of intervention instead of proactive child abuse investigation. At a time of severe cutbacks, assessment and non-statutory services were ready-made for privatisation and outsourcing, and subsequently many were closed down altogether. (Davies and Duckett, 2016)

4. A very important point is that creditable goals became, and still are seen as, *reducing* the numbers of children on registers or child protection plans – whereas, as discussed in this chapter, addressing the secretive crimes of CSA and CSE assertively would involve *increasing* these numbers. This is a fundamental flaw in child protection systems in relation to detection of child sexual abuse. It is so important that this should be exposed and widely discussed with a view to overturning the whole notion that reduction in cases means improved detection. That also means a fundamental challenge to, and an overhauling of, government targets.

5. Centralisation of social work services also involved moves from small 'patch' offices and teams, well-integrated with other local statutory voluntary and community services, and knowledgeable about that local area, towards large, one-stop, open plan buildings with little privacy. This created particular problems for the integrated care of children at risk, for their identification and for the identification of perpetrators, while in contrast neighbourhood 'patch' offices had been central to the uncovering of organised child abuse in Islington (see Chapters Five and Six; Davies and Townsend, 2008; Davies, 2009, 2010).

New technologies and online abuse images

The final, but important and urgent, reason, looking to the future, why we should be extremely cautious about either assuming complacently a real decrease in child sexual abuse or a successful addressing of it is found in several developments related to new technologies. There is the massive, exponential increase in the worldwide industry of online child abuse images. In 1990, the Home Office estimated that there were 7,000 such images circulating in Britain; now police can find up to 2.5 million images on a single computer. These images increasingly encompass violent and sadistic activities, and images of younger and younger children being sexually abused. They have been made ever more accessible to both adults and children through continuing development of new technologies and social media (CEOP, 2012, 2013)Research into these issues and knowledge about them develops all the time along with the technologies: whatever we write could quickly be overtaken. But three major sources of concern need to be flagged up. The first involves the need for ever more abusive images of children, on an international scale, including 'real-time' abuse in the so-called 'dark net'. Johnson et al (2014) highlight ways in which production and consumption involve a global supply chain, connecting to human trafficking, child pornography and prostitution, all trading on human bodies for profit. Abusive images are the public face of a larger network of sexual exploitation which deliberately recruits from the poor, disadvantaged and desperate from across the world.

The second big area of concern surrounds the effects on the wider population of boys and young men of freely available violent, degrading or sadistic pornography, with few serious age controls, in relation to their sexual behaviour with and beliefs about girls and young women (End Violence Against Women, 2012; Stewart and Szymanski, 2012). Advances in technology, including smartphones, tablets and other online devices, facilitate grooming, sexual bullying, 'sexting' (the sending or receiving of sexually explicit texts, image or video on mobile phones, computers or tablets), abuse by peers, and networking for abuse rings and child sexual exploitation. Prevalence studies of children's experience of sexual violence in the UK and Europe have suggested increased levels of sexual violence involving *peers and young adults* as both victims and perpetrators (Barter, 2007; Barter et al, 2009); Radford et al, 2011). Increasingly violent and abusive materials are appearing on the internet (Eisner et al, 2010; Horvath et al, 2012). Male adolescents' exposure to sexual explicit media has been linked to favourable attitudes towards uncommitted sexuality (Brown and L'Engle, 2009), sexual objectification of women (Peter and Valkenburg, 2009), increased sexual preoccupancy (Peter and Valkenburg, 2010), and sexually aggressive behaviour, in the case of violent pornography (Ybarra et al, 2011).

The respected psychotherapist Dr John Woods of London's Portman Clinic felt impelled to speak out publicly (Woods, 2012) on the threat after treating numerous children and young people of all social backgrounds (mainly boys as young as 12) who have become compulsive viewers of thousands of violent and extreme pornographic images. These images have included sex with children. Woods believes this is no longer a private health problem, but a public health one. Young people may become child abusers while they are still children themselves, and once these brutal images have formed a child's first sex lesson, they can be difficult to erase. An increasing part of his caseload consists of children whose behaviour has become out of control, due largely to compulsive internet porn use. He is treating boys who have abused their five-year-old sisters following frustration at being unable to live out their internet fantasies in everyday life. Yet funding cuts, he says, mean mental health services are having to make drastic efficiency savings that significantly reduce his service.

> All these cases are only the tip of the iceberg. For every young person who has come to the attention of police or social services, there will be tens of thousands more who manage to keep their habit under wraps...as a therapist, I believe the internet has now been around long enough for us to see the toll that unregulated sexual imagery is having on our children. (Woods, 2012)

Yet most parents, he says, remain in ignorance or denial; even though the largest consumer group for internet pornography is children aged between 12 and 17. This ready access by children and young people to online pornography, with its often dehumanising and degrading values, counters a widely accepted need to inform young men and women of values of respect and equality in sexual and intimate behaviour, in order to reduce CSA, domestic violence and adult sexual offences. This presents an enormous challenge for the future in terms of how far access to online materials can be controlled; in terms of monitoring the effects on young people, and ameliorating negative effects through parental, school, youth and other programmes. It needs to be done in non-patronising ways, which can actively involve young people, and respect their own ideas and intelligence.

Meaning of offender detection statistics unclear

The third source of concern about whether child sexual abuse is declining, increasing or remaining stable surrounds the meaning of much-increased numbers of offenders identified as viewing, downloading or distributing child abuse images. Numbers of registered sex offenders continue to rise: in England and Wales the 2013–14 figures were 43,664, compared to 32,347 in 2008–09, a rise of more than a third over five years, according to the MAPPA report (Ministry of Justice, 2014). There were 24,572 in 2004, 29,973 in 2006. In Scotland there were 3,314 registered sex offenders in the community in 2012–13, and 3,953 in 2015, compared with 2,984 in 2008–09.[5]

This increase may well mean we are protecting more children from perpetrators, demonstrating welcome improvements in detecting offenders, keeping some out of circulation for a time, and keeping others better monitored. Unfortunately, it could equally mean that various kinds of sex offending against children have increased; or that internet offending figures have revealed that *there always were much larger numbers of sex offenders against children than previously realised*. This is why interpreting sex offender statistics is so difficult.

There is an active debate about links between possession of online abuse images and 'hands-on' assaults against children. Current evidence on this is conflicting (McGuire and Dowling, 2013). Some studies, such as CEOP (2012), suggest viewing indecent images of children is often an important risk factor for contact offences. Other research challenges such a link, or finds small numbers of dual offenders.

However, the second category has received far more belief and publicity among practitioners. There was an outcry when the Bourke and Hernandez 'Butner' study (2009) found that while 26% of their 155-strong sample of internet offenders had a proven history of hands-on offences, by the end of treatment 85% admitted this, with an average of 13 victims per offender. But their findings precipitated intense criticism and claims that

---

[5] www.scotland.police.uk/about-us/police-scotland/specialistcrime-division/national-offender-management-unit/

the research was flawed, despite the authors rebutting these criticisms in detail (Bourke, 2012, and Chapter Two).

Temptations to reduce risk

Two temptations may reduce the perceived 'offline' risk of 'online' offenders. First, many have been shown to be respectable, middle class professional men with no previous criminal records. They have lacked established risk factors for sex offenders. That creates a temptation to feel that they are surely less likely to be dangerous. An alternative possibility, however, is that they may have been more skilled at concealing their behaviour. Second, the number of men (this is overwhelmingly a male offence) found in possession of indecent images of children continues to increase year upon year. The criminal justice system – even the police resources required to examine their computers – has been overwhelmed. There is a huge and growing backlog of cases to be investigated. In a single inquiry alone, Operation Notarise, there are details of more than 20,000 suspects, yet only a small proportion were investigated and fewer than 1,000 people were arrested in 2014 (Halliday, 2014). Making numbers manageable by minimising the dangerousness of many is not a safe way to deal with a genuine social problem.

The claim that most of those who gain sexual gratification from repeatedly viewing violent and perverse sexual assaults on young children are not likely to want to abuse children offline is at root a hope, not a scientific finding. It is fostered by the claims of offenders themselves. Evidence from studies which suggest this low risk is inadequate, relying heavily on official follow-up of known recorded sexual offences. But most sexual offences are carried out in secret, and will not be known, or if experienced will not be reported. Again, evidence that internet offenders have resisted committing contact abuse with children could be convincing only if their previous, present or future victim targets were identified, and were able to reveal if they had been abused. But most abused young people are not identified, find it extremely difficult to tell, and are often disbelieved when they do.

Accumulated knowledge of sex offenders suggests that they often offend compulsively, with often vast individual collections.

Thus we must ask how realistic it is that they would change their behaviour so drastically after being caught that 'in an average of 2.5 years only 3.9% of child pornography offenders reoffended for that offense, and those (internet) offenders with no prior criminal record ... had a contact sexual offense only 1.3% of the time...' (Seto and Eke, 2005).

Theory insults male population

The widely heard theory of accidental interest in abuse images is surely insulting to men as a whole. It suggests that while accidentally clicking on child abuse websites, thousands suddenly discover a deep-seated, unrealised urge repeatedly to watch and collect shocking images of children and toddlers being sexually assaulted or even tortured. All without any wish to try this on any actual children? The alternative hypothesis is that those who access abuse images are *already* sexually attracted to children, *already* seeking sexual gratification from watching these assaults, and have actively sought out these images. The implication, then, is that most represent a genuine risk to children. As Bourke and Hernandez (2009) asked 'are we faced with a new type of offender, or (merely) a new type of offending?'

This has major implications for calculating the current scale of sex offending against children, and the current challenges which our society and its law enforcers face in addressing it. Adult survivors of child sexual abuse have for decades tried to tell of being abused by, for instance, teachers and doctors, clergy, sports coaches, foster parents, residential care managers or TV celebrities. Their testimony is also evidence. The first survivor whom I met in the Incest Survivors' Campaign in England in the early 1980s was upper middle class, and her colleagues included victims of a 'foster father of the year'.

Revealing the true scale?

It needs to be asked if the disturbing new statistics simply reflect more closely the numbers and types of abusers who have always existed, but who previously had far less opportunity (or technology) to view abuse images, and far less chance of being caught. In the UK and indeed internationally, spiralling numbers of known internet offenders may simply be reducing the large disparity between numbers of abusers previously identified in the criminal justice system, and the high prevalence of child sexual abuse revealed retrospectively by adult survivors.

If this is so, policymakers will need to address the sheer scale of prevention and protection which they need to prioritise. And we need to reconsider the implications of this and all the developments in online abuse for our understanding of child sexual abuse prevalence.

What needs to be done?

What are some of the measures that need to be taken to assess the prevalence of child sexual abuse more accurately, and genuinely to reduce its incidence?

Research on the continuing influence of the backlash

I believe we must roll back the effects of the backlash: but first this demands more precise knowledge of its current influence in child protection. Qualitative interviewing and survey research are needed with staff at all levels in professions concerned with child protection, including social work and residential care, police, health and education. This would explore their beliefs about what they have been allowed to do (for instance if they could ask young people directly about sexual abuse). It would explore their beliefs about backlash theories such as 'false memory syndrome' or the 'satanic panic', about any professional pressures they face about working with CSA, and about their sense of personal adequacy and confidence. Peer-reviewed and 'grey' literature including that available on the internet would also be examined for the influence of 'backlash' theories.

The lessons from that research could be fed into accurate information-giving, training courses and staff development programmes, and into meeting the needs of staff for support and supervision, and for a more outspoken approach from senior managers on behalf of children at risk. The aim would be to create a secure, supported, proactive, courageous and confident workforce, armed with accurate information in their work with young people and adults on issues of sexual abuse.

Reduction of barriers

There must be a reduction of some major barriers to the reporting of child sexual abuse, and to the detection of CSA perpetrators, so that a more accurate 'baseline' picture of the actual incidence and prevalence of CSA can be achieved (and, of course, to protect more young people). For example, this means enabling adults and children to pass on information about abuse with less fear or shame, through anonymous and third-party reporting, through legal support in psychiatric hospitals and prisons, through imaginative use of social media and the development of perpetrator-focused investigation (see especially Chapters Four, Five and Six).

More, and more effective, prevention strategies

For example, this will include effective whole-community prevention policies (Chapter Six), much greater protection for stigmatised young people in care or excluded from school from sexual abuse and exploitation (Chapter Four), trauma work with sex offenders against children who have themselves been sexually abused, to reconnect them with empathy with their potential victims, and reduce further risk (Chapter Ten); and finally, government resources on a national and international scale to reduce the harm caused through the burgeoning industry of child abuse images (Conclusion).

Careful, consistent evaluations of work aimed at reducing CSA in different settings

As part of any effort to judge whether or not child sexual abuse – including organised sexual abuse – has genuinely declined, stayed static or genuinely increased, I believe it is important to stop regarding CSA as some coherent, single phenomenon. Instead we need to examine and evaluate measures to prevent or reduce it in different settings and situations. That means, for example, monitoring existing prevention programmes over time, and setting up a range of pilots or pathfinders in communities and schools. In targeted area-based prevention policies, such patterns can be analysed and evaluated in detail over, say, three, five or ten years. An evaluation of five or even ten years, after all, is hardly long in the context of the whole history of CSA in society!

TWO

Lies and deception in the backlash

The enemy counted on the disbelief of the world. (Wiesel, 1993)

In order to escape accountability for his crimes, the perpetrator does everything in his power to promote forgetting. If secrecy fails, the perpetrator attacks the credibility of his victim. If he cannot silence her absolutely, he tries to make sure no one listens. (Herman, 1992)

Introduction

The opening chapter discussed some ways in which the modern backlash against the exposure of child sexual abuse (CSA) has undermined protection of children at risk. Supporters of accused adults have used media and academic discourse to shape public, legal and medical opinion; and at times to discredit, intimidate and silence child and adult survivors of CSA, the children's mothers and professionals who have tried to protect or support them.

Theories promoted by proponents of the backlash against exposure of CSA have received widespread credibility and media publicity. Those who believed abused children and adults have often found themselves portrayed as gullible and naive. This chapter examines how credible some major examples of backlash theories have actually been: the 'satanic panic', 'false memory syndrome' (FMS) and 'parental alienation syndrome' (PAS). Some individuals particularly active against sexual abuse, and repeatedly targeted for discredit, are discussed. Continuing attempts at discredit are suggested through the example of the 'Butner study'.

Careful academic and legal critiques already exist of FMS and PAS. As discussed later, the memory debates from the early 1990s onwards inspired valuable professional analyses of amnesia and memory issues following trauma. Rather than simply repeat these, I concentrate here on sometimes glaring weaknesses in backlash theories, which should have raised obvious doubts about their reliability and credibility, yet did not. At times, proponents' claims have been the opposite of the truth. The 'satanic panic' has been less often deconstructed than the other two theories, and less often questioned. I hope to do so here.

I examine why all three such stories, despite obvious weaknesses, became persuasive to many sections of society, and why critiques of these stories which were available at the time made little impact. Finally, I offer a re-interpretation of these stories as part of an historic, concerted resistance to the exposure of sexual abuse. Such precedents place the modern backlash against exposure of CSA in sometimes vivid historical context.

Why should challenging and exposing the backlash be relevant and important to the task of improving prevention, protection and support in sexual abuse work? Child sexual abuse debates have been wars of words. The winners of these arguments have influenced both child protection policy, and wider attitudes to the credibility of child and adult survivors of CSA. Understanding backlash theories in their historical context, exposing and considering their flaws, thinking seriously about any prejudices which made them persuasive – these things are important for everyone, whether they are politicians and policymakers, child protection professionals, media people or members of the public. Critical faculties are restored, and there is more sceptical examination of future attempts to minimise CSA, to discredit its victims and those who support victims. That will better protect young people at risk, and better support adult survivors of sexual crimes.

Indeed it is my strong view that agencies, including schools, with a role in protecting and safeguarding children will not be able to protect them better from sexual abuse until those authorities stop basing their approaches, behaviours and priorities on a nervous and defensive response to powerful, intimidating backlash movements.

Theories which promote the backlash against exposure of sexual abuse will continue, although like chameleons they will take on different colours. Each time they appear, we should ask: 'Who benefits? The victims of CSA, or their perpetrators?'

The liberal discourse about CSA

Much research, professional discourse and media understanding about child sexual abuse has been characterised by a liberal optimism – that nearly everyone wants the best for children, that most people sincerely seek facts and solutions, and that conventional academic research and professional debate will uncover these. Thus, what reputable-sounding professionals (especially medical and mental health professionals, or academics) say if they debunk child sexual abuse must be considered very seriously. In heated, polarised debates, the answer may perhaps lie somewhere in the middle.

This is an odd approach because child sexual abuse is not simply a social problem. It is a serious crime: one of society's major serious, organised and financially most lucrative of international crimes, involving great disparities of age, power and resources. For perpetrators there is huge investment in continuing, in covering tracks, and in undermining attempts to reduce it.

With other crimes – such as fraud, extortion, violent assault, robberies, tax evasion or even second-hand car fixing – we do not simply take on trust what those convicted or accused, or their supporters, tell us. We do not start by assuming their innocence. We do not believe them over their victims. The answer might not lie in the middle between two sides: they might be fibbing. Researchers with people involved in illegal activities routinely consider the possibility of deception (that is, not being told the truth about crimes interviewees have committed, nor about their current criminal involvement) when constructing their research design. Nor do we with most other crimes spend endless time, debate and research assessing whether or not alleged victims are telling the truth.

It is time to stop treating CSA and its controversies as some interesting intellectual discussion where everyone shares equal integrity, and treat it as the crime that it is. That means shedding naivety and innocent, deferential respect, especially towards educated, middle class men who promulgate theories and claims which deny CSA. Were theories like FMS, parental alienation syndrome or the 'satanic panic' supported by factual evidence, or were they deliberately constructed blind alleys?

Many references in this chapter date from the 1990s, or even the 1980s. This reflects the fact that meticulous critiques of some backlash theories and claims existed at the time, and could easily have been consulted. Yet they were still not given widespread credence. This suggests that they were not what most lay people and professionals wished to hear.

Examples of the backlash

> The backlash is characterised by extreme positions, lack of supporting research data, and near-total rejection of the knowledge and experiences of childhood sexual abuse. (Conte, 1994, p. 228)

Child sexual abuse is the most defended of crimes. Numerous theories – many of them now discredited – have diminished, discredited or dismissed it since Victorian times.

1. Satanic panic

Just because it rhymes, it doesn't mean it actually happened.

'Satanic panic' theory emerged from the late 1980s and early 1990s onwards. It is a variant of the moral panic theory in sociology (Cohen, 2002; Young, 2009).

Satanic panic theory developed following very disturbing, bizarre and baffling disclosures by children of sadistic organised abuse with ritual overtones, and disclosures by adults, especially by those who had experienced severe dissociation. Satanic panic theory is elaborately designed and still very influential in explaining away organised abuse with ritual – especially occult

– elements. On the internet, it is almost impossible to find any neutral description of ritual abuse cases which does not invoke this claimed 'panic' and its theoretical claims.[1]

Yet this theory is another invention. Professor Jean la Fontaine called belief in the existence of satanism a triumph of faith over reason. But could that apply instead to uncritical belief in a 'satanic panic'?

The disturbing disclosures of some children and adults from the late 1980s onwards included accounts of extreme sexual, physical and emotional cruelties, even torture and sometimes murder, with ritual, religious or magical overtones, committed by groups – especially, but not exclusively, those with satanist or occult beliefs. The distressed children and adults might chant strange prayers, write in odd script, describe being drugged and sadistically abused at quasi-religious ceremonies, being locked in cages or coffins or suspended on upside-down crosses, or witnessing torture and killing of animals and babies. Children and adults showed extreme terror. A reputable literature documenting ritual abuse has existed over several decades (for example, Snow and Sorenson, 1990; Gould, 1992, 1995; Sinason, 1994; Coleman, 1994; Scott, 2001; Matthew, 2002, 2005; Salter, 2013a.

Constituent elements of satanic panic theory

When in the USA, cases of alleged ritual abuse were publicised, particularly in nursery settings, and when in the UK, children were taken into care in publicised cases of alleged ritual abuse in Rochdale, Nottingham and Orkney, satanic panic theory rose to prominence.

In brief, this theory claimed that stories had originated in the USA of a widespread, highly organised cult of devil-worshippers who engaged in blood sacrifice and ritualistic child sexual abuse. These rumours were said to be propagated by a surprisingly wide assortment, and a more surprising collaboration, of people including evangelical pastors, police, psychotherapists, radical

---

[1]   The SMART and the Survivorship ritual abuse pages are exceptions: https://ritualabuse.us, https://survivorship.org/ritual-abuse-evidence.

feminists and social workers specialising in child abuse. (This was despite the fact that neither radical feminists nor social workers are known for their staunch fundamentalist Christian convictions, nor for their urge to believe in the devil.)

Under satanic panic theory, it is claimed that the panic then swept across the Atlantic to Europe, with the beliefs of child protection and mental health staff fuelled or even instigated by, it is frequently said, Schreiber's *Sybil* (2009), Smith and Pazder's *Michelle Remembers* (1989), and Bass and Davis' *The Courage to Heal (*1988). Supposed links with these particular books were once again repeated in a BBC Radio 4 documentary by Aaronovitch (2015). It has been claimed that child protection staff were instantly converted to the idea of 'satanic abuse' and very zealous to prove it, even after attending a single conference on the subject. Child protection officials were said to use a range of dubious, vague, usually unspecified techniques to extract extremely bizarre disclosures from children and adults.

Promoters of 'satanic panic' theory drew parallels with historic witch hunts in mediaeval times, with the Salem witch trials or even with McCarthyism (Nathan and Snedeker, 1995; de Young 2000, 2004; Frankfurter, 2001, 2006).[2] It was allegedly this panic which led to children being snatched into care across the USA, UK, New Zealand and other countries; to respected, loving families being accused of 'satanic' child abuse; and to 'witch hunts' against respectable parents.

These stories have kept reappearing in the media and on the internet, sometimes with 'folk devil' of the backlash, Dr Roland Summit (see Chapter Three), thrown in.

> South Ronaldsay (Orkney) is where the ritual sexual abuse theory leapt from the pages of social work journals and entered the popular lexicon of the nation. ... A psychiatrist Roland Summit's controversial idea was that organised, ritualistic abuse of children was happening everywhere. ... it was out there and all social workers had to do was go and find it. And they did so with a passion of a zealot

---

[2] See also http://en.wikipedia.org/wiki/Satanic_ritual_abuse

rooting out evil. The idea crossed the Atlantic gaining professional credibility as it spread like wildfire. (Crichton, 2001)

… On demonic wings, presumably!

Reasons given for the spread of these 'wildfire' beliefs include: the influence of fundamentalist protestants and a fundamentalist religious ideology (much more applicable to USA than UK); and people seeking simplistic answers to complex social developments and economic upheaval during economic decline, insecurity and family disintegration (echoing the 'witch hunts' of earlier centuries) (Clapton, 1993; la Fontaine, 1998). Other theories included that satanism was being normalised in popular culture, film and rock music, with the potential for eroticism in devil worship (Clapton, 1993).

Many flaws in this theory

There are numerous flaws in the 'satanic panic' theory.

- There *was* no widespread panic, certainly not in the UK. The majority of professionals and lay people remained unaware of these disclosures and behaviours by children and adults, and of attempts to interpret them. Only a small, often isolated minority of police, psychiatrists and counsellors, journalists, child protection professionals and foster parents had personally encountered the disclosures. Further, most of their own colleagues were sceptical and unsupportive of their belief, even thinking they must have 'lost the plot' (see Carole Mallard, Chapter One).

Distortion of professionals' reactions

- Nothing could be further from the truth than the claim that professionals and random feminists pursued satanic abuse theory with passion or zeal. The only people I ever met who seemed pleased and vindicated by evidence of satanist abuse (satan*ist* indicates human followers of a cult, not the devil) were a few evangelical Christians, who saw satan everywhere, told me he was flying low across the fields, and prayer-marched through places like Inverness (near the notorious satanist Aleister Crowley's old house).

That anyone else would actually *want* to find or prove it, or would be pleased and zealous in pursuit, was bitterly laughable. Even for many people experienced in working with CSA, it was the worst, most disorienting and traumatising knowledge in the world. This could easily have been established by talking to professionals at that time. There was the strongest impetus to disbelieve that ritual abuse and its tortures took place, because it threatened to overturn your lifelong belief systems, your trust in the limits of human conduct towards children, your sense of safety, and your judgement of the people in front of you. I suspect that all of us can remember the very day we decided with tremendous shock that evidence before us pointed to only one conclusion, that ritual abuse of children did indeed take place. Ritual abuse cases also brought many professionals considerable fears for their personal safety (Youngson, 1993; Sinason, 1994).

- I lived and worked through this particular controversy, and neither met nor heard of any professional who came to believe ritual abuse existed through reading *Sybil, Michelle Remembers* or *The Courage to Heal*. They all, in my experience, first came to it through trying to make sense of baffling disclosures by children and/or adults. Nor can I remember over decades anyone ever reading or recommending *The Courage to Heal* for whatever it might have said about ritual abuse or 'multiple personality disorder'. Survivors read it for its helpful, respectful and imaginative support in assisting recovery from all forms of sexual abuse trauma.

- We are expected simultaneously to believe that 'satanic abuse' disclosures and allegations are unbelievable, incredible, ludicrous and completely without evidence – and would be to any normal person – and that educated professionals in child protection and mental health swallowed them whole after reading one book, or attending one conference!

Out of line with moral panic theory

- The scapegoats and folk devils in classic moral panic theory (Cohen, 2002) should have been the accused adults. But in fact they have been the professionals who took children into care and/or publicly professed a belief that ritual abuse existed. This has been another substantial flaw in the (satanic) moral panic theory. It was not at all a means of professional advancement, but often of professional discredit, ridicule and vilification.

- Another essential feature of 'moral panics' in classic sociological theory is that these are promoted, carried and encouraged by the media. But most media, after a brief flurry of salacious interest, became not supportive but hostile in their coverage of ritual abuse. Most media have *supported* accused parents, and adults who have respectable standing in their communities, in major publicised cases of alleged ritual abuse, in both the USA, UK and other countries (see Chapter Three). This is another major flaw in 'satanic panic' theory.

- The verbal disclosures, actions and behaviours of children and adults abused in ritual settings were so baffling, so esoteric and so unlike content previously heard that it would be incredibly difficult – I would suggest impossible – to generate these words, actions and behaviour through pressured interviewing techniques by professionals such as social workers. (Even had these illegitimate techniques been specified and proved to have occurred in each case.) It was in fact the foster parents of children taken into care in both Nottingham and Orkney, not professionals during interviews, who produced by far the most evidence of children's bizarre statements, drawings and actions. These were ordinary people who were baffled and disturbed by what they witnessed and heard from the children placed in their care. No convincing explanation of this point by 'satanic panic' theorists has ever been made.

- The alleged alliance of radical feminists and right wing evangelical Christians was laughable: the great majority of professionals and foster parents who met ritual abuse were neither. This could have been checked at any time.

Critical faculties lost

- Critical faculties seemed to be lost. For instance in Orkney during the child abuse inquiry of 1991–92, a series of occult bookshop newsletters, apparently published in Leeds, with titles like *The Lamp of Thoth*, circulated widely on the islands and were sent to elected councillors. I found these newsletters strewn about in the council and inquiry. 'At last the full truth about the satanic abuse allegations can be revealed!' they dramatically claimed. Whole sections of their propaganda about worldwide conspiracies by social workers or evangelical Christians were repeated as fact, even in some 'quality' papers, despite clearly coming from such a partial source.

- Again, claims were spread that one 'born-again' Christian basic grade social worker, CF, influenced the Orkney social work department and police into jointly carrying out the dawn raids. This influence by a basic grade worker was implied too in BBC Scotland TV's 'faction' drama *Flowers of the Forest* (BBC Drama, 1996). Among other, often ludicrous, aspects of this drama (listed in Nelson, 1996) the fact was ignored that even had the social worker sought this far-reaching and long-planned act, he lacked any professional power or status to succeed.

Shortcomings of la Fontaine report

- When Professor Jean la Fontaine published her Department of Health-commissioned summary report *Extent and Nature of Organised and Ritual Abuse: Research Findings* (la Fontaine, 1994) – which minimised evidence of ritual abuse in 84 cases studied – most media and the Health Minister Virginia Bottomley agreed that it 'exposed the myth of satanic abuse'.

It was set up as serious research in the wake of public furore about notorious cases, but for anyone with experience of social research, it was a breathtaking document, as I listed in previously published work (Nelson, 1994). Yet this did not appear to trigger critical appraisal.

It offered nothing more substantial in research findings than 36 pages full of anecdote and opinion, the scantiest definitions, and a bibliography in one-third of a page to summarise a substantial, reputable professional literature stretching back at least ten years.[3]

Assessing only recorded cases where an allegation of ritual abuse had been made, the report made random claims about interview flaws in cases which are not outlined. It dismisses the testimonies of adult survivors. It contains no summary of conflicting arguments in the professional literature; no interview reports or summaries with social workers, police, therapists, or voluntary organisations; no reports of interviews conducted with foster parents. Yet her statistics reveal that foster parents were the largest single category of people to whom disturbing claims were made. They are disparagingly dismissed without evidence as a group who (like social workers) already had a belief in satanic abuse. Yet most foster parents had been kept ignorant about basic aspects of the children's upbringing (Nelson, 1994).

An alternative explanation?

I suggest that there is a far simpler explanation for the conviction, which grew among some child protection staff, police, therapists, journalists and others in the late 1980s and early 1990s, that organised abuse in the form of ritual (including satanist) activity existed. This explanation accords with their actual, shocking, traumatising, month-by-month experience as evidence accumulated in cases in which they were directly involved.

The burgeoning feminist movement had strongly challenged victim blame, mother blame and the excusing of male

---

[3] The full report, though promised, never appeared: instead she wrote a book debunking ritual abuse, *Speak of the Devil* (la Fontaine, 1998).

perpetrators of child sexual abuse. It made central the gendered abuse of power, and attitudes within families and the wider society. Writers such as Florence Rush (1980) and Judith Herman (with Hirschmann, 1981) were influential in changing the understanding of CSA among practitioners and agencies. The movement gave impetus to a considerable growth in official recognition of numbers of known cases of CSA, from a one-time estimate of one in a million (Henderson, 1975).

By the mid-1980s, many professionals, including psychiatrists, psychologists and social workers, had stopped discounting abused children's and adults' disclosures as oedipal fantasy, imagination, misinterpretation, madness or lies. Open-minded listening developed trust, often for the first time, among victims, that they would be heard and might risk telling more, without being disbelieved, laughed at or committed to a psychiatric institution.

Open-minded listening

Open-minded listening to, and consideration for, children and adults opened the floodgates to professionals hearing and considering all kinds of then barely known sexual abuse, of which ritual abuse was merely one. These, we now know and accept, have included widespread abuse of boys; abuse by women; abuse in institutions, by headmasters, care home staff, priests and other religious figures; abuse by politicians; abuse by therapists treating victims; abuse of children in care sent abroad; abuse of indigenous peoples.

'The opening up of new and more sympathetic therapeutic spaces created alternative testimonial opportunities for victimised children and women, away from the medico-legal traditions that had trivialised their accounts' (Salter, 2013a). The contribution of child sexual abuse trauma to adult mental ill health was also increasingly acknowledged – for example Briere and Zaidi's (1989) study of female psychiatric emergency room patients had found a CSA rate of 70%.

Thus, professionals witnessing these disturbing, unusual, distinctive words and behaviours about ritual and occult events, instead of dismissing them, desperately tried to make some sense of them, seeking information from research reports and conferences. Ritually abused children and adults must have said, drawn and acted out strange, frightening, apparently meaningless things long before, but were likely to have been judged mentally ill or even psychotic. Obsessive-compulsive disorder specialists had already noted the oddly blasphemous religious content of many patients' intrusive thoughts (Toates and Coschug-Toates, 2002). One possibility is that a history of ritual abuse accounted for these.

Be suspicious...

I suggest in conclusion that we all ask some simple searching questions, and exercise a lively suspicion, about a 'satanic panic' story riddled with so many holes. Why has it been vital to discredit ritual organised abuse so thoroughly, and with such elaborate, inventive design? Why is this invention still evident all over the internet, to the near-exclusion of criticisms of it, and why have critics failed to get more accuracy accepted into Wikipedia entries about ritual abuse?

2. False memory syndrome

'Satanic panic' theory has an interconnection with the false memory movement. For Michael Salter, the rhetorical importance for false memory syndrome of 'satanic ritual abuse', and the chance this gave to ridicule allegations of child sexual abuse, is shown by the term being found in 140 of 144 newsletters of the False Memory Syndrome Foundation (FMSF, 1992–2011) (Salter, 2013a).

FMS has been one of the most influential backlash theories of recent decades. Uncritically promoted through most media for many years, it is still propounded today (see French, 2014).

The theory and its invention

FMS was invented in the early 1990s, as a new psychiatric condition, by accused adults. That in itself should have attracted the strongest critical scrutiny. It emerged in response to claims by adult women of child sexual abuse, and sometimes of ritual abuse, especially by fathers in educated, professional families. Such fathers were very threatened by these developments and spearheaded the membership of FMS societies. Many, though far from all, instances involved recovered memories of abuse. The FMSF was established in the USA by the accused parent Peter Freyd and his wife Pamela, following recovered memories by their daughter Professor Jennifer Freyd. By the mid-1990s FMS societies had sprung up in many countries, gaining public respectability by attracting some academics and mental health professionals, mainly psychologists, to their boards.

False memories of sexual abuse were allegedly, on a very widespread scale, put into the heads of gullible, mentally unwell women by therapists, using dubious techniques, unreasonable pressures or even brainwashing. These women supposedly found it comforting to blame their mental ill health, their troubles or inadequacies on the explanation of sexual abuse in childhood (Gardner, 1993). Numerous documents expounding and developing the theory can be read on the British False Memory Society's website.[4] As in 'satanic abuse', the women have been portrayed as weak, as blank canvases or fantasisers, driven by feminine neuroses, while therapists were malign. FMS was said to shatter devoted families.

In Salter's (2013a) interpretation, the women's movement and child protection movement at that time challenged the gender order of male control of families (Morris, 2009) and appeared to attack innocent, socially respected men. This released much anti-feminist and misogynistic sentiment (see the attacks on Bass and Davis, below). 'The claims of the accused were accepted at face value ... the ensuing backlash resulted in multiple failures to protect children and vulnerable adults' (Salter, 2013a).

The reliability of recovered memories following trauma was continually challenged by some psychologists and other academics in false memory societies (although not by the vast majority of trauma specialists). Whitfield illustrates their scattergun approach by listing 22 claims proponents made. They included: the accused looks respectable; the accused is the real victim; the therapist or therapy group is to blame; the plaintiff

---

[4] http://bfms.org.uk/

is crazy; it is not common sense; the claims are similar to alien abduction claims. There is frequent use of pseudo-scientific jargon and invented terms like FMS, recovered memory therapy or parental alienation syndrome: 'In other words, disinformation and junk science' (Whitfield, 2001).

Influential over range of settings

FMS theory was very influential in academic, media and legal debates. Academic 'expert witnesses' presented the arguments of defence teams in court as scientific fact. The journalist Marjorie Orr meticulously collected numerous examples of media giving credence to this theory, as well as collecting and publicising much painstaking academic research which challenged its veracity and claims.[5]

Hine (2000) and Salter (2013a) have documented repeated lawsuits and other extremely intimidatory actions against numerous professionals, including doctors, therapists, psychiatrists, lawyers and advocates, in the USA who believed and supported survivors, or who criticised proponents of FMS. In the UK, there was huge media publicity, almost entirely sympathetic to the accused parent, about the 'recovered memory' cases of Katrina Fairlie and of the Scotford daughters (see, for example, Nelson, 1998b; Feltham, 1999; Cramb, 2001).

In 1991, before formation of the FMS Foundation, more than 80% of news coverage in the popular press about child sexual abuse was weighted towards histories of survivors and the nature of childhood trauma. However, by 1994 more than 80 % of news coverage focused on allegedly false accusations and 'false memory syndrome' (Stanton, 1997).

Obvious flaws ignored by believers in FMS

What did many people within legal systems, the media, mental health professions and others gullibly fail to consider?

---

[5]   See www.accuracyaboutabuse.org

- Believers in FMS accepted a theory invented by the Freyd parents, Peter and Pamela, who had no qualifications to judge memory issues, over their daughter, the distinguished psychology professor Jennifer Freyd, who had many. They also ignored the published account by Peter Freyd's own brother William confirming Peter's abusiveness (Freyd, 1995). Jennifer wrote:

  > I am flabbergasted that my memory is considered 'false' and my alcoholic father's memory is considered rational and sane. ... is my father more credible than me because I have a history of lying or not having a firm grasp on reality? No, I am a scientist whose empirical work has been replicated in laboratories around this country and Europe ... (Freyd, 1993)

- Actual experts on traumatic amnesia, and a considerable and historic literature for many forms of trauma (which could easily have been checked) were widely ignored. Whitfield (1997a, 1997b) has cited 36 studies specifically confirming amnesia for abuse. There are many research findings on the existence of traumatic amnesia and recovered memories (for example, Feldman-Summers and Pope, 1994; Herman, 1995; Terr, 1995; Williams, 1995; Fish and Scott, Pope, 1997; 1999; Whitfield, 2001; van der Kolk et al, 2001).[6]
  Yet even in 2014, false memory proponents were arguing through the media: 'There is a consensus among scientists studying memory that traumatic events are more likely to be remembered than forgotten, often leading to post-traumatic stress disorder' (French, 2014).

- Indeed the wider phenomena of traumatic amnesia and recovered memories had already been well documented for decades, in cases of combat trauma and concentration camp experiences (Jaffe, 1968; Krell, 1993; Marks, 1995; van der Hart et al, 2002). Yet nobody appeared to ask why, strangely, these

---

[6] Two useful websites summarise research over decades: http://blogs. brown.edu/recoveredmemory; www.jimhopper.com/memory/

phenomena were *only* causing major controversy in cases of child sexual abuse.

- Believers in FMS failed to check whether this scientific-sounding syndrome had any scientific credibility.

  'Syndrome' refers to a documented group of signs and symptoms that characterize a particular abnormality. In this case, there have been no clinical trials, no scientifically controlled comparison groups, no research to document nor quantify the phenomena. 'Syndrome' is used simply to create an aura of scientific legitimacy. (Olio and Cornell, 1994)

  On the 'recovered memory therapy' or RMT – which title they also invented and which many media still retain – 'There are no known schools of recovered memory, no conferences on how to practice recovered memory therapy, nor are there any textbooks on the topic' (Scheflin, 1999).

No easy explanation

- As anyone working with adult survivors of child sexual abuse would know, seizing on supposed sexual abuse as a child as an answer to your troubles is not at all a comforting or easy explanation. The experience of CSA exposes people to social stigma, shame, disbelief, deeply confused loyalties, the pain of betrayal, often by people they loved and trusted most, and possible court cases where they may be vilified and dismissed. Hence many survivors take decades to disclose, while others never do so. This key fact is blatantly ignored by critics of works such as *Courage to Heal*. The critics argue that such books encourage troubled women to imagine they have been sexually abused when they may not have been (Aaronovitch, 2015). Instead, Harvey and Herman (1994) suggest that recovering memories is so agonising that survivors hold on to denial for as long as possible.

- False memory societies (and most media) failed to check awkward, but very basic, facts: for example, that often survivors whom they claimed had FMS had never seen a therapist; had never forgotten their childhood abuse (Freyd, 1996); or had found independent corroboration for their memories. Harvey et al (1987) found three-quarters of subjects in their study were able to corroborate their recovered memories of CSA. Nor did the FMS societies usually present any proof that even if survivors had been in therapy, the particular therapist(s) used methods which would have extracted such false memories. Research indeed challenged this claim (Andrews et al, 1995; Morton et al, 1995).

- Proponents of FMS also ignored survivors' experience of triggers of recovered memory which do not involve therapists at all. These can include childbirth, the death of the abuser, their child reaching the age when they were abused, media coverage of police investigations, violent revictimisation, or being in a secure personal relationship, where it finally feels safe to confront one's past.

- Journalists and others failed to check the backgrounds and the attitudes to CSA of some of the most vocal defence 'experts' in courts, even when some like Ralph Underwager had been shown to justify paedophilia (Hine, 2000; Cheit, 2014; Salter, 2013b; see also Richard Gardner below).

What could have been powerful enough to override such basic checks, and such critical questions? If by chance you as a reader believed in FMS, why did you do so? I will return to these questions because I think they are the most important ones to make about backlash theories.

3. Parental alienation syndrome

Parental alienation syndrome' (PAS) was invented by the late American psychiatrist Richard Gardner. He argued that child sexual abuse allegations were rampant in disputed custody cases and that 90% of children in these cases suffered from PAS. On his view vengeful mothers used child abuse allegations to punish ex-husbands, and to deny them custody or visits (Gardner, 1991, 1992). He theorised that such mothers often brainwashed the children into believing false claims that fathers committed abuse, and that children then contributed their own fabricated stories (Gardner, 1992, 2002).

Major flaws in theory

• The authenticity of the syndrome is not officially recognised by medical, scientific, legal and professional authorities.(Faller, 1998;Surface, 2009) It has repeatedly been denounced by research specialists as junk science:'the scientific status of PAS is, to be blunt, nil' (Emery et al, 2005).

• The 'syndrome' is not backed by evidence. Child sexual abuse allegations in custody cases are actually quite rare. The largest study of child sexual abuse allegations in custody litigation found that these formed fewer than 2% of cases. High rates of unsubstantiated maltreatment, in circumstances indicating that abuse or neglect may have happened, are found to be a significantly more prevalent problem than false claims of child sexual abuse (Thoennes and Tjarden, 1990;Trocme and Bala, 2005).

• PAS was invented by a man whose own writings revealed that he believed all human sexual paraphilias, including paedophilia, rape and sadism, served species survival by 'enhancing the general level of sexual excitation in society'. Gardner claimed adult–child sex was beneficial to the species, in increasing the likelihood that genes would be transmitted at an early age. Women's physiology and conditioning made them potentially masochistic rape victims, who may 'gain pleasure from being beaten, bound, and otherwise made to suffer', as the price they have been willing to pay for receiving the sperm. Gardner lobbied to abolish mandated reporting of child abuse, to abolish immunity for reporters of child abuse, and for the creation of federally funded programmes to assist individuals claiming to be falsely accused (Gardner, 1993; Wood, 1994; Dallam, 1998; Hoult, 2006).

- The theory ignores sound reasons why sexual abuse by a father figure could be much more likely to emerge *after* parental separation or divorce. The child may feel physically safe and secure for the first time to confide to her or his mother, while a mother's suspicions about abuse may have been the reason for the separation in the first place.

- Judging the allegations of sexual abuse, or indeed of domestic violence, as manipulative parental alienation by the mother fails to consider known patterns of manipulative behaviour in *perpetrators* of child sexual abuse and domestic violence towards partners and children. It also fails to consider that failure by fathers to meet agreed contact levels with their children after separation are much more a source of complaint and frustration for mothers than attempts to deny fathers rightful access to their children.

Influential theory despite flaws

Yet despite all the flaws in this theory, and despite its official non-recognition over the decades, it has become a widespread, powerful influence: not just in criminal and civil courtrooms, but among child protection professionals themselves (Surface, 2009). It has become a virtual article of faith that child sexual abuse in particular is widely and falsely alleged by mothers in, or where there has been, custody litigation (Meier, 2009).

In the UK, the only country I can speak of personally, *all* of us working against sexual abuse have seen many cases across several decades where divorced or separated mothers, having raised fears, or even presented evidence that their child was being sexually abused on contact with fathers, have been disbelieved by courts and social workers. They were considered to have invented the allegations or imagined abuse, irrespective of the child's own disclosures.

Often, those children have then been given into the custody of their fathers: usually the mother's contact has been curtailed or lost, and she has been considered mentally unwell in some way, emotionally damaging to her child, or even in the grip of Munchausen's syndrome by proxy. Virtually every Women's Aid, Rape Crisis and sexual abuse survivor support agency in the UK, and many a family lawyer or children's rights lawyer, has witnessed and worked with such cases. Most have tried to support protective mothers to contest the decisions made against them. Is this 'just anecdotal evidence'? Ask them, through surveys and other research.

If this theory is full of holes, if it is not in fact based on hard evidence, where does its great power come from? From strong historic prejudices, that women's and children's credibility is highly suspect, and that women are malicious accusers of men. From the adversarial courts system too, where fathers' lawyers (especially where articulate, middle class professional fathers can pay for the most effective lawyers) find it a godsend. From an entrenched historic belief among judges, and indeed many other professionals, that a father has a right to his children, no matter how he treats them (McInnes, 2014).

Vital to challenge continuing influence

I believe these prejudices have been a major, significant source of gross failures over decades to protect many children from sexual abuse, greatly weakening and demoralising their only protector. It is now vital, and a policy priority, that strong guidance on the need for impartial investigation is issued to legal professions, police, health and social work professions.

In such guidance, prejudices must be named and challenged. Fears or allegations of sexual abuse, made by mothers during or after divorce or separation, must be investigated as rigorously and open-mindedly, with as much skill and informed knowledge about patterns of violence and abuse, as any other. Evaluators from all relevant professions should have a genuine expertise in both child abuse and domestic violence. If abuse claims are verified, or subject to strong suspicion of having happened, then the safety and protection of children must be dominant concerns, with preservation of the relationship with the father a secondary concern.

Propaganda against individuals

With individuals who have been targeted repeatedly by proponents of the backlash, it will be important to consider if this might be because they have so many faults; or because they have been particularly outspoken and effective on behalf of abused children and adults.

The American psychiatrist and campaigner for abused children Dr Roland Summit has given courage and insight to many besides myself with his inspirational and fiercely committed writings (Summit, 1988; Olafson et al, 1993). He keeps appearing in backlash literature. On Orkney, journalists were told by accused parents that Summit was a major culprit in inspiring witch hunts by social workers in Orkney and internationally. It was claimed that Summit had said that if children denied abuse, this meant it had probably happened. This is a distortion of his most famous paper, 'The child sexual abuse accommodation syndrome' (Summit, 1983).

Strangely, this exact claim surfaced in 1994 in a *New Yorker* editorial: 'A psychiatrist named Roland Summit explained to the jury in the Kelly Michaels case that when children deny sexual abuse happened, the denial can be evidence that the abuses actually did occur' (Wright, 1994). Summit replied to the newspaper – which subsequently published a retraction of the claims made against him – that he had been wholly uninvolved in this American case and had said nothing to the jury. 'It would be fatuous to argue that denial is really confirmation in disguise. I have never said such a thing anywhere' (Freyd, 1996; Cheit, 2014).

Feminist devils

Search the internet for Bea (Beatrix) Campbell, the prominent British feminist writer and campaigner with a long track record of incisive investigation and campaigning on behalf of sexually abused children. The torrent of verbal abuse and accusation she faces on the internet would unsettle many a less steely advocate for children. This is nothing to the vilification faced by the feminist authors Ellen Bass and Laura Davis. They have been attacked countless times by proponents of the backlash, especially by advocates of FMS, as heavily to blame, in their lengthy and substantial self-help book *The Courage to Heal* (Bass and Davis, 1988) for recovered memories by adult women. They have also been attacked for numerous other sins. *The Courage to Heal* entry on Wikipedia is typical of this backlash position,[7] and attacks include a viciously anti-feminist review by Robert Sheaffer (1994).

The attacks continue regularly. In the BBC Radio 4 Analysis programme, 'Ritual satanic abuse: the anatomy of a panic', broadcast on 31 May 2015, the programme producer was interviewed, very unusually, on air by the presenter David Aaronovitch. Hannah Barnes claimed, in an echo of the precise allegation against Summit, that the book says "that if the person you accuse is denying it, this is confirmation that it happened". It does not say so. Co-author Ellen Bass confirmed to me (personal communication, 2015) "No, we absolutely did not say that. We never said that denial was any kind of confirmation of abuse."

Later editions of *The Courage to Heal* included a section called 'Honoring the Truth: a Response to the Backlash' (Bass and Davis, 2008) in which they refuted a range of criticisms made against the book, and clarified and qualified the much-criticised phrase in the first edition 'If you think you were abused you probably were.' It is amusing that Bass and Davis are slated for not having professional qualifications, given the faith which backlash proponents displayed in Peter and Pamela Freyd.

We need to ask if Bass and Davis have really been attacked so frequently because their book has proved so helpful and so inspiring to the confidence and recovery of adult survivors themselves, that it is now in its *20th edition*?

Continuing examples of the backlash?

The Butner Study: links between online images and hands-on abuse

It is important to recognise recurring examples of the backlash, even if these come in a different guise.

---

7 en.wikipedia.org/wiki/The_Courage_to_Heal

There must always be a healthy critical awareness when it comes to analysing the research methodology of any study. But if concerted, repeated attacks on a few books or studies are not based on genuine flaws, alertness is needed for other possible reasons for these attacks. Who benefits if the authors are discredited?

In 2009, a study by psychologists Michael Bourke and Andres Hernandez was published in the reputable *Journal of Family Violence*. This suggested strong links between viewing online abuse images of children, and hands-on sexual abuse. The findings went against most other studies to date, and a belief among many practitioners in sex offender work that viewing child pornography online had only minor links with hands-on abuse of children.

The 'Butner Study' analysed data on 155 men convicted of child pornography offences, who took part in an 18-month therapeutic treatment programme at FCI Federal Correctional Institution (FCI) Butner. When sentenced, 74% of the men denied molesting anyone. But by the end of treatment, 85% had admitted at least one assault. Bourke and Hernandez's paper was accepted and published by the journal. But the Bureau of Prisons asked the editors to withdraw the study, because it did not meet agency approval.

The study has from then on been subjected to what Bourke himself described as 'An inordinate amount of attention ... trying to invalidate the study through cocktails of myth, innuendo and rumor.' It has notably been 'rubbished' in court settings, and is now widely believed to have been discredited, or at least to be full of flaws.[8]

Detailed rebuttal of critics

However in a very detailed rebuttal, Bourke (2012) has answered all major criticisms which have now been made, and continue to be made, repeatedly of the study.

---

[8] See https://rsoresearch.files.wordpress.com/2012/01/butner_study_debunking_kit.pdf

- *Inmates were removed from treatment if they failed to disclose hands-on victims.*
'During the eight years I served as a Staff Psychologist at FCI Butner no program participant was ever removed because he did not disclose undetected contact offenses.'

- *Their sample ended up being artificially skewed in favour of hands-on offenders.*
Bourke found the reverse: those with hands-on victims were more likely to be expelled or to quit the programme

- *After publication Dr Hernandez admitted shortcomings and 'backpedalled' from the findings.*
Dr Hernandez and Bourke were 'confident there are no methodological issues that raise questions about the reliability of the information we obtained'.

- *Staff members expected each participant to add to his list of offences as he progressed through treatment.*
Participants were only expected to disclose such offences if this was the truth!

- *Almost any offender faced with the pressure built into the Butner Program would generate many possible false disclosures.*
No such pressure existed – there were no consequences if an offender said he had never committed a hands-on crime.

- *The study had a 'selection bias' because participants were chosen for treatment based on more serious offending or disorders.*
No inmates were *sent* to the programme – all volunteered. The only criterion was that they were nearing the end of their sentence.

- *The authors of the 'Butner Redux' paid the* Journal of Family Violence *to publish the article and/or selected their own reviewers.*
The Journal, he replied, is a reputable, peer-reviewed journal that accepts manuscripts on academic merit. They neither paid to have the article published, nor knew the identity of the professional reviewers.

- *In Seto, Hanson, and Babchishin's (2011) meta-analysis, the study was characterised as an 'outlier', implying something was wrong and findings were flawed.*

But Bourke vigorously concluded:

> The high disclosure rate obtained in the Butner Redux sample is not attributable to coercion, or demand characteristics, or sampling problems, or methodological issues, or selection biases, or any other rumor that has been created to 'account for' the findings. Perhaps the answer will not be found in what the folks at Butner did wrong, but what we did right.

- To justify this he rightly criticised criminological research's over-reliance on official arrest records and reconviction statistics, saying reconvictions should not be used as a proxy for *re-offence*, especially in crimes where detection rates are very low: 'Using an arrest history or conviction history to label an offender would make Al Capone a simple tax evader.' In Seto and Eke's meta-analysis (2005) for instance, most researchers had had access to only one information source about the offenders. At FCI Butner they could access a very wide range including victim statements, family interviews, polygraph information, clinical notes and information disclosed from participants (Bourke, 2012).

Why was it threatening?

Why might this study be so important and so threatening that it has brought down such fierce criticism, and many apparently baseless claims? Because if accurate, its findings could have very great implications for public safety and law enforcement, in this era where activity and communication have so dramatically shifted to an online world.

It could change the whole estimate of dangerousness of the many thousands of men, very often professional, educated and middle class, in Britain alone who are known to have viewed, downloaded, exchanged or created child abuse images. Most have had no previous criminal records for sex crimes. For example after the arrest of 660 men after a six-month police operation targeting people accessing child abuse images online, The National Crime Agency said these suspects included teachers, former police and medical staff. But only 39 of the 650 were registered sex offenders while the rest had been under the radar (Shaw, 2014).

Suppose the professional viewers now identified are the doctors and lawyers, the sports coaches, foster parents, residential care managers and TV celebrities whom *survivors* of child sexual abuse have tried to tell us for decades were their own abusers? The implications for numerous current, mainly respectable and respected, abusers, who wish to continue abusing, are extremely threatening. Is this why the Butner study has unusually, among thousands of research studies, been singled out for repeated vilification and, it appears, for the spreading of deliberate untruths?

Why did gullibility happen?

It is important to consider why theories by proponents of the backlash which have been full of holes have been so widely believed and promulgated, particularly through the mass media.

Just 'denial'?

Is the answer a massive denial of childhood sexual abuse in society? There is indeed denial, but to make such a sweeping generalisation is patronising, unfair and unhelpful. Nor will it be effective to tell everyone sternly that they are simply in conscious denial and must stop. You need some knowledge of something before you can deny it, and some forms of CSA have been genuinely difficult for many people to believe. This approach is unlikely to persuade people to change their views!

Are the media to blame?

Has this, then, simply been about gross distortion by the media? Hostile media coverage has often strongly influenced public attitudes against professionals who believed children were abused. The Cleveland case was a vivid example which set a tone for others (Donaldson and O'Brien, 1995). Some prominent individual journalists also have a longstanding, consistent record of challenging the veracity of allegations, particularly of organised or institutional sexual abuse, of questioning the guilt of the accused in such cases and expressing concern about false allegations and wrongful convictions. They include David Rose, Bob Woffinden, Rosie Waterhouse, David Aaronovitch and Margaret Jervis. At times some right wing media have had an assertive agenda to attack the social work profession, even when these acted jointly with police.

But it is too easy to blame some unified, monstrous 'media'. Not only has coverage varied, not only have the media played a major role in exposing cases of gross abuse – including the Savile revelations and some English child exploitation cases (see Chapter Four). Some prominent individual journalists also have a longstanding, consistent record of investigating and exposing CSA and child sexual exploitation cases. They include Eileen Fairweather, Tim Tate, Nick Davies, Liz McKean and Cate Deveney. Readers and viewers can also reject, ignore or fail to notice published evidence which challenges their pre-existing judgements about CSA cases, as Jenny Kitzinger's study of people's recollections about the Orkney case revealed (Kitzinger, 2000). Finally, journalists and editors are also themselves part of the public, and reflect public beliefs as often as they shape them.

Poor child protection practice?

Did belief in backlash propaganda, then, spring from inept efforts to protect children, and undoubted poor practice in investigation and interviewing in some publicised cases? Did mistakes, ill-judged or precipitate actions by authorities, especially at a time when knowledge about child sexual abuse was still emerging and most agencies were poorly prepared, discredit other cases that followed, making pro-backlash arguments more credible? Andrew Vachss (1989) highlighted several such issues, in calling on all authorities to maintain the highest standards in child protection.

Examples of poor practice have been one undoubted influence, and the most rigorous, accountable investigative practice needs to be a priority in sexual abuse. However, the problem about asserting that poor practice has been largely to blame for many people's willingness to believe 'backlash' theories is that unfortunately, examples of poor practice happen right across social policy and social care with vulnerable people. Yet they have led to nothing like the same levels of public and media condemnation, expensive inquiries, lasting influence, or subsequent restrictive legislation.

We still need to ask why poor practice in *sexual abuse work* should cause such outcry: and (an important distinction) not in all sexual abuse work. More rarely in failures to identify child *victims,* but more often in actions leading to *adults* being accused wrongly or with inadequate evidence. As the example of top-level resignations at the BBC and the very fast financial compensation to the late Lord McAlpine after his wrongful identification in a care home abuse case demonstrated (Sabbagh and Deans, 2012), it still appears much more shocking to be accused of sexual abuse than to suffer it.

The above answers, then, are relevant but too 'pat' in explaining why intelligent people of all backgrounds and professions have been vulnerable to believing tales which bear little serious scrutiny.

Uncomfortable to learn about or believe

To see through disinformation and unlikely stories, people need to be reasonably informed and aware about child sexual abuse, and prepared to consider possibilities which threaten cherished beliefs about who would commit this crime and who would not. But learning about this subject makes many people uncomfortable and distressed, especially (and understandably) the idea of trusted parents and carers sexually abusing young children, or inflicting extreme cruelties. Theories which reassure that this is untrue are thus very tempting to seize upon.

> It is as though we don't want to believe it, and so every bit of evidence that is presented to us, no matter how convincing, is then filtered out through the fine mesh of our beliefs and doubts. With this kind of internal pressure to disbelieve all evidence, our objectivity and reasoning capacities are then not open to allow us to carefully listen, consider and weigh what we hear from both sides. (Whitfield, 2001)

> Organised abuse highlights the potential of some adults to inflict considerable, and sometimes irreversible, harm upon the powerless. Such knowledge is so toxic to common presumptions about the orderly nature of society, and the generally benevolent motivations of others, that it seems as though a defensive scaffold of disbelief, minimisation and scorn has been erected to inhibit a full understanding of organised abuse. (Salter, 2013a)

For professionals, recognising abuse and maltreatment from puzzling evidence often depends on being prepared to 'think the worst' of adults. Thus Doctors Chris Hobbs and Jane Wynne described how colleagues faced with severe, shocking or even fatal, injuries to children diagnosed exotic diseases, because they could not contemplate parents wilfully harming their children in these ways (Hobbs and Wynne, 1994; and see Chapter Seven).

Yet if child and adult survivors find the courage to tell us, then we must find the courage to listen with an open mind, and challenge our own beliefs, if their accounts suggest that it is time to do so.

Historic prejudices against child and adult victims

Historic legacies of often strongly prejudiced assumptions against children and women in particular have influenced many people towards ready acceptance of backlash theories. There have been powerful reservoirs of prejudice against children, with their long history of being disbelieved in sexual abuse, as ready liars and ready fantasisers, and even as instigators and encouragers of sexual acts (see Bender and Blau, 1937; Nelson, 1982, 1987; Taylor, 2002). Especially if they display delinquent behaviours which many young victims of sexual abuse act out in their despair and alienation (see Chapter Four).

People unaware that mental ill health can develop through trauma itself can easily assume that mentally unwell adults have been weak, sickly, easily brainwashed by therapists, seeking quick answers for their illnesses, and non-credible witnesses. Into the mix has gone the strong historic tradition of prejudice about alleged hysteria, malice and emotionalism in adult women (Gaarder, 2000; Campbell, 2003; and parental alienation, this chapter), along with doubts about the credibility of men who have offended or misused drugs in reaction to their abuse trauma.

'It's against common sense'

Elements of some abuses can appear to defy 'common sense.' This point is used to discredit victims and those who work with them. Thus in ritual abuse, if children say people have died and returned to life, that a tiger was in the room, that ice turned to boiling water or that they flew across the ceiling, this is easy to dismiss – unless you know such sincere childish beliefs can be instilled through drugging, sensory deprivation and conjuring tricks (Scott, 2001; Matthew, 2002, 2005; Miller, 2014). Miller gives the example of ritually abusive groups convincing children

> that something evil has been put inside them. For example, a child is made to believe he or she has a 'black heart' – seeing the abuser holding an animal heart and then feeling severe chest pain while it is supposedly inserted. In 'brain transplants', the brain of an abuser or of a despised animal such as a rat is supposedly put into a child. (Miller, 2014, p. 324)

Techniques involving drugging, sensory deprivation and trickery are familiar in political torture, but most Britons and North

Americans (assuming their governments do not do such things!) are unfamiliar with the research connecting this with sadistic abuse. Jean Goodwin's valuable work discusses the importance of placing ritual sadistic abuse within a recognisable political, social and psychological context, drawing on relevant data about studies of sadistic criminals, and studies of war crimes and political torture (Goodwin, 1993).

It is salutary, when discussing unspeakable cruelties, to recall the words of Elie Wiesel, the Holocaust survivor and author, in response to Oprah Winfrey exclaiming how "unbelievable" his experiences were. Wiesel responded: "The enemy counted on the disbelief of the world" (Wiesel, 1993).

Second, the effects of childhood sexual trauma such as traumatic amnesia and severe dissociative disorders appear to defy 'common sense'. Backlash proponents met ready agreement if they asked 'Surely, people could not possibly forget shocking life experiences and suddenly remember at age 35? Someone must have put these ideas into their heads? And multiple personalities – are you having a laugh?' Only a minority of professionals working with trauma were familiar with the complexity of the human brain and its defences, and aware that these phenomena were common and well documented over many decades: in relation to battlefield, torture and concentration camp experiences.

Unpalatable class and political aspects

The late 1980s and early 1990s saw many more professional middle class people accused, when previously known defendants in 'incest' cases were typically the working class or rural poor. For professional people including editors and journalists, these were decent, educated 'people like us', with whom they could readily identify, a very unsettling situation and one I personally witnessed when a journalist (see Chapter Three).

Propaganda cleverly appealed to both the political right and left. Lumping feminists, Christians and ideologues together crafted targets whom groups from across the political spectrum felt justified in attacking. For strong believers in traditional, patriarchal family values, the FMS lobby appealed to a powerful ideal: close loving families, cruelly shattered by baffling, false allegations. People who respect traditional authority have found it extremely disturbing to contemplate that, for instance, religious figures and churchgoers could commit such acts.

Political liberals and libertarians have long worried that state intrusion into the private sphere undermines civil liberties: they frequently hold, too, optimistic beliefs about the sexual free agency of younger teenagers, which underplay coercion. Gay men have sincerely feared that action against sex abusers both offline and online might limit their sexual freedoms as consenting adults. The theory that claims of widespread child sexual abuse simply constitute a 'moral panic' or 'witch hunt' has thus been very appealing to liberals and progressives. Also, allegations could readily be seen as an attack on alternative spiritualities, such as paganism.

As a result...

A whole series of factors thus congealed to fog many intelligent people's critical sense. The crucial point was ignored that those adults were accused of serious crimes, thus there was a strong possibility of special pleading. Articulate, reasonable-sounding arguments and energetic media campaigns by their support lobbies were widely taken on trust. Few asked 'Who benefits from this backlash? Is it abused children? Or is it someone else?'

Interpreting backlash arguments in historical context

'The enormity of the accusation destroys its probability'

Suppose instead we start by acknowledging that perpetrators of serious crimes are not known for their willingness to admit them. And that they are now known to come from every level of society, including the most wealthy and powerful. In historical context, how might we re-interpret modern propaganda which supports accused adults, attacking the credibility of victims and those who support them?

Child sexual abuse is strikingly unusual for being repeatedly discovered, discredited, re-established and discredited over time

– in what Olafson et al (1993) have called '*cycles of discovery and suppression*'. That suggests that there must be something peculiarly dangerous and threatening about exposing it on any widespread scale: and that many interests have a continuing stake in maintaining a supply of abuse 'fodder' from vulnerable young people.

The historical context

There is a long history of believing those suspected of sexual abuse above children, and above those who support abused children and adults. There is a long history of dismissing mothers, either as active colluders in abuse or as the malicious or hysterical accusers of innocent men; and an equally long history of disbelieving women and children who are raped or sexually assaulted. Brave men and women have always spoken out on children's behalf, and have been attacked for it.

The French forensic scientist Ambroise Tardieu, in 1857, painstakingly documented and studied 632 female cases of suspected sexual abuse, mainly of children under 16 years (Roche et al, 2005; Labbé, 2005). He concluded that child sexual abuse was common and gendered; that offenders were mainly known to the child; that abuse occurred in all classes and within the family. But when Paul Brouardel succeeded to Tardieu's post, he quickly redefined the strong physical evidence he and Tardieu had documented in terms about both children and their mothers which have uncanny resonances today. As do the words of Fournier and Garnier, below.

In 1883 Brouardel stated:

> One often speaks of the candour of children. Nothing is more false. Their imagination likes to invent stories in which they are the hero. The child comforts herself by telling herself fantasies which she knows are false on every point. (Masson, 1994)

In 1885 he added:

It can happen that the parents act in good faith, but that in their ignorance of infantile pathology they take simple inflammations of the vulva to be the result of criminal sexual assaults on their child. Panicked by findings that seem to her very grave and significant, the mother presses the child with questions, and reaches ... the point where she suggests to the child an account which will then serve as the basis for the future accusations. (Masson,1994)

Brouardel argued that most accusations were false, originating in hysteria, attention-seeking, 'debauchery' or the 'extreme suggestibility' of children to their mothers' questions. Fournier implied that respectable fathers would be incapable of sexually assaulting children (shades of the FMS lobby!) Gamier's case study had a 'hysterical' young woman accusing her 'honourable' father of incest, noting 'the enormity of the accusation destroys its probability' (Masson, 1984).

Issues rehearsed in the 19th century

Shifting the blame

Thus many issues in current child abuse debates were already being clearly articulated in European medical discourse, before and during Freud's early career, when he first linked sexual abuse with mental illness in his humane and perceptive essay *The Aetiology of Hysteria* (1896); then famously retracted his conclusions – describing his professional isolation – in a decision with lasting influence on psychiatry. It is striking and revealing to consider that in such a repressive Victorian climate, the shocking idea that young children were actively sexual was *still* more acceptable than the idea that respectable fathers might be sexually abusing them.

Late Victorian feminists and sex reformers who criticised male sexual behaviour and exposed the extent of child sexual abuse were redefined as man-hating, frigid, possibly lesbian 'prudes'. Here are shades of later attacks on feminists, especially on Bass and Davis (Rush, 1980; Summit, 1988; Jeffreys, 1997).

Sandor Ferenczi, Freud's psychoanalyst colleague, believed the testimonies of abused children and the confessions of perpetrators, describing how the overwhelming power and authority of the adult leads the child to surrender (Ferenczi, 1949). He was denounced and after his death in 1933, Ernest Jones obtained Freud's approval to suppress Ferenczi's work 'Confusion of Tongues', calling it a tissue of delusions (Masson, 1984; Roazen, 2001).

Victim blame suggested children might do more than fantasise – they might actively encourage sexual abuse, as when the psychoanalysts Bender and Blau wrote that children might be the actual seducers, with their 'unusually attractive and charming personalities' (Bender and Blau, 1937). As late as 1982 when the first edition of my book *Incest: Fact and Myth* was published, child psychiatrists in Scotland protested to me that even three-year-olds had 'strong desires of an incestuous nature' (Nelson, 1982, p. 41).

In Kinsey's major study (Kinsey et al, 1953), a quarter of female respondents reported being approached sexually in childhood by a man at least five years older, with four out of five frightened by this. Kinsey dismissed their fears and was concerned that girls or 'older unmarried women' might cause men to be imprisoned for accidental exposure of the genitalia or bestowal of 'grandfatherly affection'. It was later revealed that parts of the Kinsey reports (Kinsey et al, 1948, 1953) were based on a paedophile's own diaries.

By the late 1970s, the professional 'incest' research literature I unearthed remained replete with influential theories which transferred culpability from male offenders to the victims, to their mothers, and to a working class subcultural 'way of life' (Lukianowicz, 1972). Mothers in incestuous families were repeatedly accused of facilitating and colluding in incest between girls and fathers, or in driving men into their daughters' arms through their frigidity (Nelson, 1982, 1987; Feigenbaum, 1997; Collings, 2009).

That brings home how strongly these prejudices have been historically embedded in the most highly qualified and educated professional circles, and how far from open-minded impartiality has traditionally been the discourse around CSA, which has fed into modern backlash responses.

Why might a modern backlash begin in the late 1980s and early 1990s?

This book discussed how child-centred changes in the early 1980s and especially the impetus of feminist movements saw professionals such as social workers, therapists, counsellors, psychiatrists and police listening to child and adult survivors more open-mindedly about sexual abuse – rather than dismissing the disclosures as fantasy, incestuous desires for a parent, fabrication or mental illness. This opened the floodgates to exposure of many kinds of abuse.

'Backlash' responses to these discoveries can be reinterpreted as conscious attempts to discredit as many as possible, and to target those most committed to exposing child sexual abuse and supporting survivors. If we look at the sequence in this way, a different and very suggestive pattern emerges.

Feminists – as in late Victorian times – were bound to be in the modern firing line, through their role in exposing the realities of CSA in the late 1970s and the 1980s. For accused men, feminists became targets of anger, accusation and resentment. This reached vehement levels with the attacks on Bass and Davis. It fed on popular prejudices too when 'hate figures' such as the paediatrician Dr Marietta Higgs in the Cleveland case received infinitely more attention and recrimination than her male colleague Dr Geoffrey Wyatt, who was just as involved and committed as herself (Nava, 1988; Campbell, 1998).

Backlash developments have been, almost uniformly, led by the educated middle class: the backlash coincided with indicators that respectable middle and working class parents (mainly men) did this to their own children, and to those they controlled as managers of schools, care homes, and so on.

Children are most likely to tell their mothers, along with their friends, and certainly more likely to tell them before official agencies (Crisma et al, 2004; McElvaney et al, 2012; McElvaney, 2013). Thus it likewise became important to discredit these mothers through theories like PAS, a simple task given the historic legacy of prejudice against them.

Professionals who saw or listened

If proponents of backlash theories discredit the interview techniques of professionals who question children, there is still the risk of physical signs betraying the secret, so these too need to be undermined and their medical professionals attacked.

When adult survivors begin revealing past and current sexual abuse of children to mental health professionals, they and their hearers need to be discredited. And so on. The great feminist psychiatrist, Judith Lewis Herman, has powerfully written in *Trauma and Recovery*:

> Underlying the attack on psychotherapy, I believe, is a recognition of the potential power of any relationship of witnessing. The consulting room is a privileged space dedicated to memory. Within that space, survivors gain the freedom to know and tell their stories. Even the most private and confidential disclosure of past abuses increases the likelihood of eventual public disclosure. And public disclosure is something that perpetrators are determined to prevent ... perpetrators will fight tenaciously to ensure that their abuses remain unseen, unacknowledged, and consigned to oblivion.
>
> In the past few years, many clinicians have had to learn to deal with the same tactics of harassment and intimidation that grassroots advocates for women, children and other oppressed groups have long endured. We, the bystanders, have had to look within ourselves to find some small portion of the courage that victims of violence must muster every day... those who stand with the victim will inevitably have to face the perpetrator's unmasked fury. (Herman, 1992, pp. 246–7)

It is illuminating to illustrate and document, step by step, the gradual discrediting in the modern era of various evidence of sexual abuse, and the discrediting of those who exposed such abuse.

Traditional theories

- It's an oedipal fantasy
- It's a way of life in the working class subculture
- It reflects a caring relationship
- She's that sort of young woman, you know
- Sexually precocious children are to blame
- Frigid collusive mothers are to blame
- The whole dysfunctional family is to blame.

Many of these theories were being discredited by the mid-1980s, then along came...

... 'Backlash' response to new findings

- It's a satanic panic: to discredit organised and ritual abuse, social workers and abuse victims.
- It's mad paediatricians: to discredit child protection doctors and physical signs of child sexual abuse in children, in family or nursery settings.
- It's a witch hunt: to discredit professionals investigating the middle and upper classes.
- It's false memory syndrome: to discredit therapists, feminists and adult survivors.
- It's parental alienation syndrome: to discredit abused children's protective mothers.
- It's greedy compensation syndrome: to discredit survivors of abuse in care, in institutions and in penal settings.
- They're just rebellious, delinquent young girls making a life choice: to discredit victims of CSE.

Since 2012 another backlash has emerged to undermine the waves of revelations about 'celebrity' abusers, the exposure of widespread child sexual exploitation, and police re-investigations into politicians, care homes and institutions. It is said to be another moral panic, another witch hunt, and/or a huge number of unproven allegations by people whose motives and integrity cannot necessarily be trusted (for instance Smith, 2010; Cree et al, 2014; Aaronovitch, 2015).This distrust and suspicion of adult survivors again disregards our longstanding knowledge of the great difficulty which most abuse survivors have in coming forward.

Conclusion

Protectors of children, and supporters of adults, have long been branded absurdly gullible by the proponents of backlash theories and claims. Indeed, it was implied, attending a single seminar on ritual abuse could sway them instantly, as could meeting Roland Summit at a court case – even when he wasn't there. In fact, it was surely those who 'swallowed' backlash theories who were unthinking and gullible, making no basic checks on the facts. We all – child protection and health professionals, media people, academics, general public – have the opportunity from now on to use our intelligence and our critical faculties, and to acknowledge our own prejudices. When the next backlash bus rolls along, the next enticing theory brightly lit on its destination board announcing that it probably never happened and you cannot trust survivors, feminists, therapists, social workers or mad doctors, STOP and ask three questions.

- Is this theory actually full of holes when you examine it properly?

- Which brave people is it trying to knock down this time?

- Who is going to benefit?

Professor Ross Cheit and his research colleagues spent many years painstakingly researching every detail of American cases, including court records, where organised sexual abuse (especially of young children in childcare settings) had been alleged. These cases have been widely declared witch hunts against innocent adults, but Cheit exposed numerous flaws in such conclusions. His book revealed 'how a (witch hunt) narrative based on empirically thin evidence became a theory with real social force ... which stood at odds with the reality of sexual abuse' (Cheit, 2014). Are we prepared to spend a small fraction of the time which Professor Cheit dedicated on checking if denials of the existence of child sexual abuse actually stand up?

Olafson, Corwin and Summit conclude (1993, p. 19):

> The full realisation that child sexual victimization is as common and as noxious as current research suggests would necessitate costly efforts to protect children from sexual assault. It remains to be seen whether the current backlash will succeed in re-suppressing awareness of sexual abuse ... and returning us to the 'shared negative hallucination' that has obscured our vision in the past ...
>
> If this occurs, it will not happen because child sexual abuse is peripheral to major social interests, but because it is so central that as a society we choose to reject our knowledge of it: rather than make the changes in our thinking, our institutions, and our daily lives that sustained awareness of child sexual victimization demands.

PART II

Children and young people

THREE

Fact, myth and legacy in notorious child abuse cases: Orkney in context[1]

This book is published in the 25th anniversary year of the Orkney child abuse case and inquiry

Introduction

Why should highly publicised child sexual abuse cases from decades ago remain important? Why should informed accuracy about them matter?

Because the way in which facts, or more often myths, about such cases are perceived is influential for decades – with a disproportionate, negative influence on public attitudes, on professional behaviour, and, it can be argued, on subsequent child law. The myths have fuelled suspicion, even denigration, of the social work and paediatric professions; increased the stress involved in child protection work; tightened legislation and practice in ways which make it harder to protect children at risk; and eaten into professional courage and confidence. The legacy of such cases not only influences opinion, but becomes the narrative of is true and what is false in sexual abuse.

For example, I and others working in this field continue to meet teachers, youth workers, children's panel members and social workers who still quote the Orkney child abuse case of 1991–92 as a reason not to ask a child if anyone has harmed

---

[1] Earlier versions of sections of this chapter appeared in 'The Orkney Child Abuse Case' in Noblitt and Perskin (2008).

them sexually, however disturbing the signs and behaviours may be. 'The Orkney Report said we mustn't – didn't it?' Actually: no, it did not.

Thus it remains important to analyse individual, highly publicised cases, to check the facts, and to ask if lessons drawn, influenced by media coverage, are soundly based or not. If they are not, then the lessons drawn from them – such as undue caution and timidity against exposing sexual abuse – now need to be revised too. It is also important to ask whether major child abuse inquiries – often instigated after such high-profile cases – can benefit children at risk, unless in their remit and conduct children's own safety and protection are central, including the children at the centre of the case.

This chapter argues that the Orkney child abuse case remains widely misreported and misrepresented. When criticism of clumsily precipitate professional practice is justified, as it was there, people are more likely to believe untruths as well as truths about the cases, leaving a legacy which is unprotective of children.

By repeatedly publicising misrepresentations, and by omitting significant elements of this case, the media were key players in the presentation of Orkney, as they were in Cleveland. There was little difference in reporting by tabloid, 'broadsheet' and broadcasting media. This chapter highlights the important role of media in covering child sexual abuse cases. But it is too simplistic to blame the media for all misrepresentation and public hostility. Besides, media investigation has at other times been vital in *exposing* child abuse (such as in the Islington children's homes scandal – Fairweather, 2008; the Jimmy Savile revelations – MacKean, 2013; or child sexual exploitation by gangs in England – Hall, 2013).

Journalists need to explore the reasons for prejudicial coverage of *certain* abuse cases. It appears to happen more often with forms of abuse which are hard to believe, and with accusations made against respectable, articulate parents. This was suggested by the widespread media gullibility about 'false memory syndrome', when mainly professional fathers were accused of abuse by their adult children (see Chapter Two).

A brief history of the Orkney case, and features of how it was interpreted, follows. This chapter suggests that interpretation was much influenced by previous child abuse cases in Rochdale, Cleveland and Nottingham, or rather by media representations of these. I ask if the Orkney Inquiry's conclusions, which led to more cautious interpretations of children's reliability, were fundamentally flawed. I examine how the interests of actual children were marginalised, and ask which 'child-centred' issues might instead have been pursued and funded after such a case. This has messages for other inquiries. I consider repercussions for seriously abused children after Orkney, through a major subsequent case of serious child abuse in the Scottish Islands: a case which did lead to a child-centred inquiry which provides a model for others.

Brief history of the Orkney case and inquiry

In November 1990 a teenage girl, OW, one of 15 children in the very disadvantaged W family in South Ronaldsay, Orkney, alleged sexual contact by her older brothers and a Presbyterian minister. Seven of her younger siblings were removed from home into state care by social workers under place of safety orders. They had already been taken into care in 1989 but had been returned home, to the alarm of the Royal Society for Prevention of Cruelty to Children (RSSPCC) and Scottish Executive officials, who as a result suspended the Orkney Children's Reporter Katherine Kemp.[2]

Until February 1991, a public campaign by some Orkney people against the W children's continuation in care included the clergyman and his wife, the local doctor, the M parents and Mrs T. Social workers were worried and baffled by the huge volume of correspondence being sent to the young W children, and by many puzzling messages and symbols it contained.

In February 1991, during interviews by RSSPCC interviewers and police officers, three young W children made separate allegations of organised sexual abuse and strange outdoor

---

[2] In Scotland, these officials are key people within the child protection system – receiving referrals about children who are giving concern, investigating, and deciding if compulsory interventions are needed. If so, the case goes to a children's panel.

rituals in a quarry and on a beach in South Ronaldsay, an area characterised by flat farming land and shallow, water-filled old quarries. They claimed that many adults and children were involved, including the clergyman and the M, T, B and H families. They described strange costumes, musical equipment, portable lights, trailers and a 'hooker' (a type of shepherd's crook).

On 27 February, at 7 am, police and social workers, assisted by staff from two mainland social work departments, removed nine children into care from the four families (M, T, B and H) under place of safety orders. All four families were English 'incomers' to Orkney; three were middle class. Grounds for referral mentioned group sexual activity including 'ritualistic music, dancing and dress'. Parental access was refused, along with most personal possessions. Police questioned the parents and the church minister.

A major campaign by the parents, the local doctor and others was immediately launched against these children's removal. Media involvement was almost entirely in support of the parents, who very articulately protested their innocence and made links with journalists. The first use of the phrase 'satanic abuse' appeared to be by the media, not by the authorities.

During March and April 1991 the nine M, T, B and H children were interviewed repeatedly by RSSPCC staff and police. Interviews with, and behaviour at foster parents by, five of the children appeared to confirm certain aspects of the W children's allegations. In April 1991 the proof hearing was heard by Sheriff David Kelbie. (In Scotland, these take place if the findings of the children's panel about a case are disputed.) He held that the proceedings had been incompetent, calling the case "fatally flawed", and the evidence was not heard – nor ever has been – in any civil or criminal court. The children were immediately returned home amid huge publicity.

In June 1991, after the Crown Office (which is responsible for prosecution of crime in Scotland) announced that there would be no criminal proceedings, the government announced a public inquiry under Lord Clyde. Its remit was to inquire into the authorities' actions in taking place of safety orders, removing the children from home, and detaining them in places of safety. It was to make recommendations. As with the Cleveland Inquiry, *its remit was not to inquire into the truth or falsehood of the abuse allegations.*

Until March 1992 the Inquiry sat in public in Kirkwall, taking numerous oral and written submissions. In October 1992 Lord Clyde published his report. It stressed that all officials acted in good faith, but the 135 summary comments were overwhelmingly critical of the authorities' handling of the case, including their advance planning, coordination, care planning and aspects of interviewing, such as a failure to record interviews. The report made more than 190 recommendations for future good practice.

These ranged over how investigations should proceed, when removal of children should take place, improved rights of children when detained, the proper treatment of, and information to, foster carers, training needs, conduct of medical examinations, interviewing of children, and the role of children's panel reporters and social workers (Clyde, 1992, pp. 353–63).

Many of the recommendations influenced the subsequent Children (Scotland) Act of 1995. The Act saw changes in child protection orders, a tightening of conditions surrounding such orders, and provision for removing suspected abusers from home. In March 1996 the four families, M, T, B and H, accepted financial compensation, and an apology from Orkney Islands Council.

Common presentations of the Orkney child abuse 'scandal'

However, there is not a great deal even of the above bland recital in popular representations of the case. If anyone googles 'Orkney child abuse case', they are unlikely to find a balanced, objective description or discussion of it anywhere.

Orkney is held up as a 'child abuse scandal' and a ridiculous case of 'satanic panic': 'South Ronaldsay (Orkney) is where the ritual sexual abuse theory leapt from the pages of social work journals and entered the popular lexicon of the nation' (Crichton, 2001). Such versions have been recycled in Wikipedia, in documentaries, in books, 'faction' dramas and newspaper features. The allegations, it is claimed, were completely baseless, the social workers were gullible or worse, the innocent parents suffered terribly. Coverage is heavily focused around cruel 'dawn raids'.

Repeated, but problematic or inaccurate, reporting

This includes:

- Assertions that the allegations proved completely unfounded. Thus the introduction to *The Accused!* documentary is: 'we now hear the powerful story of those wrongly accused' (Blast! Films, 2006). It has been reported – even in one social work magazine – that 'The abuse allegations against the other four families proved completely unfounded' (*Professional Social Work*, 2013).

- The adults may indeed have been wrongly accused, and the allegations may indeed have been unfounded. But the evidence was never heard nor tested in any court; and to be fair to the adults, they themselves wished it to be. Thus, to this day we still do not know if any of the abuses alleged took place or not.

- The dawn raids by social workers and police have been constantly condemned in media reports, often very emotively, such as 'Two decades ago, as the morning sun kissed the shores of a Scottish island, a squad of strangers grabbed nine sleepy-eyed youngsters from their beds' (Gall, 2011). Harsh behaviour by the officials is often alleged. Many things were criticised in Lord Clyde's Inquiry Report, but the dawn raids were not among them: 'The timing of the removal was beyond serious criticism' (14.3); 'the conduct of the workers in the removal of the children was efficient and supportive' (14.2).

- Sheriff Kelbie's decision to dismiss the evidence as "fundamentally flawed" (Waterhouse, 1996, p. 173) without hearing it is invariably highlighted. In contrast the verdict of Scotland's most senior judge, Lord Hope, that Kelbie had done incalculable damage and had breached the laws of natural justice (Herald, 2001). In news terms, an extremely strong statement by such a senior judge would supersede the actions of a discredited sheriff, yet the normal order is reversed.

• Baseless stories were planted about the role of individuals, such as Professor Roland Summit, in relation to the 'satanic panic' and periodically reappeared in print (see below).

• The police's joint role and joint decision making with social workers throughout – in the prior investigations and planning, the dawn raids and the interviewing of children from both the W family and the other four families – is either barely mentioned or airbrushed out of reports, leaving all blame attached to social workers. This cannot be coincidental, as the facts are clear.

• In the whole 1.5 hour documentary *The Accused* (Blast! Films, 2006) nothing substantial that any children from any family said or did is mentioned, nor are the foster parents interviewed about what the children said and did, which included incidents of disturbing, bizarre comments and behaviour. This is also the pattern for most reports in the media and on the internet.

New inaccuracies

New variations on what Orkney was 'about' have also been heavily covered in the media, when an adult survivor in the large, deprived and severely abused W family published a book in 2013, *If Only I had Told* (Esther W, 2013). Esther believes she unwittingly sparked the first removal into care in 1989 of her younger siblings, whose talk about sexual abuse then sparked the removal of the nine other children in the 'dawn raids'. She only admits that her violent, sadistic father was an abuser, not her brothers. In care after the father was imprisoned in 1987, she was re-abused by a care worker but did not name him. She thinks the authorities assumed the culprit was her brother, therefore removing her seven siblings. She believes social workers then coached and interrogated them into claiming satanic abuse by the four other families, whose nine children were removed in the dawn raids.

This convoluted, complicated theory received widespread uncritical coverage, including by the BBC (BBC News, 2013a). Yet valuing and listening to adult survivors of sexual abuse surely does not mean failing to challenge them respectfully, when their claims can easily be shown to be both self-blaming and untrue.

The Orkney Report makes clear it was not her own complaint of sexual abuse, but that of her sister OW, which sparked the second removal into care of the younger W children. Only after the second removal did the children talk about any rituals. It also reveals that four younger siblings showed clear signs of chronic penetrative abuse long after their father was jailed. These children had been on the child protection 'radar' for years. Coverage of Esther's book revealed a depressing lack of interest in the facts, appearing so heavily publicised because it provided further justification for the theory that social workers coached false statements about 'satanic abuse' from children.

Part of a pattern: other cases set the template – Cleveland, Rochdale, Nottingham

Interpretation of the Orkney case was filtered through a template of child sexual abuse cases during the previous few years. Thus this case needs to be set in context.

Cleveland

The Cleveland child sexual abuse case (1987–88) had recently happened, and had received notorious publicity. In Middlesbrough in north-east England, the paediatricians Dr Marietta Higgs and Dr Geoffrey Wyatt had diagnosed 121 children as having been sexually abused, on the basis of evidence which included medical findings. The case escalated into a major crisis for child protection, and precipitated an inquiry into the authorities' handling of these cases, headed by Lord Justice Butler-Sloss.

A large study of legal transcripts and newspapers into how the Cleveland crisis and Butler-Sloss Inquiry were presented in the media unearthed hugely unbalanced media coverage. Highest coverage went to lawyers' evidence for the parents, least to evidence from public bodies. Emotive headlines sustained hostile criticism of doctors and social workers, wrong-doing to the families (which means the parents), and the search for someone to blame. 'Happy families' were said to have been broken up by over-zealous, incompetent, predatory social workers and paediatricians, with innocent parents torn from their children. Parents' claims of innocence went unverified. 'Adults' voices', the study concluded, 'are always louder than the children's' (Donaldson and O'Brien, 1995).

Jenny Kitzinger's wide-ranging focus group research in 2000 found that many participants, including news editors, interpreted Orkney as the latest in a line of social work blunders. People confused details of the Cleveland and Orkney cases, and used their understanding of Cleveland to reconstruct the Orkney case, with both representing faceless bureaucracy, against the rights of bewildered families. Cleveland's symbolic power thus 'lay in its status as a template' (Kitzinger, 2000).

In this paper, Kitzinger (2000) described how the recall of focus group members was of a 'screwy' Dr Higgs carrying out discredited tests on random children's bottoms, for no reason. Orkney as 'another Cleveland' thus provoked a set of powerful pre-packaged associations: and in both cases, police were absolved by media and public from responsibility.

Precipitate removal of children into care, often before the actual abuser was identified, and in the unsuitable settings of hospital wards to contain the children would bring justified criticisms – in the Butler-Sloss report and more widely – of the way doctors and social workers took action in Cleveland. However, Cleveland foreshadowed Orkney in that facts about other important aspects of the case were widely misrepresented or ignored, in the forging of contemporary myths.

Channel 4's *Unspeakable Truths* documentary *The Death of Childhood* (1997) and Beatrix Campbell's book, *Unofficial Secrets* (1998), both highlighted the destructive role in the crisis of Cleveland's police and police surgeon who were criticised strongly by Butler-Sloss but either ignored or feted in popular media coverage. The programme and book also revealed there had been serious professional concern about many of the 121 children long before they were medically examined. One child had already been admitted to hospital seven times for failure to thrive. Nor was the reflex anal dilatation sign discredited, as widely claimed. It had been in forensic textbooks for some time, and the Inquiry Report called it 'abnormal and suspicious' (Butler-Sloss, 1988, p. 193). Nor was the sign the only or main evidence in a majority of cases.

Further, the Northern Regional Health Authority sent the Inquiry team a confidential report, based on in-depth assessments of the children by 'eminent paediatricians and psychiatrists' who concluded that the doctors' diagnosis was correct in 70–75% of the contested cases (Campbell, 1998).

But *The Death of Childhood* documentary revealed that, faced with immense, hostile publicity, the council abandoned many children's cases pre-court, even when supportive evidence of abuse and clear disclosures existed. These children were sent home unprotected. Many of the 121 were later re-referred to protective services. The documentary revealed that the council and the Department of Health took a joint decision that there should be no further follow-up of these children, and records relating to them were destroyed (Channel 4, 1997).

Rochdale, Nottingham and 'satanism'

Orkney's coverage was also influenced by two English cases involving ritual abuse allegations. In May 1990 on a deprived estate near Rochdale, police and social workers raided homes at dawn and took 20 children into care, amid suspicions of sexual abuse and a ritual sex ring. This followed bizarre, disturbed words and behaviour from a 6-year-old boy at school, for instance that he was taken to a house by 'ghosts' who gave him a special drink which made him 'fly'. He also described being locked in cages, and experiences of abuse and humiliation.

The judge, Mr Justice Douglas Brown found accusations of ritual abuse unproven, saying that social workers were obsessive and mistaken in their belief that the fantasies of a young boy allowed to watch violent videos were real. The judge criticised the dawn raids, and recommended intensive training for social workers who interviewed children about ritual or sexual abuse. Gordon Littlemore, Rochdale's social services director, then resigned. Many of the children, however, remained in care for several years (Hansard, 1991). Further details of this case – and the role of parents' campaigners which foreshadowed Orkney – can be found in Salter and Dagistanli (2015).

Campbell (1995) notes that, in the aftermath of Rochdale, 'the new cause for concern was not the spectre of cruelty to children, but the cruelty of children as false accusers 'infected by the video nasty''.

Nottingham

The Nottingham case demonstrated how 'backlash' accounts of an organised abuse case can come to dominate popular discourse, despite court convictions and the official clearing of social workers. Nine adults from another deprived estate, in Nottingham, were convicted in February 1989, guilty of 53 charges of incest, cruelty and indecent assault after their children and 18 others were taken into care. As in Rochdale, there were claims that wealthy and respected professional people were also abusing these disadvantaged children. The case raised great controversy (which continues) over whether ritual abuse also happened, because some children made bizarre, disturbing revelations to their foster carers.

Mrs Justice Booth had, in care proceedings in 1988, described their environment as sadistic and 'satanic'. The perpetrators' appeal was also unsuccessful. The police, however, were sceptical of any cult links and very critical of social services. The local authority set up the Joint Enquiry Team (JET) to try and resolve these professional conflicts, but it only exacerbated them.

The JET team, in dismissing ritual abuse, proposed that social workers had brainwashed children in interviews, had been influenced by a specialist with sex offenders, that they and/or the children's foster parents were evangelical Christians, that the children might have seen horror videos or read books featuring witches, and that the NSPCC persuaded children they were satanically abused (Anning et al, 1997).

But the social workers never formally interviewed the children, who disclosed instead to their foster parents, ordinary people who wrote down the children's bizarre conversations (foreshadowing events in Orkney). The JET team did not interview the social workers yet still proposed that they had induced children to tell these stories. The social workers and foster parents had only consulted the specialist for advice months after the children had described peculiar occult practices.

The child protection professionals were commended by the High Court and the chief executive of Nottinghamshire Council. Their work was scrutinised by the Department of Health Social Services Inspectorate; the 'brainwashing' thesis was rejected by by Nottinghamshire County Council and by the High Court. The county social services committee repudiated this JET report (Nottinghamshire County Council, 1990).

However, despite all this the JET report was widely leaked and publicised. Ever since, it has been the most heavily promoted and widely available account for the public. Its claims feature prominently in media articles and on internet accounts of the Nottingham case, as an example of the 'satanic panic'.

Cases in Cleveland, Rochdale and Nottingham, then, and their heavily negative messages set the tone for understanding and mythmaking in the Orkney case. That case, unlike Cleveland, has never been reassessed. It is time it received more accurate scrutiny.

Orkney: alternative images

Five years after the dramatic 'dawn raids' in February 1991, I telephoned one social worker who assisted in removing children from one of the four families. I apologised: "I expect you've wanted to put Orkney out of your mind, instead of continually having people ask you about it." There was a startled gasp, then silence. "Oh no no," she replied with emotion. "There's not been a single day since when I haven't thought about those children."

A rare alternative voice in the documentary *The Accused* (Blast! Films, 2006), Phil Greene, a Strathclyde care manager, described how some of the nine children behaved on the plane back home to Kirkwall, after Sheriff Kelbie had dismissed the case. They changed and became hyperactive, with sexualised talk and sexual propositions to adults on the aeroplane. Years after these events, Greene's appearance on TV was one of shock and grief. He believed he had failed children whom he had a duty to protect.

The RSSPCC's Liz Maclean described what was most distressing to her about the whole 'Orkney affair'. It was neither the disturbing words of some children she interviewed, nor the heavily publicised criticism of her own interviewing methods, nor the many difficult days she faced on the Orkney Inquiry's witness stand. It was watching one small girl cross the tarmac from the plane to a huge cheering crowd, to her own parents and massed TV cameras at Kirkwall airport. "It broke my heart absolutely," she said. "We had failed her, and I will never be able to get that sight out of my mind." (personal interview, 1992)

Buried in Lord Clyde's Inquiry Report (Clyde, 1992) is an account of this little girl's behaviour at her foster parents' house when she heard she was being returned home.

> She had been given a parcel containing cards and articles from Orkney, but she flung them all on the floor as if in a fit of rage. She was extremely distressed. She cried and indulged in very aggressive behaviour which was quite unlike her, smashing a doll on the ground. She started sucking her thumb. She seemed shocked and bewildered. She said she did not want to go home and stood like a wooden doll refusing to get dressed. She left the foster carer's house in tears. On the journey home she engaged in bizarre behaviour unlike anything which she had shown before. (Clyde, 1992, p. 206)

An eight-year-old boy from another family, when told he was returning home, asked his foster mother if it meant that all the bad things would not happen any more. He began telling her of things that happened in a quarry, indicated he had been handled sexually, and said he was worried about games that were played at home: '...the foster mother found the occasion very upsetting' (Clyde, 1992, pp. 159–60).

Although these details about the children's words and behaviour are published in the Inquiry Report, they are not in the recollection of the British public and media. The images scorched on the minds of the three workers are not the same as theirs. As we described, most public perception was of ridiculous, unjustified action taken against innocent parents by over-zealous professionals. Nor does the frequent image of heartless or faceless staff fit with their commitment. Like staff involved in other highly publicised child abuse cases, their continuing preoccupation has been with the children at the heart of the affair.

This makes them unusual, for the most striking feature of the whole Orkney saga was how marginal such children became, and how little they featured on most people's agendas – legal professionals, politicians, civil servants, journalists and members of the public.

Role of the media

How was this unfolding case portrayed at the time to the public? The agenda for public discourse and understanding was set soon after the dawn raids, and the media played a crucial role. Many journalists uncritically accepted disinformation and apparently planted stories from the adults and their supporters. Journalists who tried to keep an open mind on the allegations were an isolated minority.

However, the media were not the only influences – they interacted with officials and the public to generate one set of memories of what the case was 'about'. Biased reporting was much encouraged by Orkney social work department's refusal to engage with the media or challenge the information. Divisions between 'natives' and 'incomers' to Orkney set up barriers to local knowledge. People would often claim that everyone knew each other's business and nothing could pass undetected; in fact, the two communities often led separate lives, and were frequently critical of each other.

The language of the media coverage below may be more flowery and fanciful than usual, but the sympathy displayed was widespread. Describing the M parents after their children were removed, a *Scotland on Sunday* journalist wrote:

> Jane is thoughtful, articulate and determined, and would best be played by a younger, more vibrant Anna Massey. John – enthusiastic, helpful, deeply troubled – would be William Hurt. ... since she lost her children,

Jane says, all her senses have been heightened. 'I see every feather on a bird more clearly. I see every drop of rain showing on the trees.' ... Jane sums up their time together. 'We fell in love, we got married and we lived happily ever after. Then they took our children away.' (Ferguson, 1991)

Information relevant to the crisis, such as the history of child protection failures in Orkney and the suspension of Orkney Children's Reporter Katherine Kemp over her perceived failure to protect the W children, fell off a media agenda it did not fit.

Because most English and international media disappeared quickly, only reappearing at the end of the Inquiry, some challenging evidence which appeared had little coverage outside Scotland. Tabloid and broadsheet coverage did not differ widely, perhaps because most suspected adults were respectable, articulate middle class people, with whom 'quality' press staff closely identified. 'People like us' were being accused of unspeakable things. I myself overheard such baffled, disturbed comments by news editors and senior journalists.

In addition one strand of the media, most conspicuously at that time the *Mail on Sunday*, displayed a strong right wing political agenda against social workers. There was a striking contrast between its continuing criticisms of social workers and the easy passage given to police who acted jointly throughout. Downplaying the police role reflects the respect towards the police of most middle class people, thus the greater difficulty in making them an equal target – and in admitting that they too believed supposedly ludicrous allegations. The *Independent on Sunday* also repeatedly attempted to discredit the existence of ritual abuse (for instance Waterhouse, 1991).

Planted disinformation?

As an experienced journalist, I also encountered a puzzling scent of organised media manipulation on Orkney, which I had not met before: about the so-called satanic panic, a theory publicised by the occult magazines which mysteriously appeared on Orkney; about claimed involvement by the distinguished psychiatrist Roland Summit; and about the influence of a basic grade Christian social worker, who in fact lacked any professional status to orchestrate the dawn raids. The absurdity of these stories, and some glaring flaws in the 'faction' drama *Flowers of the Forest* are recounted in the discussion of the 'satanic panic' in Chapter Two.

Just the media's fault?

But journalists often simply reflected the greater public of which they were part. The very idea that respectable clergy might abuse children was rarely considered. Quakers and other religious groups from all over Britain sent sympathy and support to the parents and children for being, as they saw it, wrongly removed.

Besides, not everyone was receiving only one side of the story. For Scots, evidence to the Inquiry was reported every day in the main broadsheets, the *Scotsman* and the *Herald,* and usually broadcast on BBC Scotland. To pick three examples, the public read that a remarkable volume of correspondence was sent by several suspected adults to the W children held in care, containing messages which were odd or inappropriate for young children. They included being asked if they were learning German, messages to eight-year-old BW about his fixing a heater and light bulb, descriptions of him as B the Best or B the Beast, inappropriate endearments and a photo of another boy, HW, with a sexual association. Strange objects like hammers were posted to the children (Clyde, 1992, pp. 25–6).

The public read that when police conducted the dawn raid on the minister's house, they recovered from his bed a child's hot water bottle belonging to the 8-year-old BW. This had the boy's name on it along with a sexual reference (*Herald*, 1991a). No explanation of this singular find has ever been given.

When the foster parents took the Inquiry stand, they detailed unusual, disturbing words, blasphemous chants and bizarre behaviour by several children from three families. After a power failure in the home of the foster mother of eight-year-old SB, on the day he arrived, she lit candles. The boy passed his hand through the flame saying, "I like hurting myself. I like killing people". When light was restored the foster mother exclaimed, "let there be light!"The boy replied:"May the light not be upon us and God not be with us". (Herald, 1991a). He became excited and agitated (Clyde, 1992, p. 160; *Herald*, 1991b). No explanation of this singular chant has ever been given.

Foster parents gave evidence of other disturbing behaviour such as violent and frightening plays involving sex, religion, bloodshed and violence; enactment of being placed in a cardboard coffin; an obsession with killing and death, and a seven-year-old girl's sexualised behaviour and graphic enactment of childbirth (Clyde, 1992, pp. 139–41). Several children showed strong fear of churches. Full details are given in Lord Clyde's report, along with all the original allegations from three W children.

Yet none of this information appeared to impact upon the public. Jenny Kitzinger's research study (2000) found most people interviewed for the study had little recollection beyond the dawn raids and a bungled operation by social workers. They recalled almost nothing about the long Inquiry or its evidence. This suggests that people are able to reject, ignore or fail to notice evidence which might challenge judgements they have already made about child sexual abuse cases.

Extremes of official caution

The third key element in Orkney was the authorities' attitude to communicating with the public through the media. Orkney's social work department took official caution and reticence to extremes. They formed part of an island council traditionally secretive and fearful, inexperienced and unprepared for an onslaught of media interest. The department failed to communicate for some time the most basic facts, let alone off the record briefings, even with the specialist social work press. (I was reporting for such a journal at the time and at the height of the crisis I sat on the steps of the social work department and refused to move until someone spoke to me.) Thus while accused adults used the media skilfully, journalists could not obtain 'the other side of the story' even when they tried to do so.

While off the record the RSSPCC was more forthcoming and voiced its own belief that ritual abuse had taken place, it quickly adopted damage limitation, rather than admitting mistakes while maintaining concern about possible child abuse in Orkney. It dropped its investigative role in child sexual abuse, publicly played down its belief that ritual abuse existed, changed its name to Children 1st and, like Orkney and Strathclyde social work departments, declined to comment publicly on the case since – beyond saying that its practices have now changed.

Such collective silences by agencies, in highly publicised cases, continue to make an impact, and raise serious questions for child protection (Nelson, 1998a, 2000). Agencies' refusal to comment, to brief what they ethically can off the record and to obtain clients' explicit permission to correct untruths deprive the public of information which would help them weigh the evidence. Statutory and voluntary childcare agencies are the public faces of child protection. They speak for many child and adult survivors who cannot do so. If they will not stand up to be counted and face the consequences, then who else will?

Were far-reaching verdicts correct?

In Orkney, the separate testimonies of three W children, which led directly to the dawn raids, formed the basis for one of the report's most far-reaching and most-quoted recommendation, that investigators 'must not fall into the trap of confusing the taking of what a child says seriously with believing what the child has said' (Clyde, 1992, p. 72).

This in effect gives succour and justification to those who still believe children often fantasise, or even lie, about sexual abuse. Given the serious consequences of Lord Clyde's recommendation for future child protection, conclusions about the W children's credibility would have had to be particularly sound. But were they instead, to borrow a phrase from Sheriff Kelbie, 'fatally flawed'?

The basis for this recommendation lay overwhelmingly in the Inquiry team's judgement of statements and copious drawings made by three W children, aged from six to eight, in February 1991. The Clyde report details the verbal allegations in full, and describes the drawings.

Undoubtedly social workers and police should have undertaken slower, more careful and more detailed investigation of adults and children named by the Ws before deciding what action, if any, to take. But this was not the basis for the recommendation. Instead it centred on the fact that the W children came from a family with a history of abuse, 'which was likely to have affected their development'.

Professional assessment of the children by a psychologist or psychiatrist would have been prudent, says the Inquiry Report, to consider:

> Whether their perception of reality had been in any way coloured or affected by the [their] abusive experiences ... what might have seemed real to them might well not accord with what was real to others. It was not impossible that innocent incidents could have taken on a sexual overtone in their imaginations. (Clyde, 1992, p. 223)

The message is familiar. Mixed-up children with histories of abuse need their minds tested before we take their matter-of-fact statements as matters of fact. But there are several problems about using such arguments in this case.

First, the W children had more of a history of reticence about sexual abuse in their family than of fabrication or fantasy. One older boy took two years to admit to his residential school, Raddery, his father's sadistic physical and sexual abuse. Second, the report rightly criticised the fact that the nine children from the other four families were not treated as individuals. But the report itself failed to consider the three W youngsters as individuals, treating them instead as a single entity.

Children not treated as individuals

There were clear similarities in practical accounts of places, events, activities, car trips, material detail and names of adults and children present, by three children kept apart for several months (apart from one brief supervised meeting between two of them). The report's argument would mean that three separate children's life developments had been identical, that their distorted perceptions of reality had been identical. Innocent incidents would have had to take on exactly the same sexual overtones in their imaginations. Such overtones would not explain why all these children believed they had witnessed or experienced physical pain, distress and sadness. No alternative explanation is offered for what exactly the innocent incidents, which led to these reactions, might have been.

Third, did these children's accounts have a ring of imaginative storytelling and fantasising, or of concrete, mundane description? Take such extracts as:

> (MW) was asked where this had happened. She said in a quarry in a field. She drew a picture of a car and trailer travelling to the place from her home. In the trailer she drew the table and music centre. She drew car lights on and said it was dark. We asked her who would be there. She named ...[etc]

> (QW) She said Morris put his dickie into MW's fanny, that MW was crying and that afterwards she said 'phew that's over and done with!' ... she then went back and talked about where the cars stopped, and this was a big field but she did not know where it was. (Clyde 1992, p. 31)

These children describe in a very matter-of-fact way being taken from one place in certain cars and trailers by named people in certain costumes, to another place, where they unloaded specific equipment and were joined by more named adults. These, they claim, sexually abused named children. They name the same people, and equipment the interviewers do not understand, like the hooker. The children worry about accuracy. They grow annoyed when the hooker drawn is too small or when the car lights are not put in, and they make corrections. The only obvious examples of childish imaginative expression are about emotions, as when M 'drew the sun looking down with a sad face, and tears, and said that the sun was crying'.

It is not clear why such accounts were considered to need examination by a psychologist or psychiatrist. Rather, they appear to call for detailed police investigation of the *information* they contained, to see if any corroboration could be found; and to probe further whether these events happened and where, if so, and if children were given any drugged substances. Drugs might indeed have affected their perceptions.

The disturbing evidence given by foster parents, ordinary people with no axe to grind who made serious, detailed claims about children's bizarre words and behaviour in their care, was not even assessed by the Inquiry, far less validated or discredited. This evidence formed no part of the official interviewing techniques, which were so scrutinised and so criticised.

The marginalisation of real children

Indeed the most striking feature of the whole Orkney case was how rarely children, and in particular nine children at the heart of this case, were central to the concern of anyone – except to the authorities who were heavily criticised.

The socially stigmatised, 15-strong W family never appeared to raise much public interest within or beyond Orkney, although social workers continued to work closely with them, a number being placed for adoption or in long-term foster care.

The outrage in most press publicity after the dawn raids was about injustice done to adults – the children's parents, and the church minister. Not one voice was raised publicly from the Church of Scotland, this major Scottish institution, that it should investigate the allegations in case any children were at risk, or that the minister should be suspended on full pay until the matter was resolved. (Only in 1997 did the Church ratify a child protection policy of its own at its General Assembly.) Thousands of Quakers who sent letters of support to some parents and children did not seem to consider that allegations of abuse should be investigated.

The Orkney public conspicuously avoided attending the Inquiry proceedings. One local councillor explained to me that he was ashamed to say people did not want to go in case they were identified with the affair. Local people told me that it was damaging Orkney's image, but few expressed concerns for the nine children or the W children. Some told me that where the W family had previously lived, it was well known that children's screams were heard coming from their house – yet no one had apparently reported this. Orkney's tourist chief deplored the damage done to Orkney's image and its visitor business. Orkney Islands Council paid compensation and fulsomely apologised to the families concerned, which effectively prevented their giving offence by monitoring any children about whom they had remaining concerns. It is not possible to base the protection of children on fear of offending adults.

The nine children were marginalised in other ways too. Sheriff Kelbie's rejection of evidence prepared by social workers and police before it was heard breached the laws of natural justice, according to Scotland's senior judge, Lord Hope (Herald, 2001). Although acting children's panel reporter Gordon Sloan won his appeal against Kelbie's decision, he decided to abandon further proceedings. For that he was sharply criticised in the Clyde report: 'It was by no means certain that if there was evidence to support the acting Reporter's case, it would have been tainted or irrecoverable ... it is not easy to reconcile his belief that the grounds for referral were well founded, with his despair of the case' (p. 263).

When the Secretary of State for Scotland announced the public inquiry headed by Lord Clyde, its remit, about the conduct of the authorities, excluded consideration of the truth or falsehood of the allegations. It could not discuss whether or not any children were in need of protection.

One sentence of concern

The Inquiry lasted eight months, cost £6 million, exhaustively criticised the child protection authorities, and made nearly 200 recommendations in 350 pages. Most were sensible and constructive: the Inquiry team members were caring, experienced and competent people. Yet they had just one sentence of explicit comment to make about all the bizarre evidence from several children, which they had heard:

> In the case of some of the children, it is not impossible that there could have been some matters, perhaps far removed from any incidents in Orkney, which could have been troubling them. (Clyde, 1992, p. 341)

That seems a mild and cautious comment in response to one child enacting gruesome sexual plays, claiming his mother made gravy with blood, and saying he was put into coffins; to another claiming her father drank blood and kept it in the fridge; to another graphically re-enacting childbirth at the age of seven, and claiming that the baby would die; and to another reciting strange chants against God. These incidents are all described in the Inquiry Report. This last boy, according to evidence to the Inquiry on 17 December 1991, drew men with huge breasts with snakes coming out of them, kept talking about germs and washed himself continually, talked angrily in words which made no sense, talked constantly about killing people, and was convinced that his mother could hear him through the radio.

This was the boy who may have had some matters far removed from Orkney troubling him: the same boy who, on hearing he was to be sent home to Orkney, had asked his foster mother, "Does this mean that the bad things are not going to happen any more?"

Obsession with adults

After the report was published, the public discourse was all about apologies to adults, vindication of adults, resignations by adults, the need for community reconciliation among adults, and for Orkney social work department to establish its good faith among the adults of South Ronaldsay. Nothing could have been more revealing about the respective priorities our society gives to adults and to children.

When the Orkney case has been raised since, officials have fallen over each other to say how they have changed, to separate themselves from this flawed attempt to protect children. None have dared to say that even if the methods were wrong, there were grounds for concern about some of these children. For example Cathie Cowan, director of Orkney Health and Care, said 'many lessons were learned' from Clyde's Inquiry, continuing jargonistically: 'Decision-making is now based on robust inter-agency planning which minimises the risks of such events happening again' (Gall, 2011).

Only Janette Chisholm, coordinator for the W children during the Orkney case, has continued speaking bluntly (with no jargon):

> I can't decide if things happened or didn't happen. But people saying things didn't happen doesn't affect me in the slightest. Because that's my experience of what people always say. I'd be very surprised if they said it did! (BBC News, 2006c)

Important issues not explored

It is hard to imagine, as a result of the Orkney case, a fraction of the £6 million of public money devoted to the Inquiry being spent on techniques of criminal investigation, on strengthening child protection services in remote areas, or on research into organised sexual abuse in Scotland. Just as it was impossible to visualise a fraction of the cost of the 1987 Cleveland Inquiry being spent on research into anal assaults on children.

And although this eminent, caring Inquiry team was often prepared to exceed its strict remit (for instance, by including in the report some disturbing detail of children's words and behaviour), it was not prepared to do so by inserting a single sentence at the end. This could have kept open the door to future monitoring of the children's safety, and would not have reduced their valid criticisms of the authorities.

'We remain very concerned,' they could have written, about some of the evidence from certain children we have heard presented to us, and believe that further monitoring of possible risks to these children is necessary'.

Children at heart of case

It does not make sense to argue, as in the Cleveland report, that 'the child is a person, not an object of concern'; (Butler-Sloss, 1988) or as in the Orkney Report, that the nine children 'were not treated as individuals', if the actual named children involved in a case fall through a gaping hole in those inquiries. For if the entire panoply of a country's child protection system cannot protect known children in a single case, then whatever else it achieves, however many guidelines, procedures or sound practices it spawns, there is a failure at its heart.

And if we as a society – politicians, judges, public, media – are happy to sanction £6 million on a public inquiry into the behaviour of officials who sought however ineptly to protect young people, yet can neither fund a means of establishing whether or not a handful of children were horrifyingly abused, nor make a priority of seeking better ways to protect children from abusers in future, there is something profoundly skewed about our values.

How did children disappear? How might this be avoided in future?

How did the children disappear from a case which for so long absorbed professionals, media and public? That is an important question, with wider parallels.

The Inquiry's remit meant that it promoted examples of child-centred practice (such as maintaining contact with siblings and parents, keeping their own possessions). Difficult questions about child-centred practice in *protection* were submerged: such as when is it dangerous to children to allow them contact with their parents?

Second, due to its remit the Inquiry had to relegate other important considerations. 'The problem' was not about how sadistic organised sexual abuse could effectively be investigated, nor about how rural child protection could be improved, nor about how communities could work with professionals to keep children safe. Though all these three things were touched upon in the report, they occupied a small fraction of the space given to analysing, in 69 pages, *each week* of detailed preparation and the dawn raids, including serious conflict between managers and social workers. Decades later, many people still urgently need guidance on organised sexual abuse, on rural child protection or on community child protection. Few if any now wish or need to examine the tortuous daily detail of preparations for the dawn raids, which featured some poor investigatory planning and blinkered managerial arrogance.

The Inquiry Report did call for some measures against suspected adults – such as provision to remove alleged abusers, rather than children, from the home. But most other recommendations were in effect about how professional procedures could be improved to minimise risk of *unfounded* action. Thus there were numerous, specific recommendations about procedures for the careful interviewing of children.

The Orkney Inquiry Report did make other, less publicised recommendations, but these have either still to be carried out, or have been watered down and took many years to implement. For example, 'Research should be urgently undertaken into all forms of child sexual abuse, in particular cases of multiple abuse.' The report also called for a specialist resource group available to advise any social work agency in cases 'of particular complexity'. That call was repeated after the Eilean Siar case in 2005 (see below). Only in 2015 was the welcome development of a new National Child Abuse Investigation Unit launched by Police Scotland.[3]

An alternative response

A different response could have been made to a highly publicised case such as Orkney (or indeed Cleveland). There could have been a limited-term inquisitorial judicial inquiry into official conduct with recommendations for improvement; an exploration of existing best practice from elsewhere; a well-funded research programme; and establishment of protective measures like children's rights officers, children's resource centres or helplines, suitable to the area (for example, for Orkney, in the Scottish Highlands and islands, and other remote areas). Alternative strategies, however, demand a willingness to pause and reflect before responding to public scandal and public outrage. They call for political courage, and a determination to place the needs of children above the raucous demands and wounded sensibilities of adults. Those are what we need from child abuse inquiries.

Imagine if police forces had instead been resourced to prioritise sound ways of prosecuting organised abuse, including the most effective means of surveillance and evidence-gathering in remote communities, or if a pilot project had been funded to create an

---

[3] www.scotland.police.uk/whats-happening/news/2015/april/national-child-abuse-investigation-unit-launched

informed, aware, protective local community. It is only through realising how hard these things are to imagine that we appreciate how skewed our child protection system actually is. Who among the public, media and professionals will finally demand a change of priorities?

It is even more important that, if indeed some young people needed protection in places like Cleveland, Rochdale or Orkney, they retained the hope of protection and justice and restitution. It does not absolve unfinished responsibilities to real young people to apologise that social workers bungled procedures, that a sheriff behaved improperly, that the acting children's reporter should not have abandoned his appeal. There was surely a responsibility to maintain continuing vigilance, so that new evidence could be collected if it was there to be collected. If any of those children on Orkney did indeed need protection, justice or restitution, then they are still waiting for it as adults today.

Afterword: has anything changed?

In 2005, a courageous and outspoken Inquiry Report which did put children at its heart was published on shocking, longstanding abuses against three girls in Eilean Siar, or Western Isles (Social Work Inspection Agency, 2005). The case was investigated by the respected senior social work practitioners Alexis Jay and Gill Ottley of the arm's-length Social Work Inspection Agency (SWIA). There is a valuable discussion of this case and the SWIA report in Children in Scotland (2005). Alexis Jay's child-centred integrity was again illustrated later, when in 2014 she authored the report which found that at least 1400 young girls had been sexually exploited over 16 years in Rotherham, and uncompromisingly described their suffering (Jay, 2014).

The 170-page SWIA report catalogued years of graphic, highly distressing physical, emotional and sexual abuse by the father – already a convicted child sex offender – and his friends. The sisters had been on the child protection register in England as at risk of sexual abuse before they moved to Lewis in 1995. Their mother (Mrs A) had mental ill health and learning difficulties. The girls were again registered as at risk of sexual and physical abuse and neglect. Extensive assistance to support the family was set up.

Mrs A, then the girls, reported sexual abuse by the father and others. There were 222 official concerns registered about their home conditions and wellbeing – from cigarette burns to genital soreness, repeated soiling at school, and being clingy, tired and weepy in the classroom. In all 100 professionals were involved, and there were 29 case conferences, 21 statutory reviews, and 24 children's hearings.

Yet the eldest girl was not removed from home and fostered long-term until 1998, the other girls not until 2003. In late 2003, nine adults in the Western Isles and England were arrested for seriously harming the girls. This followed allegations by Mrs A which included some ritual abuse-type behaviours, wearing of robes and masks, the involvement of animals and abusive ceremonies.

In July 2004, the Crown Office dropped all charges against these adults for undisclosed reasons. Thus for more than a decade, numerous professionals and agencies repeatedly failed to protect these maltreated girls – culminating in the Crown Office dropping its criminal prosecutions. It has never explained the reason, and no one has been called to account.

The SWIA team concluded that: a) the girls all experienced severe and prolonged abuse; b) social work authorities made seriously flawed decisions and should have protected the children much sooner; and c) health authorities failed to respond appropriately to the children's needs. They made 31 recommendations, including basic safeguards when a convicted sex offender is acting as a parent. Again they made the call the Orkney Inquiry had urged, indeed more strongly: 'A multi-agency national resource should be established to assist in the effective investigation and resolution of complex child protection cases anywhere in Scotland.'

The same old coverage...?

What did most media concentrate on in relation to this case? They drew on the legacy of Orkney, and other notorious cases before it.

Until the SWIA report was published, barely a word of concern was published about these three girls, nor a hint of their actual, appalling lives and suffering. We might think the children's lives were the ones deserving of adjectives such as 'devastating', 'nightmarish' or 'suicidal'. However, the many articles published (particularly from the 'quality' press, incidentally) instead concentrated on prejudging as innocent the adults charged with these 'devastating' offences. (As in Orkney they may well be innocent, or they may not: we now have no way of knowing.)

The great suffering these (mainly) respectable adults faced was described in emotional, sympathetic detail, including suicide attempts, shattered lives, breakdowns and sobbing. In comparison with the lack of time spent over the abused girls, *Sunday Herald* reporters talked to the accused adults over nine months, who were later cleared of the ritual abuse of children on Lewis. In an 'exclusive' the reporter gave headlines included 'Ruined lives of islanders in child sex fiasco' (Martin, 2005). These articles discredited the evidence of Mrs A, a vulnerable sexual abuse survivor, by repeating unsubstantiated claims from the accused adults that she had a history of making false allegations.

Legacy of Orkney

It was left to the SWIA report to suggest what the final legacy of the Orkney case and Inquiry had been: excessive caution (some would say paralysis) about taking these desperately vulnerable girls into care:

> Professionals tried hard to help both parents. ... at this time new legislation [the Children (Scotland) Act 1995] was designed to protect children, within the context of partnership with their parents. This, together with the aftermath of the Orkney Inquiry (1992) may have contributed to the prolonged attempts to engage with the family: rather than to try to remove all 3 children. (SWIA, 2005 p. 25)

The respected media commentator Gillian Bowditch wrote powerfully of this case, a case few of the public are likely even to recall, in comparison with Orkney:

We have now reached a situation where the new legislation itself is a contributory factor to abuse. The Lewis children were abused for so long with the authorities' knowledge partly because the Children (Scotland) Act puts the emphasis on keeping children within families wherever possible.

... What do you call it when three little girls are routinely battered, burned, starved, neglected, raped and sold as sexual playthings to other adults and it is observed, documented, recorded and discussed for more than a decade by scores of caring professionals – good people – without anybody preventing it?

... What this case exposes is nothing less than the complete and utter failure of both social services and the criminal justice system in Scotland. When a social worker can discover a five-year-old sleeping in a urine-soaked cupboard, document it but fail to stop it; when a convicted paedophile can abuse three children for years under the noses of the authorities; when the Crown Office has concrete evidence of prolonged abuse of the worst kind, but fails even to attempt a prosecution, it is hard not to conclude that what we are witnessing is the collapse of a fundamental plank of civilised society. (Bowditch, 2005)

FOUR

Stigmatised young people: from 'abuse fodder' to key allies against abuse and exploitation

Introduction

Asked by a House of Commons select committee in 2012 what lay behind repeated failures in Rochdale to protect young teenagers and pre-teens from sexual exploitation, Sara Rowbotham answered simply and powerfully. She was coordinator of the local NHS crisis intervention team, which had made more than 100 largely fruitless referrals to social services and police between 2004 and 2010.

> It was about attitudes towards teenagers. It was absolute disrespect that vulnerable young people did not have a voice. They were overlooked. They were discriminated against. They were treated appallingly by protective services. (Williams, 2012a)

This chapter highlights stigmatised teenagers who have faced child sexual exploitation (CSE) or very young (especially pre-teen) pregnancy. It concentrates here on prejudiced, sexist attitudes to girls and young women and how these attitudes have contributed heavily to contemptuous perceptions of their suffering. This is not to deny that a significant minority of boys and young men have also faced sexual exploitation.[1] Many of

---

[1] See, for instance, http://mesmac.co.uk/blast-resources

the changes called for in protection and provision will also be helpful to them, although certain perceptions which they face are different (see Chapter Nine).

This chapter describes sexist vilification, contempt and blame sexually exploited girls have faced from professionals, public and media alike. It challenges theories of so-called 'political correctness' as a reason for failing to bring to justice perpetrators from minority ethnic backgrounds. I argue that the most urgent need for professionals in ensuring genuine change is to examine very searchingly of themselves why, in CSE, their clear witness of distress and huge dereliction of care persisted decades after it was made clear through practice, legislation and legislative guidance that the young people were *victims* of exploitation, and must be treated as such. That has enabled perpetrators to continue using these girls as fodder for abuse, leading to enormous suffering which now cannot be undone.

Similar prejudices have meant very young pregnancies still fail to raise the strong suspicions they always should about possible rape or sexual abuse. (Indeed, with children under 13, sexual activity can never in law be consensual.) This is illustrated by cases including that of Tressa Middleton. She was billed in the media as 'Scotland's youngest mother at 11'. She was publicly excoriated – including by some media, politicians and church figures – as an example of teenage promiscuity, the permissive society and welfare scroungers, but was later found to have been raped since the age of seven by her own brother. The interpretation of stigmatised girls, both in young pregnancy and in CSE, as sexual free agents has further contributed to failures to protect them.

This chapter calls for changes which will both protect stigmatised teenagers, and enable them to become vital allies in the fight against child sexual abuse and organised exploitation. Changes include protecting them earlier from the child sexual abuse which makes so many vulnerable; making uncaring behaviour in caring agencies serious disciplinary offences; considering closure of most residential care units; opening networks of short-term semi-formal local refuges; and establishing permanent alternatives to school exclusion. Finally but crucially, the unique knowledge and experience of these stigmatised young people urgently needs to be harnessed to the child protection system. They know who the abusers are, and where they abuse.

Moves towards all the above need in my view to be priorities among the wealth of other training packages, resources and concrete examples of good practice in CSE work: in Barnardo's reports and outreach work; in Parliamentary Inquiries and Commissions across the UK; in serious case reviews; in the excellent research by Professor Jenny Pearce and her team, which continues at the University of Bedfordshire; and in the equally excellent resources for good practice in CSE work of the National Working Group network.[2]

There are selfish as well as altruistic reasons to support change. Many troubled and troublesome young people would, if protected, cause much less trouble to communities through the anti-social behaviour, substance misuse and even at times violence that they perpetrate in response to the brutalities of their own life experience.

A history of failure to care

After an official report found that up to 40 staff at Kerelaw residential school and secure unit had physically or sexually abused children there (Frizzell, 2009), the Scottish Government Minister Nicol Stephen summed up the central message of such damning reports into care scandals:

> Too often, our most vulnerable children are the ones who are let down the most. (BBC News, 2007)

Disparaging or uncaring attitudes towards the most damaged, difficult or stigmatised young people are far from new: they have allowed numerous child abuse scandals to happen, in care homes, in religious institutions and residential schools (Shaw, 2007). Abusers target the children and know they will get away with it, because they share the same disrespect. As Ann Coffey

---

[2]   www.barnardos.org.uk/what_we_do/our_work/sexual_exploitation. htmin; www.beds.ac.uk/ic; www.nwgnetwork.org

MP said, after her own published report on CSE (Coffey, 2014) revealed that the Crown Prosecution Service justified 'no further action' by reference to the girl victims wearing 'sexualised clothes … such as crop tops':

> The perpetrators are given a very clear message that society doesn't think these children are of any account, and [that] it's not worthwhile pursuing justice on their behalf. (Murphy, 2014)

When are those attitudes finally going to change? When are those professionals who hold these views going to explain, to themselves and others, how exactly an abused child who deserves their protection suddenly transmutes before their eyes, at only 11 or 12, into a freely choosing young prostitute or promiscuous slut?

These are still 'throwaway' children. How telling to reflect that, once it was considered in many media that no murders after all had happened at the former Haut de la Garenne children's home in Jersey, media coverage – which daily had been high – almost evaporated. This was despite very serious allegations that remained of multiple physical and sexual abuses there. Since 2011 these have been subject to further scrutiny through the Jersey Care Inquiry (Scott-Clark and Levy, 2009; www. jerseycareinquiry.org).

Prejudices against 'throwaway' children are not just an ethical concern: they can have highly damaging results. Consider the murders in 2002, in an English village, of ten-year-old Holly Wells and Jessica Chapman by their school caretaker, Ian Huntley. These two children gained enormous international publicity and sympathy. Yet Huntley had already been investigated for three rapes, one indecent assault and four under-age sex cases. But he serially targeted vulnerable, stigmatised girls. When four of these girls shrank from making a complaint, their decisions were accepted and the cases were dropped. This was not some recording muddle, but a shameful failure to protect – or even to record the assaults against – certain 'kinds' of girls. Had Huntley been charged over those, his known record would surely have prevented his employment as a school caretaker, with such considerable access to children (Kelly, 2004).

CSE: facts and legislation ignored

In 1996 Britain was a signatory to the 'Stockholm Declaration' after the multi-national World Congress against Commercial Sexual Exploitation of Children. Despite the label 'commercial' the Declaration made clear that this involved remuneration, in cash *or kind*, to the child *or* to a third party, and that it was 'a form of coercion and violence against children'.

It called on all states

> to criminalize the commercial sexual exploitation of children ... and condemn and penalize all those offenders involved ... so that by the year 2000 there are data bases on children vulnerable to commercial sexual exploitation, and on their exploiters, with relevant research ... and respect for confidentiality of the child victims.[3]

Barnardo's Streets & Lanes project in Bradford had been set up in 1994 as a dedicated service for girls at risk of what was then called 'prostitution'. Its manager Sara Swann spoke extensively with nearly 100 girls aged 12–17, developing her influential 'boyfriend model' of sexual exploitation. This clearly dispelled any notion of uncoerced choice, revealing instead control and abuse by older males. Later CSE cases replicated almost exactly what she described – the ensnaring through gifts and affection, the creation of dependency, the possessiveness, isolation, control and violence, brutality and enforced sex with many males, often for several years. For Swann there were no child prostitutes, only abused children and child abusers (Swann, 2000).

Swann's original model was widely publicised through Barnardo's *Whose Daughter Next?* report (Van Meeuwen et al, 1998). Statutory guidance, published as 'Safeguarding children involved in prostitution' (DoH, 2000) made absolutely clear to

---

[3] www.ecpat.net/sites/default/files/stockholm_declaration_1996.pdf

police, social services and health services that this activity was exploitation. The guidance was strengthened in 2003 by the Sexual Offences Act, when it became an offence to arrange or facilitate child prostitution or pornography. This included 'administrating a substance with the intent of committing a sexual offence' (plying victims with drink and drugs continues to be an extremely common feature of CSE).

There have since, of course, been several further updates to law and guidance, tightening provisions further. For example, In Scotland, the Protection of Children and Prevention of Sexual Offences (Scotland) Act 2005 makes it a statutory offence to meet a child for sexual purposes following preliminary contact, or to purchase sex from a person under 18.

The point about detailing such earlier law, legislative guidance and national political commitments here is to emphasise how clear these were. Yet they continued to be widely flouted and ignored by key protective agencies nearly two decades later. We have to ask why.

Examples of prejudice

This behaviour was not a case of a 'few bad apples'. Here are only a few examples of such attitudes:

In **Oxford** a gang who targeted vulnerable girls from care, involving years of torture and extreme sexual violence, was convicted of 43 charges in 2013. The girls, from 11 to 15 years, had been drugged, raped, sold as prostitutes and trafficked while supposedly in the safekeeping of the local authority. The ring was only exposed when a police officer, Simon Morton, proactively built evidence against the men in late 2010 (see Chapter Five).

Damning evidence of blame by some care professionals emerged during the trial. One care worker at a council children's home said a girl was 'glowing with hormones,' 'played the game well' and was a danger to male members of staff. He was describing a girl who was 11 when she fell victim to men who for three years subjected her to relentless sexual barbarity. (Norfolk, 2013).

In **Rotherham**, the Jay Report calculated that over the course of 16 years, at least 1400 girls were discovered to have been victims of CSE, groomed, abused, trafficked, beaten, multiply raped and even tortured. Yet many offenders had been identified to police but not prosecuted, while people who tried to expose the abuse had faced hostility from the authorities (BBC News, 2012b; Norfolk, 2012; Holt, 2014). Jay was appalled at the attitudes of the very authorities who were meant to protect children: 'Nobody could say, "We didn't know" … when we looked in detail at cases … The level of violence and brutality that was used, as well as the sexual abuse to control and humiliate them, was appalling' (Brown, 2015).

Indeed back in 2002 in Rotherham, the confidential report of a Home Office funded research project had criticised police for 'in all cases' treating young victims 'as deviant and promiscuous' while the men they were found with were never questioned nor investigated (BBC News, 2015a). Louise Casey's (post-Jay) follow-up inspection report on Rotherham Council, a particularly blunt and damning document, was told during her inspection that among police officers

> There was no awareness. The view was that they were little slags. … the sense was that if there had been any offence it had been by the girls, for luring the men in. (Casey, 2015)

In **Derby**, CSE eventually became the subject of the successful Operation Retriever, producing multiple convictions. A Serious Case Review said professionals had treated the girls, many of whom were known by or under the care of social services, as simply rebellious teenagers. Yet the girls' background made it predictable that they would become vulnerable adolescents at risk of abuse. The Serious Case Review said earlier intervention would have made exploitation less likely. Two girls ended up with criminal convictions, treated as offenders rather than victims, the Inquiry found (Galley, 2010; Carter, 2010).

In **Rochdale**, where Sara Rowbotham's crisis intervention team made more than 100 largely fruitless referrals to police and social care, a serious case review by the Rochdale Safeguarding Children Board in 2013 highlighted failures by 17 agencies. Rochdale MP Simon Danczuk said agencies actively ignored the abuse and that social services believed these girls were making lifestyle choices. Yet in 2008 a report to Rochdale Safeguarding Children Board had identified 50 children at risk of sexual exploitation. But social workers and police focused on young people's high risk behaviour, not their vulnerability. (Williams, 2012b; Donovan, 2013). One father had called children's services numerous times, yet social workers told him she was 'a child prostitute' (BBC News, 2012a).

A failure of common humanity

What could have been strong enough to override all this legislation and guidance and, more urgently, the direct witness of suffering, injury and distress? How could that be interpreted as consent? Because until these young people are valued as much as others, there will never be enough impetus to make difficult and challenging changes in policy throughout the country, rather than in a few pockets of excellent practice.

Sara Rowbotham recalls:

> "It's the million dollar question still why they (police and social services) kept ignoring evidence. Staff were witnessing complete distress, awfulness, horrible-ness – for example the girl who came to see us after being thrown out of a car at dawn – she was covered in s★★t, she stank, was covered in bruises and love bites, had had to have sex with goodness knows how many men. I detailed it all, social services went round to her house and did an initial assessment, but that was all: the police didn't even go to the property." (personal interview, 2014)

Nor does the oft-cited lack of resources and overwork, a genuine problem particularly for social workers, explain the negligence. Admittedly as Chapter One describes, the 'Baby P' scandal in 2007 greatly heightened pressure to concentrate on child protection against abuse and neglect for babies and young children within families, rather than older children and teenagers, with a considerable growth in referrals of younger age groups. But how do work pressures and resource issues override common humanity and the witness of suffering with one's own eyes? This policy also meant more suffering for the many young girls made pregnant through rape in CSE. For those considered unable to parent – who themselves had long been left unprotected – the final cruel blow was that attention shifted to removing their own babies.

Rowbotham watched young men actually collecting phone numbers in the waiting room of sexual health services in full view of receptionists who did nothing: "Maybe they think, 'Well, those girls are no better than they should be.'" Did some or even many professionals, like them, feel the children deserved these harsh consequences – through their apparent promiscuity, or even their 'impudence' to staff? If so, what a terrible and disproportionate punishment. Let us say unequivocally that it is entirely unacceptable that people with such views should remain any longer in caring jobs.

Making free choices?

Ignoring the girls' suffering may partly be explained by the deceptively 'streetwise' image many of them presented, when in fact those putting on such a 'front' often have little concept of risk or of safety. It can partly be explained by failures to understand – inexplicably after decades of child protection guidelines – how apparent sexual promiscuity can be a confused reaction to past and present sexual abuse. It can partly be through sincere belief in older children's free agency in sexual matters, which still takes hopelessly inadequate account of coercion, intimidation and damaged self esteem, in both offline and online worlds, in these particular young people. Many young people's sexual health services, where these girls might first come to concerned attention, remain influenced by this philosophy, even with girls who would qualify as clearly vulnerable to coercion through a history of being in care or a history of previous abuse.

Narrow professional views of sexual health services' role as set by targets (such as chlamydia testing) can also be a constraint upon safety awareness. Rowbotham, herself the leader of an unusually aware crisis sexual health team, says of her experience in Rochdale:

> "In sexual health, if you answer the right questions, tick the right boxes, you are given treatment and sent on your way ...The Gillick test[4] concentrates on whether you can understand the *treatment* provided. They are spending five to ten minutes with this patient, which doesn't allow the scope to build a relationship.
>
> "Training doesn't allow nurses to be a nurse advocating *for* teenagers ... STIs [sexually transmitted infections] don't make them more suspicious. Because it is almost ordinary to see patients with chlamydia, it's so common. It doesn't cause them to ask about possible coercion ... we got very few referrals from GUM [genito-urinary medicine]. We had lots of girls who were pregnant but [services] don't even ask them about coercion. They might ask, 'How old is your boyfriend' ... of course, the girl will say something like 15!
>
> "Services were set up to encourage a positive pregnancy if they chose it; they didn't worry about *how* she got pregnant. Unless they were concerned that she wouldn't be likely to be able to parent, social services would not get involved." (personal interview, 2014)

Reaction to sense of powerlessness?

Has uncaring also been a way of coping with a professional sense of powerlessness, frustration and defeat? To turn responsibility onto the victim, who just keeps absconding to dodgy people, making risky decisions, and failing to supply court-reliable evidence? If so, this needs to be openly admitted and addressed,

---

[4] In medical law, to decide whether children up to age 16 are able to consent their medical treatment without needing parental permission or knowledge.

and staff supported to see other solutions. Giving up on a human problem is not a professional answer. And it is patient good practice with the most demanding young people – discussed later in this chapter – which, far from causing more stress among police and social workers, appears most to *raise* their morale and sense of achievement.

Racism and cultural issues

Another much-publicised reason for failure to prosecute abusers and protect children has been that the particular form of CSE involving grooming and abuse by gangs in the 'night economy', such as through taxi firms and takeaways, has heavily involved men of Pakistani or African heritage. Prosecution was said to raise fears of inciting community tensions, of being labelled racist, and of feeding the frenzy of white right wing groups. The damning Casey Report into how Rotherham Council dealt with the Jay Report found some councillors and officials expressing fear of being branded or construed as racist. The film-maker Anna Hall tried ever since 1996 to screen documentary investigations into sexual exploitation gangs in England. She faced repeated postponements for legal reasons, or after claimed fears of raising racial tensions. *The Hunt for Britain's Sex Gangs* (True Vision Films) was finally screened by Channel 4 in 2013.

Where such fears existed, victims were silenced yet again. And each time sincere white anti-racists responded to alarming information by protesting that most sexual crime is committed by whites, the issue was swept under the carpet. Of course most sexual crime is committed by whites. This particular organised *form* within the 'night economy' has not been. Pretending that something is not happening, when people can see that it is, does not reduce community tensions.

A survivor-centred approach to over-representation of some minority ethnic groups in this form of CSE is for agencies to work in close partnership with organisations within those black and minority ethnic (BME) communities to tackle and reduce this crime, and change some cultural attitudes towards women which have influenced it. They have strong support from prominent and outspoken Muslims such as Dr Taj Hargey, Imam of the Oxford Islamic Congregation, who has argued:

> The view of some Islamic preachers towards white women can be appalling. They encourage their followers to believe that these women are habitually promiscuous, decadent, and sleazy ... Their dress code, from miniskirts to sleeveless tops, is deemed to reflect their impure and immoral outlook ... (thus) these white women deserve to be punished for their behaviour by being exploited and degraded. (Dixon, 2013)

Julie Siddiqi, the executive director of the Islamic Society of Britain, has called for change in the male dominance at the top of many Muslim organisations, which may have contributed to previous silence on grooming for sexual exploitation (Dugan, 2013).

'Political correctness' unconvincing

However, even accepting that some professionals in caring agencies, some officials and councillors nervously feared stirring racism, this theory leaves very awkward questions as a *general* explanation of inaction, especially by the police, prosecutors and courts. We have to ask why such a striking exception was made in CSE, when letting ethnic minorities off with suspected crimes for fear of inciting tensions has been far from usual within policing and criminal justice? It is also frankly rather ludicrous to judge that the councillors and officials – described in reports such as Jay's and Casey's to be part of an old-fashioned, bullying, macho, sexist culture in towns such as Rotherham or Rochdale – were too politically correct! Indeed Alexis Jay herself said she never used the phrase 'politically correct'. Instead she believed the traditionalist, Labour-dominated council turned a blind eye to the problem because of 'their desire to accommodate a community that would be expected to vote Labour, to not rock the boat, to keep a lid on it, to hope it would go away'(Pidd, 2015).

Statistics challenge this theory

BME people are not treated lightly by criminal justice authorities. They are over-represented at almost all stages of the criminal justice process and disproportionately targeted for stop and search by the police. They are more likely to be imprisoned, and for longer than white British people. Further, Asian Muslims are now the main targets for suspicion about Islamist terrorism.

Between the years 2005–06 and 2009–10, total numbers of arrests in England and Wales decreased. But numbers arrested from BME communities increased, by 5% for black people, and 13% for Asian people. Analysis of all stop and searches in 2010–11 indicated that black people were seven times as likely and Asian people twice as likely as white people to be stopped and searched by police.

In 2010, 23% of white people convicted for indictable offences were sentenced to immediate custody, compared with 29% of Asian people. BME groups are significantly over-represented compared to population in the prison system, at 25%. A 2011 study based on analysing more than a million court records found that Asians were 19% more likely than white people to be given a prison sentence for shoplifting, and 41% more likely for drugs offences. Asians have also been more likely to be arrested for drugs offences, fraud and forgery.

Where religion is concerned, for many young Muslim men, stop and search under Section 44 of the Terrorism Act has become their most frequent and regular contact with the police. Statistics reveal that *Muslims are more disproportionately incarcerated than any other religious group.*[5]

These statistics put the 'fear of racism' theory into serious question. Some might say they make a nonsense of it. Therefore, has the persistent failure to prosecute BME men *for CSE crimes alone* been about the perpetrators at all? Or has it in fact been another judgement on the victims?

---

[5] Ball et al, 2011; Balon et al, 2011; Berman, 2012; Stopwatch, 2012; and www.equalityhumanrights.com/sites/default/files/documents/research/counter-terrorism_research_report_72.pdf; www.slideshare.net/smccormac7/ethnicity-and-crime.

Were they so lowly regarded and so stigmatised, so apparently deserving of the consequences of their acts, that they were unworthy of any risk of stirring racial tensions in communities? Was there also fear that arrests for CSE might disrupt the arrests of BME men for other offences – such as drugs crime – which were taken much more seriously by the police and by many of the public?

Is genuine progress in addressing CSE now being made? The increase in referrals of children in CSE to police and social services following the publicised scandals, and the increase in charging and convictions are very welcome. For example, CSE referrals to social work in England and Wales increased by 31% in 2014–15, while some police forces trebled their numbers of criminal investigations (Halliday, 2015). However, the proportion of children involved in CSE who went on to receive social services support actually dropped (Stevenson, 2015).

Pre-teen pregnancy: disparaging stereotypes

Like involvement in child sexual exploitation, very young (especially pre-teen) pregnancy has not been considered an issue that flags up the strong possibility of sexual abuse, rape or sexual exploitation. This is remarkable when we consider that, in Britain, there is no defence to a charge of sexual activity with a child under 13. The child is considered unable to give consent under the Sexual Offences Act 2003 (England & Wales) and the Sexual Offences (Scotland) Act 2009.

Very young pregnancy, however, particularly excites some media, politicians and clerical figures to blame the young women, and to use them in pursuit of political and moral agendas. We urgently need a complete change in approach, and an automatic child protection investigation for every very young pregnant girl. Although I believe all under-16 pregnancies should be looked at carefully for possible sexual coercion, I mainly consider here children in the 11–14 age group.

Sexual abuse leaves signs of *sexual* activity: obvious, yet often ignored. Research studies find a high correlation between teenage pregnancy and a sexual abuse history. In Noll et al's meta-analytic study (2009a) the probability of a pregnant adolescent having a history of child sexual abuse was a remarkable 4.5 out of 10. Research studies, such as Logan et al (2007), also find that girls who are younger when abuse occurs tend also to be younger at first pregnancy. Sexually abused girls will have even less control over contraception than those in consensual relationships, given the coercion and disparities of power. When young pregnancy is not the direct result of sexual assault itself, it may spring from the effects of earlier sexual abuse – given the well-known effects on destroying self esteem, confusing sexual boundaries and bringing greater risk of revictimisation.

Yet as Logan et al (2007) perceptively note, 'Although childhood sexual abuse has been found by a number of studies to be significantly associated with teen pregnancy ... there is little evidence of pregnancy prevention programmes that specifically address this issue.'

Tressa M: promiscuous 'chav' or victim?

In 2009, Jason Middleton was convicted of raping his sister Tressa Middleton when she was 11 years old. He had been raping her since she was aged seven (Johnston, 2010). In 2006 she had had a baby, who was adopted. At that time, she was portrayed sensationally across the media as 'Scotland's youngest mother at 11' (*The Sun*, 2006; Drury, 2006; Thornton, 2011).

The court case gave a starkly different picture to the previous notorious publicity. She had been portrayed as a shocking example of carefree young promiscuity and the failure of sex education programmes. Allegedly pregnant by a 15-year-old at a drunken party – a story put out by her family – she was painted as a promiscuous slob, and a heavy drinker and smoker since primary school, where she had been excluded for fighting. A supposed product of welfare culture and the permissive society, her pregnancy was said to signal the disintegration of public morals (Nelson and Mackay, 2015).

In reality, she had experienced an extremely unsafe childhood and, the court heard, had tried to kill herself several times. She had been in and out of foster care when younger and sold to other men for a few pounds at the age of nine, as she later revealed in her own book (Middleton and Weitz, 2015). But rape and repeated suicide attempts didn't fit with what many people wanted to hear, because like other pregnant girls she had become a metaphor for all the ills of modern society.

Politicians claimed her pregnancy highlighted 'failings that have allowed such a young girl to go on a night out, get drunk and pregnant, yet seemingly ignorant of the risks and consequences'. A spokesperson for one of the churches declared that it 'is indicative of an increasingly promiscuous culture' (BBC News, 2006a). Liberal-minded politicians still missed the coercion aspect, calling for more and better sex education for young people. The tabloid newspaper which broke the story interviewed her and her mother extensively during the pregnancy and after the birth, concealing only her face in photographs (*The Sun*, 2006). The approach taken in both popular and 'quality' media contributed to numerous verbal attacks by the public on online media comment websites on a 12-year-old child. Many of these comments – most, though not all, now removed – remained available to read for years even after the rape conviction. For example: 'We already know the little twat was drunk and knocked up and continuing to smoke – her mother was proud of her slut offspring' (Nelson and Mackay, 2015).

Part of a familiar pattern

This girl's treatment reflected longstanding treatment of other cases. Because sex and pregnancy issues among young people touch on salaciousness, welfare dependency, sexual morality, the state of national morals, the upbringing of children and teenage anti-social behaviour, impetus is greater to interpret cases in ways which support that agenda among some politicians, church figures and media.

Such pregnancies are repeatedly claimed and apparently accepted by most professionals, media and public as simply drunken one-night stands, with some (usually unnamed) teenage boy said to be the father. Publicised details of how the pregnancy started keep changing, but this fact seems to go unnoticed. Girls and their mothers are blamed, but males involved often escape comment. That strand of sexism links such cases with cases involving adult women who allege rape or sexual assault.

Other examples (this time from England) include:

- Jenny T, a 12-year-old mother, also from a family on benefits, was first said to have tried sex with a 15-year-old boy at school. Oddly, the story changed to 'a single night of experimenting with a 13-year-old boyfriend'. Media reports said she was a cause for public outrage, worry and despair (Moyes, 1997). The authorities reportedly considered that although sex with a girl under 13 was a statutory offence, 'clearly it's a peer relationship that went sadly wrong'.

- Amy C, also 12, became in press reports 'Britain's most notorious gymslip mum' and 'a national disgrace', facing moral outrage and abusive comments about promiscuous, booze-swilling welfare 'chavs' and the permissive society. She was photographed full face. Amy, another young smoker from a family on benefits, with eight brothers and sisters, claimed a one-night stand with a 'Jamaican boy', a stranger of 15. She first claimed it happened at a leisure centre, then changed this to a 'club'. She later changed his nationality to Gambian (her child was black, she was white). No charges were pursued (Bletchly, 2008; Freeman, 2010). Buried in the text of these press accounts however we read that Amy's mother had had several live-in boyfriends, her latest a Gambian who recently returned to Gambia to his wife and children.

'Chavs' from the underclass

Pre-teen mothers have received scorn and class prejudice for personifying the supposed evils of an 'underclass' culture. Blamed for the way their families lived, they are stereotyped as idle, promiscuous products of sink-estate single parents and alleged 'nanny-statism'.

Thus Alleshia G, from a family on benefits (photographed with her two small children) gave birth at 12, becoming pregnant again at 13. It was reported that this was 'by the same [unnamed] boy'. According to the newspaper 'Her story … casts a bleak reflection on a stratum of society in which the products of broken families are blithely having children when they are still children themselves.' The paper featured her £656 a month of welfare benefits. (Clarke, 2013)

In April 2014, a 12-year-old giving birth drew these remarkably savage and class-prejudiced comments from a (female) newspaper columnist:

> There aren't any more chances for this girl. It's finished … she'll be on state benefits already and by the time she's 15 she'll be destined to be forever dependent on the state – a state which forks out £20,000 a year for every single mum like her.

> There'll be no job, no carefree teenage years – just a life on the breadline where she'll spawn [sic] more babies with men who will leave her. (Malone, 2014)

But while rates of teenage pregnancy are consistently highest in areas of deprivation (Macpherson, 2013, Information Services Division, 2014), the great majority of young people in council estates, from poor backgrounds or on benefits, do not have sex at 11 or 12. Nor do they become pregnant. In any case, children are not responsible for their parents' morals or behaviour, for drug users coming to their house, or for other dangerous acts by adults. What the pregnant pre-teenagers in sensational cases have usually had in common is that they lived in unsafe situations, with parents singularly unable to protect them from predators who might regularly be coming and going to the house.

The role of the media has been very significant in these cases. With the Child Protection Research Centre (NSPCC Scotland/ University of Edinburgh) and with full support from the National Union of Journalists, Kirsteen Mackay and I wrote a booklet for the media raising issues about reporting of under-age pregnancy. We asked journalists to change their reporting of such cases, and to point out that children under 13 are by law always victims of sexual crime. As such they should neither be interviewed nor photographed. We urged the media, among other guidelines, to

- Avoid repeating popular prejudices against women who are raped, and against families on welfare benefits, when writing about girls in cases of under-age sex or very young pregnancy;
- Always consider the possibility of sexual abuse or rape in cases of very young under-age sex or pregnancy;
- Always contact organisations and individuals who work to protect young people, for comment on those stories. (Nelson and Mackay, 2015)

Always a child protection issue

In this chapter, the main concern is how agencies, rather than media, work with these young women, and how agencies make assumptions about the pregnancy. In both statutory and voluntary sectors, there appears to be an alarming complacency about accepting dubious stories of how the pregnancy happened and who was responsible; and accepting it was consensual even though consent under age 13 is not possible, and remains very qualified between ages 13 and 16. During publicity about very young pregnancy cases, I have never read nor heard on radio or TV a statutory or voluntary agency speak out, to warn that there is a child protection issue which should be addressed.

Thorough child protection investigations always need to be carried out. Sexual health agencies need to link these young women into voluntary agencies and projects for young people, where they can gain confidence to reveal over time what has happened to them.

Reforms urgently needed (1): Protect children much earlier from child sexual abuse

We should surely have expected social services and health to be well aware that child sexual abuse and other maltreatment may lie behind the behaviour of Tressa, other very young pregnant girls, and many victims of sexual exploitation: such as the early drink or drug misuse, the very young sexual risk-taking, pregnancy, repeated self harm and school exclusions for disruptive behaviour.

These have been acknowledged for decades as frequent reactions to sexual abuse, past and/or present. Hence the signs and behaviours which are given in published guidelines, to inform agencies, parents and the public. To take just one example, the Edinburgh and Lothians multi-agency child protection guidelines state that 'alerting signs' of sexual abuse can include:

> Sexual promiscuity, stealing, over-sexualised behaviour, expressing affection in inappropriate ways, display of sexual knowledge beyond one's years, drug, alcohol or solvent abuse, running away from home, lack of trust in adults or over-familiarity with adults; eating disorder, pregnancy (especially when reluctant to name father); sexually transmitted infections, bruises, scratches, bite marks to thighs and genital areas, self mutilation.[6]

So what has been the point of such guidelines for all this time? It is noteworthy that the Children's Commissioner (2015) report on intrafamilial sexual abuse recommends that all teachers are trained and supported to understand the signs and symptoms of child sexual abuse, as part of initial teacher training and ongoing professional development, and that this requirement should be in statutory guidance.

The most vulnerable

Although CSE has trapped some young people without vulnerable backgrounds, especially through skilful use of social media grooming, children of abusive and neglectful backgrounds have been particular targets. Abusive CSE gangs have consistently targeted children in the care system, young runaways, school excludees and truants, and 'throwaways' already socially rejected because of difficult or chaotic behaviour. The 18 and Under

---

[6] www.midlothian.gov.uk/downloads/file/582/edinburgh_and_lothians_inter-agency_child_protection_procedures

organisation in Dundee told the Scottish Parliamentary Inquiry into CSE of their own cumulative experience with girls involved in CSE, who had been sexually abused at home:

> As they are already taking big risks with their lives (using alcohol, drugs and running away) and have low self esteem some of them see the exploitation as a way of being in charge … of being in control … that it is better to get money for sex than do it for nothing. (The Scottish Parliament, 2014)

In the Office of the Children's Commissioner's sexual exploitation report, Berelowitz et al (2013) noted: 'So many young people told us … of their early histories of being sexually abused within the family home, and of their experiences never being acknowledged'. Indeed this was one finding which led to the OCC commissioning its two-year study into intra-familial sexual abuse in 2014 (Horvath et al 2014; Sellgren, 2014).

Prostitution marginalises and stigmatises young people who have already suffered harsh backgrounds (Levy, 2004). In the Barnardo's report about work with sexually exploited young women and men in Stockton-on Tees, 65% admitted to having experienced child abuse at home, 89% of these from a family member (Crawley et al, 2004). Andrea Dworkin (1992) memorably described incestuous abuse as a 'boot camp' and a 'training camp' for prostitution. Numerous research studies have found that a majority of women entering prostitution have been sexually abused in childhood, and studies have exposed violence and exploitation within prostitution (such as Hunter, 1993; Farley and Barkan, 1998; Kramer and Berg, 2003).

Substance misuse clues

In my own research with male survivors of child sexual abuse, half of those I interviewed were addicted to drink or drugs by their teens and a quarter before their teens (Nelson, 2009). Reasons for very early substance misuse include trying to blot out post-traumatic memories of abuse, steeling themselves for further abuse, and being plied with drink and drugs to make them complaint and dependent. That has been a feature of CSE. Yet how many of these young people had already been made dependent by abusers earlier in their lives?

Some 366 children aged 12 or under, including children as young as eight, were referred for drug or alcohol misuse treatment in 2012–13 in England, according to Public Health England (*Telegraph*, 2014). Yet the debate that followed among politicians, commentators and even charities was almost entirely about the effectiveness of drugs education in schools; about how Ministerial guidance and the new National Curriculum in England will impact on schools teaching about harmful substances; and about the risks to children from substance-misusing parents.

There was a glaring absence of discussion about what may have led children to seek refuge in substances (for example Stoltz et al, 2007). How many experienced a child protection investigation? Of course numerous teenagers experiment with drink and drugs but serious, protracted, addictive early use should *always* alert to an urgent need for help and protection. Abused children send out loud messages when they cannot speak the words.

In Scotland, a major report (Brock, 2015) on safeguarding vulnerable children repeatedly emphasised the importance of effective early intervention in their lives, and "a clearer focus on children and young people who are at risk, and where parental engagement is currently insufficient. Raising attainment for all, reducing drug, alcohol and tobacco misuse among young people, youth offending and teenage pregnancy are just a few examples. All of these inequalities impact disproportionately on children and young people who have grown up in challenging family circumstances" (page 10).

Online and offline vulnerability are connected

Much grooming and coercion in CSE, as well as in other abusive behaviour, now takes place online. While recent research has found that a considerable majority of young people have resilience online to approaches from sexual groomers, it also finds that a minority are very vulnerable (Soo and Bodanovskaya, 2012; www.europeanonlinegroomingproject.com/home.aspx).

A widespread and important research finding is that online and offline vulnerability are inter-related. For Smahel et al (2012) and d'Haenens et al (2013) the so-called double jeopardy effect means children with more psychological and emotional problems and low self esteem, with behaviours including misuse of drugs and alcohol, are most vulnerable to repetitive, compulsive and uncontrolled use of online technology and its negative consequences. They find excessive use is also associated with meeting new online contacts offline, and sending sexual messages online. Again, a wide-ranging review of young people's vulnerabilities to online grooming revealed how lonely, marginalised or excluded young people use online chatrooms to communicate with others, to compensate for social difficulties offline. They found that chatrooms, more than other online communications, put young people at risk of sexual approaches (Whittle et al, 2013).

The behaviours and the problems noted above are those of many of the children and young people discussed in this chapter. They are also common behaviours of children who have already experienced violence and abuse.

Smahel et al draw the important conclusion *that children's engagement with computers and technology should be understood within the wider context of their everyday life.* Given that past victimisation is a proven risk factor for future victimisation, Whittle et al note that revictimisation is found to be particularly a risk when someone has been a victim of child sexual abuse (Reese-Weber and Smith, 2011); and that a history of offline child sexual abuse is a specific risk factor for future victimisation online (Helweg-Larsen et al, 2011; Noll et al, 2009b; Wolak et al, 2008). Having been abused offline appears to be significantly and independently associated with online grooming, which is in turn associated with meetings offline (Noll et al, 2009b).

Further evidence for earlier intervention in CSA

Thus, ever-increasing knowledge and research about risks to young people in the online world only strengthens the point that the belated, welcome profile now given to addressing CSE makes little sense, if the priority for prevention and intervention against sexual abuse, other violence and neglect earlier in life is downgraded (see Chapter One). The Scottish Parliamentary Inquiry (Scottish Parliament, 2014) made one of its recommendations that 'social work and other child protection services give higher priority to addressing child sexual abuse … which may put them at particular risk of CSE'. Thus one crucial way to reduce CSE and the many costs of addressing it is to identify any abuse and violence which made young people vulnerable to sexual exploitation in the first place.

However, one urgent change needed here is to end the separation of child sexual abuse and CSE in the organisation of protective multi-agency services, which frequently and bizarrely separate abuse occurring within and outside the family. This makes little sense. Perpetrators frequently abuse in both settings, and family ones may indeed deliberately groom their own children in order to sell them for abuse outside the family (Itzin, 2000). In Rochdale, for example, Sara Rowbotham recalls "Social workers were batting cases of CSE they heard about back to the police, because it was abuse outside the family, and they dealt with families" (personal interview, 2014). An end to this separation where it exists throughout UK child protection services is needed. The pooling of all information through perpetrator-focused investigation and further development of MASH hubs (see Chapter Five) is likely to be far more effective in tracking both individual offenders, and organised groups.

Reforms urgently needed (2): Change prejudices for good

It is surely time finally to declare completely unacceptable in every authority destructive, prejudiced or uncaring attitudes towards troubled young people, and in particular prejudices against 'promiscuous' women and girls, among police, social workers, health staff and residential care workers.

Professional awareness

There is support through the courts for an important point made by English appeal judges, who overturned a lenient sentence on a male perpetrator. This followed widespread protest at remarks made by defence, prosecutor and judge in the Neil Wilson case of 2013, that the 13-year-old girl (a vulnerable school abscondee) was 'predatory' in her behaviour. The Crown Prosecution Service suspended the prosecutor from sex offence cases. The appeal judges argued, significantly, that 'An under-age person who encourages sexual relations with her needs more protection, not less. The Attorney General is therefore right to say that the victim's vulnerability was an aggravating, rather than a mitigating feature' (Attorney General, 2013; Nelson and Mackay, 2015). *This clearly suggested that young girls showing apparent 'promiscuity' and suggestive signs of previous abuse or exploitation deserve protection, not blame.*

Priority must now surely go to a major, country-wide campaign and training exercise (not a piecemeal programme) to convey unequivocally what law and guidance states, and to change attitudes, particularly by clarifying once again the links between a history of sexual abuse, and such chaotic behaviours. The considerable, imaginative resources of the National Working Group (NWG) Network against sexual exploitation will be invaluable. So will the direct input of young people themselves, for example through training DVDs. The NWG network is the only child sexual exploitation network working across voluntary/statutory agencies tackling CSE. It has more than 1000 practitioners from 260 organisations working with CSE and child trafficking in the UK, and has a wide range of training resources, including input from young people themselves.[7]

It will particularly be important to enlist the training of the feminist voluntary sector working against domestic violence and sexual violence, in highlighting the kinds of prejudices against women and girls which link attitudes to rape and attitudes to victims of child sexual exploitation.

I strongly believe that disciplinary measures in police and caring agencies should then take place if the disrespectful actions of the past towards troubled young people continue. The knowledge that this might happen should have a salutary influence on behaviour. I want to ask unions and professional associations representing the caring professions to support this,

---

[7] www.nwgnetwork.org

with due safeguards, and actually to stand beside the stigmatised young people instead of simply protesting about a blame culture in child protection.

Public awareness

Informing the public about the links between previous abuse and apparently promiscuous behaviour could also change public attitudes as one key part of 'bystander education' (examples of projects can be found on the NWG website: also see Chapter Six). Much of the grooming in the CSE scandals took place in plain sight of local people – at fast food restaurants, in the streets and around particular houses. It was the *interpretation* of what they saw which prevented local residents from reporting what was happening to the young people.

Laurie Matthew of 18 and Under in Dundee recalls:

> "In Charleston [estate], we ran two sessions a week with the community for 10 weeks. We raised awareness about abuse and its effects on children's behaviour. This visibly changed how local people felt about kids who acted out. Next time they saw a wee boy breaking windows, they thought about whether he had had any dinner – say they noticed his mother wasn't back until midnight, and one said, 'You know what? I'm gonna offer him a sandwich.' That was a huge change within a few weeks." (personal interview, 2014)

Reforms urgently needed (3): Radically change the residential care system

Vulnerability to sexual exploitation has consistently been found to be particularly high for looked-after young people in residential care. A Barnardo's study, for example, identified CSE as an issue for almost two-thirds of girls in residential homes in Northern Ireland who took part in the research (Beckett, 2011), a study followed by Marshall's independent inquiry into CSE in

Northern Ireland (Marshall, 2014). CELCIS concluded from its Scottish case study research in 2013 that CSE was an issue for a quarter of the care population, but 'considerably higher' for older age groups, for girls and for children placed in residential care.[8]

Inquiries, reports and consultations have reported many problems in this system about keeping often the most chaotic and damaged of our young people safe from abuse and exploitation. Some problems concern attitudes already discussed in this chapter, but other problems concern structures and powers:

- Risks of peer-on-peer abuse abuse, of introducing exploiters to each other, or of running away together to an older person's house.

- Lack of powers, or lack of clarity about their powers, to keep young people in. They cannot lock them in their rooms and even fire regulations could be cited for inability to lock the doors. In open units the young people are free to come and go much of the time and get involved in exploitation, and their advocacy organisations work to ensure their rights to free movement.

- Direct targeting of care homes by sexual predators.

- Persisting failures over many decades to deal effectively with absconding, a major source of sexual and physical danger to young people.

Taking absconding seriously

In England, a report by the Centre for the Study of Missing Persons at the University of Portsmouth found that 99.5% of those missing from private care homes (which include all kinds of care, such as for frail elderly people) were young people up to age 18. The authors noted: 'We should expect the same degree of care from residential carers as (from) a mum and dad.' They

---

8 www.careknowledge.com/the_sexual_exploitation_of_looked_after_children_in_scotland_25769805085.aspx)

believed Ofsted should sanction the homes if high numbers were going missing, and if there was no evidence of strategies to reduce absconding. They believed there were grounds for social care professionals to be able to prevent people from leaving institutional premises, including children who repeatedly go missing and are at risk of sexual exploitation: yet these children, they found, were rarely classified as at 'high risk' (Stevenson, 2014).

The report noted that 46% of children in care are placed many miles away from home, putting great distances between them and their social worker. Children are then more likely to run back to where they want to be A government consultation on improving safeguarding of children in care (DfE, 2014) recommended that out-of-area placements should only be made in the best interests of the child, and signed off by the Director of Children Services. The Scottish Parliamentary Inquiry in.to CSE (Scottish Parliament, 2014) recommended that CSE be made a specific area for inspection for local authorities, and for all organisations accommodating children.

Unless we are going to put all children likely to abscond to dangerous people into secure units – impossible both practically and ethically – is it finally time to ask if open residential units can ever protect them? If not, what is the point of placing them in these very expensive units, especially if they have been removed from home precisely because it was sexually unsafe? And especially if, as is often the case, running away is itself part of their post-traumatic behaviour, which will require intensive work to change?

In the 1980s, as a social work journalist, I visited a girls' care home in Scotland where the manager told me young male predators hung about constantly outside. I was told then by care managers that absconding was now being taken seriously, and ways to tackle it were being implemented. In 2014 I was told of Scottish residential units where almost all the girls left every evening, and became involved in sexual exploitation in the local towns (I am not at all suggesting that Scotland is worse than anywhere else, but that experience may have parallels throughout the UK). How long is change going to take?

Abuse trauma unaddressed

Nor are effects of abuse trauma addressed in the case of many looked-after children. Sometimes this failure is graphically suggested by events, particularly through high suicide rates. For example, while in the Good Shepherd's open unit in Bishopton, Renfrewshire, 14-year-old Niamh Lafferty and Georgia Rowe jumped in a tragic double suicide from the Erskine Bridge in October 2009. The Fatal Accident Inquiry report emphasised their placement in a ground floor flat with easy exits, and the paucity of staff on duty.[9] However, the body of the report revealed that their deaths were rehearsed in a cumulative, disturbing list of numerous suicide attempts, abscondings and self-destructive chaos.

These reflected classic behaviours by many children who suffer from abuse trauma, and from likely current exploitation (they kept absconding and being found in strange men's flats or cars, plied with drink and drugs). The report documented that from the age of seven Georgia showed sexualised behaviour and dissociative episodes reminiscent of fighting off assault; she reacted violently to restraint and took huge amounts of numbing alcohol and drugs, as did Niamh, while both made several serious suicide attempts.

Children with this history need two things most: consistent safety in their placement, and skilled therapeutic work by trauma specialists. A few professionals had long recommended therapy, but little ever took place. Nor was better therapy provision recommended by the Inquiry report, nor were specialists in abuse trauma consulted during the Inquiry.

Throughout care settings, fears, taboos and excuses about lack of training persist about working with abuse trauma, especially sexual abuse trauma. This is fiddling while Rome burns: like seeing as relevant whether these desperate girls lived on the ground floor, or the first. Supportive staff training and awareness-raising about trauma care need to become priorities (Nelson, 2012d).

---

[9] www.scotland-judiciary.org.uk/10/895/fatal-accident-inquiry-into-the-deaths-on-erskine-bridge

Improve or change?

Perhaps we could start yet again, and copy all the residential units with the best and safest practice with young people. These undoubtedly exist and I don't for a second want to denigrate their skilled staff. There are also interesting and important moves to house young sexually exploited and abused women in small care units, within their own home areas (rather than in remote secure accommodation) along with specially trained and longer-term staff. Examples are the St Christopher's Fellowship Safe Steps projects (Williams, 2015).

However, Laurie Matthew, director of the confidential service 18 and Under, believes that time is overdue for alternatives to be tried.

> "There is good practice [in residential care], I've seen it. But there are still so many basic problems about most units.
>
> "Someone has to care enough about these chaotic young people to go and get them as you would your own child. These need staffing up better, but not with shifts of people who keep changing, on the minimum wage, who don't understand trauma issues. You can't relate to people who are constantly changing. Their whole lives are controlled by people who don't care enough about them. And where social workers are report-writers and people who exchange information about them. The kids demand money, clothes etc and they get these things almost thrown at them in care, but that's not what they actually need: they need love. At the moment, they learn from each other how to self harm, and where to run together to dangerous people." (personal interview, 2014)

Alternatives: specialised fostering and 'wraparound care'

Laurie Matthew thinks the answer lies with a genuine 'wraparound local community' using specialised foster parents who are skilled and strongly committed to children. This is also a possible solution to the perennial problem of placement instability in looked-after children (Norgate et al, 2012). That would involve placing some effort and resources into recruitment and training: but specialised fostering compared with conventional fostering could have a new appeal for skilled people, including some from the residential sector. To Matthew, the carers would have to behave as parents would.

> "If my child went missing I would go out and search for her and bring her back. What kind of parent would let their kid get into a car with an older man? But they would also need to build trust and mutual respect, or it wouldn't work." (personal interview, 2014)

Under this plan, numbers would be manageable locally, and statutory/voluntary teams would be built around those children, including trauma therapists, mental health, drug and alcohol services, sexual health and confidential support services for the young people themselves.

Relationships were the key

Just 'pie in the sky'? Barnardo's already run specialised foster parenting with sexually exploited and trafficked children, providing support and training both to the foster parents and their allocated specialist worker. An evaluation of this pioneering scheme, the Barnardo's Safe Accommodation Project (for sexually exploited and trafficked young people) by Shuker (2014) found many positive results. This was despite the multiple abuses and vulnerabilities of the young people chosen for the scheme.

Most significantly it found that it was the development of warm, trusting relationships between young people and foster carers, reflecting compassion, unconditional acceptance and persistence while still maintaining boundaries, which proved the key to unlocking a whole series of other outcomes of safety and wellbeing. These warm and trusting relationships were at the heart of creating safe and stable foster placements.

Among the positive outcomes were: young people felt safer and protected from exploitation; their awareness of healthy relationships increased; protective factors grew, such as engagement in education and positive friendships; their physical, emotional and psychological wellbeing improved; in most placements, going missing stopped or was reduced.

Among key qualities of the carers were: providing positive attention; persisting before there was evidence of change; helping young people to communicate; responding to their emotional needs; applying boundaries consistently; making it harder to run away; talking frankly; offering therapeutic outreach; valuing cultural identities; challenging oppressive assumptions; modelling healthy relationships and offering viable, interesting activities.

Shuker's evaluation also concluded that wider use of this scheme was likely to see improved cost benefits, especially if it was used as an alternative to secure care, residential care or youth custody (Shuker, 2014).

Cost is also about human cost. There is great cruelty and human cost in traumatised young people suffering numerous placement breakdowns and being sent hundreds of miles from home. There is the human cost for inadequately trained carers and staff, who feel they have failed children.

Carers will always need skilled support. In particular, they could gain access to relevant trauma services and resources, such as that produced by Family Futures in London or the Post Institute in the US,[10] along with books and DVDs about trauma and attachment disorders. These resources would help them understand and work with the complexity and root causes of some behaviours they would meet and work with.

Peer support

Simultaneous work within neighbourhoods to change attitudes to 'difficult' teenagers also creates a protective environment for very damaged young people. For Laurie Matthew, "Peer education is also really valuable, not through using peers from privileged backgrounds but peer projects with young people

---

[10] www.familyfutures.co.uk; postinstitute.com

from their backgrounds, except a bit older." 18 and Under in 2015 launched peer support projects in Scotland called Peer Connections and Learn 2 listen. They recruit, support and train young people aged 16–19, usually from challenging backgrounds. These in turn support other young people in schools and residential units. "We have open evenings with lots of different activities to encourage the young people in and keep them engaged. We find that very quickly and naturally they start supporting each other." They have arranged for evaluations of these projects, and progress will be worth monitoring.

'Wraparound' is potentially there...

If all these changes above, in relation to supporting looked-after young people, sound unrealistic to achieve, consider that many services already exist. But they are not organised in this 'wraparound' way. For instance, Craigmillar, a very disadvantaged area of Edinburgh, social work had special responsibility for 150 young people, from an area population of approximately 8000. More than 60 statutory and voluntary organisations existed in Craigmillar when I worked there. They could easily have shared meeting the needs of these children and young people within the community from morning until night, had they collaborated closely in organising this. While some needs would be specialised, others would be more routine, like preparing breakfast (Nelson, 2004b; Nelson and Baldwin, 2004).

A radical rethink of residential forms of care for the most damaged young people puts the importance of trauma at its centre, and offers real hope of reducing distressing post-traumatic symptoms, making the young people less unsafe to themselves and others, and less vulnerable to further victimisation.

Reforms urgently needed (4): Short-term refuges essential

Why have statutory agencies so signally failed to enable and support a significant network of refuges for children under 16, 20 years after legislation permitted this under section 51 of the Children's Act 1989 and section 38 of The Children (Scotland) Act 1995? Why have only a handful in the UK survived for any time, why were they so small and so vulnerable to closure? When many thousands of children go missing each year, usually running to very unsafe people and places, the closures and failures to establish cannot be through lack of need. They must surely be through unsuitability, a lack of official willingness to refer children, and a distrust and lack of awareness of the facility among children and young people.

Has an official fear of legal difficulties with under-16s, and fear of losing their own control over a highly professionalised child protection system which often fails to protect these young people, been more pressing than the children's own needs? If so that is a shameful and continuing failure in my view. The repeated failure to take up powers has concerned the Scottish voluntary sector so much that their proposal to place an actual duty on local authorities to provide refuge was adopted in recommendations by the Scottish Parliamentary Inquiry into CSE. Members of the Scottish Parliament also urged that 'the reasons for Scotland's only refuge closing [Aberlour, in 2013] should be investigated' (Scottish Parliament, 2014, p. 26).

We urgently need to consider different models which utilise a much less formalised, a less bureaucratic and arm's-length system. The trialling of such models should be positively welcomed and worked with as an essential part of keeping young people at risk safer than they are now. Voluntary sector agencies working with sexual abuse and domestic abuse, and seen as independent by young people, should actively be invited and financed to become involved at local level. A workable system is likely to be one where small refuges are geographically very accessible, and widely known to local young people: not some single refuge for a whole country. That model has failed.

Laurie Matthew sums up her vision as:

> "Neighbourhoods could each have an identified safe flat, perhaps run by a (vetted) older person or family. A bit like a neighbourhood watch for children. A temporary refuge, where children know they will be safe ... where they are given time to think, to talk, where people listen, and give them options. Like how to keep safe for a couple of nights. 18 and

Under set an informal one up in Dundee in the 1990s, run by an experienced foster mother. We need a few neighbouring authorities in parts of the UK to have the courage to develop some through less formal networks, and to evaluate the results." (personal interview, 2014)

Reforms urgently needed (5): Make changes to the protection of vulnerable young people leaving care

Eviction and homelessness

It is extraordinary and damning that despite everything that has been known for decades about distressed acting-out behaviour in abused and damaged young people, about their mental health issues; their intensive need for support; the vulnerability of their flats for visitors promoting drugs, drink or disruption; that by 2015 they could still be given minimal support, subject to eviction for the very problems which anyone could have predicted.

A wide-ranging, hard-hitting research report by Crellin and Pona (2015) for the Children's Society found vulnerable 16- and 17-year-olds across England are still being made to leave accommodation by housing providers used by their local authority. The report found half these providers had either evicted or asked a child to move at short notice due to them getting behind on their rent and other bills, or factors like unemployment, violence or drugs. This was despite the severe risks these young people face, including sexual exploitation and violence. Instead of offering them more support when their problems increased, they were often evicted to ever more unsuitable accommodation, or even faced street homelessness.

In this Children's Society report, the organisation called on the government to introduce a raft of regulation and other measures which guarantee that all children in such accommodation are properly safeguarded. Accommodation providers, if they accommodate 16- and 17-year-olds, should proactively seek to integrate their organisation into the local structures for safeguarding. This should include making contact with the local safeguarding hub, children's services, the local safeguarding children's board and the police, if they have not already done so.

Sam Royston, Director of Policy and Research at The Children's Society, said in the report:

> It is unacceptable that children are being evicted from the very places intended to keep them safe and prepare them for adulthood, often simply as a result of getting behind on bills or lacking the support they need to cope. Instead, many are being denied the stability and safety they need.[11]

Reforms urgently needed (6): Reform school exclusions permanently

The most vulnerable young people especially need targeting for *proactive* protection – just as abusers, drug dealers and pimps target them for exploitation. Targeting them for safety during the school day is one vital need.

School exclusions are a disaster for many abused and neglected young people. A high percentage of all the female and male abuse survivors of child sexual abuse I have ever interviewed have been excluded from school, including all the male prisoners in the male research study (Nelson, 2009) – one 14 times, one starting at nursery. These are the last children and young people who should be pushed onto the streets for exposure to further sexual exploitation, violence, alcohol and drugs. Exclusion puts them at far greater risk of where they associate unsupervised with unsafe peers and adults(DfE, 2011).

In the four years up to 2009, almost 2200 children in the UK were excluded from schools for drug and alcohol abuse. Such addiction is one frequent refuge for sexually abused children. Brigadier Hugh Munro, Scotland's former chief inspector of prisons, has been among prominent public figures who call for country-wide alternatives to school exclusion. He says that in his

---

[11] http://www.childrenssociety.org.uk/news-and-blogs/press-releases/vulnerable-teenagers-forced-out-of-accommodation-and-into-crisis

experience, exclusion actively drives young people into trouble, into substance misuse or further misuse, and often into prison itself (BBC News, 2011).

There needs to be an alternative unit in each school or group of local schools which children must attend if their classroom behaviour is unacceptable: not a patchwork of some provision, or none, across the UK. Such units must not be repeatedly cut back through funding shortages. Other best practice examples throughout the UK in ending or reducing school exclusions need to be adopted as national priorities. Plenty of committed teachers would like to work with challenging children, and gain their trust to help them reveal whatever is wrong in their lives. That effort is likely to prove more than cost-effective.

Reforms urgently needed (7): Create protective sexual health services

Sometimes sexual clues are the best, most glaring clues that silenced young people can ever give. The time is overdue for a sound understanding of coercion, and ways of addressing it, to be built into *all* sexual health services. These understandings need to be seen as important, integral elements of sexual health services, which in turn need to be seen as integral parts of a system that keeps young people safe from harm. Giving out the technical means of preventing STIs and teenage pregnancy are not nearly sufficient. Governments need to take the lead on this.

Sara Rowbotham discussed her own team's successes in engaging vulnerable, disaffected teenage girls and enabling them to admit what was happening. It was not about very expensive elaborate provision, but about ordinary good practice, genuine respect, genuine caring, listening, and accessibility within local communities:

> "We originally build our reputation in a portakabin! It was run down then, we weren't a crisis intervention team then but a condom distribution and needle exchange. It had its place in the community and people knew about us. We worked with pregnancy,

information and support ... professionals referred young people to us. Pregnancies were really common.

"Normally services are appointment-based and if you miss so many appointments you are at the back of the queue again. Lots of young people's services are organised like that! That is disastrous for these young people and shows no understanding of their problems. We went and found them if they missed an appointment. It was clear we needed to double-check that the kids didn't need to come back.

"Clues that they were being abused or exploited were ... they might be connected to kids we already knew about ... or their initial behaviour made me feel concerned ... they might swear at the workers (other services might ban them). One girl did disappear fast when she knew we were going to report, but she was back in a couple of weeks. If you tell young people at the start that confidentiality doesn't mean keeping secrets, they know whether to go on telling you ... I think they wanted it to stop. We would say, 'This is all wrong isn't it ... this has got to stop,' and most let us report, then ... yet only recently [in Rochdale] have they proposed a protocol for GUM consultants, that repeat infections are a marker for safeguarding concerns." (personal interview, 2014)

Stigmatised young people: allies in catching perpetrators

An essential tool in this armoury of methods and techniques to entrap perpetrators of sexual abuse and exploitation will be freely given intelligence information from stigmatised young people themselves. Runaways, persistent school truants and excludees, homeless young people, and those in residential and foster care, in psychiatric units, prisons and secure units possess much information about abusers and abusive networks, from their own childhoods and adolescence. Sometimes, they will literally know where the bodies are buried. Yet these are also the very groups whose credibility and reliability have traditionally had the lowest rating.

They need instead to become one of the central elements in identification and prosecution of sex abusers. Child protection structures in every area of the country need to make them so. Ignoring this mass of potential information makes no sense whatsoever.

But if they are to be consulted for their experience and their witness information, they first have to be approached with genuine caring and respect. Then much wider, more imaginative means including use of social media, anonymous helplines, and limited but genuine, well-publicised amnesty for offences committed under abusers' duress are needed to enable them to transmit information safely and less fearfully. They have been silenced by self-blame, intimidation, violence, the experience of being disbelieved, distrust of and by professionals, and involvement in criminal activities, which leaves them fearing prosecution themselves. In order to free them to speak, we have to acknowledge and then counter the fears they actually have.

A number of possible methods of enabling them to transmit information more safely and less fearfully are described in the next chapter, which also suggests young people's third sector support agencies need respect and close involvement for their skills, experience and trusting relationships with young people. Most important, everyone working with these young people needs genuinely to believe that they have value, and have the potential for change.

Finally, but very important: a vital part of enabling stigmatised young people to be allies in convicting perpetrators will be *genuine* enforcement of the change in attitudes to them as witnesses, outlined in the guidance on prosecution of cases involving sexual abuse, by the former Director of Public Prosecutions Keir Starmer in 2014. Under these guidelines, prosecutors are told to focus on the credibility of allegations, not on whether victims make good witnesses: what an indictment on our legal system that this even has to be said. A list of 'myths and stereotypes' about behaviour previously thought to undermine the credibility of young victims is included in the guidelines, so that prosecutors can challenge use of such preconceptions in court (BBC News, 2013b, 2013c)

Rewarding for staff...

Changed ways of thinking and working are likely to make work with 'difficult' sexually abused and exploited teenagers not more stressful and difficult, but the opposite. They also make it much more likely that these young people will reveal the information they have about perpetrators.

In one example, five men and boys were found guilty of the rape and sexual assault of girls in Peterborough in 2014. Estelle Thain, a senior children and families social worker there, had been named social worker of the year. She found work with the young women was hugely beneficial to staff morale also. She wrote:

> Relationships are key to all social work, but they are absolutely vital when you are supporting children who have developed strong emotional connections with people they trusted, who went on to abuse that trust.
>
> Looking back it's clear that unlocking abuse is all about time and patience. When it was identified there was child sexual exploitation in Peterborough, (Welch, 2014) the city council set up a dedicated team to work with the victims and police ... We supported them through experiences that caused them distress or anxiety. Once the girls felt they could depend on us they then felt able to reveal the awful details of what they had experienced. Once the police investigations began, it was critical to maintain that trust.
>
> If there was one piece of advice that I would offer a social worker who was in the early stages of identifying CSE, it would be to put all your time and energy into developing close relationships with the victims. [Also] to ensure there are close working relationships with partner agencies. There was never a culture of secrecy; we shared everything. The past 18 months have perhaps been the most challenging of my career – but they have also been the most rewarding. (Thain, 2014)

Postscript: shooting the messenger?

In 2015, Sara Rowbotham was asked: what are you doing now? There were staff cuts in her team, which included her own post:

> "In Rochdale they 'reconfigured the service' and said they didn't need someone with my level of skills any more…in the reorganisation, they have 'lessons learned' from all this, but to this day, I have never been asked to contribute." (personal interview, 2015)

FIVE

Models for ethical, effective child protection

Sarah Nelson and Liz Davies

Safety and security don't just happen, they are the result of
collective consensus and public investment. We owe our children,
the most vulnerable citizens in our society, a life free of violence
and fear. (Nelson Mandela)

Introduction

This book has outlined several major concerns about failures
of current UK policies, practices and principles in protecting
children from child sexual abuse (CSA). Some people, including
survivors of CSA, may understandably be disillusioned with the
capacity for reform of the statutory child protection system,
and seek alternatives outside it. But it seems to us that a *good*
statutory system has to be at the centre of society's attempts to
keep children safer; it essentially supports other vital community
and voluntary sector activities to protect children; and it crucially
inspires confidence in the public, conspicuously practising the
principles it professes to believe in.

This chapter offers some practical examples to follow or adapt,
which will make for more effective, genuinely child-centred
child protection systems, particularly but not solely in addressing
sexual abuse. It suggests, first, that child protection authorities
need to simplify and redefine their core aims, giving strong,

clear direction and focus to everything they do. Core aims, values and ethical principles should be able to fit on a single page; these should infuse, underpin and inform child protection guidelines and procedures, and the beliefs and approaches of child protection staff working with children. For if staff do not truly take such core aims them on board, then guidelines and procedures – which may at times need to be complex, especially in complex abuse (see Davies, 2008, 2009, 2010) – may simply not be followed. A prime example of that problem involved the widespread ignoring of clear legislation and guidance about child sexual exploitation, when derogatory and blaming attitudes to these vulnerable young women heavily dictated their lack of protection (discussed in detail in Chapter Six).

The chapter then divides into two inter-related parts. The first considers some policies and practices which can overcome a basic problem: that children and young people find it exceptionally hard to disclose sexual abuse – at least in ways which adults can readily understand. The second part is complementary: examining policies and practices which can better identify sexual abusers through 'perpetrator-focused' strategies of investigation. We believe many disillusioned professionals would be keen to work within such models, because these will better reflect how they wanted to work with vulnerable children and young people in the first place.

Simplifying and redefining core aims and principles

Here is a suggested 'top ten' template for all policymakers and practitioners to follow in child protection. This would encourage them to follow truly child-centred practice in everything they do.

1. To promote healthy environments, living conditions, communities and relationships positively, in order to improve the wellbeing and safety of all children.

2. To protect children from harm, abuse and neglect, from a basis of informed knowledge and awareness.

3. To do so in ways which respect children's perspectives, concerns and fears, their dignity and their intelligence.

4. To identify harm to the child, and to identify perpetrators of that harm, as early as possible.

5. To respond, in all child protection processes, to the way children *actually* behave, think, feel, react and speak at different stages of their development.

6. To enable children to tell about harm, abuse or neglect actively, in an environment where the child feels as free as possible from fear and shame.

7. As adult protectors, to involve children actively in reaching solutions to secure or increase their own protection.

8. To understand and respect without prejudice the diverse ethnic, religious, social and sexual identities of children and young people, without using supposed features of such diversities to justify non-intervention into allegations of harm, abuse and neglect.

9. To respect children and young people's rights and agency, while being aware that at times this can justify non-intervention through faulty assumptions of uncoerced choice, when they are in need of protection.

10. To support all these aims by taking all action possible to allocate the resources and staffing which can make them a reality for children.

Part 1: Helping children and young people to disclose sexual abuse

Proven problems of child disclosure

There are many problems about tackling child sexual abuse effectively, but children and young people's fear of disclosure is one of the greatest. This makes current British child protection and criminal justice systems largely 'upside down', in still relying heavily on waiting for children and young people to tell. But most sexually abused children and young people do not, or at least not in ways which adults can easily understand, nor which have the phraseology and consistency of timeline, in giving their accounts, that criminal justice and courts demand.

Thus are systems based on the opposite of the way in which real children behave. All professionals involved have to ask themselves hard and honest questions about why this manifestly unsatisfactory situation has continued over decades when the problem has long been known – and even harsher questions about whom exactly it benefits. We need belatedly to turn the system back again like an egg timer, so that it does not protect the backs of anxious professionals, but is built round the way young people *actually* react, think and speak.

Research into disclosure issues to date has revealed two key findings: that among children delays in disclosure are common, and that a significant proportion of children do not disclose that they have been sexually abused until adulthood, if at all (Pipe et al, 2007). Many also deny that they were abused, even when the abuse has been corroborated and substantiated (Williams, 1995; Sjöberg and Lindblad, 2002; Malloy et al, 2007). They are even less likely to disclose abuse by a parent (Hershkowitz et al, 2005). In my [SN's] research projects young women and men gave numerous reasons for having stayed silent as children and teenagers: indeed during a single discussion, the young women's group revealed 14 different reasons (Nelson, 2008, pp. 11–14).

These included self-blame; intense shame, especially in relation to their peer group; fear of reprisals; lack of control over events after disclosure; not having the words; in denial; not trusting anyone; fear of getting in trouble; fear of being disbelieved; mixed feelings towards the abuser. It has also been found that boys are even more reluctant to disclose than girls (Nelson, 2009; Ungar et al, 2009).

Goodman-Brown and colleagues' research (2003) found similar inhibitors, and revealed how young people must continually make 'first disclosure decisions' – evaluating trust, response and the consequences of telling in each new relationship.

Active withholding

The research with children by McElvaney et al (2012) identified three key dynamics: active withholding of the secret; the 'pressure cooker effect' of conflict between wishing to tell and wishing not to; and the confiding itself. This means, they argued, that in supporting children to tell, the need for the secret to be contained and controlled must be respected.

Active withholding involves not wanting people to know, denying when asked, difficulty in saying the words, and confining numbers of people told. Non-disclosure appears to be *active* withholding, which may give a sense of control and safety in an unsafe world. The *pressure cooker effect* concerns the great emotional strain in being unable to tell, in wanting yet not wanting to. The secret may thus be blurted out suddenly and distressingly without prior planning or support. As for *confiding*, few children apparently tell the people whom child protection systems urge them to tell, such as police, social workers or teachers. Priebe and Svedin (2008) in their large scale study of adolescents, found that of those who disclosed abuse, 43% of boys and 38% of girls mentioned 'friend of my own age' as the only recipient of disclosure.

Even warm and approachable teachers can be difficult to confide in, given the level of shame which teenagers in particular feel: Dana Fowley, victim of multiple rapes since the age of five, agonised that her helpful teachers at secondary school would think very badly of her if she told (Fowley, 2010). Research and practice by voluntary sector organisations find that friends and mothers are the main recipients, whereas statutory bodies are rare recipients (Crisma et al, 2004; McElvaney et al, 2012; McElvaney, 2013).

Why is there such persistent failure to acknowledge reality, to question the reasons why, and actively to support the main recipients of disclosure? It feels only like wilful disregard of that reality.

For McElvaney and colleagues, children need to be seen as more than evidence-providers, whose own needs and concerns are often ignored. Many children cannot provide that evidence anyway. Under current investigative and criminal justice systems they frequently retract, or their evidence is found insufficient, and they may remain unprotected or even returned to abusive situations. Prosecution and conviction rates for CSA are notoriously low.

Optimal conditions for disclosure of CSA

Ungar and colleagues (2009) summarise these optimal conditions as: having access to someone who will listen, believe and respond appropriately and effectively; having knowledge and language about what abuse is, and how to access help; having a sense of control over the process, in terms of anonymity (until they are ready to be identified) and confidentiality (the right to control who knows); and being asked directly about any experiences of abuse.

What does the research, therefore, suggest about techniques and projects which might successfully enable children to tell?

The need to be asked: courage against backlash pressures

Hershkowitz et al (2005) note that 43% of their sample of 30 children disclosed abuse only after they were directly asked. Jensen et al (2005) found that disclosure followed someone recognising the child's cues, and probing further. McGee et al (2002) followed up respondents who disclosed child sexual abuse for the first time during their survey. Asked why they had not disclosed before, many said it was because they had not been asked. This has also been my own research experience in many years as a researcher. It is quite clear that many children do not disclose abuse unless they are asked.

Such seems to be the fear incited by backlash propaganda claims that adults put words into children's mouths, that many professionals (as discussed in Chapters One and Two) seem to think they cannot ask a child anything if they suspect CSA, however strong the signs. This is from fear of contaminating the evidence (evidence which they do not even have!) or of somehow putting ideas into the child's head. Yet if teachers saw bruises, burns or a rash on a child, they would not hesitate to ask. It is vital that, if we are to move from a situation which has become as ridiculous as it is dangerous to children, senior managers in all caring professions from now on reassure their staff that it is all right, indeed responsible, to ask a child they are worried about an open question about whether anyone has hurt them sexually (that is, one which does not in any way suggest a named person as possibly responsible). Just as they would ask if anyone has hit them, if children came into school with bruises on their bodies.

Respecting children's needs, priorities and fears

Sexually abused children are extremely concerned about confidentiality, and its immediate breach silences many from disclosing. As Margaret McKay, the respected former director of Children 1st and Childline, would forcefully emphasise whenever she addressed child protection conferences: "When the adult a child has chosen to trust says immediately, 'Sorry I'll have to pass on what you tell me,' it's like shouting 'STOP! DON'T SPEAK!'"

This does not mean children want us to do nothing. Nor would inaction be possible. But they do want as much confidentiality as possible, and more control over the *pace and timing* of what happens after they tell. They actively need help in overcoming a mass of fears, loyalties and confusions, in order to speak freely. They also deserve to be respectfully consulted during investigations – they often have valuable information, ideas and location details, which would help to trap their abusers.

'Brick walls' to communication with the child must also be overcome before any child can be expected to disclose abuse.

For example, when the police officer and social worker interviewed Victoria Climbié in hospital following unexplained serious burns to her head, 'Victoria presented as shy and withdrawn and she was reluctant to answer any of the questions that we were asking her' (Laming, 2003, 6.253). Victoria had not been made safe, and should not have been expected to speak about the harm as no legal safeguards were in place to protect her. Her 'carer' could have collected her at any time and taken her back home. The serious nature of threats to children by perpetrators may be unacknowledged by professionals, and even lie outside their understanding. Adult survivors inform us of the extent to which abusers will go to try to guarantee the child's silence.

Examples of practice to adopt or adapt

The examples below would address, in various ways, the serious problems which sexually abused children and young people currently experience in telling:

- Expanded confidential services and third-party reporting via the voluntary (third) sector.

- School and youth club joint work with police and social work (statutory sector).

- Stop to Listen: a statutory voluntary collaboration.

- The Children's House (multi-agency, multidisciplinary) model (Scandinavia) and Children's Advocacy Centers (North America).

Developing the voluntary (third) sector

Confidential support projects

Whether or not statutory agencies are themselves prepared to operate a greater degree of confidentiality for children under 16 suffering sexual abuse, the development of more voluntary sector projects across the UK who *are* prepared to do so could actively be supported, and at least part-funded, at government level. They would become active contributors to child protection systems, but only one valuable part. Statutory agencies would be expected to cooperate with and liaise with them.

Such projects would broadly replicate existing features of the 18 and Under (Dundee) and Childline models, which still remain remarkably unusual in the UK.[1] These allow young people as long, and as many calls, contacts or visits, as they need to build

---

[1] www.18U.org.uk; www.childline.org.uk

confidence to overcome fears of disclosure, and eventually to report. They only break confidentiality – unless the child has given explicit permission to do so – where there is imminent danger to a young person or their siblings (and in Childline's case, if they even know who is calling them).

18 and Under provided an example. A 17-year-old girl had slowly been able, over several visits to the agency, to reveal for the first time sexual abuse which was happening in her home. 18 and Under explored options with her. She then turned up with a toddler, and admitted the child was hers. On finding out that the toddler was in the same house, workers told the young woman she must either call police and social work, or they would have to, since the toddler could not be left in such a risky situation. The 17-year-old chose to call the police herself.

18 and Under have also passed on information about perpetrators to police, in order to protect other young people, without revealing the identities of the young people giving the information: a system also used by Barnardo's Safer Choices and one we believe is important (see 'perpetrator-focused strategies', later in this chapter). 18 and Under have found that when allowed this build-up of confidence, time and continuing support, there has rarely ever been a retraction from young people in the 20 years of the project's existence.

Such projects could include locally based helplines, where the counsellors know the area, and know how best to assist the child at a local level.

Confidential projects above could be new, but more likely would be extensions of, or adjuncts to, existing voluntary sector agencies: for instance, organisations with expertise and experience in working with young people, and /or survivors of sexual violence.

Self-referral would be the norm: referrals by others would need to have young people's consent. Families, friends and professionals such as teachers would be encouraged through publicity to suggest to children that they get in touch. Non-abusing family members and friends who received disclosures could also gain advice and support. The projects would use imaginative ways of reaching young people, including all the developing opportunities of social media.

What would confidential agencies need?

These changes will not happen so long as voluntary agencies feel vulnerable and unprotected, and so long as the statutory sector fails to support them. They need:

- genuine official acceptance by that sector, without pressure to reveal the names and details of abuse victims, unless victims agree;

- a mutually agreed definition of high risk situations when confidentiality would need to be broken;

- regular reliable funding, for staffing, telephone helplines, on-site services and training;

- genuinely independent monitoring and evaluation;

- the power to designate local refuge accommodation (subject to inspection); and

- agreement that the voluntary agencies can pass on 'soft' intelligence about individual or organised perpetrators, and sites of abuse, from victims, without having to identify these victims. This system operated successfully between 18 and Under and the police service in Dundee (until it was no longer permitted when new police management took over – who apparently demanded that details of the child making the allegation always be given).

This confidential voluntary sector provision could be progressed by, for example:

- identifying the number of projects needed which would give accessibility to children and young people in different areas of the UK (with plans for a rolling programme);

- identifying all existing confidential services for sexually abused under-16s in the UK;

- running a consultation with Childline, 18 and Under and other identified confidential services on specific issues of organisation, funding, practice, difficulties encountered, and so on, which need to be addressed by new projects;

- circulating proposals to voluntary sector organisations for children, young people and survivors of sexual violence who might wish to take part; and

- Assisting the launch, support and monitoring of new projects.

Third-party reporting

The same voluntary sector organisations, or others who wish it, could also become official 'third-party reporting' agencies for young people reporting sexual abuse, throughout the UK. (These could of course be used by adults too.)

The third-party reporting facility already exists widely in the UK, where frightened or ashamed victims of race hate or homophobic crime can report through voluntary sector organisations without having to reveal their identity unless they wish. For example in Scotland, Stonewall's advice on third-party reporting lists numerous third-party organisations, including six Citizens Advice Bureaux in Highland alone.[2]

It does not make sense that sexual crimes against children should not automatically be considered for such schemes. There appears no logical reason for the omission, given that the schemes are offered for other hard-to-report crimes, and given that numerous telephone lines exist to report less serious crimes like fly tipping or 'fiddling' of welfare benefits. What does this say about society's current priorities, and about tenacious prejudices against the truthfulness of children in sexual crime?

Not all organisations currently involved in third-party reporting will wish to, nor feel competent to, take on a child abuse reporting role. However, some will. The main need will be for widespread advertising and publicity that it exists, and the availability of staff training.

Phonelines and social media

There also need to be anonymous phonelines, anonymous online forms and the imaginative use of social media methods to enable and increase the reporting of sexual crime. It will be important to consult young survivors of such crime in designing these communication methods. Anonymous reporting is of course already possible through Crimestoppers. However, they have rarely highlighted sex crimes in campaigns (although they now support several police campaigns against CSE). Remarkably, no results at time of writing are found for 'sexual crime' in the search facility at the top of their website.[3] Crimestoppers need to have clear, well-publicised launches of specific facilities for reporting sexual crime.

Again, Crimestoppers' *Fearless* website for young people is well-intentioned, but most of its text seems directed to potential offenders rather than victims, with dire warnings about the lengths of likely prison sentences. This is hardly likely to appeal to frightened, self-blaming victims of sexual abuse and exploitation.

School and youth club work with police and social services

Few children appear to reveal child sexual abuse to staff in school or youth club settings, especially to more senior staff. Yet schools, by virtue of the time children spend there and teachers' accumulating knowledge of individual children, have great potential to provide safe environments for disclosure of sexual abuse. The following are two approaches which have proved successful in facilitating disclosures of abuse and violence, and enabling follow-up.

The multi-award winning VIP (Violence is Preventable) programme for children and young people by the voluntary sector agency 18 and Under, Dundee, has programmes, toolkits and games developed for different age groups, for disabled people and for a range of minority ethnic groups. It has now been delivered to more than 26,000 children, and has included more than 90 Scottish schools in the past three years. About a third of

---

[3]   www.crimestoppers-uk.org

children revealed bullying, peer violence, domestic violence or abuse, including sexual abuse, after VIP sessions. The VIP project has developed a toolkit to train teachers in schools and nurseries, and others, in its use.[4]

An evaluation by the University of Dundee listed some key elements of its effectiveness:

• Disclosure was one active goal of the programme, and disclosures were expected to occur (hence there was proper preparation with school staff). Presenters used wide, not restrictive, definitions of abuse for pupils. Their tone and body language was open and warm. They facilitated peer-to-peer talk in the class about issues of harm, giving children space and time to talk. They were not afraid to ask explicit questions about harm. Responses were received without judgement or blocking.

• Presenters had high levels of motivation and unity of purpose for the safety and protection of children, and an absence of myths and prejudices about abuse. They had considerable knowledge about child development and child protection, e.g. definition, signs and symptoms and what they meant. They were also skilled in child-centred communication. (Barron and Topping, 2010)

• Whole-school environments conducive to informed awareness and confidence among *all* staff, and conducive to disclosures among abused children, were created for several years after 1992 in Harrow by Liz Davies' social services team and a police team, working closely together.

The police officers bolstered conventional 'keep safe' schools programmes in two ways. They returned to classes every year with their messages about safety and harm: thus young people got to know them personally and the messages were repeatedly reinforced. They also deliberately included phrases which abusers typically said to children to groom them, to bribe or blackmail

---

[4] www.violenceispreventable.org.uk

them, and to enforce silence. This often led to younger children, in particular, blurting out that a perpetrator had said this to them. They received numerous disclosures of physical and sexual abuse. The programmes described 'yes' and 'no' touches rather than 'good' and 'bad', enabling children to report behaviour which felt abusive, but which they may not have defined as bad or harmful.

Meanwhile, social services and police did whole-school and nursery school awareness-raising about harm, neglect and abuse, being sure to include low-status staff like dinner ladies and janitors. This indicated the trust and confidence the joint team had in such staff. It helped them to be alert to problems, and not to fear such disclosures, but to listen and to pass them on sensitively. Such work connects closely into the whole-community prevention schemes discussed in Chapter Six.

Youth questionnaires

Box 5.1 is an example of a questionnaire Liz Davies developed with the police child abuse investigation team officers, and used in settings such as schools, youth and sports clubs where it was suspected some children may have been abused by a staff member (or members). This can narrow down the numbers of children who need following up, and who may eventually need a 'court-reliable' ABE (Achieving Best Evidence) interview as a victim or witness. Questionnaires must be age-appropriate and imaginatively accessible for specific groups, for example, disabled children and children whose first language is not English. Children would be told that what they wrote was confidential, apart from being shared with the investigation team.

'Wraparound' projects

The following three examples are of more comprehensive, 'wraparound' projects: they may include disclosure, investigation, continuing support, and possible preparation for any court case.

Stop to Listen (formerly known as the Confidential Space model, but more accurately acknowledging that confidentiality cannot be total) was originally proposed and developed in Scotland by Children 1st (formerly RSSPCC) with Sarah Nelson.

Box 5.1: Sample youth club questionnaire (CSA preliminary investigations)

Dear ....

I understand that you attend the local youth club. I would like your help by answering a few questions about this club. When you have finished please give this to your parents who will return the form to me. Thank you for your help.

1　Are you a member of the youth club?
2　Have you left the club? If so why?
3　How long have you been attending the club?
4　What do you like doing best at the club?
5　What activities do you most enjoy at the club?
6　What activities do you least enjoy?
7　Please explain why you do not enjoy these activities
8　What are the names of the adults that work in the club?
9　Is there an adult you particularly like? If so please name who this is.
10　Is there an adult you particularly do not like? If so please explain why.
11　Has anything happened at the club that you did not like? (Yes/No)
12　If you answered 'Yes' to question 11 then please explain what you did not like and why.
13　Have you ever been worried by anything at the club? (Yes/No)
14　If you answered 'Yes' to question 13 please explain what it was that worried you.
15　Is there anything else you would like to say? (Davies, 1997)

Children 1st had long been aware of the high value young people placed on confidentiality, their wish for some control after sexual abuse had been revealed, and the low level of current disclosures and convictions for child sexual abuse (Children 1st, 2006). Children 1st drew in a 'critical friends' steering group in 2013 from the statutory, voluntary, Scottish Government and academic sectors. Steering group members were invited for their expertise, their ability to influence and their potential to join up initiatives in Scotland which currently seek to improve responses to child sexual abuse.

This steering group explored definitions, workable models, development funding, problems and barriers, ages of children, agencies involved, possible pathfinder sites and resourcing. The group saw how sexual health services had successfully promoted confidentiality in order to attract young people to their services.

By early 2015 the group had actively won the collaboration of very senior officers from Police Scotland, and officials from four interested local authorities, and had acquired a Trust grant for a development worker, who started work in November 2015. Pathfinder schemes are now being explored and developed across the four local authority areas. Key tenet of any model that is adapted are that it must fit with local structures and must be delivered by statutory services, though the contributory experience and skills of the third sector will be crucial. The distinctiveness in being an adaptation within the *statutory* child protection sector means the pathfinder schemes may herald significant change within statutory systems in future.

Stop to Listen is not about doing nothing after a child's disclosure, but about responding in ways which respect young people's own development, their fears and reactions. It aims to:

- offer children better means of finding safety and support;

- improve the quality of evidence gathering, through patience and through reducing fears which lead to retractions of evidence;

- raise the morale and sense of efficacy of professionals involved in child protection;

- focus on *outcomes*, and the active participation of young people;

- disseminate the lessons of these pathfinder projects throughout the UK's child protection systems;

- offer confidence-building training and support to professionals.

Pathfinder areas will negotiate basic protocols on limits to confidentiality, with the principle of open, transparent discussion with the young person involved if confidentiality has to be broken. Pathfinders will initially involve children of 12 and over. This was a compromise reached with more cautious members of the planning group.

Models for teams may vary

The four local authority projects are likely to explore and test slightly different models in terms of how far they recruit to a new, skilled and experienced multi-agency team involving police, social work, health, education and the voluntary sector, and how far they draw upon the skills of existing child protection teams, child protection committees and other key stakeholders. Close links must be established with specialist units within Police Scotland dealing with sexual crime, with the National Sexual Crimes Unit, and other specialist teams relevant to child sexual abuse and CSE. That includes the Police Scotland Child Abuse Investigation Unit established in 2015, which has a central base and regional teams overseeing local ones (Police Scotland, 2015).

All pathfinders will aim to develop support, including local refuge if needed, while disclosure and investigation takes place. This includes specialist support for, for instance, children from BME communities and those with special needs. A specialist steering group will oversee the work of the Stop to Listen pilot areas and will commission independent evaluation and monitoring.

This will be an exciting development to follow and, along with other innovative schemes launched across the UK, will have potential to spread much more widely, creating a permanently more child-centred system of protection, and enabling far more children and young people to speak out.

Building on existing or former good practice

It is important to note that a scheme like Stop to Listen is not some revolutionary scheme launched out of the air. Rather it makes greater, more explicit use of flexibility already in the system, while promising a considerable extension of that. (See for example police work in building trust slowly and patiently with damaged and often alienated young women in CSE investigations such as Derby and Peterborough – Chapter Four.) Barnardo's Safer Choices project in Glasgow, and other voluntary sector projects, works with young people and police to build up their confidence gradually, develop their safety and identify abusers.

Again, in the Islington children's homes case, social workers patiently built trust with teenagers who began drifting into the accessible, shopfront neighbourhood office in the early mornings, after being out all night. Their information, and the flexibility of working hours which encouraged it, began the entire process of uncovering the extensive, notorious Islington children's homes abuse scandal in 1992 (see later in this chapter for more detail of the perpetrator-focused strategies in Glasgow and Islington).

Again, in Tayside, a Scottish police officer consistently visited young people's residential units from her local family protection unit, building trusting relationships with girls involved in CSE. It took six months to two years' work but resulted in successful prosecutions, and support for young women to make other choices. When she was replaced and senior police management personnel changed, the scheme was dropped.

Preparing for court: the Barnahus Children's House model (Scandinavia) and Children's Advocacy Centers (North America)

Even with schemes such as Stop to Listen, the experience which often follows their use – of the adversarial court system – will continue to be harsh for children and teenagers involved in sexual abuse and exploitation cases. The final models discussed here enable disclosures to be taken forward for use in court prosecutions, in a child-friendly but rigorous way. Such models are likely greatly to reduce the traumatic potential of court hearings, and ensure that the children receive the therapy and support they need. The Barnahus model has been actively considered by the Scottish government and Scottish prosecution authorities in 2016, for possible adoption or adaptation.

These examples suggest the importance of British child protection systems being *routinely* open to learning from good practice in other countries. One implication is that busy child protection staff need access to accurate, accessible, jargon-free summaries of research and evaluations of good practice in international child protection. To provide this is not undue or extravagant expenditure for social work, health or police authorities. It is about a mindset of openness, informed curiosity and a lack of arrogance about one's own child protection system, as well as about wishing to learn more imaginative use of new technologies.

Children's Houses were pioneered in Iceland in 1998, and now more than 40 extend across several European countries, mainly in Scandinavia. The Children's House (CAC Barnahus) is a multi-agency, child-centred environment for investigation, interview and therapy. Staffing includes a psychologist and prosecutors, as well as police and social workers. Facilities for medical examinations include a gynaecologist, paediatrician and registered nurse.

Investigation, support and other major issues are dealt with under one roof, and children are treated with respect throughout. The whole house is modelled with a keen eye on their particular developmental needs. The EU has recommended introduction of Children's Houses throughout Europe (Guobrandsson, 2013).

It may be unsatisfactory that, often without other evidence, the child's story represents the only source of information for the case but, if so, interviews become more crucial to successful outcomes in terms of prosecution. In most European states the responsibility in dealing with child sexual abuse is divided between several agencies, encouraging repeat interviews in unsympathetic settings, and a sense of revictimisation. Aggressive, lengthy defence questioning in court is of course an even harsher problem.

Instead of the child having to adapt to the needs of different agencies, his or her needs come first in the Children's House. To prevent repeated interviews, the environment is designed to make the child feel secure and comfortable, and there is joint investigative interviewing. For criminal investigation of CSA cases the child needs to give his/her testimony for a Court Judge.

This can be carried out in the Children's House if the Court Judge decides, so that the child does not have to testify in a court.

Trained professionals carry out the interview observed, through closed circuit TV, by representatives of the police and prosecution, the defence lawyer, the child's legal advocate and the child's social worker. The interview is visually recorded for multiple purposes, including medical examination, and a therapeutic service is also available. It thus provides a comprehensive service for the child and family (non-abusive members) under one roof. This ensures professional criminal investigation and 'due process' for the suspect, without compromising the principle of the best interest of the child (Davies, 2011; Farestveit 2012).

At evaluation the Barnahus models have been found to deepen understanding about the complexity of applying a child-centred approach and perspective in child protection, and generated valuable knowledge for the further development of these centres (Rasmussen, 2011).

The Children's Houses aim, through their work and their growing experience, to strengthen expertise on sexual abuse of children and disseminate that expertise to both professionals and the general public. Surely a valuable aim too, for all the other examples of working in child-centred ways with young people outlined above?

Example: how it works in Oslo[5]

Norway's population of 5.1 million is roughly similar to Scotland's: the Greater Oslo population is 1.5 million, roughly similar to that of Greater Glasgow. Pre-trial judicial hearings to take evidence are allowed for groups such as children under 16, and alleged victims of sexual abuse. There are now 11 Children's Houses across Norway.

Oslo's Children's House was established in 2009. Like others its primary purpose is to support the criminal trial process. The hearing is under the control of the judge. Also present will be the interviewer; counsel for the

---

[5] Information from this section comes from a Visit Report by Tim Barraclough, Scottish Courts & Tribunals Service, to Stop to Listen, 7 October 2015.

complainer; substitute guardian for the child; defence lawyer; police/prosecuting lawyer; police investigator; adviser from the Children's House; and children's welfare services. Interpreters are becoming an increasing requirement as Norway becomes more multicultural.

The interviewer meets all these officials beforehand, and potential lines of questioning are discussed. The defence counsel can say what questions they would like to be asked. The police interviewer, who must have a policing degree and further training, will already have established any particular special needs the child has. The interview itself follows well-established protocols based on the latest academic research into child psychology and interviewing. The questioning has to be appropriate to the age and development of the child: Oslo police have developed particular expertise in interviewing pre-school children. Breaks can be taken for the interviewer to discuss with the judge and other participants what further lines of questioning might be appropriate.

After the interview, the child is given a medical examination by specialist hospital staff. At times information useful to the investigation emerges during this as the child may now be more willing to talk to the doctor or nurse about any injuries. He/she is also assessed for any further welfare or child protection measures and support needed.

Among many benefits identified in evaluation is the wraparound service provided in a reassuring, non-threatening atmosphere, high quality technology and the ability to access quickly any additional therapeutic and medical support needed, making the experience of the interview much less traumatic.

Oslo Barnehus has a budget of approximately £1.74 million a year. Its 21 employees include three psychologist specialists, ten clinical social workers or child welfare workers, and a psychiatric nurse. It has administrative and technical officers. Most other Children's Houses are smaller, according to population. It carries out several hundred forensic interviews per year in relation to sexual abuse, and hundreds more in relation to other offences.

Children's Advocacy Centers in the USA and Canada have multidisciplinary teams from areas such as law enforcement, medicine, legal professions, mental health, child protection and victim advocacy work with children at risk. They provide forensic interviews, victim support, case reviews in one place. About three-quarters of children who appear there are seen in relation to sexual abuse (Cronch et al, 2006). The centres feature developmentally appropriate play areas, accommodation for children with special needs, decor and activities recognising diverse cultures, private interview rooms, and Children's Advocacy Center staff or volunteers to provide support (Cross et al, 2007).

Moves in this direction are already happening in the UK but they need to be supported at government level and further developed. The evaluation of the Triangle project in Brighton (which undertakes ABE interviews for very young and/or disabled children for the police) identified several good practice elements. These included use of skilled intermediaries to enable communication with children – even the very young – throughout the investigative and court process; a child-friendly environment adapted to different age groups; active participation of young people in decisionmaking; and centralisation of the process in one place (Davidson et al, 2012).[6]

Costs, funding and resources

Costs of implementing all or any of the above schemes will vary, but undoubtedly all will require funding input. That will concern governments and statutory services. In arguing for them we must be assertive and informed about the very considerable current and often hidden costs of child sexual abuse and its effects throughout life, in human and financial terms, and the savings that can be made through effective early intervention. Not just savings for the future, but savings through reduction of current problems for children and young people.

These costs include services for mental illness, physical ill health, alcohol and drug services, welfare benefits through disability and incapacity, offender services (including very expensive youth offender establishments and residential care)

---

[6]   See also www.triangle.org.uk

and social care (Saied-Tissier, 2014). There is great potential to channel some Early Years and Preventive Spend funding streams, drug and alcohol service funding, gender-based violence funding and other relevant streams into what will increase early detection of CSA earlier intervention for children and young people's recovery, and earlier intervention into problematic behaviours some young people develop in reaction to abuse. Major charitable trusts are likely to respond to well thought out, child-centred projects, especially in the wake of increased awareness of silenced children in the wake of the shocking Savile revelations and the CSE scandals in England.

Part 2: Developing a perpetrator-focused strategy

The first part of this chapter has suggested a range of ways in which children and young people can feel safer to come forward, reveal who is abusing them, and obtain continuing support.

The growing emphasis in child protection – and in child welfare generally – has been on the need to share ever more information about ever more children, however intrusive this may be. That is not the answer to child protection failings (Davies, 2013). We need to develop (or in some cases return to) *a perpetrator-focused strategy* to protect children more effectively, one which is not merely *reactive* but *proactive*.

Focusing on perpetrators does not mean ignoring the children. It does mean that information collected about them needs to be relevant, not random or intrusive. In the cases of Victoria Climbié and Peter Connolly, multi-agency and forensic analysis was lacking of relevant unexplained, repeated and unusual injuries, patterns and indicators over time; just as there was little focus on investigating the *adults* in the children's lives (Laming, 2003; House of Commons Health Committee, 2003; Haringey LSCB, 2009).

The second, interlinked part of this chapter highlights examples of such a strategy, which would contribute vitally to prevention by:

- focusing on systems which can remove abusers from the lives of children;

- Increasing resources to investigate serious crimes against children;

- protecting more children as a result, given the known incidence of child abuse, and how poorly this is reflected in numbers of investigations made or convictions obtained. It is estimated that fewer than 1 in 50 sexual offences against children result in a criminal conviction (Stuart and Baines, 2004). In particular, children under five, disabled children and children for whom English is not their first language are often excluded from legal processes, leaving the most vulnerable failed by the criminal justice system (Utting, 2005).

We give examples here of key elements of good practice in some successful perpetrator-focused approaches from the 1980s and early 1990s. We then consider some examples from 2010 onwards using similar principles, but made more effective through drawing on technologies not previously available – particularly social media.

We draw out some principles of organisation for the future, and urge all authorities to adopt best practice in perpetrator-focused strategy, armed with the information and experience now available to them.

Open-mindedness and joint investigation

Essential for everyone involved in a perpetrator-focused strategy is a keen and open-minded interest in pursuing abusers in order to protect children, free of prejudice and open to the possibility of their coming from *any* type of family or background. They also need to develop informed knowledge of how abusers act and manipulate both children and adults, in both individual and organised abuse. Teams need to contain expertise on the use and manipulation of online technologies by individual and organised abusers, nationally and internally.

That in turn leads to a better recognition and understanding of the linkages among paedophile networks, institutional abuse, child sexual exploitation, trafficking, ritual abuse networks, the illegal adoption trade and the worldwide trade in online abuse images of children. There must be detailed analysis of information about known or alleged perpetrators. A child abuser is likely to have more than one victim: thus, protecting one child may well mean protecting many.

A perpetrator-focused strategy calls for confident professional specialists working together in multi-agency teams. In particular, it is vital that social workers work return to joint investigation with law enforcement agencies (Davies, 1997; Davies and Townsend, 2008). Responding to the needs of children for protection will not be met by prescriptive and hasty, inadequate assessment but only through going back to joint investigation with police and other agencies. In England this would involve compliance with the protocols in a previous version of *Working Together* (DfE, 2006), because the term *joint investigation* is no longer included in the most recent statutory guidance (DfE, 2015) as child protection systems have regrettably moved away from the concept of police and social workers working together to investigate significant harm.

Police involvement now focuses on actual crimes (Laming, 2003, recommendation 99) and the social work focus is on the assessment of the child's needs. This policy change has led to a gap in the professional response in relation to the joint investigation of child abuse. In our view, the model now adopted through the Hertfordshire Constabulary and Local Authority Joint Child Protection Team, where joint police–social services working has once again been established, should be adopted throughout the UK.[7]

The call for joint investigation was supported by the House of Commons Education Committee's *Children First: The Child Protection System in England* report (2012): 'We strongly encourage all local authorities to consider the merits of moving to multi-agency co-location models. For best practice this should include co-location of local police child abuse teams with children's social care.'

The development of MASH hubs, multi-agency safeguarding centres for children's referrals, are a promising move towards

---

[7]   www.itv.com/thismorning/hot-topics/child-protection-the-front-line-mark-williams-thomas

reasserting genuine multi-agency working in child protection. They were set up to reduce failures to share important child protection information among key agencies. Professionals from police, social work, health and education typically share an office, with their respective IT systems, and have links with other systems such as the probation service. At present they are a valuable but limited 'triage' for collating and risk-assessing safeguarding concerns and pass further action on to others. At time of writing, they do not continue the investigation themselves (Durbin et al, 2011).[8]

Damaging hierarchies

Collating small clues, worries and snippets of evidence from a range of people, and working together to recognise and evaluate their significance is key to protecting children, and to identifying and convicting perpetrators. Information from lower-status staff and members of the community must also be given greater respect. The 'exaggeration of hierarchy' has been damaging, whereby referrals from high-status professionals such as lawyers and psychiatrists gain far more attention than those who may be much closer to the child, such as neighbours and childminders (Reder and Duncan, 2008).

Thus multi-agency professional teams need to work in a trusting and respectful collaboration with alert, informed communities and their organisations, in which child and adult survivors of child sexual abuse have much to contribute. Adult survivors and care leavers themselves should be represented on Local Safeguarding Children Boards and Child Protection Committees, and should be consulted by specialist teams. This is not in order just to contribute to training, but in order to share the sometimes unique information and experience they have about abuse and abusers.

---

[8]   See also www.communitycare.co.uk/2011/06/03/multi-agency-safeguarding-centre-for-childrens-referrals/

Examples from the past

Islington's multi-agency investigations

In her social work role Liz Davies played a major part in investigating a large network of organised child sexual abuse in the London Borough of Islington, in the community and within the care system (there were 12 children's homes in the borough), in the early 1990s. She also 'blew the whistle' on the abuse and on the cover-up of what was taking place. Islington had become the 'epicentre' of the Paedophile Information Exchange (PIE) the British pro-paedophile activist group. They actively promoted in academic circles the legitimacy of paedophilia, and networked widely in the UK and internationally to advocate for a lowering of the age of consent, and to argue and campaign for the 'rights' of children to have sex with adults.

Agencies and individuals worked together to share information, to target the abusers and to protect children. The media played a vital role in this exposure.[9]

Imagine for a moment how effectively the coordination and awareness below would have identified CSE, in the English towns and cities (see Chapter Four) where there have been scandals of official inaction.

- *Social services* at that time operated a 'patch' system, 24 offices covering a few streets each, based in accessible shopping centres with flexible opening hours. Staff from different agencies, statutory and voluntary, already knew each other. They worked closely with local community groups. Yet the 'patch' system of offices was later discontinued.

- *Children's services* received direct statements from children, families and the community. There was liaison with residential social workers, foster carers and childminders. They located missing children, and investigated jointly with police.

---

9   See www.theneedleblog.wordpress.com/operation-greenlight/london/
islington/islington-care-homes and www.lizdavies.net/islington-child-abuse-scandal

- Some of the *disaffected, abused young people* began approaching the particularly accessible social work offices, slowly establishing trust, and began to reveal what was happening to them.

- *The probation service* shared information about known child sex offenders and current concerns about young offenders.

- *The police* did likewise. Information also came from the Paedophile Unit, the Police Child Abuse Investigation Team, the Community Safety Unit, and schools involvement officers. Police carried out joint investigation with social workers.

- *Schools* shared information about known child sex offenders targeting children at school gates. They noted indicators and patterns of abuse relating to school students, while education social workers knew about young people repeatedly absent from school.

- *Health visitors, school nurses, midwives and GPs* shared relevant information, historic and current, about families and children who concerned them.

- *Paediatricians* noted indicators of CSA and collated health information from other health professionals

- The *GUM clinic* (sexually transmitted diseases) and *Family Planning Service* (pregnancies/terminations) shared relevant concerns.

- *Child psychiatry* carried out therapeutic work with traumatised victims of child abuse, and adult psychiatrists with adult victims of the same networks.

- *Housing and Environmental Health* shared information about houses and flats used by child sex abusers and procurers, and local disturbances and incidents.

- *Local authority and other local lawyers* made connections across cases.

- *Journalists and the local newspaper* were sources of archived information about local child sex abusers, and later were vital in exposing the abuse and the cover-ups, giving an important example of *positive* use of the media.

- *Families and the local community* were actively encouraged and trained to form a network of protective adults. They were the 'eyes and ears' when professionals were not around (Davies, 2014).

While the above collaborations involved investigating organised abuse, and many child protection investigations will not be so complex, the basic principles of active collaboration and mutual trust remain valid for investigations in general, which are usually difficult in CSA, because of the secretive nature of the crime.

The whole-community work by Liz Davies, her social work team and police services in Harrow was valuable to all types of investigation. They used a whole-school approach, believing that lower-status staff like dinner ladies and school caretakers were just as vital as managers in being alert to children's safety. (It is notable that many years later the Children's Commissioner (2015) report made the strong recommendation that all schools now implement a whole-school approach to child protection, where all staff can identify the signs and symptoms of abuse, and have the knowledge and support to respond effectively). The Harrow joint teams demonstrated that training of senior to junior staff in all professions, widespread publicity, open question-and-answer nights in communities, the ability to discuss concerns without giving your details, coupled with strong warnings and penalties against vigilantism, could bring a tremendous public response.

'Most people wanted to do something to help. They would ring up and say, 'we've seen a man there who has 4 boys sleeping over with him.' We managed to stop vigilantism: 'ring this number instead if you see anything that worries you'" (Davies, 2004; see also Chapter Six).

Peter McKelvie's team

Peter McKelvie was in charge of a specialist social work team in Hereford and Worcester, dealing with child sexual abuse, and working with police, from 1988 onwards. In Chapter One we described how it was closed down almost overnight in 1995. Yet it had received about 4000 referrals, successfully convicted 38 paedophiles, closed seven boarding schools and found frequent CSA within families. It had unearthed a very large paedophile ring, with senior professional men involved. The closing down of such work raises very awkward questions about potential influence by powerful people in society, just because teams were not failing, but rather achieving striking successes in child protection.

> "The difference was absolutely stark, between the numbers [of abused children] we were identifying through our team and the numbers before; children do not on the whole disclose. It increased dramatically, by hundreds of percent." (personal interview, 2014)

What were the main principles behind the success of this joint work with police, which might now be adapted elsewhere? He reflects:[10]

- "I had a very stable team. Handpicked people, and we learned on the job."

- "I had tremendous support from my director, David Tombs, who gave us lots of time to work."

- "We worked in a different, proactive way instead of sitting back and waiting for someone to report. For example, if there was gossip about houses where children were seen to be congregating, we would investigate."

- The joint team gathered at strategy meetings all possible information about suspected perpetrators and children at risk.

---

[10] All quotes from personal interview, 2014.

- The team worked proactively with communities, giving talks about their work and inviting feedback.

- They similarly went out to talk with teachers, nursery staff, health visitors, and so on, helping them to identify and articulate signs and behaviour that worried them, and monitoring the children rather than rushing in:

"We knew a significant number of children were sexually abused and would never talk. So people became aware of what children were doing or drawing for instance ... and when they had worries about them, we would call a strategy meeting with the health visitor say, her line manager, police, and relevant professionals – contact the GP to see if e.g. there was a history of urinary infections ... to see if there was any more information available ... we would then keep an eye on this child (not rush in): 'These are children we need to be watching...'"

- They had a meticulous approach to evidence gathering: "We never got accused of making false allegations, because we had done our homework. We had no unsuccessful court cases. It is the easiest crime to commit, and the hardest to prove. If you look for it, doing realistic and careful investigation, it will be there..."

Peter McKelvie advocated a national unit to coordinate inquiries – staffed with police and social workers – to identify paedophile rings across the country.

Some current examples of perpetrator focus

Barnardo's Safer Choices Project, Glasgow[11]

This young people's project has identified many victims and perpetrators of child sexual exploitation through close and trusting relationships with victims and agencies, particularly police, in Glasgow and Renfrewshire, and imaginative techniques

---

[11] www.barnardos.org.uk/saferchoices.htm

Box 5.2: Perpetrator-focused mapping and investigation techniques

- Investigative interviews
- Corroborative evidence
- Scene of crime evidence
- Surveillance
- CCTV footage
- Profiling of suspected or known perpetrators
- Mapping of locations for abuse
- Car registration numbers, methods & patterns of grooming
- Photographic evidence
- Forensics
- Medical evidence
- Witness evidence (Davies, 1997)

of evidence gathering. Their children's services manager, Daljeet Dagon, has been the main driver of this.

- Safer Choices is a street-based service, so they observe lots of activity and potential perpetrators on the streets especially in 'hotspots' where young people hang around. They share that information with the police, daily or nightly.

- They build up trust slowly with the young people without demanding information, and encourage any level of information they can give, such as the nicknames of victims and abusers.

- They have provided the police with a *victim association map*. This identifies young people connected to one another, and some adult perpetrators young people had talked about.

- They identify some young people as *conduits* – young people who act as a link between the perpetrators and the victims, and have often been victims themselves in the past – and share this information with police.

- They urge the police to use *harbouring notices, anti-trafficking legislation* and all the different perpetrator-disruption techniques and legislation now available.

- All this work gains support from the fact that in Glasgow the main child protection agencies try to identify young people at risk of CSE, devise a management plan, and co ordinate a care plan and risk management plan for them.

- In Renfrewshire, Safer Choices persuaded police and social workers to pull together a victim, offender and location working group. This Vulnerable Persons' Operational Group meets every four weeks and identifies victims and perpetrators of sexual exploitation, so that there is a plan of intervention to deal with both.

Taking the initiative in Oxford

Detective Chief Inspector Simon Morton's singlehanded drive to launch a serious inquiry into the organised abuse of young girls in Oxford is as an inspiration and example to others of what can be set in train with determination, proactive approaches and an understanding of *relevant* information-gathering about both victims and perpetrators.

In autumn 2010, he became concerned about how many girls were repeatedly disappearing and then reappearing in Oxford. *He had no complaints from victims but decided to investigate further.* He called a meeting with social services, who spoke of rumours that girls were spending time with older men.

Morton had begun inquiring knowing nothing of repeated failed investigations by Thames Valley into single incidents reported over years by some young victims, who, with some abusers, had crossed police and social services' radar multiple times. Many from both professions knew certain groups of Asian heritage men were grooming schoolgirls. But no one was putting the evidence and intelligence together.

One victim made two complaints in 2006. In 2007 and in 2008, another told police and social services she was raped by a named abuser. She was allegedly told it would only be possible to get the men on drugs charges.

Morton set up Operation Bullfinch, two social workers were seconded and they pulled in all the intelligence in the police and local authority system. They began to identify men around the girls and on his whiteboard, Morton wrote a string of names and realised that this was an organised crime group.

Once he identified the perpetrators as an organised gang – some already known to police for drug dealing – he determined to go after them *without* victims' accounts, using police tools such as covert surveillance, telephone monitoring, informants and corroborative evidence. He took advice from the UK human trafficking unit and the Child Sexual Exploitation and Protection centre.

He trawled medical, social services and school records of possible victims. He went back historically to get every detail of girls who came forward in the past and gradually gained more officers to work with him. In simultaneous raids 13 men were arrested and put in custody.

Understanding their fears of violence and retaliation, only then did Morton go to the victims he had identified through meticulous research, telling them he already had men in custody and believed the girls were victims. Then 80% of the victims, feeling themselves safer than if the men had been on the streets, spoke to police and some were prepared to testify in court. Evidence included not only the victims' accounts, but DNA evidence, identification evidence, and corroborative accounts from witnesses.

Seven men were found guilty in May 2013 on 59 counts, including rape and facilitating child prostitution, and sentenced to a total of 95 years in prison. After the convictions and further inquiries, the number of known victims has continued to grow considerably (Gardner, 2012; Laville, 2013).

The techniques used by Safer Choices and those initiated by Inspector Morton, along with the consistent arguments of Liz Davies in relation to proactive investigation, have been supported in major documents from the Office of the Children's Comissioner in its research reports on sexual exploitation in gangs and groups. They recommended proactive intervention through *problem-profiling,* where agencies combined intelligence, experience and data to flag up and break up networks which exploit children. This approach, they argued, should become the norm, rather than waiting to be told that a child is being exploited.

The problem–profile should be led by police and children's services working with other agencies to collate data about children at risk, along with intelligence from covert policing and information from sexual health clinics, residential care homes, youth groups and schools. It should include *proactive evidence gathering* and mapping of locations of abuse, the motivations of perpetrators, and multi-agency intelligence leading to identification and apprehension of perpetrators, and monitoring of non-convicted suspects (Berelowitz et al, 2013).

Taking the lead online: mixed blessings?

Meanwhile, perpetrator-focused strategies have been highlighted by both journalists and survivors themselves taking initiatives online. Established investigative journalists have increasingly developed websites and used social media to pull together and present past and current information about alleged sex abusers, particularly in pursuit of institutional abusers and influential figures in society.[12]

Adult survivors of sexual abuse and rape have also increasingly used social media to identify perpetrators and corroborate their own single accounts with each other's, for instance in the build-up to the successful prosecution of long-time abuser Charles Napier, and re-investigation of the former Paedophile Information Exchange network. They have identified connections among abusers, locations for abuse, and movement among those locations, and mobilised quickly to demand action (Davies, 2014).

These are important and promising developments. However, use of social media by victims of sexual violence to identify perpetrators can be both positive and problematic in outcome, for both victims and for those named as perpetrators.

---

[12] For example, www.spotlightonabuse.wordpress.com

Michael Salter's paper on justice and revenge in online counter-publics (2013b) highlights this. Exploring three case studies where girls and women used online platforms to make extrajudicial allegations of sexual violence and abuse, he illustrates how naming in social media has led to criminal charges being successfully taken against perpetrators (for example, after the rape of Alexandria Goddard, who blogged her abusers' names). When Savannah Dietrich named her gang rapists who had received only trivial sentences and was charged with contempt of court, a huge online campaign on her behalf led a different judge to rule in her favour and increase severity of the sentences.

Risk of class prejudice and misogyny

But Salter found that some voices are privileged over others'. He described how Kim Duthie, abused by football players, suffered class prejudice and a blatantly misogynist view of her character and behaviour after she posted compromising photos of the players online. She did not conform to a respectable educated model, and her erratic behaviour – possibly in response to abuse and violence itself – further damaged her credibility. Many survivors of sexual abuse are not 'respectable' in public eyes either. The torrent of online vilification suffered by disadvantaged, pregnant pre-teen girls (see Chapter Four) illustrates these widespread prejudices.

> The reproduction of sexist interaction and speech
> is common in online forums, and indicative of the
> masculine ethos that predominates in online content
> and interaction. (Salter, 2013b)

The verbal abuse and naming of the rape victim of Welsh footballer Ched Evans once again illustrated the depth of sexist prejudices: she has been forced to move house several times, and has had to be given a new identity. On the other hand and in contrast, she has also drawn widespread support on social media, after which several football clubs backed down from signing Evans (O'Connor, 2015)

Again, websites which have sought to name alleged paedophiles, particularly if the websites were set up by people with unusual world beliefs, overt racial prejudices or strong belief in conspiracy theories (which is not to deny that conspiracies exist!) have proved very problematic contributors to exposure of child sexual abuse. Apart from the human rights issues they raise for anyone wrongly named as a perpetrator, the problem is that half of what they say may indeed be accurate, and the other half not. But we can never be quite sure which half is which!

It is likely that the balance achieved between positive and negative outcomes will become much clearer over time as use of these increasingly sophisticated and accessible technologies develops; and as British judicial systems respond to challenges which are both practical and ethical.

A final caution......

Finally, this chapter (like Chapter One) has made very obvious that many successful methods of perpetrator-focused investigation are not new, but were either closed down in the past or phased out. If they are resurrected in modern form and prove successful in identifying perpetrators, then given the organised opposition to exposure of child sexual abuse (see Chapter Two), it will not be enough this time to be complacent that their structures and successful methods will continue. Instead, we must positively expect attempts to discredit or dismantle them, or gradually to starve them of leadership and funding. Forewarning allows for pre-planning, to steel the political will and professional determination to sustain such projects: so that what they achieve will not once again be as short-lived as it is impressive.

SIX

Community prevention of CSA: a model for practice

Sarah Nelson and Norma Baldwin

Introduction

'Child protection is everyone's job' is a familiar sentiment, heard from statutory child protection services throughout the UK. In Scotland, this has been expressed by the mantra 'It's everyone's job to make sure I'm all right' (Scottish Executive, 2002), and in England and Wales by 'Every child matters' (DoE, 2003). Yet this sense of shared concern and responsibility is often accompanied by feelings of helplessness and inadequacy, in personal and professional discussions about keeping children safe from sexual harm.

This chapter builds upon our belief that protecting children from sexual exploitation and abuse cannot be considered in isolation, but is one key element in an integrated approach to supporting children and families within their communities. It cannot be separated from the range of social factors which influence children's development and life experience. That is an international approach to children's wellbeing, and to the comprehensive way in which it needs to be secured. It is re-emphasised in the United Nations' Millenium Goals (UN, 2006; Stahl et al, 2006).

Such an approach means acknowledging the realities of poverty, inequalities and deprivation, alongside culturally harmful attitudes to gender, race and diversity, as well as the predatory and brutalising behaviour of some individuals and groups. Thus joined-up strategic planning, which takes account of all available evidence of connections among personal, community and societal influences, is needed. That vitally includes fostering and supporting genuinely informed communities in protecting children and young people from abuse and exploitation, and involving young people actively in their own safety.

Contrast with individual approaches

This approach contrasts with the individually focused, narrowly professionalised approaches to child protection which have long dominated public policy. We analyse this critically in the first part of this chapter. Such systems have been unable to make substantial progress in preventing harm and abuse. While investigation will still be needed in individual cases, and must be of the highest quality we can achieve, systems based almost entirely on a case-by-case approach can never tackle the root causes of the 'bottomless pit of need' (Baldwin and Carruthers, 1998). Yet even where locally based, community-wide protective services are implemented, they find it hard to maintain funding stability – usually being the first to be cut during hard economic times. Witness, for example, the 'roller-coaster' existence of family centres, and the struggles of local Sure Start projects to maintain their outreach work.

The NMCS model

Having first contrasted individualised approaches with community development approaches – which have already proved successful in diverse communities – we then offer our model as a way forward for policy and practice. This detailed preventive community strategy is Neighbourhood Mapping for Children's Safety (NMCS; Nelson, 2004a; Nelson and Baldwin, 2004). Though based on our original projects in disadvantaged areas of Edinburgh and Coventry, it can valuably be used by communities of any social, ethnic, urban or rural background.

NMCS is rooted in the conviction that an overarching view of the needs of communities and neighbourhoods, based on detailed local information and understanding of the links between different sorts of harm to children, is crucial in developing effective child protection strategies (Baldwin and Carruthers, 1998, 2000; Atkar et al, 2000). NMCS uses coordinated mapping exercises, to gather and interpret information relevant to young people's safety from sexual crime within a given geographical area. It involves agencies and communities in partnership in identifying problems and in seeking solutions. It addresses the need for broad-based attempts to reduce sexual offending against children and young people.

NMCS is relevant to reducing opportunities for abuse outside the immediate family context, or in public spaces – for example in the 'street grooming' which has become such an urgent topical issue in child sexual exploitation or in local clubs and recreational settings, or in abuse by some young people against others in places where teenagers gather.

It is also relevant to reducing (and protecting against) intra-familial abuse. When sexual crime is named and openly discussed, when people become more informed and aware about it, they are empowered to begin talking about what has happened in their own families. They are empowered too when supported by community groups and agencies to address any abuse which they themselves experienced. They become more knowledgeable about signs of distress in their own children, and about signs that some people are unsafe with their own children. In addition, many perpetrators abuse both within and beyond their families. When these offenders are identified, then children are protected in both contexts.

Some lessons learned from the first projects to develop the NMCS concept are discussed, in order that future projects may incorporate best practice, and avoid pitfalls. It is particularly important to find ways of ensuring that the improvements recommended by partnerships of local people and agencies in NMCS projects are implemented, as far as possible.

Individualised, targeted approaches to child protection

Shortcomings of reactive, case-by-case approach

Despite support for community development approaches to child and family welfare over at least four decades, including recommendations from two major reviews of the role of social work (National Institute for Social Work, 1982; Seebohm, 1968), the UK continues to develop individually oriented, reactive approaches to safeguarding children and young people. These focus on a minority of families with children already judged at risk of significant harm. But these services are endlessly overstretched trying to react to each individual case. The temptation then (see Chapter One) is to raise the thresholds for intervention to cope with demand, which will simply put more children at risk. Individualised approaches repeatedly fail to identify cases which are 'under the radar'. Case-by-case approaches also make it particularly difficult to recognise and collate any *organised* abuse against young people. Organisations often struggle to make the most obvious connections, and some have an alarming capacity to draw a veil over sensitive, complex problems.

Many among the media and public were precoccupied, when the inquiry into child sexual exploitation (CSE) in Rotherham was published (Jay, 2014), with how such a shocking level and scale of exploitation could have continued for so long. Alexis Jay's report illustrates key points relevant to this chapter, about failure to develop strategic inter-agency responses and policies, based on detailed information about – and involvement with – groups and communities affected by CSE:

- an individualised approach to cases in key agencies;

- vast amounts of information available, but not analysed or used to inform long-term, inter-agency policies;

- patterns not observed and acted upon by key agencies;

- children and young people not listened to, dismissed or disbelieved;

- poor communication across agencies; and

- those working directly with young people seen by other agencies as exaggerating, and given little influence.

Participation of, and consultation with, children and young people is much emphasised in modern child protection, but this is largely through their involvement in this individualised system. Even then (see Chapter Five) the deep concerns they express about confidentiality have not been listened to. Young people's collective experiences, their major concerns within particular neighbourhoods and within different ethnic and cultural groups have rarely been given prominence in developing protective systems.

In Rotherham, detailed information offered since at least 2002 about exploitation and the concerns about individuals and groups raised by teachers, youth workers and researchers were given little attention, or were disbelieved (see Chapter Four). There was also lack of attention to wider aspects of this exploitation – its connections to other criminal activity, in relation to alcohol and drugs, to sexism and racism, to punitive attitudes to young people, to their economic, housing and support needs, to inadequacies in the care system. This resulted in continuing harm and exploitation.

Little change in official policy

Similar failings have been identified over decades, yet have so far failed to lead to a radical shift in approach. Meaningful consideration of community-level factors was absent from successive public inquiries, including that after the death of Victoria Climbié. Only one of the report's 107 recommendations focused on community-level factors (Laming, 2003). In *Working Together to Safeguard Children*, the 200-page statutory section contains only a few paragraphs about the potential impact of neighbourhood factors on children's safety (DfE, 2015). In the *Every Child Matters* agenda, only one of 165 requirements mentions issues beyond the child's individual or family circumstances (DfE, 2003). The *National Guidance for Child Protection in Scotland* (Scottish Government, 2010) was updated in 2014: only a few paragraphs specifically consider communities. Their tone is instructional, rather than collaborative or supportive.

Gordon Jack comments: "It seems the default position, reinforced by these periodic tragedies, that we must put all our energies into identifying individual cases..." (personal communication, 2013).

Alienation from local communities

Individualised approaches have been accompanied by an increasingly narrow professionalisation of child protection work. This has damagingly reduced a meaningful role in child protection from most low-status professionals and ordinary people, such as neighbours or extended families. This undermines official rhetoric that it is 'everyone's job' to protect children. Communities are often viewed with suspicion and anxiety by official agencies as simply likely to commit vigilante attacks against suspected or known sex offenders rather than contribute in any positive way to a safer environment. Neighbours concerned about children's welfare may be suspected of malicious intent: Professor Sue White's study of social work teams found that in some busy teams, there was routine categorisation of anonymous referrals as malicious, and indeed referrals from neighbours and family members were also often treated as suspect (White et al, 2008).

When sexual abuse is suspected and investigated, children are expected to tell professionals such as teachers or social workers, whom research suggests they rarely approach (Crisma et al, 2004; Nelson, 2008; McElvaney et al, 2013.

There is understandable pressure to protect the quality of evidence in alleged sexual abuse cases by ensuring investigations are conducted by highly trained staff, but current procedures are often ineffective. There will always be problems about gathering enough evidence for a prosecution in sexual crime cases. Prosecutions are rarely successful and may still not be enough to keep children safe. When there is a media and public backlash against failures to protect children, organisations look for better individual solutions, often taking refuge in repeated and exhausting reorganisations. "The view is that whenever something goes wrong, it must be to do with the systems, and we need to reorganise again!" (Gordon Jack, personal communication, 2013). We need to look urgently, instead, for other ways to minimise risk and prevent harm.

Increasing professionalisation has isolated social work agencies within neighbourhoods. In the 'patch' social work system developed in the 1980s but now largely abandoned, social workers had more opportunity for informal contact and were more connected with a range of local services. Yet distrust of communities, especially poorer ones (for instance over violent vigilante action against suspected sex offenders) can be a self-fulfilling prophecy. If people receive little or no feedback, and have little influence on what happens locally, then mutual distrust, suspicion, anger, and the temptation for some in communities to take action themselves against the few identified sex abusers increase.

Development of community approaches

The background

Community approaches, in contrast, use existing networks to protect children, and respect the knowledge, experience and skills of local people, both adults and children. They promote safer, healthier environments and behaviour, through shared understandings and collective responsibility.

A substantial critique of the individualised approach to child protection services has been developing in the UK and USA since the 1980s. This has drawn on research which demonstrated the importance of family support services and community-wide strategies to raise the general level of child care, health and safety within neighbourhoods (Garbarino and Sherman, 1980).

There has also been increasing emphasis on the importance of listening to young people's own knowledge and experience, and involving them in designing future services. Greater recognition of the rights of children has been enshrined in the UN Convention on the Rights of the Child. The Convention charges states with providing environments which promote health, education, shelter, safety and financial security for all. UNESCO and the World Health Organization (WHO, 2008), in their international efforts, are strong advocates of a community development approach.[1]

These documents emphasise the effectiveness of informal education and community participation in inspiring and supporting social change – where human rights, education, health and environment issues cross-cut child development and protection, and the empowerment of girls and women. Tunstall et al (2011) argue that community-based approaches to social problems (nationally and internationally) have a strong and lasting track record.

Vulnerability to cuts

The major UK political parties *all* argue for strengthening local communities, building on their social capital and altruism. Yet these broadly based initiatives are often the first to be cut, with services returning to their default position, focusing on individual cases. In England and Wales, the Local Safeguarding Children's Boards (LSCBs) were established in 2006 in part to ensure a wider agenda, with a duty to investigate how best to meet the needs and lessen risks of harm for children in their localities. LSCBs are now the key system for organisations to come together to agree on how they will cooperate with one another to safeguard and promote the welfare of children. The purpose of this partnership working is to hold each other to account and to ensure safeguarding children remains high on the agenda across their region. Yet according to Blewett (2011), research by France et al (2010) suggests that consistent, full involvement across all agencies, cannot be relied upon: they are still mainly focused on (individualised) serious case reviews. Most

---

[1]   www.tostan.org/community-empowerment-program; www.un.org/millenniumgoals

Boards at that time had not embraced the wider safeguarding agenda. These issues parallel criticisms made in the Jay Report.

We argue the need for this wider safeguarding agenda. With the Munro Review (2011), we emphasise the importance of early intervention and wide-ranging support services, developed in parallel with those individually focused services which are effective.

In this individualistic climate, the Scottish Government's Early Intervention initiatives (Scottish Government and COSLA, 2008) are a welcome move in the direction indicated by research. They attempt to shift the emphasis towards prevention, family support and easily accessed neighbourhood services, encouraging integration and coordination across sectors. Targeted funds support a twin-track approach.

This contrasts with diminishing commitment in England to support such community-based initiatives as Sure Start. Even in some (English) reports focusing particularly on young people's participation there is surprisingly narrow emphasis on improving individuals' experience within the existing child protection system, rather attending to young people' views of how needs and risks may be addressed (SCIE, 2006). In Scotland there are at least strong policy commitments to build upon which focus on the whole child in her or his environment, taking account of their social and economic conditions (DfE, 2003; Scottish Executive, 2006). GIRFEC (Getting it Right for Every Child) emphasises ensuring that children's experience informs policy and practice.[2]

Despite proven successes...

Such commitments are important since despite some promising rhetoric, and despite excellent models provided through reseach, community-oriented practice has remained on the margins of mainstream provision within the UK (Baldwin and Carruthers, 1998; Jack and Gill, 2003; Jack, 2004; Spencer and Baldwin, 2005; Barber, 2007; Gill and Jack, 2007). Community initiatives have proved difficult to sustain *even if successful,* despite official

---

2

emphasis on 'evidence-based practice', and were not taken up by governments as models of best practice or used as the basis for formal guidance.

Examples with links to NMCS

During the 1990s the Canklow estate project in Rotherham used community-based social workers to enhance support networks of local families, especially informal support such as play schemes, youth clubs, women's groups and adult education. A five-year evaluation found significant reductions in the numbers of children in care or on supervision orders. Workers had helped to reduce mistrust between them and child welfare professionals, enabling people to seek help earlier (Holman, 1993).

Other projects based on this critique, which aim to understand and support children and families in their social, cultural and economic circumstances, at least keep these debates alive. Examples are The Henley Safe Children Project (Baldwin and Carruthers, 1998 – see below); the community-based prevention work of 18 and Under, Dundee; One Parent Families' Scotland's Dundee Community Family Support Project; Families and Schools Together (FAST); Safety Net, Brighton: Working with Communities to Keep Children Safe; and many of the Headstart and Sure Start initatives.[3] Most of these projects continue into the present day, although with endless difficulties in competing for scarce resources (Spencer and Baldwin, 2005; Bartley, 2007; ResPublica/Action for Children, 2011).

Another example which foreshadowed the Craigmillar project was NSPCC's Tilbury project. This was launched in 2000 amid a local culture of distrust of child protection professionals. The local authority, Area Child Protection Committee (a forerunner of LSCBs) and a local Sure Start programme were involved. Aims were to promote community responsibility for protecting children, to ensure high awareness of risks to children and provide strategies to tackle them, to increase children's confidence, and

---

[3]   www.18u.org.uk; www.opfs.org.uk/service/dundee-community-family-support-project/; www.familiesandschools.org; www.safety-net.org.uk

break barriers between professionals and communities. Time was spent building relationships among councillors, youth services, employment services, regeneration initiatives, crime projects, street wardens, the community police and others. A community conference reached a common agenda. (ResPublica/Action for Children, 2011). The programme helped community groups to develop their child protection policies, and ran 'protective behaviours' programmes for families, and child protection training for professionals.

Situational crime prevention

Yet another influence on community strategies against sexual crime – highlighted especially in the physical environment aspects of the Craigmillar NMCS project in Edinburgh – has been the development of *situational crime prevention* (Wortley and Smallbone, 2006; Clarke, 2009; Kaufman et al, 2010; Leclerc et al, 2011). This still-developing body of research and practice has drawn on the theoretical frameworks of Cornish and Clarke (1987) among others, to apply opportunity-reducing techniques to child sexual abuse. It aims to make committing offences, especially opportunistic ones, more difficult and inconvenient, to increase the risks of detection and to strengthen potential victims, by educating children about protective strategies. The best-known aspects of SCP are probably measures such as extra lighting to reduce dark areas, or reduction of bushes around play areas to reduce neighbourhood crime in general. But it can also include safety policies and background checks in organisations working with children, and the reduction of other possible facilitators of sexual violence.

Neighbourhood mapping for children's safety: case study 1 – the Henley Project

We have discussed above some important 'building blocks' of what was to become the Henley Project (Baldwin and Carruthers, 1998, Baldwin and Spencer, 2000) provided the detailed backdrop for developing NMCS, as it was later progressed in Craigmillar, Edinburgh. It focused on mapping neighbourhood difficulties, and understanding the experience of local people.

The Henley electoral ward of Coventry had then the highest proportion of child protection referrals in the city. Information was gathered from national and local surveys: on health, income, employment, housing, services and resources. Mapping of many factors could be taken down to postcode level – this revealed a correspondence between the highest scores on deprivation and numbers of child protection referrals. It also showed that there were clusters of referrals in the postcode areas with the highest proportion of under-18s.

This detailed information was presented to local authority and health policymakers. Local people were supported in presenting their experience of the project's impact on their daily lives and what local changes were needed. They were able to translate the broad statistical picture of deprivation, needs and problems into a detailed account of what it was like to bring up children in this neighbourhood.

The Henley Project worked intensively with local people – mainly mothers of young children – and with social welfare, health and housing professionals. It aimed to take account of demonstrated links between disadvantage and many aspects of harm, including poor health and low educational achievement, child neglect and crime; and to draw on the expertise of local groups in preventing and responding to harm. It led to planned inter-agency strategies of: neighbourhood and family support; action with young people for a safer environment; principles of partnership with communities; and positive action to build on the strengths of families and communities, drawing on their own resources and expertise.

Local mothers, along with other community groups and supported by the local authority strategy, were instrumental in developing networks of family support and childcare provision over several years. They were heavily involved in setting up social, health and educational groups and projects to enhance employment opportunities. They gained funding to improve parks and play areas for children and were involved in efforts to make the area safer and reduce youth crime and anti-social behaviour (Baldwin and Carruthers, 2000; Gardner, 2003). Funding continued from the local authority and NSPCC.

Minority ethnic involvement

A major gap identified in the early work in Henley was the lack of involvement of minority ethnic groups. The project had collaborated with a city-wide African Caribbean group to consult and do outreach work with the small number of African Caribbean families in the Henley area. However, this could not address what might be substantial differences in areas of Coventry where there was a high proportion of families of south Asian heritage. The Hifazat Surukhia project was set up with funding and support from the Barrow Cadbury Trust, University of Warwick, NSPCC and local authorities to work closely with minority groups in Coventry, Birmingham and Sandwell to look at concerns about protecting children (Atkar et al, 2000).

Research and development workers who spoke minority languages led the initial work, consulting with young people, women's groups and community leaders. Workers were clear about the need to open up discussion about cultural expectations and taboos. Many of the issues around under-reporting of sexual abuse, the shame of victims and the lack of follow-up of alleged perpetrators identified later in the Rotherham report (Jay, 2014) and in the report of the Children's Commissioner about intra-familial sexual abuse (Horvath et al, 2014) were raised by the participants in the Hifazat project. NSPCC and local authorities in the West Midlands followed up this work with long-term outreach and support within minority communities.

Knowledge, energy and creativity of local people, their commitment and altruism throughout these years of community development work were crucial. Local individuals and groups provided time, wisdom and resources to tackle difficulties and problems they had identified.

Neighbourhood mapping for children's safety: case study 2 – the Craigmillar Project

What is NMCS?

A Neighbourhood Mapping for Children's Safety research project was developed in Craigmillar, a disadvantaged area of Edinburgh of approximately 8000 people, suffering redevelopment blight (Nelson, 2004a; Nelson and Baldwin, 2004). Although designed specifically for this urban area, its principles and processes can be adapted to any area.

Building upon – though further developing – the Henley principles, NMCS involves coordinated mapping exercises about features of the area and population relevant to children's safety. It highlights factors which invite risk, or offer support. Important questions include: which aspects of the physical environment increase the risk of sexual or physical harm to children? Are some spaces unsafe due to the behaviour of certain groups? How might places where young people congregate be made safer? Which agencies or individuals could best support children and protective parents? How can young people participate to ensure that their knowledge informs initiatives?

NMCS builds upon existing profiling by local authorities, health authorities and central government. It can involve many professionals and lay people, working together: thus a secondary school geography class might map derelict buildings in the area. A women's support group might check, record and evaluate the child protection policies of local sports facilities.

A designated researcher and a planning and implementation group, drawn from statutory, voluntary and community organisations, needs to work with specialist consultants such as planners, social geographers and environmental experts. They set goals and timescales, allocate tasks and supervise project work.

Launching the Craigmillar Project

Womanzone, a voluntary sector community health project based in Craigmillar and working against sexual violence, had long been keen to progress a sexual safety project. It provided the base for a research project of just under a year (this limited timescale was dictated by tight funding constraints). A steering group, which included the Craigmillar Social Inclusion Partnership (SIP), police, social work, community education, health, local voluntary sector and local residents, met regularly to take the study forward. Sarah Nelson was the researcher and Norma Baldwin the research supervisor.

Aims of the Craigmillar Project

These were to identify community needs, strengths and problems relating to the safety of children from sexual crime by:

- mapping demographic, socioeconomic and physical features of the Craigmillar SIP area;

- consulting local people and agencies on how they saw the main risks, problems and solutions involved in keeping children safe from sexual crime;

- considering any attitudes and cultural beliefs which might support or undermine young people's safety;

- analysing findings, and preparing recommendations for partnership action by agencies and the community; and

- publishing a report, and launching this at a conference in Craigmillar.

The consultation

The researcher held 54 interviews and group discussions with agency staff and service users, and distributed community questionnaires to adults and young people. She attended inter-agency meetings, events and programmes and observed the work of youth projects.

Findings in Craigmillar

Demographic features
- Estate population approx. 8000
- High percentage (25%) under 16
- Majority of children lived with lone parent/carer
- High proportion of carers were young mothers
- 61% of high school pupils had free school meals
- Many adults and children had disabling conditions
- High numbers of 'looked-after' children
- Many children had lost parent(s) through bereavement, for example drug overdoses, HIV/Aids
- Only significant minority ethnic group numerically were Gypsy-Travellers

Physical features
- Compact area, accessible and with good transport links;
- Severe redevelopment blight – many derelict flats used by heroin addicts, unsafe open spaces, dangerous rubbish
- Parks, 'green' footways which did not feel safe
- Large residential project for disabled people
- Large retail park and entertainments complexes nearby

Cultural features
- Tolerant environment for people of different faiths, ethnic groups and abilities, and strong sense of community.
- Common, falsely reassuring residents' belief that local 'jungle wolves' would drive out paedophiles (in fact such incidents were rare and could, in any case, only apply to the few offenders who were identified).
- Many local people were related, fearing recriminations or betrayal of loyalties if they reported violence or abuse: for example, "You daren't say anything because everyone is somebody's cousin!"
- Many disadvantaged residents were very suspicious of police and social workers.

Strengths
• Numerous support agencies (a recent survey had mapped 80 agencies in the area)
• Long tradition of community campaigning
• Known networks of communication and support
• Strong arts and drama tradition through Craigmillar Festival
• Areas of high social need can access extra funding

Findings of consultation with agencies and local people

People's perceptions of risk were not confined to sexual crime, but also included dangerous physical environments, physical violence, neglect and the risks of school truancy. Risks are frequently interlinked. While agencies and residents shared some common concerns, some noticeable differences in emphasis emerged.

Shared concerns

• There were many alienated or vulnerable teenagers. On any school day, 20% of local high school pupils were absent. Teenagers wandered the area, a few broke into unsafe buildings or even slept rough.

• Many vulnerable younger children were at risk of neglect, especially those of the many drug users who attended the local health centre.

• There were considerable socioeconomic and health problems.

Agencies' additional concerns

• High thresholds of risk were needed before the formal child protection system would intervene. Some agencies, including doctors, felt it was almost pointless to raise concerns about child neglect. The social work department was overstretched: the local office alone had 180 'looked-after' children in its care. Despite the team leader's enthusiasm for collaborative work, social work was quite isolated within the area: little collaboration had developed among the numerous agencies to support this vulnerable population.

- There were many vulnerable parents, especially drug users and women affected by child sexual abuse or domestic violence. They needed support for their own trauma issues.

- Parents or carers could not easily access or afford safe childcare, unless they were in work or training.

Local people: additional concerns

- Environmental dangers existed, especially unsafe buildings due for demolition, and derelict areas.

- Convicted sex offenders were placed in certain local high-rise flats.

- They perceived dangers to children from highly visible groups, such as drug addicts and alcoholics on the streets.

- Insufficient information existed for carers on how to keep their children safe.

Craigmillar: the recommendations

Recommendations needed to consider notable features of the mapping and consultation exercises. There was a particular need to support carers in keeping their children safe, given high numbers of young mothers, young carers and grandparents (since many children had lost parents). Again, surveys showed 38% of people described a limiting long-term illness, disability or infirmity. Disabled carers and disabled children may face extra barriers in keeping youngsters safe. Research has consistently found greater vulnerability in children and young people with disabilities, and inadequate involvement of such young people in expressing their own needs and opinions (Stalker et al, 2010).

In Craigmillar, difficulties in speaking out against relatives, and the strong distrust of officials, also suggested intermediary agencies and phonelines might help those who with information on sexual crime.

The mapping and consultation exercises produced 26 recommendations for change. An implementation group, linked to existing area initiatives, was recommended, with five small working groups to progress these recommendations. Its aim would be to focus on: physical environment; vulnerable and excluded youth; education, campaigning and publicity; support services for adults; and information and reporting systems relating to sexual crime.

These are some of the recommendations made, and approved at the Craigmillar Conference at the end of the project.

Physical environment recommendations

- Pressurise public and private redevelopment agencies to speed up demolition or change of use.
- Develop safety projects in local parks and green spaces, and temporary youth activities for derelict land.
- Launch a safety initiative in the retail park, to engage the private sector. The large retail/recreation complex is attractive to children and young people (thus to potential sexual predators). The park's security team focused on preventing theft or damage. An awareness-raising initiative for recreation facility managers, shop managers and security firms would improve children's physical and sexual safety. This might prove attractive for school students or youth clubs to design, with support.

Comment on physical environment issues

Two examples from elsewhere of *physical improvements* exemplify possible achievements from such a community development approach:

- Derelict land, prey to continual dumping, was leased to the Penygarn Residents Association (near Pontypool). Woodlands Field Ltd was created and in 2008 a neighbourhood learning centre was built with a training room and IT suite. It became a thriving community hub engaging many visitors and users. The centre runs employment schemes, healthy eating programmes, Sure Start and youth support, and a multi-generational allotment project (ResPublica /Action for Children, 2011).

- Primary school 'Safety Squads' are run by the Safety Net community project in Brighton. The local park did not feel a safe place to play. Bevendean Squad researched playgrounds in other areas; all children voted on what equipment they wanted, and after they campaigned to the council, a new playground was built. Older children made them feel unsafe again by spraying graffiti. The council agreed to remove it, and funded a video where children put their safety concerns to others – including the graffiti culprits (Res Publica/Action for Children, 2011).

Vulnerable and excluded youth recommendations
- Appoint outreach youth workers.
- Develop daytime facility for non-attending/excluded pupils.
- Initiate round-table agency talks on intervention thresholds.
- Set up a drug users' children's safety project.
- Add a youth protection concierge to existing neighbourhood wardens (who tended to interact with young people who were causing a nuisance, but also noticed vulnerable young children on the streets at night).
- Improve coordination of existing services, to keep children out of residential care: thus some agencies could prepare breakfast, accompany children to appointments, and so on.

Comment on vulnerable and excluded youth issues

This set of recommendations particularly highlighted how an NMCS scheme may identify problems, such as child protection policies, which can only be tackled through inter-agency or cross-departmental action or at regional or national level – not purely at area level. (In these cases, however, local communities can still be involved in campaigning for change.)

Most schools reported very low rates of sexual abuse disclosures and referrals over several years. Staff often wrongly believed child protection guidelines prevented staff asking children any questions about sexual abuse, even if they strongly suspected it. There were extremely limited support services for young people needing help with sexual concerns, abuse or exploitation. Major agencies thus need to ensure that if they encourage children to share concerns and disclosures, that their staff are able to hear them; and that they put in place services which can listen and deal with the abuse revealed, address criminal justice implications, and offer therapeutic support.

Recent revelations about the way in which paedophile rings, for instance in children's homes, and CSE gangs would traffic and collaborate, across the UK and beyond, also point to the need for national and international action by criminal justice services, as well as the need for local identification.

Education, campaigning and publicity recommendations

- A play and exhibition, building on the area's very strong arts and drama tradition
- A safety video, drawing on video-making experience in youth and adult education
- Self-defence courses, to be available at the local sports centre
- Multi-agency collaboration, to design informative safety leaflets and posters for disabled adults and children
- 'Choose the best prevention programme' initiative, where a residents' group would visit several UK community prevention programmes, report back and, with agency support, design a funding proposal for their own local programme.

Comment on issues related to education, information-giving and campaigning

Education and campaigning provides an important opportunity to address attitudes and values in communities which promote or tolerate domestic, gang and sexual violence and abuse, including racist violence. This gives the opportunity for innovative projects to tackle racism and sexism, along with bystander education.

Challenging boys' and men's attitudes

These needs relate to young people too. While major problems were not identified in the Craigmillar project, much evidence has emerged since about extreme sexual violence towards girls in many urban gangs, and by peers against each other, suggesting a profound need to challenge these attitudes through community work. The OCC study (Berelowitz et al, 2013) into sexual exploitation in gangs and groups graphically exposed the sexism and brutal sexual violence, including beatings and frequent gang rapes, which many girls face when involved with neighbourhood gangs. Girls as young as 11 and 12 were sometimes victims. Some senior gang members passed their girlfriends around to lower ranking members or even the whole group. Gang members often groomed girls at school using drugs and alcohol, which disinhibit young people and create dependency, and coerced them to recruit other girls through social networks.

Hence recommendations to tackle any such attitudes would need to be included in any future NMCS scheme. A range of community projects now confront – in a challenging but supportive way – these attitudes, and encourage and enable young men to meet their children's needs positively. One example is Young Fathers.[4] The Blast Project offers many resources for working with boys and young men, not just as potential victims of abusers but as potential perpetrators, challenging attitudes to young men which may lead them to excuse such perpetration.[5]

Carlene Firmin's study (2015) of young people, their schools and neighbourhoods found that professionals often concentrated on assessing the victim of sexual assaults, not the perpetrator, and tried to solve the problem by moving the victim around. 'Each case was treated as an individual incident, rather than what it might be telling the school community about what was acceptable or not. No changes were made to the school environment.' But spaces outside the home, used by young people, need intervention in response to peer-on-peer abuse: 'we need preventive work in social spaces' (Firmin, 2015).

---

[4]   www.youngfathers.info/contacts/service_providers.htm
[5]   http://mesmac.co.uk/blast-contact-us

The study identified the importance of creating safety in public spaces such as transport hubs, parks and schools, and the influence of peer groups in young people's decision making. That is a central feature of NMCS projects. Firmin's research has explored young people's experiences of gender inequality, and the impact these experiences have on their welfare and their contact with services. She heads the MsUnderstood Partnership (Girls against Gangs) between the University of Bedfordshire and Imkaan. They are working with 11 local authorities to develop their responses to violence and abuse between young people.

Bystander education

Meanwhile, the sexual exploitation (CSE) scandals in English towns such as Rochdale, Rotherham and Oxford have sharply highlighted problems of official inaction and failure by adult community bystanders to report 'in plain view' grooming of under-age girls, or particular local houses used for exploitation. Negative judgements about 'delinquent' or 'promiscuous' young girls have hampered realistic child-focused responses (see Chapter Four). Yet helping ordinary people to be informed and vigilant, and addressing their prejudices against groups like the stigmatised teenagers involved in CSE, is vital to keeping young people safe.

A literature has developed on bystander education (such as Banyard et al, 2007) – on techniques that maximise the likelihood that bystanders will engage in helping behaviour. This has received new impetus with the revelations of CSE. The National Working Group (NWG) network has promoted some valuable bystander education tools for local communities and local businesses, such as hotels, guest houses, bars and restaurants who might observe grooming or suspect sexual activity on their premises. One example is the DVD and educational materials 'Say Something if you See Something'.[6]

Bystander education tools could and should be incorporated into any future NMCS community project, increasing the

---

[6] www.nwgnetwork.org/youth-participation/what-do-we-do/say-something-if-you-know-something

likelihood of community members taking an active role in prevention and intervention.

Using active bystanders

We can also learn from some striking examples of 'active bystanders' who emerged unexpectedly in the Craigmillar project. Observant supermarket checkout staff and cinema ticket sellers told the researcher their worries about particular children they recognised, wandering round cinemas during the day; or depressed young mothers they had come to know, buying alcohol in the mornings. Yet such staff had little or no locus in the formal child protection system. The Royal Society of Arts' analysis of existing social networks and connections in communities (ResPublica/Action for Children, 2011) found that dustmen and postmen were better connected than local councillors; that the best connections to the most isolated individuals and families were shopkeepers and cab drivers; that pubs and sports facilities were at the heart of large local networks. Yet, again, such people and networks have had little or no locus in the formal child protection system. They need to be appreciated and their wisdom and experience drawn upon. Abuse survivor groups are equally valuable in being able to feed into and inform the statutory child protection system, yet they are very rarely used in such a potentially important role.

Support systems for adults: recommendations

- Low-cost, safe childcare and sitter services for lone parents and grandparents.
- More support services for both female and male survivors of CSA.
- An expansion (including staff training and support) of the existing and popular Phonelink service, which in Craigmillar phoned older people and adults with mental health problems regularly to ensure that they were safe.

Comment on support systems for adults

These recommendations reflected the problem that very many people in a disadvantaged area could not afford the often high costs of safe babysitting. It also suggests that if we expect local people to report sexual crime and to face up to difficult issues about child sexual abuse in their own families and neighbourhoods, it is very important to provide as local a service as possible, actively to support those affected by abuse and violence. A history of sexual abuse, of course, affects parents in many types of area, across many social, ethnic and religious backgrounds.

Information and reporting systems on sexual crime: recommendations

• Production and regular updating of leaflets by statutory agencies, explaining their policies on housing and monitoring sex offenders
• A booklet, regularly updated, listing the child protection policies of major local agencies
• A pilot proposal for identifying 'contact points', such as
  – confidential anonymous 'hotlines';
  – mailshots (and now we would add their social media equivalents) similar to those used to identify drug dealers; and
  – use of third-party trusted individuals or specific local agencies.

Comment on reporting of sexual crime, and vigilantism

Since the Craigmillar project, third-party reporting of homophobic crime and racist hate crime have been established in many parts of the UK. This acknowledges how reporting of both is undermined by fear, intimidation, shame and embarrassment, like sexual crime. The scheme could, and should, be extended to cover sexual crime.

These recommendations, more broadly, recognise residents' genuine fears of convicted sex offenders, when wide community notification cannot be offered. They also recognise the need for ways to be provided in which people reluctant, distrustful or fearful about contacting police or social workers can relay information about current or historic sexual crimes against children.

Although this may seem counter-intuitive, awareness-raising can often be most productive when tensions are high about known sex offenders, and after violent incidents. For instance in Midlothian in 2005, a notorious and brutal rapist faced two angry protest marches to his isolated cottage. After his release from prison, local agencies had a responsibility by law to manage and rehouse him. Campaigners launched a huge Facebook campaign and discussed refusing to pay council rents or council tax if he was not moved. Midlothian Council's Equalities Unit took the initiative and held productive and informative discussions in local communities – former mining areas whose cultures were very male-dominated – about violence against women, about overcoming the difficulties of speaking out in small communities, and about innovative methods of community safety (Nelson, 2012c).

Such initiatives are important, given that angry vigilantism (especially by abuse survivors themselves) can divert attention and priority from the far greater numbers of still-*unidentified* abusers within that community. Thus, when mass DNA testing after a rape in one small Scottish highland village identified an elderly man, only then did numbers of women feel able to come forward to tell police that he had abused them as children (BBC News, 2003).

The aim must be to work in partnership with local communities to agree how information about sexual offenders can be handled responsibly, and how local people can help hard-pressed official agencies by noticing and reporting any worrying behaviour, without attacking a suspected offender or his property. Such non-vigilantism agreements worked constructively while Liz Davies worked in joint social work/police teams in Harrow (see Chapter Five).

Using NMCS in different types of area

It is clear that, even in less than a year, the mapping and consultation in Craigmillar produced large amounts of valuable data, community enthusiasm, and a cascade of recommendations for improvement. Many of these will be applicable to other areas of social and economic deprivation. However, the NMCS mapping technique can also be adapted to very different geographic or demographic areas. Such exercises give great scope for imagination and creativity within innovative partnerships of researchers, local adults and young people, agencies and statutory or voluntary organisations.

Remote and rural areas

Consider first some of the features and issues which might be identified through mapping and consultation in remote and rural areas.

Physical features and amenities of such areas might include marinas, caravan or chalet parks; a village halls network; schools, closed school buildings or derelict farm buildings; poor public transport networks.

Demographic features might include retired people with useful skills; teenagers and migrant workers doing poorly paid work in hotels or fish farms; local extended families, and small utopian communities.

Strengths might include a long tradition of mutual help through small communities, church organisation and rural voluntary sector; a range of human resources and skills; and innovative use of new technologies possible for communication and learning.

Problems might include isolation from services, including safe public transport; traditional beliefs might hinder open discussion of family violence; privacy may be difficult (for example, care professionals might be your relatives); migrant workers may face unacknowledged racism; people may believe sexual abuse 'doesn't happen' here!

Thought-provoking mix

We can already see a thought-provoking mix of possible risk and support points, positive and 'denying' attitudes, and opportunities to improve children's safety. Marinas and chalet parks can be idyllic for holidays, but can also be hard to monitor and provide cover for individual or organised paedophiles. Amusement arcades can be an enjoyable attraction for young people but can also be targeted by abusers. Utopian communities can find it difficult to believe sexual predators may exist within such an idealistic group, and may as a result fail to ensure routine protective measures and everyday vigilance. Extended families can be a vital support or a means of silencing, through loyalty or intimidation. Isolated buildings can be a haven for dangerous predators, or converted for safe community activities. Tourists can be worrying 'unknown quantities', or invited into fundraising and publicity events for children's safety, like drama by young people: taking innovative ideas back home with them.

What might a NMCS project recommend after mapping some of the features above? Here are some suggestions: readers will be able to think of others.

Examples of recommendations: remote and rural

- Drama, music and arts events during tourist seasons and festivals and Highland games could show visitors the safety work of the community – and serve as a warning to any unsafe visitors.

- A travelling roadshow could prompt discussion on children and young people's safety issues at village halls.

- Travelling banks, libraries or food vans could carry safety publicity leaflets and posters – in more than one language for, for example, migrant seasonal workers.

- A support phoneline, website and social media link could be set up or extended, for adult survivors of sexual abuse.

- Old schools and derelict buildings (where possible) could be converted for community use, including after school clubs – especially valuable in areas where mothers may work early evenings in hotels and restaurants.

- Marinas, caravan sites and holiday chalet parks could have to record names and addresses of everyone who is staying, with registers regularly inspected, along with periodic police surveillance exercises.

- A community minibus could take teenagers to and from fish farms so that they do not have to hitch-hike on isolated roads.

- Innovative technologies can access protective help for children and young people, in utopian communities; on remote farms; for transient hotel workers; where strict cultures act against speaking out on family problems; for giving migrant workers a link with speakers of, for example, East European languages.

Prosperous middle class towns

There is not space here for a similar exercise to the above, but more briefly: in prosperous middle class towns we might find rich human resources through their reserves of professional skills and experience. These could be 'audited' to assist in innovative safety projects. There might also be a strong network of church groups, older people's groups and mother and toddler groups for awareness-raising and mutual support. There might be boarding schools whose child protection policies could be rigorously checked, but which would also offer useful human and physical resources from staff and young people alike.

On the other hand the potential isolation of mothers, particularly those facing violence or suspecting child abuse, would need to be acknowledged. Unrecognised needs of minority ethnic people living or working there would need attention. Assumptions by authorities and families that respected professional people there would not commit sexual crimes would need to be challenged. Many families might hesitate to think of social work or domestic abuse support services as being 'for' them, so they might need supportive outreach work to change these assumptions. Netmums and other online forums could also play a very positive role in informing and supporting middle class mothers (as well as others!) on issues relating to child abuse and domestic violence.

In another example, work in areas with BME minority populations, on children's safety issues, can not only build upon the sensitive past work with communities, achieved, for example, in Henley (Coventry) and through the Hifazat Surukhia project. It can also draw upon current best practice in working alongside

BME communities where some men of that community have taken part in organised sexual exploitation.[7]

Advantages of NMCS, compared with other community prevention schemes

NMCS can generate more effective and comprehensive community prevention than projects which concentrate mainly on information, publicity and education work – as the majority do.

- Some communities have isolated or victimised both survivors, and women needing support to deal with the emotional turmoil of suspecting their partner of abuse. Current community prevention projects in Britain and the USA tend to minimise personal difficulties in dealing with the whole subject of child sexual abuse, placing an onus on individuals and families themselves to learn about signs of CSA, and to lobby and campaign. Adult survivors may need the help of sexual abuse support organisations to tackle difficult personal topics, and take part in building community strength, *before* they can challenge or campaign.

- Strong media messages alone may not change underlying attitudes about such an emotive issue as child sexual abuse, and one where many people appear to find it difficult and distressing to change their beliefs about who abuses and who does not. For example, an independent evaluation of the Darkness to Light anti-sexual abuse project's mass media campaign found it had significant impact on short-term knowledge, and when using hypothetical vignettes of abuse situations. But there were no differences in *actual* behavioural responses at follow-up. 'Results of this study imply that media campaigns alone may not significantly affect primary prevention of CSA' (Rheingold et al, 2007).

---

[7] See, for example, www.safenetwork.org.uk/resources/pages/bme_communities_cd_rom.aspx

- We believe that information and awareness-raising about sexual crime against children needs instead to be embedded – as a key element in NMCS – within a supportive, comprehensive community programme. This fully acknowledges people's problems in speaking out, allowing adults and young people to identify and address attitudes in their community which threaten the safety of children. We are arguing for local grass roots involvement, sufficiently differentiated and thoughtfully planned for people of different social backgrounds, religions or ethnicity to be involved.

Lessons to improve future NMCS projects

Acceptability

The Craigmillar study met a very positive response, despite the sensitive subject. The launch conference for the report of findings was enthusiastically supported by local people and organisations. Local authorities may be too cautious about engaging communities on this issue. However, the positive approach of 'keeping children safe' and campaigning to prevent a range of harm to children appears still more acceptable than campaigning solely against sexual abuse or sexual crime. This matters particularly where there are diverse religious and ethnic minorities, according to the experience of the Henley Project, of Safety Net Brighton, and of the Hifazat Surukhia project with Asian families (Atkar et al, 2000).

There were key problems in relation to implementation in Craigmillar, and this was part of the learning process for future problems.

Timescales

Just under a year (a timescale constrained by funding problems) was not long enough to build trusting relationships with the main minority ethnic community in Craigmillar (gypsy-travellers) nor to engage fully with them on difficult issues like attitudes to girls' education, sex education and domestic violence. The Henley Project also found it was more difficult and time-consuming to engage with men in the community than with women. Yet given that the majority of child sexual assaults are committed by men, it is of course vital to find constructive ways of engaging males in any projects which aim to protect children.

Funding

If NMCS projects are to be set up as independent studies, we recommend that they are funded for 18 months minimum for the mapping, consultation and recommendations process. Alternatively, Safeguarding Boards and Child Protection Committees could look at ways of building continuous monitoring and planning for NMCS into local strategic plans. It is especially important that thorough preparatory work is done with minority communities, taking account of language and communication needs. Project boards or steering groups need to include active members of minorities (Baldwin and Carruthers, 1998; Atkar et al, 2000). It can be harder to access or gain trust in communities of cultural and religious diversity: longer timescales assist community consultation, and enable trust to be built.

Researcher and research support

The researcher needs to be funded full-time, seen as independent, and based within a respected and financially stable organisation. Educational institutions and established young people's organisations might be considered. The researcher needs necessary office facilities, administrative support and the ability to draw on expertise, for instance of planners or geographers, at points during the project.

Methods of consultation

In Craigmillar, using questionnaires as a form of public consultation had very limited success, especially among young people. Only a minority of questionnaires were returned. There are methodological problems with questionnaires, especially in diverse or multiply disadvantaged areas where literacy levels or understanding of English may be limited. There are also larger questions about who 'represents' either adults or young people in any community. Group discussions and individual interviews proved much more successful in Craigmillar. An imaginative range of methods is needed for this sensitive issue, including focus groups, quizzes for young people, work with schools and youth groups and the innovative use of social media.

The Henley Safe Children Project developed wide-ranging means of community consultation over 15 months, including focus groups, structured interviews and open meetings, and through encouraging local residents to consult through their own networks. It prepared carefully to facilitate meetings, for example by providing crèche facilities.

Implementation problems

These are key issues. They need to be thought of in advance of a project.

In Craigmillar, maintaining momentum and achieving a phased programme of change, rather than the small piecemeal improvements which took place, and despite efforts by bodies like the Craigmillar Social Inclusion Partnership, proved impossible from the base of a small, overworked voluntary organisation (Womanzone). Implementation thus proved the only disappointing aspect – but an important aspect – of a project which had otherwise motivated communities and agencies. As a new and unfamiliar venture, it was handicapped by the lack of influence of its original base in the support agency Womanzone, which later closed down, and by its precarious funding.

This is an important lesson for the future. Communities need to see that NMCS is not simply a paper exercise, however much enthusiasm and confidence is generated. Poorer communities, especially, have often been disillusioned by the failure to maintain initiatives.

Advance commitment

Key services cannot commit in advance to total implementation, nor to open-ended funding, particularly in a climate of cuts. However, it is strongly recommended that all NMCS projects seek prior commitment from social work, education, police and health services, through their local children's services plans, and involve local councillors, local safeguarding boards and child protection committees, to take genuine account of NMCS findings and recommendations in their planning processes.

On the Asian project (Atkar et al, 2000), the local authority and NSPCC agreed in advance to look very seriously at the recommendations and commit themselves to moving forward. The Henley Project survived well for several years under NSPCC auspices, developing safe spaces for children and other supports and improvements. The NSPCC made it one of its major projects when Home Office funding ran out. It had also built up and trained a pool of local volunteers, who helped to sustain it.

The experience of these projects shows that key principles of NMCS can be incorporated into existing strategic planning mechanisms of health and local authorities.

Pathfinders elsewhere

It will be important to pilot NMCS studies in different types of area, such as prosperous small towns and remote rural and island areas. This would generate valuable information about what the most effective, workable size of area and population, and authority or neighbourhood boundaries might be; what are the most productive forms of public consultation; what are effective models of implementation, and the best ways of working with social heterogeneity. These pathfinder studies would form the basis of NMCS audit and mapping templates, and training packages for local authorities. These would support much wider implementation of NMCS projects.

Conclusion

NMCS has developed from a long history of community development work, which despite global evidence of its effectiveness in achieving social progress (Tunstall et al, 2011; Power and Willmott, 2007) has had insufficient impact on the highly professionalised, individualised systems of child protection in the UK. While we urge reform of the current individualistic child protection system, and while other chapters of this book have suggested how it can become more genuinely child-centred, we are not calling for it to be dismantled. Rather, it needs to accommodate and address the many diverse factors associated with harm to children and young people.

Major attention needs placing in all communities – and in popular culture – on our images, expectations and understandings of children. Social and environmental risks in their localities, sexual exploitation and abuse, alcohol and drug use and availability, peer pressures, gender roles, gang cultures, should all be in strong focus. NMCS can be a powerful tool in drawing attention to these issues within communities and neighbourhoods, and in suggesting realistic, practical and cost-effective ways of working together to protect young people from harm and to increase community safety and cohesion.

All political parties claim commitments to the wellbeing of children and young people. They claim to support more localised approaches to social problems, encouraging citizen responsibility and involvement. The aims and principles of NMCS match stated government and opposition priorities in partnership working, promoting social inclusion and social capital.

One suggestion from ResPublica/Action for Children (2011) is that the (then) government's Big Society programme offered the potential to promote these. They suggest various 'community building' initiatives with a specific focus on keeping children safe, preventing the need for acute and crisis intervention. In updating statutory guidance for local authorities, they urge, attention should be paid to the role of youth services, children's centres, parks and playgrounds in keeping children safe and building social capital. Local organisations such as schools, police, fire services and employers can be rich resources for building networks of trust and help around children.

ResPublica/Action for Children also emphasised that high expectations bring out the best in people – children, teenagers, mothers, fathers, grandparents, older people. Almost everyone – even the most vulnerable – can give if they are supported and appreciated in doing so.

NMCS can provide a genuine foundation for 'it's everyone's job to make sure I'm all right'. The Scottish Policy document

Getting it Right for Every Child (Scottish Executive, 2006) aims to have in place a network of support to promote wellbeing, so that children and young people get the right help at the right time. This network will always include family and/or carers and the universal services of health and education. Many will draw support from their local community. Most of the child or young person's needs will be met from within these networks ... *Only when support from the family and community and the universal services can no longer meet their needs will targeted and specialist help be called upon* (emphasis added).

This connects with a commitment to early intervention, as part of a comprehensive programme to recognise and respond to needs and risks: and which recognises the need to spend on preventive services to avoid expensive interventions later.

Are we serious about preventing abuse?

NMCS is a positive response to recent scandals, crises, and failures to listen to and protect young people. If we are serious about providing more effective responses to widespread sexual exploitation and abuse, we need at last to listen to what young people can tell us about better ways of keeping themselves safe. We can draw on the detailed intelligence they and local people can provide, and work in genuine partnership to formulate and implement realistic strategies.

Local people show immense commitment to their children, young people and neighbourhoods. They can provide the resources of time, knowledge, imagination and skills to reduce risks of harm; and support environments in which children flourish. Can we at last learn to listen to one trenchant voice in the Victoria Climbié Inquiry (Laming, 2003), to campaign for a more positive future?

> [Victoria Climbié] has become an embodiment of the betrayal, vulnerability and public abandonment of children. The inquiry must mark the end of child protection policy built on a hopeless process of child care tragedy, scandal, inquiry, findings, brief media interest and ad hoc political response. There is now a rare chance to take stock – and rebuild. (Beresford, 2003)

PART III

Working with adult survivors of sexual abuse

SEVEN

Physical ill health: addressing the serious impacts of sexual violence

Introduction

In this chapter I challenge conventional theories of the links between child sexual abuse (CSA) trauma and physical ill health.

The chapter explores the extent and possible causes of widespread physical ill health and chronic pain among adult survivors of CSA. This contributes to their suffering and disability throughout life, becoming an additional burden and stigma. Yet their physical health has received far less research attention than their mental health. Tenacious theories of 'somatisation' and 'secondary gain' explain away these often serious disorders, yet there are flaws in both theories. The greatest problem adult survivors of CSA have found in accessing respectful, appropriate healthcare and support is the assumption that their ill health must be psychosomatic, or even 'hypochondriacal', due to their actual or assumed mental health problems.

I argue the case for the little-considered, direct effects of sexual violence through injury, damage and sexually transmitted infections (STIs). I offer suggestive evidence on this for researchers to pursue. Future research into causes, treatment and recovery should investigate further these direct effects of sexual violence upon the body; the neurobiological impacts of serious early life trauma, where changes in the autonomic nervous system increase vulnerability to pain, infections and auto-immune conditions; and complex dissociative processes in face of violence and torture.

I call for much greater collaborative research and practice, nationally and internationally, with those working in fields as disparate as sports medicine and the care of political torture victims; for closer links between paediatrics and adult medicine; and for qualitative research with CSA survivors, on any connections they themselves discern between their childhood experiences and their adult health.

I believe that such changes, along with the rejection of prejudicial, gender-biased assumptions about CSA survivors in healthcare, will make more appropriate and effective the treatments and therapies available to them. It will not be sufficient in itself to carry through, in medical practice, excellent recommendations already available to healthcare professionals for sensitive approaches to abuse survivors: about ensuring that healthcare offers a safe welcoming environment, confidential services, the availability of chaperones, an awareness of 'triggering' examinations, and sensitivity in questioning about assault history (for example, Teram et al, 2006; Schachter et al, 2009; McGregor et al, 2009; Nelson, 2012b). Such thoughtful survivor-centredness in routine practice is very important, but it is only part of what is needed.

Open-minded research into the causes and extent of survivors' ill health will also have considerable implications for *prevention* and early recognition and intervention in CSA. Accepting the extent and seriousness of sexual violence, and the severity of its health impacts, is likely to increase the perceived seriousness of CSA in society. The case for rigorous primary prevention and earlier intervention will be strengthened, especially if research brings increased knowledge of some physical warning signs of CSA, which might be detected in childhood or teenage years.

Medically explained and unexplained conditions: what research tells us

In a systematic review of reviews, Maniglio (2009) found survivors of child sexual abuse are significantly at risk of a wide range of medical, psychological and sexual disorders. Talbot et al

(2009) in their study of older patients found CSA was associated with higher burden of medical illness, worse physical function, poorer activities of daily living and greater bodily pain. In their startling estimate, the effect of severe CSA on illness burden was roughly comparable to adding 8 years of age; but for impairment of daily living activities and pain, the figure was 20 years. Larson et al's large study (2005) found that nearly half the abused women with substance misuse and mental health problems reported serious physical illnesses. In an important series of studies by Leserman, Drossman and colleagues they devised an abuse severity measure following physical and sexual abuse (Leserman et al, 1997) for types of condition commonly undermine health in people who experience CSA. These are *medically explained*, and *medically unexplained, or functional conditions* – that is, where no clear organic cause can at present be found for the illness.

'Medically explained' conditions, for which organic causes have been found, and where the incidence of sexual abuse has been shown to be higher than among non-abused people, include: certain cancers (Stein and Barrett-Connor, 2000; Norman et al, 2006; Fuller-Thomson et al, 2009); arthritis, inflammatory and general auto-immune diseases (Norman et al, 2006; Kendall-Tackett, 2007); diabetes (Romans et al, 2002; Kendall-Tackett, 2007); heart disease (*Dong* et al, 2004); epilepsy (Greig and Betts, 1992); pelvic inflammatory disease (Champion et al, 2005), and morbid obesity (Williamson et al, 2002).

'Medically unexplained' and functional symptoms

Survivors of child sexual abuse are frequently affected by troubling somatic conditions for which no medical explanation has yet been agreed. A *functional* disorder impairs normal bodily function, but examination cannot detect an obvious disorder. Yet these conditions can be exhausting, debilitating and disabling, and can occur across several organ systems of the body. They prove stigmatising for CSA survivors, bringing frustration to both patients and doctors, easily leading to disparaging images of a so-called 'heartsink' patient. They often coexist with mental health problems such as depression, anxiety and panic disorders or dissociative disorders; and this is precisely why their conditions have been so readily interpreted as psychosomatic, or even hypochondriacal.

In a literature review and scoping exercise (Nelson et al, 2012), which also contains a detailed list of references to more than 100 academic research papers studied, the medically unexplained (MUS) conditions most frequently associated with histories of CSA identified were found to be:

- MUS across several organ systems, such as gastro-intestinal, gynaecological, neurological, upper respiratory, chronic fatigue;

- chronic pelvic pain or other sites of chronic pain, for example, headache, lower back pain, temporomandibular, or multiple sites (fibromyalgia);
  gastro-intestinal (GI) symptoms;
  non-epileptic seizures (sometimes known as pseudoseizures);

- respiratory problems not responsive to asthma medications; throat, mouth and oesophageal disorders. (Nelson et al, 2012)

Service users in support projects

Research has already revealed that sexually abused people are vulnerable to worse physical health than non-abused people. However, when I took part in Scottish physical health support projects in 2012 with female and male survivors of child sexual abuse at two survivor support agencies – Open Secret in Falkirk and Kingdom Abuse Survivors' Project (KASP) in Kirkcaldy – I was shocked and unprepared for the levels of illness, chronic pain and disability we uncovered. Far from being hypochondriacal obsessions, these were revealed hesitantly by the survivor groups over months, often with shame or embarrassment – especially when they concerned genital, urinary or anal problems. Both of these survivor support agencies state that in their experience over many years, more than 80% of their clients have suffered significant health problems.

Among 23 adult female survivors the following were reported. Irritable bowel syndrome (IBS) was almost universal and hysterectomies were frequent.

Other conditions included ulcerative colitis; fibromyalgia; chronic pain throughout the body; slipped disc; chronic neck and back pain; spinal degeneration; migraines; repeated flu-like symptoms; arthritis; non-malignant tumours; asthma & respiratory conditions; hypothyroidism; gynaecological infections, pelvic inflammatory disease and prolapse of womb; breast abscesses; psoriasis; pelvic floor problems; chronic pain in genital & anal areas; anal tearing; very painful periods; prolonged menstrual bleeding; fibroids; spondalitis; painful urination; incontinence; urinary infections and severe bladder problems; kidney pain and kidney infections; hydranitis; sinusitis; diverticulitis; painful and difficult swallowing; alopecia; chronic fatigue. The majority have been unable to do paid work, and depend on welfare benefits (Nelson, 2012b).

In my research study with female survivors (Nelson, 2001) one woman with eight abusers as a child had had 15 gynaecological-related operations, then a full hysterectomy. Her memorable description was of being 'ripped apart at nine'.

Among eight adult male survivors at Open Secret and KASP, the main conditions were IBS; chronic pain including spinal pain and temporomandibular disorder; chronic fatigue; respiratory problems; and ear and kidney infections. One male survivor has epilepsy, one sciatica, two noise-sensitivity and other environmental sensitivity. Most are currently unable to do paid work. Another male survivor of multiple abusers as a child has experienced lifelong back and rectal pain, IBS, eczema, neuralgia in face and jaw areas, osteoarthritis and lung disease. Powerful reflex gagging after oral abuse means he cannot get false teeth fitted. He has been unable to work for decades, and depends on welfare benefits (Nelson, 2012b).

These are, of course, only two striking examples. But there are no factors to suggest why these support agencies would contain more clients with ill health than any other agency or service. They are open to, and attract, a wide range of female and male survivors of CSA from the community. It will be valuable to survey a range of other survivor support agencies, nationally and internationally, to see if these findings are replicated.

Disruption to daily life and work

The following two examples strongly suggest how conditions heavily linked to both sexual and physical abuse histories can bring persistent suffering, and disruption to ordinary relationships and everyday tasks. These can make survivors of child sexual abuse feel they have been doubly punished. Many are punished a third time, by attitudes among medical and mental health professions.

Peters et al (2008) studied women with intersticial cystitis and painful bladder syndrome. They found 58% of participants reported CSA, 65% physical abuse, and 43% domestic violence. Most had had pain for five years or more. More than a quarter had caesarean births, more than three-quarters had had a miscarriage, stillbirth or abortion. Almost a third reported three yeast infections per year, while 48% had had a hysterectomy. Deep pain with sex was reported by 77%, deep burning pain after sex by 68%. More than 40% had IBS and stress urinary incontinence. They reported on average four pelvic surgeries. The researchers concluded that this group of patients were 'in desperate need of care' (Peters et al, 2008).

Vulvodynia in adulthood – pain or discomfort at the entrance to the vagina – has been strongly associated with sexual and physical abuse as a child (Harlow and Stewart, 2005). It can cause intractable, knife-like pain, affecting intimate relationships, work and recreation. Vulvodynia can cause hypersensitivity to clothing or touch, and even limit simple activities like sitting and walking (Newman, 2002).

Wide range of possible reasons for ill health

The search for reasons why child sexual abuse survivors might suffer disproportionately from physical ill health, compared with non-abused people, has often featured single theories. Yet many factors might have a bearing on different conditions. These might also point to the need for different types of intervention.

Thus, taking even the first four theoretical explanations below, neurobiological changes might be the main factor in auto-immune conditions; psyche–soma interconnections for tension headaches during stressful therapy; dissociative processes for the temporary paralysis of a limb; and historic stress injuries, inflicted by heavy adults upon small children, for some back and neck conditions.

Possible reasons for ill health include:

- Direct effects of sexual violence, and sexual transmission of infections.

- Neurobiological effects of prolonged early life trauma.

- Links between psyche and soma, in the experience of health and wellbeing, illness and pain.

- Dissociative processes, following triggers to their abuse history.

- The physical effects of mental health effects. Examples would include repeated self-injury, self poisoning and suicide attempts; depression, bringing lack of self-care or exercise and poor diet; eating disorders – which can also damage specific areas like digestive systems and the gullet (oesophagus); and obsessional attempts to clean body areas felt to be polluted by sexual abuse, such as through the use of bleach (Nelson, 2001).

- There are known health impacts from heavy smoking and other drug and alcohol misuse. This is to self-medicate distressing post-traumatic symptoms, but also because perpetrators themselves often ply victims with substances. Dube et al (2003) found that up to two-thirds of serious illicit drug use were accounted for by effects of childhood sexual or physical abuse.

- Effects of miscarriage, abortions (legal or otherwise) and stillbirth, following CSA in young girls.

- Health effects of homelessness and street living, if a young person flees from abuse, for example, exposure, poor nutrition, skin infections and street assaults.

- Fear and avoidance of preventive health checks, especially 'triggering' checks to genital and oral areas, which can mean that early signs of treatable disorders are missed.

- Prolonged psychiatric medication and polypharmacy for mental health problems. These can have many side effects, especially weight gain and the diseases of obesity (Allison et al 1999; Newcomer and Haupt, 2006; Nelson, 2011; Bak et al, 2014). Some Open Secret clients were prescribed 13 different daily medications (Nelson, 2012b).

- Repeated, fruitless investigations and exploratory operations, in the sincere search for causes, can also create health problems (Arnold et al, 1990). Multiple surgeries can lead to adhesions, scar tissue which can make tissues or organs inside the body stick together. They can be caused by infection or inflammation, but also by surgeries and operations, especially in the abdomen and pelvic areas. They can cause problems such as abdominal pain, bowel obstruction or infertility.

Theories that stigmatise

Sexually abused patients will often already attract disapproval because of unhealthy behaviours such as smoking, drug use or binge eating as self-medication against distressing post-traumatic symptoms, and because they often fearfully avoid preventive health checks which can trigger memories of abuse. Two prominent theories, relating to somatisation and secondary gain, have further stigmatised them, often resulting in inadequate or inappropriate treatment, or a lack of treatment. Thus urging doctors and nurses to ask about a history of abuse is not *in itself* sufficient to improve their care, because prejudices about child sexual abuse survivors may influence judgements, diagnoses and suggested treatments. We must challenge these prejudices too, asking medical professionals to be as open-minded as they would be towards any other patient.

Somatisation

Holistic approaches to health and ill health across the world, of course, link psyche and soma, and reject a rigid mind–body dualism. Few open-minded people could disagree that psyche–soma interconnections clearly exist. Indeed all of us have experienced them: even basic reactions like being sick just before an important exam or driving test.

The concept of 'somatisation' (Lipowski, 1988) where emotional stress is believed to translate into – or be expressed through – bodily symptoms, developed via older concepts of 'hysteria' and conversion symptoms. While holistic understandings and approaches can be complex and sophisticated, 'somatisation' has often been applied loosely, crudely, without informed knowledge and often prejudicially to explain physical symptoms, in CSA survivors and others who suffer mental ill health (Nelson, 2012; Nelson et al, 2012). Walker (1997) states an understanding widely employed in the literature: 'Psychosocial distress is frequently expressed in the form of medically unexplained physical symptoms, a phenomenon known as somatisation'. He talks of social distress 'masquerading' as physical symptoms. Ehlert et al (1999) actually describe somatisation as a 'psychiatric disturbance'. Survivors' *mental* states have thus been interpreted as the primary factors in influencing or even producing the *physical* symptoms.

However, as suggested later, a different reason is possible for the coexistence of physical and psychiatric symptoms in victims of abuse.

One of several problems identified in the literature review by Nelson et al (2012) of MUS in survivors of sexual abuse was that the authors of research have not themselves usually been specialists in sexual abuse issues. Nor have they usually either collaborated with survivor support agencies, nor carried out qualitative research with survivors themselves.

Applied loosely and prejudicially

The experiences from survivors confirm that many medical professionals have often jumped to an assumption of 'somatisation' before even conducting tests. This emerged as by far the biggest issue for survivors in my own research (Nelson, 2012b):

> "Doctors all assume it's emotional distress. But surely it's not normal to have so much pain that you can't sleep. I have pain in my hips, neck, fingers, feet, toes, my joints ... I have had headaches regularly for years ... I had IBS for a long time also, as a teenager especially. I have bad periods and they can last up to 2 weeks." (Laura, early 20s)

> "When I was 16 and suffering terrible stomach pains, I was in hospital and the nurses' attitudes towards me changed when they saw my records [revealing CSA]. They said, 'we would like you to see our psychological doctor ... we know your pain seems real, but it's strange the way the mind works' ... and they hadn't even done my tests!" (Carol, late 20s)

> "I went to the optometrist with eye problems, but he just kept talking to me about my mental health. I asked him 'are you a psychiatrist then?'"(Margaret, late 40s)

As a result dismissive treatment or non-treatment has further alienated some survivors from health settings about which they were already nervous. Nelson et al's (2012) literature review concluded that this key concept of somatisation was problematic, stigmatising and gender-biased. There were varying definitions in studies, or a failure to define it at all. The term has many critics too among medical professionals (Burton, 2003) while even those who formerly found it useful have increasingly questioned aspects of its value (Sharpe and Mayou, 2004).

Because sexual abuse survivors among MUS patients are disproportionately more likely to be both female and psychiatrically unwell, they have also been particularly susceptible to bias and prejudice (Barsky et al, 2001; Malterud, 2003), and somatisation disorder is diagnosed approximately ten times as often in women as in men:

> Given the looseness of definitions, it is a short step to diagnosing any patients with unexplained symptoms as having a somatoform disorder ... the verb 'to somatise' and the noun 'somatiser' are unusual in the vocabulary of medicine because they imply that patients are performing a deleterious action on their own bodies ... only the stigmatizing term 'somatiser' implies that patients are the authors of their own bodily suffering. (McWhinney et al, 1997, p. 748)

Independent effects on ill health

Banyard et al (2009) examined studies of trauma and physical health. After controlling for family variables and current psychiatric diagnoses, they found that the relationship between childhood abuse and several health problems remained significant, and that both child sexual abuse and child physical abuse had an independent effect:

> We concluded from our researches that the higher rate of depression found among adults who experienced childhood abuse was not the primary factor for their increased pain reports. *Both depression and pain need to be appropriately addressed within the context of medical and psychological treatments.* (Banyard et al, 2009, emphasis added)

Brown et al (2005) also found that the association between sexual abuse and impaired health continued, even after controlling for depression or other psychiatric problems.

In conclusion, the theory that mental or emotional stress has been translated into physical symptoms has strongly influenced the way relationships between abuse survivors' psychological and physical symptoms have been theorised. Yet little concrete evidence of the existence of such a process has actually been adduced. It remains unclear why so many practitioners and researchers should assume that the sometimes extreme sexual and physical violence suffered by victims of CSA would necessarily translate only into a psychological effect, which then translates back into a physical symptom!

Catastrophising

Another popular theory has been that that depression, anxiety and post-traumatic stress disorder (PTSD) symptoms generally can lead people to catastrophise their health, and to amplify their physical symptoms. 'Catastrophising' is a term used in cognitive behavioural therapy (CBT), to describe a specific thinking pattern that is very common in people who suffer anxiety. Based on very limited evidence, people may assume the worst-case scenario about their health, creating additional anxiety and panic that they have a more serious condition than they do.

However, this theory contradicts experience with most child sexual abuse survivors, who are more likely to ignore than to overstate their health needs (see below). It has also been disproved in experimental pain studies. There, sexually abused people have shown *decreased* sensitivity to experimentally induced pain (Fillingim and Edwards, 2005). Some survivors found clinicians making these assumptions about amplifying pain, even when evidence in their medical records suggested the reverse!

> "My mother and I were told by a dentist at age eight that I had surprisingly high pain threshold. But in my late teens I was told by a psychiatrist, when he learned about my abuse, that I had a low pain threshold!" (Laura, early 20s, personal interview 2012)

The development of neurobiological theory has of course suggested other, more complex reasons why survivors of abuse may experience some chronic pain conditions.

Neediness, dependency and maladaptive coping

A second popular theory has been that deficiencies in early care and attachment lead to needy patterns of healthcare-seeking and dependency, to attract the care and comfort survivors of child sexual abuse lacked but longed for as children (Fiddler et al, 2004; Waldinger et al, 2006). This is viewed as bringing CSA survivors secondary gain, adopting and enjoying the so-called sick role, fulfilling their dependency needs. That raises an image of rather weak, needy creatures, who at best deserve sympathy and compassion, or at worst form doctors' classic 'heartsink patients'.

A minority of survivors with 'borderline personality disorder' symptoms related to attachment can indeed can be very needy and demanding. But for anyone who has had prolonged contact with CSA survivors, this image is strikingly at odds with most. Far from needily seeking healthcare, many survivors actively avoid it because of dismissive, prejudicial or triggering treatment in the past. Fatalistic stoicism is far more commonly met than dependency, and resilience in the face of chronic pain more evident than weakness. In interviewing survivors about their health, I consistently find that most claim to be 'OK' before gradually revealing numerous problems. Asked to explain, they say they always had to put up with it:

> "I felt ill for most of my life, it's like background music for me. I just get on with things." (Rebecca, 40s, personal interview 2014)

> 'My attitude has been 'we don't learn to live, we learn to exist'. Normal is to us where we're at." (Adam, 40s, from Nelson, 2009)

They often strongly dislike, blame or feel alienated from their bodies, as powerfully recorded in Leslie Young's insightful paper 'Sexual abuse and the problem of embodiment' (1992). 'Julia' in *The Memory Bird* recalled:

Being abused made me separate my body from myself in self-defence. Self-hatred has made it impossible for me at times to listen to myself or believe I am important enough to have health needs. Denial has made me simply cut off physical sensation, dismiss pain as 'being silly', and value self-neglect as proof that I was strong. (Malone et al, 1996, pp. 85–6)

... I realised I believed my body had betrayed me, by having pleasurable feelings when my brothers were abusing me. Therefore I hated my body, and if it did anything I didn't want it to do, I would simply ignore it. And I did that to the point of nerve damage in my legs and a ruptured disc. (Bass and Davis, 1988, p. 212)

I suggest that when survivors of sexual abuse do seek healthcare frequently it is not because they are either 'somatising' or in need of a nurse's comfort to compensate for lack of caring in childhood. It is because they have so many things wrong with them and so much pain: and keep hoping that someone, sometime might discover the causes and solutions.

Two major theories: neurobiology and dissociation

Two major, complex and specialist areas are described briefly below. They are in continuing development. Neither, however, is likely to provide a *general or comprehensive* explanation of the range of disorders to which survivors of CSA are vulnerable.

Neurobiological theories

Neurobiology may well come to explain why many survivors of both child sexual abuse and child physical abuse suffer disproportionately from conditions such as hypothyroidism, diabetes, heart disease and auto-immune diseases. This ever-developing field has found that severe stress and maltreatment, especially in the critical formative years of childhood, produce a cascade of neurobiological events which especially affect the hypothalamic-pituitary-adrenal (HPA) axis. This has consequences for areas such as the hippocampus and amygdala. Neurobiological sequelae of early severe stress and maltreatment have been linked with endocrine, auto-immune and metabolic disorders (Teicher et al, 2003; Charmandari et al, 2005). New technologies such as functional MRI (magnetic resonance imaging) have enabled scientists to identify the chemical and structural differences between the central nervous systems of abused and non-abused young people (Teicher et al, 2003; Weniger et al, 2008).

For example, both high and low levels of cortisol, released in response to stress, have damaging effects. Cortisol is needed for nearly all dynamic bodily processes, including glucose levels, protein synthesis, thyroid and immune function. If proteins are not properly broken down the body can see them as foreign and the immune system attacks them, bringing auto-immune disorders, also caused by high levels of inflammatory proteins in the blood after severe stress. Flooding with cortisol in response to high stress can also mean that the body fails subsequently to produce enough. When this happens, people are more vulnerable to viral infections and thyroid deficiency (Altemus et al, 2003). Research by Danese and McEwen (2012) has also furthered understanding of these interconnections for people who suffered childhood abuse. Fuller-Thomson et al (2009) found a robust association between child abuse and osteoarthritis in adulthood, even controlling for other risk factors.

Doctors Garner Thomson and Khalid Khan (2008) write of how important it is not to label such disruptions to the system as 'psychosomatic', 'functional illness' or 'hypochondriasis'. They argue that real, measurable physiological disruption is an inevitable result of chronic stress. Any implication that it is 'all in the mind', they say, does a disservice to the person, and is likely to increase their stress.

In order to help CSA survivors, the challenge is to identify which of their symptoms and disorders may reflect neurobiological changes; and to discover which particular interventions, treatments and therapies as a result might alleviate these. That will vitally include listening to survivors themselves, some of whom have campaigned vigorously for more effective treatments, notably Sandra Whyte and her colleagues in their petition to the Scottish Parliament in relation to endocrine disorders (Whyte et al, 2012).

Dissociative processes

Anyone who has worked with child sexual abuse survivors over a long time is aware that very many experience baffling pains and symptoms like temporary paralysis of a limb, long after they were hurt as children. Symptoms can be severe, sudden and dramatic; they may also disappear later. Surges in symptoms often happen when survivors are finally in a safe relationship; while they are triggered to remember; or when sensitive therapeutic bodywork reconnects them with their alienated bodies. My own research participants, who suffered vaginal, anal or oral abuse or physical torture, have experienced acute pain in a forearm which the abuser burned on the cooker decades before; have woken with waves of knife-like anal and genital pain; have experienced a bafflingly paralysed left leg or an unbearably painful throat, among other examples.

These are often described (and understood by sufferers) as body memories, or as experiences stored in the body, although medical professionals tend to see 'body memory' as an unscientific term. Much developing work on dissociation after trauma continues to shed greater light, and more scientific understanding, on these experiences.

Rehabilitation of the theories and insights of distinguished 19th century psychologist Pierre Janet, and reconsideration of 'conversion symptoms' as dissociative, have usually emphasised *mental* processes relating to the disruption of memory, consciousness and identity. But especially through the work of Onno van der Hart, Ellert Nijenhuis and colleagues (Nijenhuis, 2001, 2004; van der Hart et al, 2004), it is now recognised that dissociation can also apply to lack of integration of *bodily* functions, movement and experiences. Research on somatoform dissociation has highlighted the freeze effect, which creates anaesthesia and analgesia in both animals and humans who cannot resort to 'fight or flight'. Acute pain is felt only afterwards, if they survive. Some CSA survivors experience extreme pain many years after violent sexual assault. Sack et al (2007) found a specific association of *sexually* related symptoms with sexual traumatisation: 'Our findings also fit well with the assumption that dissociative mechanisms play a significant role in the etiology of somatoform symptoms in traumatized patients.'

Dissociative behaviour can also involve re-enacting actual abuse incidents. Mental health staff and counsellors are familiar with clients regressing temporarily during therapy to a terrified child and cowering in a corner. But it is also possible that re-enactment can be expressed through a bodily disorder. One clear possibility is that the accelerating body movements, pelvic thrusting, distress, crying and closed eyes often seen in non-epileptic seizures are re-enactments of actual sexual assault in sexually abused patients and that in these cases patients have a *dissociative* condition (Greig and Betts, 1992; Bowman, 1993); although I am not suggesting that re-enactment of sexual assault explains non-epileptic seizures in all patients.

In order to help CSA survivors, the challenge through knowledge of this field is to identify which of their symptoms and disorders may reflect somatoform dissociation; and to discover which particular interventions, treatments and therapies might alleviate these.

The seriousness of violence inflicted

The next section of this chapter concerns the direct effects of sexual violence on the body, for example through infection, untreated fractures or soft tissue damage.

One basic problem about theories of somatisation or dependency is that in making a diagnosis, it is rare that what *actually* happened to people's bodies is traced. This is very unlike the situation after, say, sports injuries, many war injuries or car accidents, where often there will be records and people will also be asked for the details. In sports and exercise medicine, a complete history is taken for diagnosis and management of the injury. Detailed assessments are made of soft tissue lesions or chronic overuse injuries. Specialist treatments are available, and management of sports injury is considered key to optimal recovery. People who break a bone can find, in the orthopaedics speciality, a great deal written and practised about diagnosis, treatment, rehabilitation, exercise, therapy and medications.

Severity of assaults

If we started to think about what actually happens to children in sexual abuse, we would include the effects of smothering, pulling legs and hips about, straining necks and shoulders, penetrating undeveloped areas of a child's body, tying up to avoid escape, or having a heavy man's weight on a small child's back, neck or chest. (Former rugby players, often left with a legacy of neck and back pain, are not likely to be told that such pain is psychosomatic.)

In addition I was aware through my own research and others', through survivors' own writings, through growing international knowledge about organised sadistic abuses and what is now a massive captured collection of online abuse images featuring brutal assaults, that many survivors describe greater violence and at a younger age than is often assumed. Deliberate infliction of pain can include bondage, burning, mutilation, biting, electric shocks, suffocation, bestiality and insertion into the anus or vagina of objects such as bottles, crucifixes or screwdrivers. This can often be accompanied by extra physical violence such as blows to the head, ears or mouth.

Examples of the severity of violent acts are common in the professional literature on child sexual abuse: for example, in Gitta Sereny's account of Mary Bell's suffering (Sereny, 1998); in Sara Scott's account of ritual abuse (Scott, 2001); in Dana Fowley's account of family and group abuse in Edinburgh (Fowley, 2010); and in the violent ordeals over many years of 'Alice Edwards' and 'Rachel Pearce', who later suffered chronic physical ill health (Itzin, 2000). Such acts are more akin to domestic torture than to minor assault. They seemed likely to leave not just psychological damage, but lasting physical damage and injury, including the consequences of infection and re-infection.

If serious injuries and assaults are not considered, not only is physical ill health likely to be misdiagnosed, but the seriousness of sexual brutality against children is actively concealed.

Similar professional attitudes to political torture

There are close similarities between psychological approaches to survivors of child sexual abuse with physical ill health, and to survivors of political torture. These two groups have much in common: it may be years since the assaults; rape may now leave few signs; and many physical complaints are similar – for example, musculoskeletal, abdominal, or sexually related (Forrest, 1995). Responses have been similar too. Amris and Williams (2007) write that emphasising the importance of psychological aspects may result in insufficient somatic pain diagnoses and treatment, with considerable risk of chronic pain not being addressed in its own right. Worryingly, they note, some centres working with torture have taken an entirely psychogenic model of pain, with few offering access to a pain service.

Reasons for possible similarities of attitude are discussed later in this chapter.

Risks of sexual violence and injury

There are several reasons why injury and infection from abusers might have more serious long-term results than accidental childhood injuries in non-abusive families, who seek prompt healthcare:

- Because they may be undiagnosed and untreated through concealment, neglect or lack of concern for the child. Thus the long-term effects of poorly healed fractures, and of injuries and untreated sexual infections in genital, anal, oral and throat areas need to be considered.

- Because the same assaults may be repeated hundreds of times on similar areas of the body, over months or years.

- Because penetrative assaults on prepubertal bodies are likely to cause internal damage, which may be particularly hard to discern.

- Because repeated, unproductive investigations of assumed MUS and unproductive operations may then lead to increased production of adhesions. This area as a source of pain needs much more investigation.

Rethinking the interconnections: a key issue

The usual hypotheses for the coexistence of physical and psychiatric disorders are that B leads to C (for example, having rheumatoid arthritis or multiple sclerosis may make you very depressed) or that C leads to B (obsessive-compulsive personalities may develop bowel disorders; or traumatised people who cannot speak their anguish may somatise it).

But a third possibility is regularly overlooked: that child sexual abuse (A) may independently have produced *both* the physical disorders (B) and the psychiatric problems (C). The way this is consistently overlooked is very surprising, since this genesis would, after all, be widely accepted in a victim of street rape, gang rape or war rape who has genital injuries, a sexually transmitted disease and post-traumatic stress.

Thus in research studies, if many people suffering a particular health condition also display psychiatric symptoms, this may indicate that large numbers of sexual abuse survivors are congregating undetected in the samples.

A paper which originally prompted me to think 'outside the box' about such possible interconnections was Clouse and Lustman (1983). They researched patients with abnormal contractions and motor responses of the oesophagus, and found that a remarkable 84% also had psychiatric diagnoses. They called for more investigation of what the link might be between emotional disturbances and such disorders. I wondered what had happened to the patients to cause them all this psychiatric disturbance, and wondered how realistic it was that mental distress would be 'somatised' through this strange physical symptom. Had something else perhaps independently caused both the physical symptom and the psychiatric disturbances? This directed me to wondering about possible damage, through sexual abuse, to the throat area and its cluster of organs.

A second paper which prompted me to think about similar issues was Lapane et al (1995). The authors noted a link between depression and infertility in women, and concluded that depressive symptoms may play an important role in the pathogenesis of infertility. I wondered if instead the samples might contain a high percentage of sexually abused women, whose abuse had brought about both the depression and the infertility as a result, for example, of gynaecological infections or injury.

The nature of oral sexual abuse

My 2002 paper on physical symptoms and sexual abuse (Nelson, 2002) described discovering from a number of child sexual abuse survivors their experience of oral sexual abuse. Before onset all had their heads pulled roughly into unnatural positions which hurt their jaws, necks, shoulders and backs. One had clamps placed in her mouth. During the assaults all experienced displacement and pain to the teeth, and jaw pain; one had her jaw dislocated. All, surprisingly, described penetration as being down the throat, not simply inside the mouth. This caused panic, near-suffocation and the need to learn shallow breathing to survive. It affected vocal cords as well as the ability to swallow. One woman recalled:

> 'Your throat is incredibly painful. I couldn't eat for days, or even drink without great pain. I couldn't talk for days either. My whole 'voice box' felt swollen. Your gagging reflex goes haywire. Afterwards, as a child, I used to scrub the inside of my mouth; I even tried to scrub the back of my throat.'

Since I wrote this paper other sexual abuse survivors have confirmed to me that their oral sexual abuse in childhood was akin to 'throat rape'. Such an experience would certainly be likely to produce mental distress, and possible psychiatric symptoms, in its victims.

What become key areas for investigation?

Some suggestive papers

What would happen, then, if we selected the main bodily sites of sexual assault as key areas of investigation for baffling physical health problems in child sexual abuse survivors? That might seem an obvious question, but it does not seem to have been. Some papers are several decades old: the clues have sat there for a long time without, it seems, being followed up. Suggestive findings in the examples of papers below do need finally to be followed up by medical researchers and medical specialists.

Disorders of the throat, oesophagus, mouth and jaw

The possibility that 'throat rape' of children is relatively common, however distressing or distasteful to think about, opens the way to reconsider a range of often baffling and allegedly 'psychosomatic' conditions relating to the throat area, vocal cords and oesophagus.

So many important organs – pharynx, larynx ('voice box') and oesophagus – are clustered closely in the throat area that damage to one part could readily affect another, while this whole area of the body is vulnerable and easily damaged. Feinberg and Peterson (1987) note that intubation, placed in the airway for surgery or ventilation, if carelessly done, can damage the vocal cords, leading to laryngospasms and injuries including scarring, inflammation and laryngeal granuloma (inflammatory growths). Intubation tubes are considerably thinner than a penis.

Voice disorders have been described as a prototype of functional disorders or MUS. There is an established literature linking dysphonia with psychological factors. It is also admitted, however, that laryngologists find it hard clinically to distinguish organic and functional voice disorders.

Paradoxical vocal cord dysfunction (PVCD): Here, the vocal cords close when people breathe in (reversing normal function), causing noisy, wheezy breathing termed 'stridor'. Normally such closure only occurs when people swallow, or when they defend their airway from intrusion. It has also been assumed to be associated with gastroesophogeal reflux disease (GERD) (Powell et al, 2000). They noted redness at the back of the throat in the young people they studied. Otherwise, PVCD has been described as a psychosomatic disorder, which mimics symptoms of bronchial asthma attacks, usually being misidentified and mistreated as such. It has attracted prejudicial names such as hysterical croups, hysterical aphonia, psychogenic cough and Munchausen's stridor.

The psychosomatic explanation, however, is simply an hypothesis, since it is not at all clear why stress or emotional upset would cause people's vocal cords to behave paradoxically. The much simpler possibility is that something has been forced crudely down the throat.

A sexual abuse history was acknowledged in all four PVCD patients studied by Freedman et al (1991) and suspected Brown et al, (1988). Starkman and Appelblatt (1984) noted that laryngospasms could occur in borderline personality disorder – itself closely correlated with histories of child sexual abuse. Although Freedman et al asked if one patient's oral abuse contributed 'to the specificity of her vocal cord dysfunction', they were exploring symbolic, not literal, meanings of the symptoms.

In a teenager unsuccessfully treated for severe asthma with recurrent wheeze since she was four, a major psychological component was considered likely; she eventually disclosed longstanding sexual abuse. 'It is postulated that her physical symptoms were a somatic manifestation of underlying sexual abuse, and that the 'asthma' was in reality vocal cord dysfunction' (Edwards and Maddocks, 2000). Her improvement in the 'asthma' and other somatic symptoms appeared to follow the ending of the sexual abuse. If so, this would raise the possibility that PVCD was less a psychological response than a direct physical response to penetrative oral abuse – which stopped happening because the abuse had also stopped.

It is interesting, and surely deserves follow-up research, especially since diagnosed eating disorders are common in CSA survivors, that Stacher et al (1990) suggest achalasia (a disease of the oesophagus muscle) may be misinterpreted as anorexia or bulimia. Clinical evaluation of eating disorder patients should, they say, take a thorough history regarding swallowing and vomiting, in case of a possible oesophageal motor disorder: 'In some patients weight loss is so prominent that achalasia may be mistaken for anorexia nervosa, particularly in adolescent girls ... the issue is complicated by the fact that ... *psychiatric symptoms are common in patients with esophageal motor abnormalities'* (Stacher et al, 1990, emphasis added).

Facial and mouth problems

Temperomandibular disorders and other atypical facial pain are very often considered psychogenic (Pankhurst, 1997). Feinmann et al (1984) exemplified a circular argument by calling atypical facial pain 'psychogenic' in itself, then finding that it was accompanied by psychiatric disturbance in 55% of cases! And yet despite this, Feinmann and colleagues admitted *that pain recurrence appeared independent of mood state* (emphasis added).

The American Dental Association says that numerous temporomandibular problems are caused by (physical) trauma, such as a blow to the jaw or a whiplash injury, or by repeatedly opening the mouth too wide. If your mouth is forced open, ligaments may be torn. Recalling again descriptions of oral sexual abuse, it is suggestive and distressing to note how many survivors' drawings in their own writings such as *The Memory Bird* (Malone et al, 1996) feature children with huge, dark, wide-open mouths.

Chronic pain: do positional problems contribute?

Chronic pain can of course have many causes. Temporomandibular disorders can produce tension headache, earaches, toothache, and even neck shoulder and back pain. One line of inquiry being followed by researchers into the effects of political torture concerns positional torture and soft tissue damage.

It is common to meet child sexual abuse survivors with fibromyalgia, who experience pain throughout the body, and CSA survivors have disproportionate rates of fibromyalgia compared with the non-abused. An insight here, given how often survivors describe having their necks pulled into unnatural positions as children, might come from the effects of whiplash injuries in other contexts. Writing on fibromyalgia, Donald Liebell (2009) states that the greatest concentration of nerve connections in the human body is in the upper neck. Misalignment, he argues, can lead to nerve compression, affecting the whole nervous system. The great majority of patients he has seen had a neck injury, often many years before onset of their symptoms.

The number of CSA survivors who have suffered neck injury during abuse – perhaps routinely so – needs to be investigated.

> 'He would put me across his lap on a bed ... then he would bend your head right back, so if anyone did come in, he could pretend he was tickling me.' (Laura, early 20s, personal interview 2012)

> 'When I was 5 they would sit on a chair and I had to kneel between their legs and they would yank my head and neck back for oral abuse.' ('Mary' in Nelson, 2001)

Anal problems

The following papers again give suggestive indications of physical injury, which need to be followed up.

Engel et al (1995), on unwanted anal penetration as a physical cause of faecal incontinence, found that in both men and women, anal penetration can cause permanent structural and sphincter damage. All patients in this study had evidence of internal sphincter disruption. Morrow et al (1997) found clear links between encopresis (soiling) in disturbed boys in residential treatment, and anal sexual abuse.

Leroi et al (1995), on anismus as a marker of sexual abuse, studied 40 women, whose disorders of the lower GI tract had been diagnosed as functional. All had experienced sexual abuse. He found anismus in 39 of 40 participants, but in only six of 20 healthy controls. Anismus is failure of the normal relaxation of pelvic floor muscles during attempted defecation, with paradoxical sphincter contraction. It has also been called spastic dysfunction of the anus. Arnold Wald (2012), writing on IBS, discusses one theory that IBS can be caused by abnormal contractions of the colon and intestines, hence the term 'spastic bowel'. Vigorous contractions of intestines can cause severe cramps.

Could one cause of such abnormal contractions be repeated violent penetration of prepubertal children?

Ian Warwick's research (2003) with male survivors of child sexual abuse found that bowel disorders and anal pain were very common, and that 25% of his research sample had had colonoscopies, which they had found retraumatising.

Gynaecological problems

A *majority* of sexually abused women I have met over decades have suffered gynaecological problems, including chronic pain, fibroids, endometriosis or infertility, and many have had hysterectomies. Sexual abuse support agencies confirm this experience. For women such problems can also have profound influence on their sense of identity and their self esteem *as* women. Kaliray and Drife (2004), in a review of gynaecological problems and sexual abuse, list findings about numerous conditions including bladder and yeast conditions, pregnancy complications, dyspareunia, unusual uterine bleeding, severe premenstrual syndrome and chronic pelvic pain. Indeed interpersonal violence in general, both sexual and physical, is known through international research to put victims at risk for a range of gynaecological health problems.

Very strong associations, in particular, have been made between a sexual abuse history and chronic pelvic pain (CPP) in women. One problem is that often the exact nature of the CPP is not closely defined, since it can cover many areas and sources of pain, including endometriosis, pelvic inflammatory disease, or adhesions. It is estimated that 50% of such pain still remains as unidentified pathology.

Endometriosis is an interesting case, in not being considered an MUS or functional disorder – even though many sufferers also have mental ill health, and even though its causes are still mysterious. This is simply because bodily changes can be identified on examination. From my own observation and that of sexual abuse support agencies over many years, many adult women survivors of child sexual abuse appear to have endometriosis, which can cause severe pain. In this condition endometrial tissue, which normally grows only in the uterus and is shed during menstruation, may grow on the fallopian tubes, ovaries, peritoneal cavity or, in rare cases, outside the pelvic area. But why this should happen is unclear.

Could one cause possibly be linked to repeated penetrative abuse of a child's body, especially a young child's body, by a penis or by objects? There may be hints in that obstruction of the cervical canal and fallopian tube scarring are known predispositions to endometriosis, and because prolonged IUD and tampon use have also been implicated.

Urinary problems

Again, observation suggests urinary problems are very common indeed in adult survivors of sexual abuse. Papers by Peters et al (2008) and by Harlow and Stewart (2005) were discussed at the opening of this chapter. Peters et al found that in their clinic population of 76 women with interstitial cystitis, 86% reported sexual abuse in childhood. Link et al (2007) found sexual abuse to be associated with urologic symptoms – not simply in patient samples, but in a large, diverse community-based random sample of both men and women.

Conditions like incontinence can of course feel particularly shaming, humiliating, and disruptive of normal daily life and work. In my own experience of discussing physical health problems with both women and men, incontinence of bladder or bowels is one of the last problems which survivors will admit. Major campaigns against some devices to alleviate such problems and pelvic floor complaints, such as transvaginal mesh implants, have also revealed how extreme pain and suffering can only compound the consequences of such conditions.[1]

Denise Webster (1993, 1996) has warned that interstitial cystitis, which includes pain and spasms without obvious bacterial infection, risks being misdiagnosed psychiatrically because of diffuse symptoms and through prejudice, since it is a woman's condition. Inflammation of the vulva, urethra or anus is reported.

---

[1] www.scottish.parliament.uk/GettingInvolved/Petitions/scottishmeshsurvivors

Disorders in several organ systems

Many child sexual abuse survivors have baffling symptoms in not one, but several, organ systems. Richter (2001) found more than half the patients with painful oesophageal motility disorders also had IBS. They often had 'psychological abnormalities'.

Do people experience pain in several organ systems because they have some widespread 'somatisation disorder' for psychological reasons, and therefore require psychological help? Or is it because they have been damaged through sexual assault in several of these bodily sites, which are often close together?

Beck et al (2009) found that multiple pelvic floor complaints were correlated with a sexual abuse history. In the study, the female patients with this history had significantly more complaints in three domains of the pelvic floor – urinary, defecation and sexual function – compared with the non-abused.

Devroede (1999) describes how the pelvic floor is closely involved with urologic, genital and distal intestinal tracts, so that dysfunctions can overlap in sexual, genital, defecatory and urinary behaviour. Unsuspected pathology can lie outside the spectrum of activities of one speciality. Thus, he calls for urologists, gynaecologists, gastroenterologists and colorectal surgeons not only to exchange, but also to be aware of the pathologies of neighbouring specialities. I urge this in the recommendations.

Why this silence about the obvious?

Impossible to see or hear?

Why has the obvious likelihood of physical damage and injury through sexual assault not been pursued? And why are so many of the interesting and suggestive research papers quite dated, apparently not followed up?

We could ask for instance why the encopresis-affected boys (Morrow et al, 1997) were not asked obvious questions about abuse: suffering instead many humiliating physical examinations. We could ask why the humane team of Arnold and colleagues (1990) did not ask an obvious question about what had happened to the young woman with urinary incontinence and rectal bleeding who was examined by baffled gynaecologists, urologists and genito-urinary specialists. We could ask why it has been easier to make a metaphorical interpretation of sexual abuse survivors developing PVCD than a literal one. I have wondered why, since I published my paper which discussed the nature of oral sexual abuse (Nelson, 2002), only child sexual abuse survivors, and professionals working with political torture, have ever contacted me about it, and said that it was accurate. I received in more than ten years no other professional contacts, nor to my knowledge has research been pursued during that time about, for example, the child protection implications of PVCD.

Genuine ignorance

There is still a widespread assumption that most child sexual abuse is about inappropriate touching and fondling, rather than more serious sexual assaults on various parts of a child's body. Perpetrators do not publicly reveal the acts they commit. Many survivors do not give details through shame, embarrassment, traumatic amnesia, or their wish to spare the professional listener shock and distress. Sensitive researchers do not press survivors for physical detail of abuse. I had never asked any victim what happened in oral sexual abuse until I wrote my 2002 paper – and only after a survivor friend trusted me with some information about it.

Too distasteful and distressing?

Widespread ignorance may be cemented in place by understandable reluctance to contemplate very distressing or disgusting acts against children. What cannot be contemplated cannot exist. Many professionals still find it unthinkable that parents and close relatives can inflict very sadistic practices on children. Thus, in their work on violent child abuse and fatal child abuse in Leeds, Doctors Chris Hobbs and Jane Wynne recalled this inability to contemplate what the physical signs indicated:

> The premeditated and sometimes repetitive way
> that adults may deliberately burn children made us
> consider torture as the only accurate description.
> However, several medical colleagues were unwilling
> to entertain this possibility, and diagnosed unlikely
> or exotic diseases. (Hobbs and Wynne, 1994, p. 215)

Taking on board the messages of physical signs can also have unpalatable political and social consequences, which can bring a backlash against the reliability of physical signs. For example in her analysis of the Cleveland child abuse case, Bea Campbell (1998) pointed to the implication of the reflex anal dilatation (RAD) sign: that anal abuse, including of male children, by heterosexual men was much more widespread than had been assumed.

Dr Amanda Williams, who works with victims of political torture, has described her experience that findings in her own field often proved unwelcome, particularly if they reflected on governments who denied that they sanctioned torture. The messengers became the unpopular ones: "Somehow in medicine, I think some sense of otherness attaches not only to survivors, but to those who advocate for them and raise issues" (personal communication, 2012).

But there is surely less and less excuse for being wilfully blind given that we now have not thousands, but millions of child abuse images online – many of which show sexual acts being committed against children to suit every perverted or violent taste. In terms of considering possible effects of these on the body, there needs to be recording and research, however distressing the subject matter, as well as international attempts to combat this trade, and protect children at risk.

Tenacious psyche-soma theories

Another reason for not considering the obvious is that there is no major body to speak out strongly for it, through an 'unwitting conspiracy' among people from very different influential groups. They all find it difficult to look – even when this is necessary – beyond a tenacious belief in very close psyche-soma interconnections:

- Many *orthodox medicine practitioners* have limited knowledge of child sexual abuse or of particular mental conditions. Many also find it difficult to admit not knowing what exactly is causing a medical problem. As we saw from remarks which survivors have experienced in medical settings, a bowdlerised, popular, unsubtle understanding of psyche-soma links has been tempting to fall back upon when faced with so-called 'heartsink' patients, whose conditions remain baffling and who are mentally unwell.

- *Psychosomatic medicine specialists*, while usually sympathetic to victims of sexual abuse, may have limited knowledge of it. Their belief in psyche-soma interconnections can amount to dogma. They lead most of the research, publications, and treatments for medically unexplained symptoms, and they suggest diagnoses and solutions. They have a vested interest in promoting and funding the (admittedly underfunded) *psychological* therapies as solutions.

- *Many therapists, counsellors, and voluntary sector support groups using complementary and holistic approaches* are knowledgeable about child sexual abuse, but share a sincere belief in psyche-soma-spiritual interconnections, which can also amount to dogma. They often understandably wish to de-medicalise conditions which result from social conditions or life experiences, and seek alternatives. But sometimes these conditions do have medical components, diagnoses or solutions.

Some additional problems

Other significant and practical problems have hindered detection and recording of physical health issues following child sexual abuse which need to be addressed by much closer multidisciplinary working, and by better lifelong recording and record-keeping.

- Defects, disorganisation or gaps in lifelong medical records, and lack of communication between paediatricians and practitioners in adult medicine, all work against continuity of observation, recording and interpretation.

- The division of adult medicine into many specialities makes it difficult even for alert, curious practitioners to see the 'whole picture'. For example, an ear, nose and throat specialist is unlikely to be considering problems in the oesophagus, let alone gynaecological problems, in a patient with a baffling disorder of the throat.

Recommendations for future action and research

What kinds of research and collaboration might further elucidate the links between childhood sexual assault and physical health problems in later life, and which governments, health authorities and major research funders could support?

- Where papers have been summarised here that suggest damage caused by sexual assaults may be major influences in disorders considered functional or psychosomatic, specialists in the relevant medical areas should carry out research into this possibility.

- Concrete evidence of types of assault, from samples of the huge quantities available of seized online child sexual abuse images, should be recorded and analysed. They are not currently examined in order to detect assaults that might have long-term physical effects, or to explain baffling conditions, but for other criminal justice purposes – which have understandably had priority. There is room for both.

- The physical descriptions of assaults which child sexual abuse survivors have already put on record (both in research and in police investigations) should be gathered, collated and analysed. Sensitive research with CSA survivors and their support agencies, using both quantitative and qualitative methods and with respect for confidentiality, should also take place on types of childhood assault they experienced, and any links they see with their own health conditions. Researchers (including me) have applied for funding for such research, but it has repeatedly been declined.

- Consultations among GPs, nursing staff in general practice, and survivors through their support organisations could be very valuable in devising and piloting sensitive means of conveying to health staff types of childhood sexual injury which the survivors experienced. This information could help in diagnosis and treatment of conditions.

- Prospective (longtitudinal) studies of the physical health of children and young people whose sexual abuse history is recorded should take place.

- Collaborative research is needed with specialists working against political torture, and with international specialists working with physical health problems after child marriage. This is on the impact of certain types of assault, especially repeated assault, and on the best possible evidence-based treatments and pain services.

- Studies should be made of the techniques used by the expanding field of sports medicine in its detailed examination of stress injuries, repetitive injuries and other forms of damage, with a view to adapting these for abuse-related injury.

- Multidisciplinary groups of professionals with a special interest in the medium- and long-term health effects of child abuse should be launched, to meet regularly and work collaboratively on research about causes, diagnoses and treatments, with a central body to organise conferences and seminars. These multidisciplinary groups could include, for example, paediatricians, interested GPs and dentists, and specialists in psychosomatic medicine, gynaecology, forensic, GI, urinary, respiratory and chronic pain conditions. They should consult and listen to the cumulative experience of third sector agencies working with abused children and adults. Valuable examples of the benefits of such could be learned from existing Special Interest Groups (SIG) such as Pain Related to Torture, Organised Violence and War – part of the Association for the Study of Pain.[2]

Why open this Pandora's box?

Uncovering the reality and detail of sexual assaults against children is distressing for professionals, including researchers, to hear, and for survivors to recount or admit. Why do we need to pluck up the courage and 'go there'?

- There has already been more than enough silencing in child sexual abuse. If we feel disgusted and distressed, imagine how much more disgusted and distressed victims feel. Turning a blind eye can only continue to aid perpetrators everywhere.

- The experiences of child sexual abuse survivors, who have so often been branded somatisers, hypochondriacs or heartsink patients, would be validated; they would be seen as victims of serious crime; this would increase the respect and dignity they would receive in healthcare settings.

- Informed knowledge, understanding of the full range of causal factors, and long-term research collaboration with specialists in related fields would grow.

- There could be several specific child protection improvements, with sexual abuse being picked up earlier in life, and with a renewal of interest in physical signs in children suggestive of possible sexual abuse. PVCD is one example given here. Paediatricians might at last receive the professional and public support to work closely with specialists in teenage and adult health.

- Informed knowledge could point to a range of possible treatments and therapeutic interventions, including those

---

[2] www.iasp-pain.org/SIG/TOVW

learned from orthopaedic practice and sports medicine, which could be piloted and evaluated. There would be better prospects of ameliorating the pain and suffering of CSA survivors, and the length of time that they endured these.

- If the full facts about the seriousness and impact on physical, as well as mental, health of sexual assaults in childhood were realised, this would increase the perceived seriousness of CSA in the eyes of society, strengthening the priority for prevention and deterrence. It would be more likely to become a major public health issue, as serious and widespread as mental ill health; and to move beyond psychosomatic medicine, into the mainstream of NHS services.

EIGHT

Producing radical change in mental health: implications of the trauma paradigm

Introduction

Our psychiatric hospitals, secure hospitals and outpatient psychiatric clinics are packed with the victims of crime – especially with victims of child sexual abuse (CSA). This fact continues to be heavily obscured due to dominant medical model paradigms in mental health. As a result, such hospitals and clinics remain major parties to the concealment of the extent and impact of such crimes.

This chapter considers the persistence of biomedical models of mental ill health despite repeated and continuing evidence for trauma aetiologies, and discusses some reasons why this evidence has been consistently ignored. It argues that it is very important, but not sufficient, to challenge biomedical models of mental illness, to challenge current diagnostic labelling, and to oppose coercive techniques of restraint: as many committed critics within and beyond the mental health professions have already done. It is also very important, but not sufficient, to provide – for survivors of abuse and indeed survivors of other serious life adversities – adequate, humanistic, caring, appropriate therapeutic and support services, and genuinely to involve service users in shaping those services.

But the major implications for *prevention* of the crimes which continue to make so many people mentally ill must also, at last, be fully acknowledged and acted upon. Given the major role accorded to prevention in many other areas of public health, it is after all extraordinary and unusual that they have not been. Thus our mental health systems, with forceful prompting from governments and health authorities, need actively to contribute to multidisciplinary efforts to prevent and reduce CSA.

This chapter suggests some directions for such work. They include new working alliances with those working against other forms of violence and abuse, nationally and internationally; the redirection of some significant resources; a regular means for survivors of CSA in all mental health settings to pass on vital information about perpetrators; and funding for new forms and topics of research.

This chapter argues that governments, senior policymakers and commissioners in mental health – working with those professionals and service user groups who urgently seek change – must do all they can to enact and enforce change, rather than continuing to defer to powerful professional lobbies, particularly that of biological psychiatry. They need to do this not because somebody has told them to, but because they finally find it intolerable and unacceptable that our mental health hospitals and clinics should continue to be warehouses for the victims of serious crime. Victims who are more often punished and stigmatised again by the system we have at present, instead of being routinely protected, supported, and offered routes to justice.

Historic resistance to a trauma paradigm

The long history of resistance to the trauma paradigm of mental illness is well known and documented, but this powerful summary from Ann Jennings, with reference to sexual abuse trauma, is particularly trenchant:

> Resistance to a sexual abuse trauma paradigm has existed for more than 130 years, during which time the etiological role of childhood sexual violation in mental illness has been alternatively discovered and then denied. In 1860, the prevalence and import of child sexual abuse was exposed by Amboise Tardieu,

in 1896 by Sigmund Freud, in 1932 by Sandor Ferenczi, and in 1962 and 1984 by C. Henry Kempe.

"Each exposure was met by the scientific community with distaste, rejection, or discreditation..... Freud, faced with his colleagues' ridicule of and hostility to his discoveries, sacrificed his major insight into the etiology of mental illness and replaced his theory of trauma by the view that his patients had 'fantasized' their early memories of rape and seduction. ...100 years later, in spite of countless instances of documented abuse, this tradition of denial and victim blame continues to thrive. Psychiatrist Roland Summit refers to this denial as 'nescience' or 'deliberate, beatific ignorance'. (Jennings, 1994, pp. 6–7)

The rise and rise of biogenetic models

Under the biogenetic model of mental illness, services and research have been dominated for decades by a reductionist focus on biological phenomena, with minimal consideration of the *social* context within which genes and brains operate. Respected progressive voices such as Pilgrim (2014) have described how this model has been led by supposedly scientific diagnoses based on collections of symptoms, and by a search for technical 'fixes' to disorders which have attracted huge research funding. Radical psychiatrists like Pat Bracken argue that ethics, values and meaning in theories of mental health and illness have become secondary in this biogenetic quest (Bracken and Thomas, 2005, Rapley et al, 2011). Research on rats about aspects of schizophrenia has received more funding than research into psychosocial factors in mental illness, such as a history of child abuse. These psychosocial factors have been seen as having scant influence, except grudgingly as a possible vulnerability factor (Read et al, 2009; Read and Bentall, 2012, Bentall and Varese, 2012).

Hugely expensive drugs bill

The psychoses have been located firmly within the biomedical model, subject to heavy investment in antipsychotic medications. The dynamic among biogenetic psychiatrists, academic researchers and the international pharmaceutical companies has increased the power and wealth of such companies. These have extended the markets for their drugs, despite evidence either of dangers to health, or of failure to make any difference to patients' conditions (Moncrieff et al, 2005; Goldsmith and Moncrieff, 2011; Middleton and Moncrieff, 2011). The pharmaceutical companies have extended their markets through for example the considerable recent expansion of the 'bipolar disorder' diagnosis in American children, and through the addition of 15 new disorders in the DSM-V manual.[1] In the UK, this has contributed to what is now a massive NHS drugs bill for mental conditions (Ilyas and Moncrieff, 2012; Busfield, 2013).

A study of prescriptions and costs of drugs in the UK between 1998 and 2010 found rising trends in prescriptions per year in almost all psychiatric drugs, with patients also receiving longer drug treatments. Antipsychotics overtook antidepressants as the most costly psychiatric medication, with costs rising by 22% per year, even though many patients prescribed did not have a psychosis at all. Increasing prescriptions of lithium and sodium valproate may, Ilyas and Moncrieff suggest, reflect the mysteriously increasing diagnosis of bipolar disorder. Significantly, the study found no reduction in prescribing since the Increasing Access to Psychological Therapies programme was established in the UK in 2006 (Ilyas and Moncrieff, 2012).

Biogenetic theories can be comfortable and non-challenging for governments to approve, as they sidestep awkward political and social questions about how human beings treat each other, and the impact of living conditions, unemployment, life experiences and racist responses to ethnic diversity (Fernando, 2011). But so too, we should remember, do some non-drug therapies, particularly the CBT dominant among 'talking

---

[1] http://dsm.psychiatryonline.org/doi/book/10.1176/appi.books.9780890425596

therapies'– useful as this can be with some conditions, and at later stages of recovery. So too do some often-heard ways to reduce depression, which put the onus on the patient: eat healthily, take exercise, laugh more!

Doubting biomedical models: abuse survivors' negative experiences

The many survivors of sexual abuse with whom I have worked have not had a lot to laugh about. Their overwhelmingly negative experiences of mental health services must inevitably raise scepticism about the effectiveness of many medications, of current assessments, and of the accuracy of psychiatric diagnoses.

Reid et al in 2003 established clear research links between hallucinations/delusions, and a child abuse history. In my qualitative research with both women (Nelson, 2001, 2004a) and men (Nelson, 2009; Nelson et al, 2013) who survived child sexual abuse, all had experienced mental ill health, often including hallucinations and other psychotic symptoms. *All* had attempted suicide as children, teenagers or adults – often several times. Yet the experience of myself and others working with sexual abuse, of attending major anti-suicide conferences over the years, is that proven links between suicide and sexual abuse (Wiederman et al, 1998; Dube et al, 2001; Oates, 2004) rarely received a conference 'slot' – if these links were mentioned at all.

The survivors in my studies had received a bewildering range of diagnoses, which kept changing. These included depression, anxiety, postnatal depression, borderline personality disorder, schizo-affective disorder, schizophrenia, paranoid schizophrenia, bipolar disorder, seasonal affective disorder, dissociative disorder, and post-traumatic stress disorder. Few had even been asked about a history of CSA or other maltreatment.

Most had been given a range of psychiatric medications, often several at once. Most had suffered significant side effects and drug dependency. Polypharmacy raised severe problems in relation to drug dependency and general health (Nelson, 2012b).[2]

For example, following his father's violent sexual assaults and a traumatic army gang rape, Gordon[3] was repeatedly admitted to psychiatric hospital. Despite some excellent individual staff, he recalled a bewildering number of diagnoses and medications, debilitating effects, failure to explore his trauma, and disbelief:

> "I was told I was being treated for schizophrenia, personality disorder … I was having flashbacks, seizures, ranting and raving … I would re-enact flashbacks to the rape and my childhood. I was (once) on 35 tablets a day … anti-depressants, tranquillisers, painkillers, anti-psychotics … it suppressed all emotions. I was totally lethargic, slurred speech, drooling at the mouth." (Nelson, 2009; Nelson et al, 2013)

Adam, victim of extreme sexual abuse by multiple perpetrators, was once on five powerful drugs:

> "The heaviest I've been (after medication) is just under 30 stone. I didn't function … slept for long periods … up to 18 hours a day, and was up at night. And crazy driving … I was off my cage, there was no way at all that I was going to be driving safely." (Nelson, 2009; Nelson et al, 2013)

At the other extreme, several were refused admission to hospital when they felt they needed it, or were refused a diagnosis, because 'only' life experience, not diagnosed mental illness, was the problem. Roy recalled:

---

[2] Polypharmacy involves current use of multiple medications. These will be necessary for some people, and it will constitute best care for them. However, polypharmacy is also linked with prescribing too many, or unnecessary, medicines – at dosages or frequencies higher than are needed, and with some unfortunate side effects.

[3] All names have been changed.

"Despite this terrible feeling that I had, this portent of doom that hung over me like a cloud all the time, she [psychiatrist] says: 'there's nothing wrong with you, on you go. You're fine.'" (Nelson, 2009; Nelson et al, 2013)

Psychological assessment via endless forms and tick-boxes was particularly disliked, after which they were often told that talking treatments would be too distressing. Tina, assessed for eating disorders, memorably captured the way patients had to fit into services, rather than the other way round, after she filled in a psychological assessment form: "Well they put me out … and it was like, cheerio! I had to circle things and I think they thought I wasn't right for them."

Clare, a victim of CSA and then of sexual abuse by a mental health professional, recalled:

"I sat for two hours answering questions … at the end of it they said … 'I don't think you're suitable for psychotherapy.' I said, 'why would that be?' He said, 'don't you think it would upset you too much?' I thought, rejected because I'd be upset? That's why I'm here, to speak to someone, because I'm f–in' upset!" (Nelson, 2001, 2004a)

Female and male survivors in my research studies showed many similarities in naming aspects of services which they found unhelpful or damaging. These included employing only medical models of mental illness; dealing with emotional pain by polypharmacy; not asking about a possible CSA history; disbelieving or dismissing this history; failing to offer 'talking treatments' to address their trauma; giving a stigmatising borderline personality disorder (BPD) diagnosis, which could repeatedly exclude them from services; making formulaic assessments; and retraumatising them through physical restraints or other punishments. Women especially noted the lack of physical safety in acute wards, men the lack of practical support with daily living (Nelson, 2001, 2004a, 2009; Nelson et al, 2013).

Research evidence for the trauma paradigm

Biomedical models have poorly reflected the care needs of mental health service users, particularly survivors of childhood trauma. Yet there have been growing challenges to this model from research as well as from service users themselves, *even while* the medical model has increased in use and influence. There has been research evidence for decades that a high percentage of people with mental ill health experienced serious childhood adversities, with child sexual abuse prominent. For example, Craine et al (1988) found more than half of female state hospital patients studied had been sexually abused as children or adolescents. In most cases, staff were unaware of their patients' CSA histories. Although 66% of the abused patients met diagnostic criteria for post-traumatic stress disorder, none had received that diagnosis.

Links with borderline disorder

Judith Herman's valuable, groundbreaking work on complex trauma kickstarted an increasing recognition of the similarities between this trauma and borderline personality disorder (BPD). Even before Herman's classic work *Trauma and Recovery* (1992), Herman et al (1989) had found that 81% of patients with BPD interviewed for their study revealed major trauma, 68% sexual abuse. Darves-Bornoz et al (1995) had found more than a third of women diagnosed with schizophrenia had been victims of contact child sexual abuse. Kessler et al's major review analysed data from 21 countries and concluded that 'childhood adversities have strong associations with all classes of disorders'. Those associated with maladaptive family functioning were the strongest predictors of disorders (Kessler et al, 2010).

Links with the psychoses

While trauma histories have become more widely accepted by conventional psychiatry in conditions such as depression, anxiety and phobias, the painstaking research of John Read and colleagues has been vital in revealing high rates of child abuse history in patients with the most serious conditions, the psychoses. This has been a major challenge to the biogenetic model. Child abuse has been found to be related to most severe levels of disturbance and dysfunction in adulthood. Hallucinations and delusions, including instructions to kill oneself, have been much more common in psychotic patients with an abuse history than in those without (Read, 1998; Read et al 2001, 2003). Varese et al's meta-analysis (2012) provided important confirmation that childhood adversities increase the risk of psychosis. Meanwhile, a huge contribution to this particular understanding of psychosis has also been made by service users and ex-users in the Hearing Voices Network, which now extends over 20 countries.[4]

Challenges to diagnostic reliance and 'schizophrenia'

Critiques of diagnostic reliance in general have increased within and beyond the professions of psychiatry and psychology (such as Kinderman et al, 2013).

The very existence of a diagnosable illness called 'schizophrenia' is increasingly questioned. The Critical Psychiatry Network,[5] a professional pressure group which has also argued powerfully against coercion and restraint of psychiatric patients, argues that the diagnosis has no scientific basis, is harmful and stigmatising to patients, and a barrier to recovery. Complex experiences, say these psychiatrists, are stripped of their meaning by identifying them as symptoms, paying scant regard to cultural contexts and personal narratives. The Network points out substantial evidence linking the experience of hearing voices and other psychotic experiences to trauma and abuse in adults and children (Romme and Escher, 1993; Read et al, 2003; Romme et al, 2009; Bebbington et al, 2011).

Advances in neuroscience

Meanwhile, major and continuing advances in neuroscience have challenged biomedical model explanations for changes in the brain and nervous system, such as a decrease in hippocampal

---

[4] www.hearing-voices.org
[5] www.criticalpsychiatry.co.uk

volume, or hypervigilance. These have been linked to the effects of severe stress and trauma in early childhood. The stress-regulating functions of the HPA axis have been found particularly important. This topic is also discussed in relation to physical health (Chapter Seven). Research findings in this field have been reviewed by researchers such as Twardosz and Lutzke (2009) and de Bellis and Zisk (2014)while Anda and his team have explored the convergence of neurobiology and epidemiology on survivors of sexual abuse (Anda et al, 2006).

Read et al (2009) proposed *a traumagenic neurodevelopmental model* for psychosis. They explored developing knowledge about how epigenetic processes turn gene transcription on and off, through mechanisms influenced by a person's social and environmental experiences. Read et al believe that to understand emerging evidence of the relationship between adverse childhood events and psychosis, these epigenetic processes, especially those involving the stress-regulating functions of the HPA axis, need to be integrated with research on psychological mechanisms through which childhood trauma can lead to psychotic experiences.

These continuing advances in neuroscience hold out increased possibilities that the needs of many people in the mental health system will be recognised and diagnosed as the result of *trauma,* not of a biogenetic condition. However, two significant dangers need to be guarded against. First, there is the risk that these advances are used only to advocate and research quick technological 'fixes' for traumatised patients – without following through the implications for prevention of child abuse and other human brutalities, or meeting the needs which traumatised adult victims have to enable recovery. The second danger comes if concentration on brain changes prenatally, in infancy and early childhood comes to dominate in neuroscience, resulting in further personal blaming and stigmatisation of poor and disadvantaged mothers (Edwards et al, 2015).

Advances in understanding of dissociation

In dissociative experiences, there is disconnection among the usually integrated human functions of consciousness, memory, identity and perception. Pierre Janet, in the 19th century, was the first clinician to show clearly how dissociation can be a direct psychological defence against overwhelming experiences, and how dissociation plays an important role in post-traumatic experiences (van der Hart and Horst, 1989). Janet's rehabilitation has continued to promote great interest, and continuing research, into the role of dissociation after trauma in our understandings of mental illness and 'personality disorders'. This is especially so for the most severe, such as dissociative identity disorder, which has been explained in its complex impact on body and mind by distinguished investigators such as Bessel van der Kolk and Ellert Nijenhuis (van der Kolk et al, 2001, 2005; Nijenhuis et al, 2003; van der Kolk, 2014).

In examining complex PTSD and dissociation, Van der Hart et al (2004) described how being traumatised interferes with the development of a cohesive personality structure in children. In trauma-related dissociation, two divided parts of the personality influence the way in which intrusive re-experiencing of traumatic events, and avoidance or numbing can alternate. Traumatic memories are not integrated properly. They are mainly 'somato-sensory', intensely emotional, hallucinatory, fragmentary, and involuntary. Dissociated parts of the personality that are fixated on defence tend to intrude when someone is faced with a real or perceived threat. Dissociative symptoms can include amnesia, loss of emotion (numbing), loss of some cognitive functions, traumatic memories and nightmares, rages, self harm and uncontrolled emotions.

Certain symptoms of what has been diagnosed as schizophrenia – hallucinations, hearing voices commenting or arguing internally, thought insertion and withdrawal – are common in patients with dissociative disorders (Dell and O'Neil, 2010). Exploration of these processes is shedding new light on, among others, the precise aetiologies of hallucinations and delusions (Read et al, 2001, 2003). This expanding body of research is again challenging biogenetic models of the psychoses.

Why resistance to the trauma paradigm?

In face, then, of all these challenges, and in face of research evidence from so many sources, the key question becomes why the medical model of understanding madness and its amelioration through 'diagnose and drug' remain so dominant. I believe it is important that all mental health professionals, of every status, ask themselves this question, and speak out to us and to their colleagues about the answers.

Defence of greed and status quo?

On the international power, influence and self-interest of major pharmaceutical companies, Read et al (2014) make the harsh judgement that such companies' main motive has been 'the morally blind economic imperative to increase profit for shareholders and bonuses for themselves'. In one example, in 2012 GlaxoSmithKline was fined US$3 billion, after admitting a scheme to hide unhelpful scientific evidence, to manipulate articles in medical journals and reward sympathetic doctors, in order to increase sales of psychiatric drugs to children (Foley, 2012).

The British psychologist Mary Boyle (2011, 2013) goes further in provocatively arguing that mental health services actually function to deny the importance of child abuse and neglect, domestic and sexual violence, discrimination, poverty and unemployment. And that these events mainly involve relatively powerful groups – governments, corporations, men, white people, adults – damaging less powerful groups. The medical model, she says, camouflages this social control, giving politicians the perfect excuse to do nothing about reducing social problems underlying distress.

I have already argued (in Chapters One and Two) that a powerful continuing incentive to the denial of sexual abuse has been the benefit which many abusers of all classes gain from access to children and young people, for both individual and organised sexual abuse. The dismissal until recently of sexual abuse memories in psychoanalysis as fantasy, along with persisting attempts to deny the processes of recovered traumatic memory through the invention of false memory syndrome and the intimidation of therapists (see Chapter Two) are memorable examples of the role of denial of sexual abuse in mental health. Also, while most mental health staff themselves are of course not abusers, their profession like all others contains perpetrators in their own ranks, with many potential victims among these particularly vulnerable clients.

Self-protection?

Staff can also protect themselves with a silencing response when, with insufficient support, they must witness the pain of people who have endured terrible things, otherwise risking vicarious traumatisation and 'burnout'. There is, too, an awkwardness, embarrassment and sense of inadequacy in addressing child sexual abuse trauma in particular. This contributes heavily to the widespread, defensive response 'we mustn't open that can of worms', and to persistent failure to ask routine questions about sexual abuse trauma, even when such inquiry is professionally advised (Jacobson and Herald, 1990; Goater and Meehan, 1998; Nelson, 2001; Nelson and Hampson, 2008). Professionals who are survivors themselves, but who have not addressed their own pain, can also find it extremely difficult to open themselves to reminders and triggers.

I gathered, during my research projects, numerous examples of mental health staff and social workers' reasons for not asking clients about a history of sexual abuse, and for not working with that abuse. These appear in the box below. It suggests considerable nervousness and discomfort with the subject among the very professionals who care for traumatised people. It reveals strikingly the persistent silencing of survivors, and the many excuses for doing so. It suggests the pervasive influence of actual teaching 'not to go there'. Sue Hampson and I never managed to pinpoint where such an instruction came from and comes from originally

We don't have the skills

We don't have the training

We don't have the resources

We don't have the staffing

We don't have the time

We might encourage false memories

He's always telling wild stories

Saying he's been abused is part of his illness

She's always talking about it, but I think
it's attention-seeking

Asking about sexual abuse?

It's not part of our remit

We're not funded for that

We're not allowed to ask that

It's not on our list of outcomes

She would decompensate if we asked about that

He'd break down completely

She'd start slashing herself

It'd make him MUCH worse

Patients might commit suicide and we could be sued

She's been assessed as too vulnerable

We've been trained not to go there, that it might do more
harm than good

It's not proper psychiatry – just life circumstances

There's no evidence base for treatment

Not sure it would be helpful, you know

The environment isn't suitable, another place would be better

They're not with us long enough

We'd rather refer them to someone skilled

There's nowhere to refer them

The abuse wasn't that serious

Nothing much happened – wouldn't it be more damaging to make a fuss?

It's better to put the past behind you

We can't open that can of worms...

Kids will only tell us when they're ready

Asking would be too intrusive

We'd have to do something about it then

We'd trigger a court case, she wouldn't want that

We'd have to break confidentiality, they don't want that

Such a can of worms to open in a small community

Such a can of worms to open when you work with the family

You can't just go round accusing people!

I'd be too embarrassed

Couldn't deal with that stuff myself

Too close to home for me

It's so common, we'd be overwhelmed...

(that remains an important question). But the precise expression 'mustn't open that can of worms' occurred so often that we illustrated the cover of our booklet, which described sensitive ways of asking about a sexual abuse history, with a 'can of worms' image (Nelson and Hampson, 2008).

Tasks for the future: treatment, support and prevention

Support towards amelioration or recovery: the need for parallel services

There have been several welcome developments in mainstream psychiatry, like the increased willingness of conventional psychiatry journals to publish trauma-informed papers (such as Read and Bentall, 2012) and the fact that researchers now have to declare drug company income. Despite this, I firmly believe the evidence from the persistence of the biomedical model through control, pseudo-scientific diagnosis and vast global industries of medications, and from continued ignoring of the clear role of trauma, is that sufficient reform of services to people suffering life traumas is never likely to come from within conventional services. It will only occur in a minority of services and pockets of imaginative practice, nationally and internationally – however excellent these continue to be.

I cannot share the psychologist Andrew Moskowitz's confidence that a new paradigm in mental health is finally emerging, with a central role for trauma and dissociation. He believes conditions are right, recalling that Kuhn (1970) argued that paradigms change when: (a) a period of crisis develops in which the paradigm fails to adequately answer questions considered fundamental; (b) phenomena not clearly compatible with the paradigm are observed; and (c) a suitable alternative paradigm explaining many of the previous findings and anomalies comes to light (Moskowitz, 2011).

The problem is that all those conditions have already been met for many decades in mental health without change happening, and because such powerful forces and interests are ranged against it. Sexual abuse, most of all, is remarkably defended and denied in all spheres of life. Many staff and patients will have the experience that radical and progressive work with clients has actually gone backwards in many psychiatric hospitals and clinics, as the medical model has predominated. To take one example, the Royal Edinburgh Hospital was once a centre for imaginative nurse-led groupwork with patients, and for more egalitarian teamwork among staff (Nelson, 2001).

Thus a strategy of setting up more and more parallel services – including residential and respite centres – beside conventional services may prove a more productive route to change. This means progressive professionals, psychiatrists, psychologists and psychiatric nurses coming together nationally and regionally, setting up or joining such establishments, instead of trying to reform from within, and supported by as many funders and commissioners of services as possible. In alliance with third sector mental health organisations and major user groups such as the Hearing Voices Network,[6] they would run parallel services. Some of course do this already, but far more are needed. The more parallel services that exist and work well, the more they will woo others to join. Pressure to change will also be placed on conventional services.

Staff would, I believe, substitute current frustrations and low morale for the excitement and professional satisfaction of fulfilling their commitment to service users, while many disillusioned former staff would return enthusiastically to mental health work as a result.

What do service users want?

This is surely not a counsel of despair but of realism, because so many even of the simple changes have failed to happen. Consider what survivors of sexual abuse say they have found most helpful about good mental health services, and what they would like to see. These are straightforward, low-tech, often financially inexpensive things, which also reflect what many other service users – not necessarily victims of trauma – value. So why are they still rarely happening, or only in pockets of good practice?

---

[6]   www.hearing-voices.org

Many of my own research findings with both abused women and abused men have reflected other studies too (such as Dale, 1999, O'Leary, 2009, McGregor et al, 2010). Survivors of child sexual abuse most valued staff who were:

- secure about boundaries, but related with warmth, empathy and kindness;

- able to ask about abuse history without fear, and had courage to 'stay with' distress;

- were informed about the effects of CSA, or keen to learn;

- showed respect, belief and acceptance;

- understood gender issues for both sexes;

- gave them time to talk – even small amounts of time were much valued;

- respectfully consulted them on their treatment, trying to reach agreed decisions about it; and

- were imaginative and eclectic in techniques to address the impact of trauma.

Survivors found sympathetic, informed GPs vital, even life-changing gateways to good services.

The survivors sought:

- warmth and personal safety in mental health environments and settings;

- more 'talking treatments' without strict time limits, particularly counselling or other therapeutic approaches focused on the needs sexual abuse survivors themselves bring; and

- crisis and respite houses, outside hospital settings.

The most consistent research finding in both women and men was that staff who helped most to improve their mental health did *not* come from any one professional background, discipline or therapeutic approach. Instead they ranged across volunteer and paid counsellors, mental health social workers, voluntary sector project staff, psychiatric nurses, psychologists and consultant psychiatrists. Their personal skills with abuse trauma, their patience, respect, good communication, empathy and courage proved key to aiding recovery (Nelson 2001, 2009, 2013; Nelson and Hampson, 2008).

This information challenges professional hierarchies, and current professional qualifications and training in mental health. It will be threatening and subversive to many professionals who value status and hierarchy. But it is surely attractive to other staff who value working in more egalitarian, multidisciplinary team settings.

Not a diminution of specialist skills

This finding does *not* imply that specialist training and therapies are unimportant in assisting survivors of child sexual abuse trauma.

Issues faced by some survivors in particular need more prolonged, highly skilled therapeutic interventions: for example in work with forms of dissociation after severe and complex abuse, psychotic episodes or non-epileptic seizures. Nor does it mean that ameliorating distressing symptoms is unimportant – using medications with discrimination and in full consultation with patients, and continuing to explore the positive impact of techniques such as Eye Movement Desensitisation and Reprocessing (Edmond et al, 1999; Edmond et al, 2004; Korn, 2009) to reduce post-traumatic symptoms. Parallel services need to include very skilled multidisciplinary work with sexually abused people with dissociative disorders and voice-hearing. Compassionate trauma work with patients in state and secure hospitals is especially urgent, building on the valuable, highly gender-informed work of Dr Sam Warner with women in secure hospitals (Warner and Wilkins, 2004; Warner, 2009).

Rather, the message is that learning specialised techniques (or being highly qualified) is not sufficient *in itself*, without respect, genuine empathy and willingness to listen.

Broadening alliances

In developing more parallel services, progressive mental health staff working with sexual abuse can make active alliances with reformers whose main concern is the relationship of poverty, bad housing conditions or unemployment to mental ill health; and with those working against domestic violence, political torture and combat PTSD.

This is not least because we can agree many basics of that agenda: the power of narrative in understanding and healing in mental health (Mehl-Madrona, 2010; Kalathil, 2011);[7] the central role of values and ethics; positive belief in recovery (Roberts et al, 2006); the importance of user-informed services and consultative working; the reduced use of medications; widespread crisis and respite centres; and opposition to coercion and restraint. We have excellent models to draw upon of humane and compassionate care, such as Phil Barker's widely respected Tidal Model (Barker and Buchanan-Barker, 2004).[8] This is the recovery-focused approach developed collaboratively by professionals and service users, which involves their continuing collaboration throughout the recovery process, including at points of maximum distress (Brookes, 2006; Lafferty and Davidson, 2006).

In making alliances across professionals and lay people the Critical Psychiatry Network, some of whose leading members published the important paper *Psychiatry beyond the current paradigm* (Bracken et al, 2012), can play important roles. So can SPS UK,[9] part of the International Society for Psychological and Social Approaches to Psychosis, (Martindale, 2012) which supports psychological approaches in their own workplaces: approaches ranging from psychodynamic, cognitive behavioural,

---

[7] See also http://mentalhealthrecovery.omeka.net/exhibits/show/andrew voyce/recovery/the-power-of-narrative

[8] www.tidal-model.com

[9] www.ispsuk.org

arts-based, and family to holistic approaches. So can so many psychiatric nurses who currently leave statutory settings disillusioned with being simply the controllers of patients, and dispensers of medication.

Professionals can make close alliances with user groups in the burgeoning Recovery Movement and with groups such as the First Person Plural (dissociative survivors)[10] and the Hearing Voices Network (HVN). If a relatively disempowered, often marginalised group such as HVN can achieve such success and such remarkable expansion (with nearly 200 support groups in England alone), then surely progressive mental health staff can be inspired to maintain and redouble their own efforts?

However none of these valuable changes will be sufficient, I believe, without strong and determined political direction, and without clear understanding of the importance of prevention. It is not enough to help people recover better from things they should never have had to suffer.

Governments and health authorities must lead on system change

Senior professionals in our current mental health systems have had adequate time to make the changes in diagnosis and treatment suggested by evidence of the trauma paradigm, and evidence of the humane treatment, therapies and settings which service users value. Therefore, central and devolved governments in the UK, along with other funders of services and research, commissioners, senior managers, health and social work authorities must, I believe, contribute vitally to changing mental health systems and services, funding parallel services, and promoting the prevention of trauma.

However, too few national and local politicians and health managers will see sufficient need for change, or have the will to enforce it, without the confidence and knowledge to stop deferring to medical model psychiatrists, who remain so influential in mental health services and as leads in mental health teams. They need to be informed in order to take on the powerful lobbies, and their relationship with the international

---

[10] www.firstpersonplural.org.uk

drugs companies. Informed – and thus disturbed – about all the evidence which challenges conventional treatments and diagnoses, and which demonstrates such a high prevalence of trauma victims in the mental health system.

Ensuring that they have this knowledge will call for concerted lobbying, and the supply of accessible information, by the many critics who are coming together. This will be the central merit of repeating and summarising evidence for the trauma paradigm, and for the failures of expensive medications. Such evidence needs to be presented to them repeatedly and accessibly.

Plan for progressive change

Central and devolved governments throughout the UK need to announce a 10–15 year plan for progressive change, based on the clear public statement that a high percentage of mental ill health is the result of traumatic life experience, particularly childhood abuse trauma. They need to announce that services and research will gradually be reorganised in accordance with this knowledge, including knowledge of, and response to, gender issues in mental health. They need to announce that service users will be fully respected for their needs as victims of crime; that it is now in the 21st century totally unacceptable that psychiatric hospitals remain warehouses for victims of crime; and *that mental health services must therefore be about prevention of crime, as well as about amelioration of symptoms.*

They have the power

Governments have the power, if they use it, to reduce funding to the pharmaceutical companies and to set strict curbs on NHS spending for psychiatric medications. They have the power to redirect their own funding to different priorities, to give incentives for the research they want to see, and to reduce funding on what they do not. They could oversee the establishment of research projects into contested or little-funded areas, such as possible links between severe organised forms of sexual abuse and dissociative identity disorder or non-epileptic seizures.

Along with regional health authorities and commissioners of services they can fund professional secondments into the parallel services, and fund evaluations of those services. They can ensure that service users, always including sexual abuse survivor groups, are genuinely involved in management and training within mental health services, and that these services respond to users' expressed wishes for services.

Shifting significantly the undergraduate and postgraduate training of psychiatrists, psychologists and psychiatric nurses is likely to be a gradual, medium- to long-term task. However, shorter training modules and professional development courses can be made compulsory. Supportive and reflexive courses in working with child sexual abuse trauma are likely to be more effective and longer-lasting in their impact than stern instructional approaches.

Implications for primary prevention and detection of abuse

Considerable health resources and publicity are devoted to the wider prevention of ill health, not just against the dangerous diseases of former times but in campaigns against smoking, poor diet, the damaging effects of sunburn or sexually transmitted diseases. How odd that this now long-established principle does not seem to apply to mental health!

Important as improvements in dignity and respect, in therapy, treatment and support of mentally distressed people are, they do not in themselves reduce the basic causes of much mental ill health. We have to go one step further at long last.

An invited editorial in the *British Journal of Psychiatry*, having summarised the research on trauma and psychosis, concluded that

> The implications of our having finally taken seriously the causal role of childhood adversity are profound. ... The most important implication is in the domain of primary prevention. (Read and Bentall, 2012)

The introduction to this book highlighted the inadequacy of pursuing recovery and healing in serious crimes such as child sexual abuse. Nonetheless, survivors need and deserve the best possible therapy and support, which at the moment most do not receive. Therefore, an ethical approach in mental health may be to see pursuing the greatest recovery possible as one major part of addressing sexual abuse, with the contribution towards primary prevention and criminal justice the other major, and irreducible, part.

Thus changes needed go further than accepting the trauma dimensions of mental illness and personality disorder diagnoses, beyond treating clients effectively and sympathetically, beyond training and supporting mental health staff better to work with CSA trauma, or providing crisis houses. They go beyond funding trauma therapies in many settings, including prisons, secure units for young people, children's residential units and projects for young offenders, important as these are.

The implication of the trauma paradigm is that a very great deal of mental illness is preventable; and that mental health systems thus need to involve themselves centrally in the business of prevention, and contribute funding and resources to prevention.

They would thus be saying upfront: 'Our contributions are directly relevant to the reduction of mental ill health, and to the improvement of mental health and wellbeing in all our communities.'

The importance of *prevention* is, it seems to me, especially highlighted by the complexity and the length of treatment necessary for recovery (or amelioration) of people with, for instance, severe dissociative disorders, after extreme childhood abuses such as ritual abuse (Sinason, 1994; Mollon, 1996; Noblitt and Perskin, 2008). Professionals find these areas absorbing with regard to research and treatment, dialogue and debate, conferences and publications. I am not disparaging the sincerity and dedication of skilled clinicians in saying that; but they need to remember that such patients are going through hell meantime, have done so for many years, and will probably do so for some years more. Could we not spend a fraction of all that time and effort, all of that fascinated interest, research and resources in trying to prevent such extreme violence and abuse in the first place?

Prevention, protection and earlier intervention

Within mental health settings

If mental health institutions and services are filled with the victims of crime, it makes no sense that questions of protection and justice for them are not considered. It makes no sense that they are not consulted in detecting and preventing further crimes against themselves, other vulnerable adults and children. A history of abuse trauma in so many patients and clients also increases the priority for mental health settings to become the safest, least abusive places that they can be.

I propose the following principles and practices to make a much greater reality of prevention, protection and early intervention.

All mental health services need to see themselves, and to be seen by other agencies, as contributors to national and local multidisciplinary child and adult protection strategies; to have a locus in local and national forums and committees for child and adult protection; and to offer a route, if service users wish, to give information about perpetrators to criminal justice agencies.

Most psychiatric hospitals have offices for various services already – such as social work, chaplaincies, service user advocacy, minority ethnic support and third sector drug and alcohol services – but remarkably, not to my knowledge regular legal advisers and police *for* patients. Police officers are frequently placed in hospital A&E units, to protect staff *from* drunk and aggressive patients. But some patients and their families equally need their protection.

An office containing a police, legal advice and victim support person, all trained in sympathetic communication, should be set up in all psychiatric hospitals and secure hospitals, from a team which also does outreach to young people's mental health units, wards for suicide attempters, and outpatient clinics. The outreach team member(s) would explain what they do, and respond to service users' requests to speak to them. Non-threatening leaflets and posters, and contacts through phone, email and social media should be widely advertised and displayed in mental health settings. Patients/clients would then know this team is available, if they wished at any time to tell someone about harm done to themselves or others, or to discuss possible criminal action against someone.

Information about perpetrators would clearly fall within the concern of the police and, at times, of social work. Mental health staff, chaplains, occupational therapists and others – while helping to advertise the service – would not need to feel professionally compromised by asking such questions themselves. The specialist unit would handle reporting of crime, and it would liaise with child and adult protection teams. If staff grew worried about accounts emerging during treatment, accounts which strongly suggested current or recent abuse, they would consult the unit and encourage the service user to talk to the unit. This process would need to be integrated with the staff's existing child protection procedures.

That of course means considering open-mindedly what mentally ill people were saying to them – not regarding accounts of sexual abuse as fantasy, delusion, or even a symptom of their psychotic illness!

> Sometimes, people are extremely unwell with schizophrenic illnesses and when they are unwell, they say they have been sexually abused. But if you sit down and ask them to talk about it … the accounts are very bizarre … and sometimes when they get better, it is clear there never was sexual abuse … it is part and parcel of their illness, in other words. (Consultant psychiatrist in Nelson, 2001, p. 48)

Taking child protection more seriously

Child protection issues, including child sexual abuse, must be fully and routinely considered as factors in mental distress in *all* child and adolescent mental health settings and services. That means recognising and working with effects of trauma as integral parts of their practice. At times that will involve a full child protection investigation by relevant agencies. It also means thinking through the implications, and considering who in a young person's circle is safe, and who may not be.

The goal of working closely with whole families in mental health practice is admirable, but it should not supersede the goal of keeping young people safe. Young inpatients with eating disorders should clearly not be sent home at weekends from psychiatric units if they are in fact being abused within their own families. In residential or respite settings, there should always be the most serious consideration about who visits the young person; about the people they stay with; and about what the young person's *own* expressed wishes and fears are. Sensitive inquiry should always be routinely included in units working with symptoms where links with sexual abuse have been established, for example eating disorders, self harm, and suicide attempts: especially when these symptoms are prolonged and repeated.

It becomes vital that mental health settings, most of all inpatient settings, provide physical and sexual safety to patients. It is vital that measures to ensure this are finally given priority, including rigorous staffing checks, full awareness of gender issues and the establishment of the long-overdue single sex wards throughout (DoH, 2002; Mental Health Network, 2010); and that settings do not replicate by violence, sexual assault, harsh physical restraint, deprivation of choice or other authoritarian practices, abusive behaviours which many patients have already suffered.

Wider involvement in prevention and early intervention

Research must address prevention

Mainstream current research in mental health appears little to consider primary prevention, that is, the prevention of problems and experiences which create a risk of mental ill health happening in the first place. This needs radically to change. A PsycINFO search in January 2012 revealed that of 111,674 research papers ever published on 'schizophrenia' or 'psychosis', only 96 (0.09%) focus in any way on primary prevention, with most discussing only secondary prevention (of young people *already* identified as at high risk). Remarkably, even then, only one paper identifies *childhood abuse* as a target for primary prevention (Bebbington et al, 2011), and only one focuses on poverty (Read, 2010; Read and Dillon, 2013).

Mental health research resources need a substantial diversion into research which contributes towards the protection of children, young people and vulnerable adults from violence and abuse. Here are a few of many possible examples.

1. A research programme with mothers who seriously harm or kill their babies or young children is needed. The condition 'Munchausen's syndrome by proxy' has come under increasing criticism. It was always in my view highly speculative, lacking in evidence and gender-biased in its assumptions that it was about attention-seeking among women and their secondary gains in achieving hospital care. The diagnosis has also been used against protective mothers, in claims that they foster so-called 'parental alienation syndrome' (see Chapter Two). I believe the time is overdue for research into the possibility that killings or serious harm to babies or young children may instead be dissociated behaviour by women who have suffered severe childhood abuse: who may be acting out scenes they have either witnessed, or have been forced to take part in themselves. Another possibility is that killing their babies, along with attempted killings of themselves, could constitute efforts, as they see it, to protect their children from future attacks in multi-generational abusive families. Earlier identification of severe abuse histories might, if so, save the lives or the health of many babies and children. These are speculations which deserve research exploration.

2. Research involving paediatricians, and informed by adult survivors themselves, is needed into possible links between physical signs and symptoms in some children and the presence of sexual abuse. That could result in earlier detection and protection, and better mental health outcomes in later life. Examples include paradoxical vocal cord dysfunction (PVCD) and other baffling and persistent respiratory, mouth and throat conditions currently attributed to psychosomatic causes (see Chapter Seven).

3. Research is needed into the persistent intrusive, abusive, often violent thoughts suffered by many people with obsessive-compulsive disorders, and by others who hear voices, and

their possible links with a history of sexual abuse. The Hearing Voices Network has already, through its roots among service users themselves, established connections with the voices of perpetrators of violence and abuse. But the puzzlingly blasphemous content of some intrusive thoughts of a sexual and violent nature (Toates and Coschug-Toates, 2002) need more exploration as a possible indicator of occult types of abuse.

4. Collaborative research on Attention Deficit Hyperactivity Disorder (ADHD) in children is needed to explore fully the role of abuse trauma in this condition, or the misdiagnosis of PTSD as ADHD (Weinstein et al, 2000; Briscoe-Smith and Henshaw, 2006; Stewart, 2015); and the child protection implications of this.

1. Research is needed into the extent to which postpartum psychosis and any prolonged postnatal depression is related not to hormonal or similar changes, but rather to the triggering effects of childbirth on child sexual abuse trauma (Wosu et al, 2015a, 2015b).

2. Mental health professionals should be encouraged and enabled to build research and practice alliances with people nationally and internationally who work to protect children and address trauma in children and adults. Examples are organisations working internationally for child welfare, against political torture, against child marriage, and against the use of child soldiers and other exploitations of children and young people. Sharing expertise and learning, holding joint seminars and conferences, shadowing and mentoring are just a few valuable examples of possible collaboration.

Prevention schemes

Not only do mental health resources need to contribute to primary prevention of the child abuse which influences so much mental ill health, they also need to be directed into *positive* promotion of sexual and physical safety in children and young people. This effort would then become part of the wider drive towards an integrated public policy which nurtures mental health and wellbeing, and promotes mental health as a public health discipline.

Mental health services (like other disciplines) should be contributing some of their funding and resources to schemes such as community prevention and safe environments for children (Chapter Six), to methods of enabling children to reveal sexual abuse (Chapter Five), and to early intervention work with children at risk.

The financial implications of these changes

It is not up to advocates of reform to provide governments and services with a ready-made model of how changes suggested in this chapter could be afforded. They have their own experts and specialists. However, some comments are useful to consider.

Some increased spending would be needed, certainly for a period, to increase inadequate therapeutic trauma services for sexual abuse survivors with mental health issues, to support parallel services and contribute to better child protection. There would also be costs in ensuring inpatient safety such as the genuine ending of mixed wards, which has been urged for decades, and in measures to place a police and legal advice office in every psychiatric hospital (although criminal justice services ought to share those costs).

However, increases in talking therapies would decrease the vast and spiralling current costs of drug treatments for mental disorders. Research funding could be redirected rather than increased, while in the medium to longer term these measures would be expected to bring considerable savings. Good, free or low-cost, widely available therapeutic services can improve the ability of people to take part in education and the workforce. They can reduce dependence on the drugs and alcohol so often used to blot out abuse trauma. That would in turn reduce the major problem of addicted parents, and the huge child protection costs of social work supervision and the removal of their children into state care.

Widespread therapy and support are also liable to reduce the desperation and anger which can lead some survivors into crime (see Chapter Nine), and reduce the current high costs of repeated crises and hospitalisations in mental health and addictions services, where underlying problems are not properly addressed. Police, social work, drug and alcohol services could and should in turn make a contribution to such 'preventative spend'.

Ann Jennings (1994) delivered a particularly sharp critique of the financial wastefulness of failing to address sexual abuse trauma in mental health services. The high costs she gave then, 20 years ago, would now need considerable updating! (Bonomi et al, 2008). In one detailed estimate for example, Saied-Tissier (2014), for the NSPCC, assessed a figure for the UK of £3.2 billion in 2012.

> Incorrect diagnoses and treatment exacerbate the condition of traumatized patients, making them dependent on the system's most restrictive and expensive services. An analysis of 17 years of Anna's records shows that she was hospitalized a total of 4,248 days. The total cost for this hospitalization, figured at $640 a day, was $2,718,720. Had she lived to the age of 52, these costs would have nearly tripled to $7,390,720. Not included in this analysis is the cost of social services, police, ambulance and legal/court services, conservator and patient advocacy services, residential treatment, psychiatric and therapist sessions, crisis services, day programs, and intensive case management. With studies showing prevalence rates as high as 81% of hospitalized patients with histories of sexual and/ or physical trauma, the fiscal implications to exploring a trauma paradigm are obvious. (Jennings, 1994, p. 8)

Governments and policymakers thus need the courage to argue forcefully that these changes will eventually bring welcome economies, rather than engaging in the usual effort of government departments to avoid spending for the future, and passing spending cuts on to each other.

Can our politicians, policymakers and mental health professionals at last find the courage and will to make such radical change in mental health?

NINE

Pathways into crime after sexual abuse: the voices of male offenders[1]

"Nobody ever asked me what was wrong when I was in care or prison ... nobody said, 'why are you doing this?' I was always in trouble – dishonesty, fire raising and property stuff. It's all children in care, who've been abused, who end up in prison ... it makes my heart bleed that there will be more children." (Pete, ex-prisoner)

"There was nine of us in the 'List D' school who suffered that [sexual abuse] and later nine of us later got life sentences, because we didn't know anything else but badness." (Paddy, life prisoner)

Introduction

Abuse and offending

What might the connections be between being sexually abused as a child, and becoming an offender? And why should understanding the connections be important? For many reasons: because earlier protection from abuse might make many of these survivors less likely to commit crimes, protecting future victims; because reactions to child sexual abuse (CSA) trauma might explain 'meaningless', even fatal, violence, increasing the

---

[1] I am greatly indebted to Dr Ruth Lewis and Dr Sandy Gulyurtlu for their work for the male survivor life history study, including interviews and analysis of the offenders' accounts and lifegrids.

urgency of earlier therapeutic support which might save lives; because all CSA survivors, whatever they have done, deserve help to reduce the effects of their trauma; because many young offenders might be enabled to change their lives; and because most offender services and penal institutions remain very poorly equipped to meet – or even to recognise – the needs of sexually abused prisoners.

Most male and female survivors of sexual abuse do not offend. It's very important to stress that. However, very many convicted offenders have sexual abuse histories.

Research has shown that sexually abused young people have higher risks of offending than non-abused young people (Dembo et al, 1992; Jumper, 1995; Tyler, 2002; Levy, 2004; Johnson et al, 2006; Fergusson et al, 2008). CSA is an *independent* risk factor for offending (Swanston et al, 2003; Feiring et al, 2007; Felson and Lane, 2009; Duke et al, 2010). Abuse histories are strongly associated with substance misuse – which can itself involve users in illegal activities. Sexually abused boys and men are many times more likely than non-abused ones to report the early use of alcohol and illicit drugs (Eley Morris et al, 2002; Simpson and Miller, 2002; Dube et al, 2005; Nelson, 2009). However, the possible risks of sexually abused young people becoming perpetrators of *sexual* assault (see Chapter Ten) have attracted much the greatest research interest. Far fewer studies have explored possible links between a sexual abuse history and other, non-sexual offences.

Although the main emphasis has been on sexual abuse histories in female prisoners, it's already estimated that a high proportion of male prisoners has also suffered CSA. In a sample of 100 incarcerated males, a US study found 59% reported having experienced CSA. (Johnson et al, 2006). Fondacaro and Powell (1999) surveyed 211 inmates in the USA and found that 40% were survivors of CSA. Few had had their needs addressed, nor had support to overcome their anger and the impact of their abuse. Prison counsellors such as Ilene Easton (later in this chapter) have found very high numbers of male survivors of sexual abuse in Scottish prisons. This chapter focuses on such male survivors.

The influence of sexual abuse trauma on later offending has been suggested in high-profile criminal cases, as well as in research. When William Goad from Plymouth was convicted in 2005 after decades of brutal sexual abuse against hundreds of boys, Judge William Taylor remarked that many of Goad's victims, now adult, had been in court before him "again and again and again". Their recorded crimes included grievous bodily harm, violent assaults, burglary, blackmail and drug-related crimes, and stretched back to their teens following Goad's assaults. The judge concluded: "They have a hopeless existence going from day to day, drug to drug, and that's all they care about – oblivion. They have no job, they know nothing other than to steal, they have nothing to look forward to" (BBC *Panorama*, 2005).

This chapter first considers violence involving homicide. It discusses a major study of killings of gay men, and why these are suggestive of explosive attacks by male survivors of sexual abuse, triggered by post-traumatic reaction to sexual activity. The study deserves wider-ranging, follow-up research, for it may point to a still largely unrecognised problem, which would urgently demand more investigation in order to protect potential victims. Many young men may also be wasting taxpayers' money and their own lives undergoing long prison sentences for crimes which might have been avoided, had there been strong sexual abuse prevention policies and earlier intervention.

However any understanding of interconnections between childhood abuse and offending needs to include CSA survivors' *own* narratives of pathways into that offending. (France and Homel, 2006). Yet these are still rarely explored. The second part of this chapter goes on to consider Scottish prisoners from my own life history research study (Nelson, 2009). Life history studies allow for detailed exploration. The men discuss a variety of responses to CSA which led them, directly or indirectly, into offending when they were children or teenagers. The impact of anger and rage, of rejection and brutality, shame and self-denigration, and desperate, failed attempts to draw attention to their abuse, is traced in their own behaviour. They explain why counselling in prison has proved very helpful in reducing their aggression, their fear and their tendency to scapegoat. These findings all merit further research with wider groups of male survivor offenders.

The prisons counsellor then summarises her work and her approach. The chapter ends with recommendations for future policy and practice.

Killings of gay men: a suggestive pattern?

Violent attacks

In October 2011 Ryan Esquierdo, a teenage first offender, violently killed Stuart Walker, a popular gay barman, in Ayrshire, then set his body alight.

Meeting by chance one night, they talked about the teenager's confused sexuality. Consensual sex caused Esquierdo to panic: flashbacks of sexual abuse triggered uncontrollable rage and extreme, explosive violence. Derek Ogg QC, defending, said the killing was "not a gay hate crime" but "far more complex", adding that Esquierdo felt "utter bafflement and horror that he could inflict such violence".

The Crown accepted his plea to culpable homicide through diminished responsibility, after psychologists' evidence that he was in the throes of a flashback and PTSD following sexual abuse as a child. He was still jailed for 12 years (Drainey, 2012; Nelson, 2012a).

Thomas McDowell strangled, then dismembered, the body of a trainee rabbi he met in a London gay bar in July 2002. At McDowell's later trial, it was revealed that he had been severely abused by a man as a child and grew up hating homosexuals. He admitted manslaughter through diminished responsibility. The judge recommended that it might never be safe to release him (*Daily Mirror*, 2004).

Attacks on lesbian, gay, bisexual and transgender (LGBT) people are a significant social problem. Research by Stonewall found that one in five LGBT people in Britain have suffered homophobic hate incidents (Guasp et al, 2013). Gay men have sometimes faced extreme violence, even death, in response to even tentative advances they made to young men.

Might cases such as Esquierdo's hint at a frequent underlying reason for some young men's 'motiveless violence', which needs attention now to prevent many more tragedies happening?

The Bartlett study: hints of abuse histories

A research study by Peter Bartlett, which I believe is valuable and should urgently trigger further and wider research, has painstakingly explored Crown Prosecution Service (CPS) files on the killings of 77 gay men and the conviction of 78 perpetrators (Bartlett, 2007). While he does not presume to draw definite conclusions he does conclude that issues of personal history 'seem inescapable'. There are many indications that the perpetrators may have been sexually abused young men.

High risk populations

The killers came from populations known to be at high risk of sexual abuse. The assailants appeared 'remarkably vulnerable'. Three in five were aged under 30: they were drawn disproportionately from poor, marginalised social groups. Half the perpetrators had attended special school or borstal, or had been in care. They had behaviours frequently found in males who 'act out' after coerced sex. Most had a history of offending, anti-social behaviour and offences suggesting hostility and anger, while their lives were said to have little direction.

In contrast to the killers, three in five of the men's victims were over 40, and one in four was a professional. They had usually invited the killers back to their own home, where most killings happened, during sex or after an invitation to sex.

Ambivalence and shame over sexuality

Assailants showed confusion or shame about their sexuality and their sex acts with gay men, along with a lack of understanding that they could refuse sex. Their recorded life histories were incomplete, but up to a third were known to have been paid for sex in the past. In a striking phrase, Bartlett writes of a 'lack of information in reports of perpetrators' understandings of their sexual self'. Frequently they agreed to sex then became disgusted, nauseated and ashamed, reactions which appeared to trigger the violence. They did not feel they could ask the man to stop. It appeared that sex was perceived by them as a matter of inevitability.

Lack of apparent motivation

Rarely did crimes appear premeditated – most men used a weapon that came to hand, or their fists and feet. There was little convincing evidence, despite police beliefs, that robbery, blackmail or dispute about payment for prostitution was the motive. Nothing of value was usually stolen. Half of the victims were strangers and many others may only have been known for 24 hours. Although Bartlett speaks of 'sexual homicides', these were not killers who gained *sexual* satisfaction from wounding and killing. The violence tended to be reactive and private. What then might it have reacted to – and why might the violence have been so extreme? For exceptional violence and aggression was common, such as stabbing a victim 40 times.

Exceptional violence

The men could usually provide no coherent explanation for their violence. Often they remembered little of the killing, or they described being taken over and losing themselves in violence. The defendant nearly always complained to police of an unwelcome sexual advance or act, along with self-disgust, before 'flipping' – for instance grabbing a knife from the kitchen.

Sudden explosive violence around a sex act, loss of memory or a sense of being taken over and out of control could fit with a possible post-traumatic response. Given the high number of near-strangers, did the victim represent something or someone else, rather than being killed for himself?

Occasionally in the CPS reports studied by Bartlett a sexual abuse background is specifically mentioned: one psychiatric report referred to the trigger as 'a series of homosexual assaults the assailant states he suffered in his youth'. Yet only 13 of 61 psychiatric reports available about perpetrators referred explicitly to a child sexual abuse history (Bartlett, 2007).However, this low figure would not be surprising, given the intense shame most young men feel in revealing such victimisation; given that the penal or care institution was unlikely to have asked about such a history; given that police are unlikely to have asked this after the killing; and given that medical models and personality disorder theories still dominate in mental health services, with scant attention to past trauma (see Chapter Eight).

I believe that those offenders still available for interview in penal or other settings should now be re-interviewed about their childhood histories as part of further research into motivations for killings of gay men, in order to protect gay men, and to focus on prevention and earlier intervention for male victims of sexual abuse.

Further clues from my research

My own Edinburgh University research (Nelson, 2009) – and the experience of organisations working with traumatised offenders – further suggests that there may be many abused young men convicted of serious violence, against men they thought to be gay, or men who had merely looked at them, as they would put it, 'in the wrong way'. Abused by men, they bottled up their anger for years, blaming all gay men for their own abuse by paedophiles; ashamed to tell because it is not 'masculine' to be victimised; worried that they might be gay and again not properly 'masculine'; suffering untreated PTSD, hypervigilant and fearful against apparent threat, unable to understand their own explosive violence.

The Nelson study

Distrust of gay men was apparent in *most* of the heterosexual or sexually ambivalent male survivors we interviewed for the life history study, not just for the subgroup of prisoners (Nelson, 2009).

This wider study, in which I was assisted by Dr Ruth Lewis and Dr Sandy Gulyurtlu, was with 24 male survivors of child sexual abuse. It explored child and adult disclosure, education, work, health, relationships and sexuality as well as offending, aspects noted as important in research on the effects of sexual abuse of boys (Holmes and Slap, 1998; Valente, 2005; Hopper, 2008). The aim of the study was to improve services for male survivors, through gaining their own perspectives on their care, support and intervention needs through the lifecourse. Life history methodology enabled the survivors to pinpoint what *for them* were the most significant events, impacts and needs, during their lives. It can also provide more accurate timelines than other research methods (Creswell, 1998, Dhunpath, 2000; Cole and Knowles, 2001; Denzin and Lincoln, 2003).

The men were interviewed twice, the first using a 'life grid' (a chart with age-bands along one axis, and issues such as education, work or relationships along the other). The life grid assists recall and aids rapport, especially about sensitive topics (Parry et al, 1999; Berney and Blane, 2003; Wilson et al, 2007). Second interviews further explored the main themes emerging from the life grid interview.

The offender subgroup

The convicted offenders we interviewed had all, it emerged, been sexually abused by multiple perpetrators. Violence played a part in most of their own offences. In this chapter they describe their pathways into offending following sexual abuse.

The subgroup was purposively sampled because an earlier male survivor needs assessment in the Lothians (Nelson, 2004c) revealed that professionals working with male offenders had found a high prevalence of sexual abuse in their childhoods. Information was also emerging from work in Scottish prisons by voluntary sector agencies, such as Open Secret and Stop it Now Scotland.[2] Although they were a small sample, their experiences and reflections give pointers to wider research – and to preventive interventions.

Six men were aged 18–23; one was in his early 30s, one in his early 40s (details of their abuse history and offending in Table 1). It emerged that they had all experienced deprived early lives of poverty and disruption, and all had also been in residential or

---

[2] www.opensecret.org; www.stopitnow.org.uk/scotland.htm

Table 1: Characteristics of the offender subset at time of interview

Participant*	Age Group	Current status	Type of offence imprisoned for	Known CSA perpetrators
Danny	18–22	In prison	Series of violent offences from childhood, including life-threatening violence; arson	Male family friend Local ice cream man Mother's boyfriend
Dean	18–22	In prison	Violence, organised theft; drug related	Female staff member and older boys at care homes Male babysitter Abducted from street for a week, repeatedly raped by multiple gang members
Hunter	18–22	In prison	Theft, minor violence	Older boy Male foster carer
Liam	18–22	Recently released from prison	Violence (and one sexual offence, not discussed here)	Brother
Mike	18–22	In prison	Violence, drug related	Local family members Other boys in care Abducted from street and raped by multiple (male) gang members
Ryan	18–22	In prison	Series of violent offences including life-threatening violence	Older boy Male residential school teacher Unknown family members
Pete	30–35	Out of prison	Violence, drug related	Male youth club worker Male residential care worker
Paddy	40–45	In prison	Serious violent offences	Staff at residential schools (male & female)

* All names are pseudonyms.

foster care, a setting where several had suffered sexual abuse. They differed from most non-offenders in our study in the severity and repeated nature of the abuse and ill-treatment, both by their families and by officialdom.

All participants in the study had to have access to support before they could take part. The prisoners all had a counsellor and were asked in confidence by her if they would like to participate.

The narratives: pathways into offending[3]

Anger and rage

Anger and rage were very common reactions to child sexual abuse expressed by the male survivors throughout the full study, not just among the offender subgroup (Holmes and Slap, 1998; Hopper, 2008). It was 'bottled up' inside, particularly when they felt unable to tell. The male survivors, as they put it, *"lost the rag"* or *"snapped"* under particular stress. Anger was frequently directed at themselves, through self harm, but among the offenders it had also been directed at property, at authority figures, at fellow prisoners and strangers.

Violent to themselves

Anger or despair made some commit quite serious violence on themselves or on objects.

When in jail Pete – sexually abused by a youth worker and a residential care worker – was overcome by terrifying thoughts that he might perpetuate a '*cycle of abuse*' against children. This was behind the violent head-banging, which staff thought was due to mental illness.

> "Then I went right behind my door and stayed in solitary confinement for a year, – I chose it, I was frightened … I pictured myself sodomising a baby. I'd never do that and never would … so I started smashing my head off the walls of my cell … trying

---

[3] All the quotes in this section from pp 328-43 are taken from Nelson (2009).

to get it out of my head and that. What triggered it off was, there's a saying, 'a victim of a victim' ... and I thought: have I to do that (assault a baby)? Am I expected to do that, because it happened to me? Then I started smashing my head against all them walls, trying to get it out of my head."

Violent to others

For the offender group, outbursts became a frequent reaction to anything or anyone seen as a threat. Several had been jailed for violent offences, even for attempting to kill. Danny and Ryan had a childhood history of violence. Others had become involved in a downward spiral among dangerous or desperate people.

Pete described "lashing out" constantly as a child and teenager, committing many offences: "I think (for boys) it's a way of expressing what happened without saying it."

Mike, multiply abused as a child and teenager, would smash car windows:

SN: "Can you help me understand what you felt at the time, why you were doing all these things?"

Mike: "Anger. And instead of taking it out on other people I took it out on objects."

After suffering a brutal street rape, he was asked if he had gone for medical help: "No, I didn't want any, I just went nuts instead."

The most common form of aggression appeared to spring from anger, hurt, confusion and despair. Ryan used frequent violence throughout his life, and this continued in prison.

"I got kicked out – every residential I've been in, and all the secure units. Smashed up, I just always started battering young offenders, battering prisoners, I set fires, smuggled drugs ... a lot of crimes, just been a pure idiot."

Liam, who smashed up his care unit room after being disbelieved and laughed at by a staff member when he revealed his sexual abuse history, disclosed that as a young teenager he had violently attacked his abuser, his brother. Afterwards:

> "I went off the rails. I attacked a staff member (in the children's home), pinned him against the wall and put a knife to his throat."

(Liam had also been convicted of a sexual offence at age 14, but had several violent offences which are highlighted here.)

Danny, abused by multiple perpetrators, had committed serious and violent offences since childhood, including once setting a classroom on fire:

SN: "Do you remember just before [you set fire] what it felt like?"

Danny: "I'd been angry like with everything, and I blamed it on everybody else ... I think it's more to like see something destroyed, because part of you's been destroyed."

Angry, disillusioned reaction was often increased by harsh treatment received in residential care. Paddy, sexually abused by both male and female staff at residential schools, recalled:

> "I didn't know anything else but violence, that's the way things were in a 'List D' school [former Scottish residential schools for children referred from children's panels]. I'd just go home full of anger and full of hatred. There was nine of us in the 'List D' school who suffered that [sexual abuse] and later nine of us later got life sentences, because we didn't know anything else but badness."

Projection and hypervigilance against women, gay men and sex offenders

The men had also projected their anger on to others who had not harmed them. Ilene Easton, the prisons counsellor, describing their attitudes to gay men, said her sexually abused clients throughout male prisons became "very homophobic".

Liam perceptively considered his past aggression to strangers who had merely glanced in his direction:

> "I can't tell anybody [about the abuse] because everybody will look down on me and I'll be a piece of dirt ... so I walk along the street and somebody looks at me; as everybody does, they look about. I'd go over and hit him. It was a case of I was angry, he's looked at me, he's not looked at me in any other way but I'm going to blame it on him. You looked at me, I'm angry: you're getting hit."

Female partners, or women generally, also became victims of projection, blamed for their mothers' failure to protect them from abusers such as the mother's violent boyfriends. Liam explained why he thought many abused young men were violent to their own girlfriends, like his brother was:

> "The way I looked at things when I was young, and I know he thinks the exact same way ... is every woman is going to be the same as our mother. And my mum was an alkie ... and all the rest of it [she sold sex to men at home]. And I was completely different in the way I treat women because I always thought my mum's behaviour was a result of the way that she had been treated."

Ilene Easton found woman-blame to be problematic among a *majority* of the hundreds of male survivors she had worked with in prisons, even when males had been their abusers. She explored the roots of this (usually, blame of their mothers for failing to protect them) with them during the trauma work, believing this was vital: "I have to say the feminist in me wants to work with males because potentially the majority are going to have girlfriends, children, wives, mothers, and if their behaviour isn't sorted?…"

'Meaningless violence'

One of the hardest things for most people to understand is why some young men attack people, even strangers, in the street or pub for no apparent reason. Respondents tried to explain. Fear of further sexual assault was found to play a significant part, confirming previous studies such as Leeb et al (2007).

The young men in my study were hypervigilant, easily misinterpreting innocent signals during conversation, social situations, or attempts to help the survivor. They were particularly vigilant against men they thought to be gay. Mike, multiply raped and abused, explained the sense of being on guard against every real or imagined threat:

> "When you swear to yourself that if anything like that you've been receiving is going to happen to you again, you'd kill them because you'll not let it happen."

Paddy was asked why survivors lashed out at innocent people who were not trying to hurt them:

> "Because the person's maybe breached that barrier that, that's round them, you know… They're on the defensive … as soon as somebody steps through that the only thing in your head is lashing out and protecting myself because they think that that person is trying to hurt them… I've had enough of that when I was a bairn."

If child sexual abuse is common among male prisoners, this offers another perspective on why known sex offenders might regularly be attacked and need protection in prisons. Paddy admitted:

"I've always had a problem there, you know ... even in jail I've attacked them all the time ... through the YOs [Young Offenders] and all that. Before I actually met Ilene [counsellor] I was an angry person. I was a very angry person."

'Vicious circles' of rejection and brutality

Repeated rejection and brutality as children and teenagers increased the seriousness and frequency of offending in some, by increasing their anger, alienation and sense of futility. Their out-of-control behaviour at home led to residential care, a return home, rejection by those they loved, yo-yo instability and harsh treatment back in care. This produced further violent reactions, cynicism and a reduced responsibility towards other people.

Dean, for example, had been sexually abused at age seven by a female carer at a children's home, tried to tell but was not believed. He was then sexually abused by a male babysitter. Back home, his parents could not cope with his behaviour, and he was soon in care again. By this time, he felt "Nobody wanted me, I was lonely and my mum and my family didn't want me."

By the time that Dean suffered a traumatic week-long abduction and multiple rapes by a gang while on the run from another children's home, he was disillusioned that anyone would believe or protect him. This very serious crime has never been reported nor investigated.

Triggered by physical restraint

Another trigger to violent or aggressive reactions was behaviour which re-enacted past sexual or physical abuse. Thus Pete, who had been anally abused, reacted violently to male psychiatric nurses restraining him, pulling his trousers down and injecting him.

Paddy was asked if prison was more, or less, difficult to cope with if people had abuse in their past:

"A lot more difficult because people in authority are the ones that ruined my childhood. So you put everybody in authority in the same bracket. And when you come into the jail ... you're 'they'll be just the same as what happened to me when I was younger.' When you've been battered and kicked up and down the cell... your mind goes back to when you were a bairn, you know."

'Acting the big man' to restore self esteem

Reflecting on their violence, a few offenders described becoming bullies as children and teenagers, trying to 'act the big man' and silence doubts about their masculinity, their sexuality or their victimhood.

When Danny was sexually abused by a neighbour the only way he dared get back at him was by bullying his son. He joined a gang of older kids at 11:

> "They were 13, 14... smoking cannabis and gang fighting ... and I was with older ones who – I used to think to myself – they're looking up to me and it felt good. And it was like I always had to prove my point."

The prisons counsellor recalled her cumulative experience with male offenders:

> "For many of these young men, they've experienced trauma with domestic violence. And because of it they felt so isolated. 'Who can I tell?' They've felt there was no one. So what do you do with that pain? You swallow that pain. The difficulty is they feel so powerless they become rageful, with knives, with fighting, with gang culture, and many only in gangs for a sense of belonging."

Sometimes a successful criminal career, in terms of financial gain and peer kudos, appeared to give the young men a sense of control and power, at least for a time. Dean described the excitement and "big money" in running a large car theft operation as "a good life at that time" – despite needing to take huge daily amounts of drink and drugs to dull his extremely traumatic memories.

A strategy to stop the abuse

Some survivors offended as a deliberate strategy to try and gain attention for what was happening, when they could not disclose directly. But this didn't work. Female survivors often tried this too: one from the Beyond Trauma study (Nelson, 2001) even ran along her private school roof in a desperate attempt to attract attention, but still nobody asked her what was wrong. This points up the great importance of thinking about the meaning of repeated, unusual behaviour in children.

Pete actively tried to get sent into care, then to prison, to escape his perpetrator, a local youth club worker. Dean kept hoping that "creating havoc" in class would encourage somebody to "sit down and ask me about what had happened but I just didn't know how to go about it..."

Innes (not a member of this offender subgroup, but who briefly attracted a criminal record) shoplifted to try to get sent away and escape his abuser, sending out oblique signals for help. But all it gained him was a criminal record at 14. He shoplifted for ages without being caught, was finally picked up and reprimanded, then got a suspended sentence:

SN: "Didn't anyone then ask you why you were doing it, your probation officer, social worker?"

Innes: "I didn't have a probation officer because it was a suspended sentence; obviously when I was caught and taken home it was basically, 'I've caught him doing this, blah, blah', and then the police were speaking to my mum and dad, and I was left out of the picture."

Other problems

Poverty

For some survivors from deprived backgrounds stealing had a more basic and poignant purpose. Pete recalled that he began stealing at 7 or 8 because his mother was mentally ill, there was no food at home and he had to resort to eating cabbages from fields. He gave his mother some of the money he stole.

Effects of school exclusions

The damaging impact of exclusion from school for sexually abused young people was discussed in Chapter Four. All but one of the convicted male offenders in the study had frequent exclusions from school: one had 15, another had six. Mike was excluded at age six, for letting down a teacher's tyres, Ryan from nursery school for sexualised behaviour. Possible causes of Ryan's very early sexualised behaviour did not seem to be explored:

> "My sexualised language and behaviour, like peeing in plants, when I was four or five ... just flashing at people, shouting and swearing, talking to the [nursery] staff with sexualised language and abuse."

Dean was diagnosed ADHD at school for being "hyperactive and out of control".

The young men's attempts to show something was very wrong increased the likelihood of exclusion for disruptive behaviour. That led them to fall behind with schoolwork, lose interest, and risk humiliation in front of classmates. Liam was often excluded, mainly for fighting, and reckons he missed about three years of schooling. He was once expelled for assaulting a teacher who pulled him back from a fight:

> "Everyone just thought I was aggressive and violent, because that's the way I was – (but) I made it that way, so that nobody could come in.'

Helpful, respectful treatment at two other schools later enabled Liam to gain several educational qualifications, and to stop rebelling against authority figures.

Street environments for excluded children encouraged involvement in unsafe situations and crime. Hunter, who had a refugee background, was often excluded from school for disruption. He would roam the streets with others, indulging in petty crime and stealing. He considered the negative, dangerous consequences of exclusion for vulnerable children:

> "Eventually every time I just took to the streets ... I used to get up and go and get my [excluded] pals and get some booze. Half of them never even went to school."

Drug-related criminal activity

All the offenders had misused substances heavily, often daily. They took these mainly to try to blot out nightmares, flashbacks and overwhelming feelings. But this meant regular stealing and involvement in criminal subcultures. Being 'high' on substances encouraged violent, unpredictable reactions.

> "The drink is just to forget. The drugs as well. With drugs, you just keep topping it up all day then you don't come out [of it]." (Mike)

> "Obviously people will just try to blank out, even ... that wee couple of hours. But then that moves on to a couple of days and then to a drug habit, and... because they're too used to blanking out, they don't want to face the reality of what happened." (Paddy)

Dean resorted to stealing to survive and pay for drugs to blot out his very traumatic memories. After the violent gang rape, he ran away from a harsh residential unit:

> "When I ran away I didn't care what happened to me. Because I had nothing to look forward to and I

had nothing in my life, just bad memories so I didn't really care, I just took drugs and drink."

He joined – and was protected by – criminal networks and became heavily involved in car theft. He was "blotting out stuff from my past":

"Every day of my life ...I was taking drugs ... drinking every day from I woke up in the morning ... I was taking cocaine to work, I was taking Valium to bring myself back down... and I was drinking."

This powerfully recalls Judge Taylor's comments about the victims of abuser William Goad: "They have a hopeless existence going from day to day, drug to drug, and that's all they care about – oblivion...they have nothing to look forward to" (BBC *Panorama*, 2005)

Heavy drinking increased boys' vulnerability on the streets when they ran away from care. Mike was abducted and savagely attacked, physically and sexually, after wandering the streets "completely legless". Danny described how heavy drug-taking in itself gave him psychiatric symptoms which made him more prone to violence:

"I attacked someone in a house – I was on lots of drugs at the time – Ecstasy, cocaine, heroin, Valium... and I was really messed up, and I thought people were talking about me. I was starting to get a bit paranoid. I basically thought that these people were laughing at me... aye, I just lost it."

Remorse and moral feelings

The men largely disclaimed remorse for their criminal acts. Asked why they thought they lacked these feelings, they said that repeatedly both their families and authorities had failed to help or protect them earlier. So they felt bitterly that they had no reason to help others in return.

Mike and Dean, two young men who had been traumatised and betrayed numerous times already in their lives, spoke honestly about this.

Mike: "I felt sorry for the, the... some of the things I've done but most of them, no, because people don't feel sorry for the things they've done to me."

SN: "But it wasn't the same people, was it?"

Mike: "No, but the way I see it is, is if they done that to me and they've no remorse and all that then why should I have remorse for anybody else no matter who it is? I've got no feeling anymore. Except if ... if I seen a woman getting battered... I wouldn't let it happen, I'm dead against that."

Dean, who nearly died in a car crash through driving with no care for himself, admitted:

"I'd no feelings for anybody, do you know what I'm talking about, I've not got remorse for anything... I've got remorse for people I care about, I've got feelings for people I care about, to a certain degree."

"The way I'd seen it was... the people in charge of me took a liberty with me ... all right, [other people] weren't there, they didn't abuse me and that, but they were still, they're still authority... they're all the same people." (Paddy)

But it is untrue that these offenders had lost their moral sense altogether, or fitted descriptions such as 'psychopathic'. They all revealed several strong moral feelings without prompting. They wanted to be good fathers, unlike nearly all their own fathers. They felt extremely angry at sex crimes against children and offered thoughtful suggestions about how better to protect children. They also rejected offending against people they knew and cared about, including people who had helped them in prison.

Unfortunately there had not been many such people in their lives, but they warmly recalled by name a caring relative, teacher, care worker or counsellor. (I experienced the incongruities of their attitudes to people they liked: two young men who had stolen cars for a living, on hearing that I had had two cars stolen in recent years, were shocked and said this was awful. I did point out to them that if they hadn't known me, they might have been the ones stealing my cars!)

Counselling caused them to lose their emotional numbness when they were painfully addressing their own abuse. It thus appeared that bitterness at past official inaction, and at betrayal or repeated cruelty had undermined a significant part, but by no means all of their moral sense towards self and others. This finding surely has important implications for constructive work with abused offenders. It also points to the value of assisting them to access childhood records. Discovering from these that some professionals cared greatly for their welfare after all, and tried to help them, can positively impact on their faith in other people (Nelson, 2009). Findings that repeat or violent offenders do retain a moral sense also suggests that there should be far more caution in readily applying diagnoses like 'anti-social personality disorder' to such offenders.

Trauma counselling

All the men considered they had benefited greatly from their trauma counselling. They were able to talk about severe past sexual trauma for the first time; they realised they were not to blame; they rediscovered feelings for others and had new optimism that they could plan for a different, positive future. Several also found their cognitive abilities improved a great deal and they began to write powerful poems and prose about their lives. They all felt that addressing their traumas, distressing as it was, had been the key to their ability to make changes. For some, that change was limited, simply lessening their aggression towards other prisoners and staff. For others it meant moving away from a troublesome home area on release, taking a college course, and pursuing new careers.

The prisoners all independently said remarkably similar things about the value of the counselling. They had managed to tell the counsellor about very traumatic things, often for the first time. They had found it possible to trust, and they felt respected, without pressure to reveal intimate details of their abuse. They greatly valued the confidentiality and the counsellor's independence from the prison authorities (she worked for a third sector organisation). They all managed to reduce their aggression and self-blame, and to question some attitudes, such as those towards young women. They all had greater hopes for the future, even though several had previously been deeply depressed and suicidal. It will be very useful therefore to explore what they found the most helpful aspects of their counselling, when programmes are planned more widely for sexually abused offenders.

Liam summed up factors he found most helpful:

> "She'll sit and explain what she does, who she is, the confidentiality rights… she never, ever pushed and pushed and pushed. If I brought something up that I was finding really difficult, she'd leave it and come back to it. But she would ask me when I says it, what I was finding hard about it.
>
> "You can go at your own pace… I just jumped straight in with both feet. [Confidentiality] was really, really important to me. If I talk about going out to abuse somebody … then she's obligated [to report] obviously… but it was never anything like that. I was always more concerned about somebody talking about what I was disclosing."

The counsellor's approach

> 'We as a society are suffering, every one of us are victims [of the offenders' rage]. So that work which is going towards protecting potential victims has to be recognised.'

A detailed interview was also carried out with the abuse trauma counsellor working in the two prisons involved, for an overview of key issues her work with male offenders had raised (available in full in Nelson, 2009). Ilene Easton has counselled hundreds of sexually abused female and male prisoners, mainly with the Open Secret organisation based in the Forth Valley area of central Scotland.

Counsellors from diverse backgrounds who work in prisons will use their own approaches, but some key aspects below may prove useful to adopt or adapt.

Frequency of CSA history in male prisoners

"In X prison as one example, if you were even saying a third, you know, it's 200-and-odd, but I know it's going to be a lot more than that. I couldn't keep up with the numbers when I was there. And at one point I had to start and take down the posters [advertising my service]."

Basic principles

"First, respect. Absolutely.

"I will go in, shake their hand always, ask them where they prefer to sit [for privacy]. I always tell them, whatever their offence is I find it abhorrent... [I say] 'But your behaviour isn't all of you, it's a part of you, and it's choices you made based on experiences. So by making different choices you can change the behaviour.' If they're constantly told, 'You're telling me I'm a thug, well, I'll be a thug all my life... there's no hope for me, I'm a thug.'"

First meeting with depressed prisoners

"I say 'I expect you feel pretty anxious, how about if I tell you within half an hour you'll start to feel better?' Then I will say, 'And, you know, in one to ten where are you right now? One being shit and ten being over the moon and jumping for joy'... normally it's about a two, three. And half way through I'll say, 'One to ten, where are you now?' And they'll always say, 'four, five', and I will then say, 'How did you manage to get yourself from three to five?' This is what the empowerment is..."

Easing discussion of the abuse

"What I always tell them is, 'You will be in charge of what we discuss in this room,' and you instantly, spontaneously, see a smile, and you see the shoulders relax. And I tell them that I have no need to ask them questions about their abuse but should they have a need that they want to speak about [it]... I am more than willing to hear it, share it, and support them through."

On being independent of the prison

"Someone external... These people have had psychologists, CPNs, [community psychiatric nurses], psychiatrists, and they'll tell you, 'I know the questions they're going to ask me, I've got the answers ready.' They like [the independence] especially [that] the paperwork is going out of the prison."

Giving confidentiality but explaining its limits

"They're always told right away ... 'Should you tell me about any vulnerable young person that you know may be in danger then you understand that that is information I cannot contain, and I would support you in reporting that, and if you can't I have no option.' [But] I have been truly amazed at the number of survivors, females and males, who say ... 'I'm going to report him... what he's done to me that he might be doing to somebody else.' I think it's because someone's in to support them, someone's there for them."

On challenging prisoners' self-blame

"I often say, 'Do you feel you made this happen?' 'Yes.' 'So you felt very powerful, that you had this power to make this man abuse you?' 'Mm.' And I would then say, 'I find it interesting you didn't use the same power to stop them then.' And they then realise, 'I never had any power. I was in fact powerless.'"

Ilene Easton's conclusion

"At the end what clients say is, 'I don't want to manage my anger, I want to get rid of it. Yes, I need help with my drug and alcohol problem but I need to work on why I started.' ... Every client is the same. They want to stop doing what they're doing; and they're approaching me for that reason."

What needs to be done?

All the offenders in our study turned out to be victims of repeated, severe, often unreported and uninvestigated sexual crimes as children. They gave examples of a range of pathways into offending after abuse; and while many factors influence outcomes, had they been protected as children, the future for themselves and for their victims might have been very different. There is particular urgency about the possibility that earlier intervention in abused boys' lives might reduce explosive violence through rage and fear when they become young men, causing serious injury or death. Yet their behaviour continues to appear to our criminal justice system, and to most of society, as just 'meaningless violence'.

The answer is not to excuse young men's violent assaults or other crimes, although identified PTSD should bring more compassionate lengths of sentence. Spotting what is wrong much earlier in abused boys, helping them to reveal abuse earlier and to address difficult issues of sexuality and masculinity without shame – and of course strengthening primary prevention, so they are not abused in the first place – will be far more important.

Prevention and early identification

The men's narratives gave many clues, from their behaviour and reactions, about what was happening to them as children. These suggest how better to protect boys from sexual harm.

The possibility of a child sexual abuse history in children who misuse alcohol and drugs at a young age, who abscond repeatedly from home or care, who show early sexualised behaviour or who repeatedly behave disruptively at school has been recognised for decades. Why then are these still not acted on? Since most offenders in our own study were under 23 at interview, they had grown up under recent (not distant and unreformed) child protection systems. That surely gives more cause for concern.

Routine questions about CSA need to be asked in youth settings throughout the UK when children behave in these ways, and a child protection investigation should always be seriously considered.

Helping boys to tell

Given the shame and humiliation sexual abuse tends to bring in boys, helping them to reveal the abuse will also be very important. Some proposals were outlined in Chapter Five. But they need to be 'proofed' for boys as well as for girls; settings and activities boys use must be targeted; and new technologies and social media (and older means of communication) that boys use need targeting too.

In one imaginative (actually 'low-tech') example by Barnardo's, Paul Richardson, their Middlesbrough outreach worker, described a safety initiative where he texted boys who advertised their sexual services and contact details on toilet walls. He asked them if they needed help to escape this trade (Doward, 2004). A simple idea, and the contact information was provided; why did no one think of that before?

Addressing homophobia

Since one major source of self-silencing in boys is fear of being – or being thought – gay, and given links between homophobia and violence against gay men, work is urgently needed with boys in schools and youth settings on these issues. It is vital to reduce the conviction that being sexually abused is shameful to masculinity, that homosexuality or even uncertainty about your sexuality is shameful, or that gay men in general are to blame for paedophiles' behaviour. Anti-violence initiatives among young men throughout the UK, such as the Violence Reduction Unit in Scotland,[4] need to take this issue seriously on board as part of their work.

Alternatives to exclusion

Exclusion from schools needs to be recognised as a potentially disastrous strategy for all sexually abused children, making it far more likely they get involved further with dangerous people, will become more open to sexual exploitation, and more vulnerable

---

[4] www.actiononviolence.com

to offending. Boys heavily outnumber girls in exclusions. Work on alternatives to exclusion in every school needs to have much higher priority, backed by significant government resources and commitment (see Chapter Four).

Programmes must address trauma

Unless programmes to reduce young people's violent or disturbed behaviour in care settings, residential schools or young offenders' institutions explore and address childhood traumas, they may continue having limited success. This ignores the elephant in the room. The same is true in adult prisons. Staff in all these settings need training and continuing support to change what is often avoidance of such issues, as being somehow too difficult or distressing. Avoidance also makes it harder to acknowledge and openly address coercive sexual behaviour among residents themselves.

Anger management programmes and substance misuse programmes need to explore and address the root causes of aggression and addiction, not just the symptoms. Trauma work is important too to improve the safety of partners and families of aggressive men.

In Scotland, third sector agencies such as Open Secret and Stop it Now (Scotland), and practitioners such as Sue Hampson,[5] have been working imaginatively for some years in prisons with sexual abuse trauma, and in supportive staff training. But this work is piecemeal, and very vulnerable to funding cuts or time-limited resources. It needs, instead, top-level government commitment: it needs to be seen as an essential, cost-effective tool in prisoner rehabilitation.

Young men (and women) can also be given the means to write and be involved in other arts work on the topic of abuse, and not just for therapeutic reasons. Knowing you are helping others, campaigning, and channelling anger constructively is empowering, especially for young people who have had little opportunity in their lives to experience empowerment.

---

5   www.safetosay.co.uk

Research

A needs analysis should urgently be carried out throughout male prisons, young offender institutions and community provision for offenders on the prevalence of a child sexual abuse history, and on the needs of offenders and support staff in addressing CSA trauma. But male offenders are only likely to admit their abuse if surveys are sensitively carried out, with high confidentiality. Penal institutions and prison service ethics committees need to shed their fears that somehow any research on sexual abuse histories with offenders will stir up uncontrollable emotions and consequences. These emotions already exist: powder kegs, which may explode at any time.

Second, sensitive research with killers of gay men should be carried out as a follow-up to Dr Bartlett's study, to establish the prevalence of a sexual abuse history and the background to these killings in their own lives. Such research may give important pointers to reducing these killings.

Explore backgrounds sensitively

A possible child sexual abuse history needs *routine* recognition and sensitive inquiry by criminal justice, but also by other services which form a 'revolving door' for many men (and indeed women) with repeat offending. That includes social services, homeless agencies, mental health crisis services and substance misuse agencies.

Do not replicate violence and abuse

Finally, the triggering effects of repeating abuse and violence in institutions need to be fully and finally acknowledged. This is also an ethical issue. It replays the past to use violent restraint, enforced medication and other coercive practices. These are likely to increase tension and violence in institutions, and discourage people who have already experienced great violence from considering other ways of reacting to stress. Only strong, committed management from the top of institutions will enforce change.

If we want to stop traumatised young men from behaving brutally to others, then we as a society need finally to stop teaching them repeatedly how it is done.

TEN

Rethinking sex offender programmes for survivor-perpetrators

Introduction

How can convicted sexual predators be made less dangerous to children? Public and professional concern about that question has been heightened by the highly publicised convictions of 'celebrity' offenders such as Jimmy Savile, Rolf Harris and Stuart Hall, who appeared repetitively to abuse over decades; by the ever-increasing numbers of convicted sex offenders in the UK; by a series of national and international child sexual abuse scandals in institutions, including the Catholic Church; and by the huge, ever-growing international industry in abusive images of children, aided by a range of modern and ever-developing technologies.

The Bourke and Hernandez (2009) study of internet offenders viewing child abuse images (see Chapters One and Two), which found that 85% of the men in their sex offender treatment programme eventually revealed hands-on abuse with an average of 13 victims per offender, raised further serious questions about possible risks posed by *online* sex offenders to children in the *offline* world.

There is an urgent need for dialogue between feminist and other approaches towards sex offender work. In this chapter I discuss those male sex offenders who have been both perpetrators and victims. I believe that revising our thinking towards work with male survivor offenders will reduce future risks to children. These changes will challenge our assumptions, but need not betray our principles. I go on to discuss ways in which feminist approaches can truly inform general sex offender work: that will also, I believe, reduce future risks to children.

Feminist traditions and sex offenders

I write from a feminist tradition. We have not viewed work to change known sex offenders against children as a priority for reducing child sexual abuse (CSA). Feminists have spoken with, and for, women and children as survivors, first and foremost. Gendered power relations in society have been seen as the key to permitting and encouraging sexual violence to persist largely unchecked and undetected. They are also seen to sustain woman-blame, through social and legal structures. Radical political and social change have thus been viewed as the drivers which will improve the safety of women and children.

Also, given that only a small percentage of male offenders against children is identified, we have considered primary prevention work far more effective than work with known perpetrators. Primary prevention includes work in schools and communities – to influence socialisation of young men and women into genuine mutual respect and equality – along with the creation of more equitable legal and criminal justice systems for women and children.

Thus, while staff who work with sex offenders will include feminist practitioners, feminist influence in shaping or seeking to improve sex offender programmes has been marginal. In fact some feminist organisations working with physically and sexually abused women and children have seen this work as a positive diversion from their limited, much-needed, resources. Most remain sceptical about the effectiveness of the work, especially since the very term 'treatment' conjures images of a disease or compulsion, a conclusion about sexual abuse which they reject.

Why question our approach?

Without abandoning our priorities above, I believe it is time for feminists to have closer concern with, and involvement in, programmes for known sex offenders, especially offenders against children. It is also time to question some cherished beliefs. There are several reasons for this.

- It has become ever clearer to any of us who have worked with child sexual abuse over a long time, that many male perpetrators are also survivors of CSA. We need to decide if we go on dismissing this as an influence, or if it could be addressed to help potential victims. Also, if survivors have always been our priority, how is it ethical to exclude those particular ones?

- While still obviously a minority of all perpetrators, there are now far more known sex offenders who are potentially accessible to work with than ever before. In 1999 there were approximately 3,000 people on UK sex offenders' registers; there were more than 48,000 in 2014, with numbers growing each year (Ministry of Justice, 2014).

- Evidence has been consistent that young people under 18 form a significant proportion of perpetrators, a quarter or more (Finkelhor et al, 2009; Finkelhor, 2012). Do we give low priority to changing their behaviour? If not, how do we decide on a cut-off age beyond which treatment is considered undeserved or unimportant?

- We need a stronger voice in influencing the growing body of mainstream work with known sex offenders, because there are so many unsatisfactory aspects of this work, particularly in the way that it ignores feminist insights. That must cast doubt on how effective it can be.

Rejecting relevance of victimisation

Feminist organisations working against sexual violence have on one point agreed with those who run mainstream sex offender treatment programmes, and with non-abusing survivors of child sexual abuse. All have resisted accepting that a sexual abuse history is relevant to committing sexual crime.

First of all, this is thought to imply a simplistic 'cycle of abuse' theory, whereby abused children will become abusers themselves. The melodramatically styled 'bite of the vampire', this mechanism has been variously understood as modelling, social learning or 'acting out'; as identification with the aggressor, to restore personal power; as misdirected rage; and as a compulsion or addiction, perhaps through imprinted arousal patterns (Glasser et al, 2001; Cohen et al, 2002; Epps and Fisher, 2004; Hall and Hall, 2007).

Central to the feminist rejection of 'cycles of abuse' theory is that it ignores major political, social and cultural influences, particularly gendered power relations. Rightly, 'cycles of abuse' cannot explain rape used as policy in war, in racially or religiously motivated attacks, nor in political torture. Cultural beliefs about the inferiority of women, and about proper and improper behaviour in women – not 'cycles of abuse' – have been highlighted in publicised sexual exploitation cases of vulnerable teenage girls in England by some men of Pakistani heritage (see Chapter Four).

For feminists, cycle of abuse theory has also been seen to excuse male behaviour, reducing impetus for measures to combat sexism and violence against women and children. Through failing to challenge structural inequalities, it seems politically safe. Thus distinguished feminist Professor Liz Kelly has said that in cycle of abuse theory 'attention shifts from the centrality of power and control to notions of sexual deviance, obsession and addiction … to the medical and individualized explanations, which we (feminists) have spent so much time and energy attempting to deconstruct and challenge' (Kelly, 1996, p. 2).

I myself previously wrote:

> The theory's most serious fault is that it is ahistorical, unconnected with the wider society and its values … where did all this abuse spring from? The only answer is from the parents, and the great-grandparents, and ultimately, one supposes, from some caveman and his collusive wife. But why did the men behave like that, what made them think it was acceptable? (Nelson, 1987, p. 78)

Again, adult survivors of CSA are hugely concerned at being stigmatised when many among professionals and public assume that abused children will become abusers – even though the logic of that assumption is clearly false. If 15 out of 100 sexually abused children become perpetrators, every perpetrator will indeed have been abused: but 85 abused children will not have become perpetrators.

Mainstream sex offender programmes in the UK, where cognitive behavioural approaches have dominated, have also resisted working with abused adult offenders' victimisation. Reasons include fears that it might be used as an excuse to avoid responsibility for their sexual crime among offenders who already tend to minimise; through suspicion that offenders' claims may be untrue; and through the cognitive behavioural tendency to concentrate on current cognitions, rather than on the roots of behaviour and beliefs. Also, staff often feel untrained, nervous and inadequate to carry out trauma work with sex offenders – just as staff so often feel untrained, nervous and inadequate to work with sexual abuse survivors in mental health services (Nelson and Hampson, 2008).

The problem of evidence

These are all very valid concerns. The problem is that their ideological force has largely blocked constructive discussion of *any* influence of childhood sexual victimisation. Yet I and many others working with child sexual abuse have over decades met growing numbers of young and adult men who, we became aware, were both survivors and abusers. We can no longer ignore this: we have to re-examine our previous reluctance to consider the possible influence of being a childhood victim.

We have particularly noticed victim-perpetrators in the most prolific forms of sexual abuse such as the repetitive assault of numerous young boys; and in highly disturbing or sadistic forms such as organised ritual abuse, or the assault of babies and toddlers, with its thriving industry of online abuse images. Male survivors have also described being attacked by boys 'acting out' their own experience of sexual abuse in residential care or at boarding school (Corby et al, 2001; Nelson, 2009). Thus the question becomes increasingly uncomfortable, the 'elephant in the room'. Do we continue to ignore, minimise or dispute findings about sexually abused perpetrators, and any possible influence on their beliefs and behaviour?

Feminists working with violence and abuse have previously met the challenge of new, initially unwelcome evidence. Examples include violence by women in same-sex relationships (Kelly, 1991; Ristock, 2002) and in organised ritual and sadistic abuse (Scott, 2001). Besides, some feminist writers have already suggested how a feminist understanding of the *structural* nature of sexual violence can inform work with offenders, yet still take humanistic account of their *individual* situations, experience and psychological needs in bringing about personal change (Featherstone and Fawcett, 1994; Lancaster and Lumb, 1999).

Information has now grown considerably, through male survivor testimony and through inquiries into children's homes, boarding schools or the churches, that suffering CSA is a significant issue for men too. Research now suggests a prevalence of 13–18% of males experiencing CSA (Dube et al, 2005; Hopper, 2012). That is both an ethical acknowledgement of the abuse of males, and a practical point that perpetration by a minority of sexually abused males now becomes more feasible, in terms of the numbers involved.

Research studies have found that the percentage of child sex abusers who were sexually victimised as children varies widely depending on methodology, ranging from 28% to 93% (Glasser et al, 2001; Hall and Hall, 2007). It is already known of course that an extremely high percentage of female sexual abusers (not the subjects of this particular chapter) have themselves been sexually abused.

However, men who predate serially on very large numbers of boys, and men perpetrating the most violent, hostile or perverted forms of violence towards women and children, appear from research to have particularly high rates of childhood sexual victimisation. Hilton and Mezey (1996) found that the more deviant the (secure hospital) patients' behaviour, the higher the rates of past assault.

They also found, as did Cohen et al (2002) and Briggs (2003), that perpetrators tended to abuse victims in ways and at ages *which replicated the abuser's own abuse trauma*(emphasis added).. Might this, for example, give a partial explanation for the high proportions of *male* victims of abusive Catholic priests, who were trained in all-male seminaries from a young age – closed, authoritarian environments very vulnerable to sexual and physical abuse? (Nelson, 2013).

Disconnecting two confused debates

I believe we first need to clarify what this discussion is about, because the debate has been full of confusion and muddled thinking. It is about a child sexual abuse history among known sexual abusers: not the percentage of all sexually abused children who become perpetrators.

Research produces varying, imprecise estimates of how many sexually abused children go on to abuse, from 7% to 26% (see Skuse et al, 1998; Cohen et al, 2002; Steel and Herlitz, 2005).Yet only large scale prospective studies, over decades, could begin to approach accuracy about this. Even these prospective studies would be inadequate, since most CSA survivors are not identified as such while they are children.

We should be asserting instead what we do know, from research and practice: that a substantial majority of sexually abused children, female and male, do *not* go on to abuse others. Thus where child safety is an issue, such as when CSA survivors apply to work with children, they should be assessed without prejudice, and by the same criteria as everyone else.

An influence, not a cycle

The case, then, is clearly very weak that victim-to-perpetrator abuse can be described as a 'cycle' at all. If a majority of sexually abused males do not go on to abuse others, and when childhood victimisation has been shown as only one of several influences turning some victims into perpetrators, how can such generalised terminology be justified? Additional influences include witnessing repeated domestic violence, and having absolutely no one to turn to for support as a child or teenager (Glasser et al, 2001; Bentovim, 2002; Cohen et al, 2002; Salter et al, 2003; Wilcox et al, 2004; Easton, in Nelson, 2009).

Rather, it appears from research and practice experience that victimisation can significantly *influence* the belief systems and behaviour of some perpetrators: especially the form, the severity and the particular targets of their sexual crimes. These are far from trivial questions for victims who have become, or may become, targets. They deserve that we explore the issue.

What type of role and influence, then, might sexual victimisation have on the minority of sexually abused males who become perpetrators?

Part of male socialisation

Clearly, traumatic early sexualisation does not inevitably make males physiologically addictive to abusing, since many male victims experience difficult or even compulsive sexual feelings, yet channel these without assaulting others. Thus male survivors of child sexual abuse have described endless superficial one-night stands, the loneliness and shame of compulsive masturbation or the self-degradation of repetitively seeking anonymous sex in public places (Lisak, 1994; Hunter, 1995; Nelson, 2009).

Nor surely (to meet the earlier concerns of Liz Kelly and myself, quoted above) is victim-to-perpetrator experience some 'individualised' deviant process, unrelated to society's wider values. Both the widespread perpetration and the acceptance of sexual violence have been part of traditional male and female socialisation, which feminists have long sought to expose and combat. That work has been a huge part of their political struggle, nationally and internationally.

When some male victims go on to abuse others, they can be seen to adopt the messages given by their abusers about what traditional masculinity is, what wider power relationships are between adults and children, and what kinds are violence are legitimate or justifiable. Many male CSA survivors' descriptions of their abusive childhoods tell of a macho masculinity which informed them by word and act that it was acceptable to do this to women and children; that it was their responsibility, not the abuser's; that men cannot control their sexual desires; that violence is acceptable, giving males power and status; that you are nothing if not the powerful one; and that a male victim who stays a victim is a 'poof' and weakling, someone less than a man. (Lisak et al, 1996; Sorsoli et al, 2008; Nelson, 2009).

When these become part of victim-perpetrators' attitudes and beliefs towards women and children, the 'bite of the vampire' becomes mental rather than physical. What problem could there be in feminists accommodating that, as part of a process of male socialisation? Perpetrators will still need to take responsibility for their actions and the process of change. However, both their abusive experience and their reactions to it will be acknowledged as interconnected with society's wider culture and values.

In support of this argument it is valuable to consider why few females appear to move from being victims to becoming perpetrators of sexual crime. If the effects of being sexually abused involved some physiological compulsion to act it out – or some undefined collapse in moral values and self-control – we might expect more victimised women to become sexual abusers. But if the key does indeed lie in male socialisation into beliefs and attitudes, then abused women clearly have neither the impetus nor the expectation to live up to 'macho' male values.

They would not expect to identify with the powerful abuser, nor to gain power and status by so doing, nor would they believe their desires were uncontrollable. They would not feel more of a woman by becoming an abuser, nor less of a woman for being abused. The experience of CSA does not challenge their gender identity, as it does to males, and no female survivor over decades has ever told me that it did: for the depressing reason that across the world, violence and victimisation remain integral to so much of female experience.

Effects of severe early life trauma

It is neither betraying principles nor adopting medical quackery to be open to new knowledge and insights, and to consider another likely influence on some victim-perpetrators. One area where knowledge and understanding is continually growing involves the long-term mental and physical effects of serious early childhood trauma. This is a huge topic, and space prohibits in-depth discussion here. In short, severe abuse and neglect in the early years of life produces post-traumatic effects and neurological influences which can, for some, include emotional numbing; loss of ability to empathise with self or others; distorted attachments; repetitive re-enactments of trauma, as victim, victimiser or both; unresolved grief and fear, leading to aggressive or violent behaviour; and a mix of fear and sexual arousal to abusive situations (van der Kolk et al, 1996a, 1996b, 2005; Creeden, 2004; de Zulueta, 2006; Beech and Gillespie, 2014).

This process has already been explored and widely accepted in work with juvenile sexual offenders (Jonson-Reid, 2001; Hutton, 2007). McMackin et al's study (2002) found very high rates of trauma exposure among juvenile offenders, with 77.5% exposed to three or more types of trauma. Sexual abuse was seen in all but 12.5% of the sample, with 47.5% exposed to both sexual and physical abuse. Mean age of onset for sexual abuse was seven years. The overall rate of PTSD was 84% for those who suffered both physical and sexual abuse.

Trauma-associated effects of fear, helplessness and horror were linked to their offending. That suggested a close relationship between their trauma and their offence cycle. Professor Simon Hackett considers it both standard and widely recognised that addressing adolescents' own victimisation is crucial to their treatment. (Hackett, 2002; Hackett et al, 2006, 2013). Given that numerous adult perpetrators began abusing as children or young teenagers, are we saying then that at some particular age these influences cease to exist? That argument seems hard to maintain.

Neurobiological findings about trauma do not mean that such effects are unchangeable, nor are they handy excuses for assault. They surely mean that we should now consider if they do contribute to some repetitive, abusive behaviour. Current sex offender programmes largely fail to acknowledge this influence. So we need to ask what kinds of skilled work might succeed in doing so.

Cognitive behavioural programmes by their nature rely on challenging existing thinking patterns, and teaching people to think differently, thus altering emotions and behaviour. But what if an offender's brain is not currently in a place to understand? What, in particular, if there are blocks to achieving the 'victim empathy' which sex offender programmes have traditionally sought to instil?

The empathy conundrum

That is a particularly important question in relation to some recent meta-analyses of studies which examine key factors in sex offender recidivism. These meta-analyses have questioned the whole importance and validation of 'victim empathy' in preventing reoffending (for example Hanson and Morton-Bourgon, 2005; Mann and Barnett, 2013).

This questioning is likely to encourage the reduction of victim empathy content in future programmes. I believe that would be a very mistaken direction to take. A critique of the positivist assumptions made in such meta-analyses cannot be attempted here: there is space only to raise questions and issues which I hope other people specialising in sex offender work can explore thoroughly.

- What is the whole value of using known reoffending as the criterion for making such vital judgements, when most sexual offences are neither reported nor admitted?

- How can these studies possibly discern exactly which factor out of many influenced a perpetrator to reoffend, or influenced him to *avoid* a reoffence?

- How relevant are conclusions of meta-analyses if they do not specifically consider either sex offenders against children, or survivor offenders: men who themselves have a victim status?

- Have perhaps existing 'victim empathy' modules been deficient in the first place? There is even an admitted lack of general agreement on what the phrase means. Might modules which encourage 'victim identification' be more meaningful for survivor offenders (feeling, as well as knowing, that the pain I inflict is the same as my own)? Ward and Durran (2013) also have a useful discussion on broader concepts of altruism in work with sex offenders.

Given the emphasis in conventional sex offender programmes on learning skills, Creeden (2004) says the current focus on a cognitive behavioural, relapse prevention model ignores the neuro-processing obstacles that make it difficult for many to learn, remember, and retrieve skills they are taught to avoid committing abuse. Often, he says, clients learn to *say* the right thing (about their 'thinking errors') but never integrate these cognitive lessons into their relationships and behaviour. Techniques less loaded to verbal learning are 'perhaps the most obvious change we can make in our treatment with these clients' (Creeden, 2004).

Stein (2006) challenges offender treatment programmes to address serious childhood trauma, instead of just trying to correct cognitions in a cognitive behavioural model. She thought-provokingly concludes that severe trauma has created *dissociated moral feeling* in those offenders who have been seen as without conscience. That process, she argues, undermines moral integration, by perpetuating the illusion that one is not morally implicated in what one does. Stein's important work argues for the integration of dissociated memories and emotions as the first goal of therapy. Her work challenges ideas of psychopathy and sociopathy in children and adults.

If Stein has indeed perceived the reason why some men assault very large numbers of children repetitively and repeatedly over decades, without any apparent feeling or connection with their victims' obvious distress, there could be few more important tasks for child protection than finding a means of emotional reconnection.

Through such developing knowledge about effects of serious childhood trauma, I believe we need to open our minds to new possibilities. For instance might those viewers of abuse images of children on the internet who are *not* also hands-on perpetrators include many child sexual abuse victims, repeatedly visiting without resolution re-enactments of their own childhood trauma? Martin Henry, manager of Stop it Now Scotland, has found a majority of men on the organisation's internet offenders' programme in Edinburgh disclosed a history of CSA.[1]

---

[1] www.stopitnow.org.uk/scotland_internet_offence_services.htm

That question is not asked in order to sympathise with people who sustain an enormous international market in brutal assaults against children and young people. It is to argue that, with research and more widely available trauma support, we might reduce their behaviour, and safeguard more children.

Only an excuse?

However, a widespread belief blocks willingness even to consider with sex offenders the effects of early childhood trauma. This is that perpetrators' claims are 'just an excuse': that they are probably lying, seeking easier treatment, or avoiding responsibility for their actions. That concern has also been a major influence on the reasoning that accredited, cognitive behavioural sex offender programmes should not address offenders' own trauma at that time (Adams, 2003; Ward and Moreton, 2008).

There are several problems with this. First of all, wishing something to be untrue does not make it untrue. Choosing to believe some survivors about their past but not others is neither ethical nor consistent. Giving credibility to people's accounts of their childhood experience, and respecting their needs as survivors, have been central values for feminists who work with violence and abuse. We should pause very hard before we align ourselves with influential lobbies who dismiss and demean the testimony of sexual abuse survivors (see Chapter Two).

Just as there are considered to be the deserving and undeserving poor, so, according to such thinking, there have been deserving and undeserving victims of child sexual abuse. Yet Ward and Moreton (2008) argue that ethically, survivor-perpetrators deserve 'moral repair' as much as anyone else. Addressing these offenders' own abuse, and defending the values violated in their own abuse can, they argue, also make them more aware of the legitimate claims of their own victims. For Ward and Moreton, it's entirely possible to meet our ethical obligations to sex offenders who were abused, while expecting them to accept responsibility for their own acts. These ethical arguments, and their implications for social work values and practice towards sex offenders, are thoroughly and sensitively developed by Cowburn and Myers (2016).

Second, disbelief in offenders' accounts of childhood abuse is unlikely to be soundly based. That males would willingly invent and broadcast a CSA history runs strongly counter to research and practice experience that they find such admissions even harder, more threatening to their sexual identity, and more humiliating than women do, with great fear of ridicule from male peers – especially in 'macho' prison settings (Cowburn, 2002).

An influential American paper has been widely publicised to justify disbelief in sex offenders' claims. Hindman and Peters found that when a polygraph (lie detector) was used with them, claims by 65% that they had been sexually abused in childhood dropped to 32%. (Hindman and Peters, 2001). It has been widely misreported that these polygraphed offenders were told they would return to prison if they lied. On the contrary, they had been given immunity from further prosecution, whatever their response to the lie detector had been.

Fabrication of an abuse history runs so counter to research and practice experience with males that alternative explanations of this influential paper must be considered. The strongest possibility is that these sex offenders already felt unsure if their childhood sexual experience *was* abusive, so 'played safe' under polygraph challenge and changed their answer. Sex offenders are consistently much less likely than non-abusing victims to call their abuse – even when very young – harmful or non-consensual. Yet when they actually describe what they dismiss as 'sexual advances', 'experiences', 'encounters' or 'involvements' these do appear abusive, often severely so (Waterhouse et al, 1994; Cohen et al, 2002; Briggs, 2003). Briggs also that found that sex offenders were on average abused for a longer time, by significantly more people, than non-offending CSA victims. Denial of harm, of course, crucially helps sex offenders to deny that they harm their own victims.

Darryl Fisher, formerly with the Lucy Faithfull Foundation and the probation service and now an independent consultant, has screened for trauma symptoms in male sex offenders.

> "Probation officers say to me, 'So the next time they abuse a kid, they can say, it's my trauma, not me.' But I have never met a man who justifies abuse by his

own trauma. I've never ever met anyone who's used that as an excuse. You have to persuade them that there is any connection." (personal interview, 2013)

Ilene Easton has been employed to counsel male and female prisoners in Scotland who have suffered CSA trauma. In 11 years she has counselled more than 900 prisoners: a majority of the males were sexual offenders. She recalls: "The sex offenders I have worked with have totally disconnected ... they've known intellectually (that they were abused) but ... never acknowledged in there, deep inside, the effect."

Jay Adams, with 25 years of sex offender work, wrote:

> It has not been my clinical experience that sex offenders ... try to use their own victimization as an excuse for their deviant behaviour ... one of the most difficult parts of therapy is breaking down their denial that they were abused, or that the abuse damaged them in any way. Sex offenders are often deeply affected by processing their own abuse and seeing the connections with their offenses ... more than anything else, the field of sex offender treatment needs more research on the relationships between early victimisation and later sexual offending. (Adams, 2003, p. 85)

Trauma work with sex offenders

When sex offenders have also been victims, what can be the effects of making the reconnection? The positive experience of trauma counsellors working with adult sex offenders in both Scotland and England deserves further research, evaluation and trialling. These schemes could fit very well with the values of the more humanistic *Good Lives* models of offender work currently being developed in the UK (Walker et al, 2007).[2] In Scotland the new programme informed by the Good Lives model is known as Moving Forward Making Changes. Such models explore

---

2   www.goodlivesmodel.com/information

offenders' needs for intimacy, friendship and self esteem, and plan for a positive future: a 'strengths-based' model. However, even within this model there has been little development so far of trauma-based work. Modules exploring trauma may not be effective either if 'dropped in' at various points of the programme. Where survivor offenders are concerned, they may need to come first.

Ilene Easton's remit has been to work with any prisoners on abuse trauma issues, not specifically to tackle sex offending. However, she has observed considerable change in many sex offenders she has worked with when they have begun addressing their own sexual trauma.

In a detailed account of her techniques (Nelson, 2009, pp. 120–8), Easton finds initially an emotional disconnection from their own abuse: "they never acknowledged in there, deep inside, the effect." They were also convinced that they were somehow responsible for their own abuse. These beliefs in turn enabled them to convince themselves that their own victims were responsible. But when they realised their own powerlessness as children, most sex offenders gradually reconnected with the pain, betrayal and trauma of their own childhoods. Until they respected and forgave themselves, they could not respect their victims "Their perpetrator taught them how to gain power, because they remember that feeling of helplessness and how powerful they saw the perpetrator."

But they did not feel powerful for long: "That's why most of them had to go back and do it more than once... it isn't their power to keep."

Easton also found that the minority of abused men who became abusers seemed to differ even from other sexually abused prisoners in their lack of childhood support:

> "In my experience, when I work with people in the community there's always some sort of support for them somewhere, they've not all had idyllic childhoods either, but there's been someone, a gran, an aunt, someone supportive, that may not have ever known, but that love and nurturing was there for

them. The ones I've worked with seemed to have lacked any form of nurturing." (Nelson, 2009)

Easton found that with a majority of the sex offenders she worked with, dismay at their crimes was often awakened for the first time, through achieving genuine fellow feeling and identification with their victims and acknowledge their own victimhood without shame and blame; it also enabled them admit responsibility and to avoid scapegoating, particularly of women if their own mothers had failed to protect them. Thus she sees this trauma work as directly protecting women and children (see Chapter Nine).

Insight into offending

Ilene Easton, like Darryl Fisher, does not claim that this work has changed every victim-survivor, and a minority have remained unchanged. But she has seen remarkable improvements in insight and empathy, as has Fisher in his trauma work with sex offenders. Working with men assessed as posing high or very high risk of sexual recidivism, he discovered these often had undiagnosed chronic trauma symptoms, largely through abusive and neglectful early childhoods.

> "If you are trauma-aware, it can help you a lot to understand all the paraphiliac stuff, and the connections between their early experiences and the risk they now present. [Understanding their trauma] also offers the means to understand why some men repetitively offend against male victims and stranger victims: it's to do with trauma re-enactment." (personal interview, 2013)

For Fisher, trauma symptom screening can help produce effective risk assessment and interventions with men who previously resisted orthodox sex offender work. He is clear from his professional experience that for some men, addressing trauma symptoms first through trauma counselling, and their abusive behaviour second, helps them most effectively to understand their behaviour and lowers the risks of reoffending. Orthodox approaches with such men may have no meaning:

> "Asking an offender to address issues of victim empathy is somewhat of a losing task for someone with an impaired sense of self, arising from chronic trauma symptoms. For some men, you will almost be speaking a foreign language." (personal interview, 2013)

Martin Henry makes clear he carries out preliminary, not specialised, trauma work with offenders in Edinburgh who view child sex abuse images online: he does believe though that his work also has value in enabling offenders with childhood trauma to become ready to address that specialist work.

> "Insight is a precursor to change, not the change itself. Many of the men don't understand what drives them to look at this stuff. Dual-status men draw a narrative of their lives, talk about positive as well as bad experiences ... so, gaining understanding of what have been the things along the way that have propelled them. Working at the point of crisis is the optimum time ... at the point of arrest, not ages later ... when the often catastrophic impact this has on them, their jobs and family means that this is a prime opportunity to begin interventions." (personal interview, 2014)

Examples of trauma work with survivor-perpetrators deserve more research, with piloting and evaluation of similar work elsewhere. So too does work on abuse and trauma in violent or sexual offenders, by the S.W. London Academic Network (SWAN), headed by Dr Gill Mezey and other specialists. It is co ordinated by the Centre for Abuse & Trauma Studies at Kingston University.[3]

---

[3]   www.cats-rp.org.uk

Need for inner motivation

UK Prison and Probation Service programmes have worked to enable offenders to develop strategies for self-control, as well as enforcing external controls. They aim to 'ethically reconstruct' offenders, to recognise high risk situations for their own relapse and to make strategies to avoid future offending. But self-control relies on having continuing *motivation* to prevent relapse.

That seems to me a central problem about virtually all these programmes. If their sex offences give them pleasure, a sense of mastery and sexual gratification – if also for some, the effects of serious trauma block ability to acquire identification with the pain and suffering of the child – why then should they find the internal controls to stop abusing? Inner motivation involving feeling and emotion surely need to be strong. That is why I believe screening for sexual trauma, and work to address it when it is found, is important.

This work can also encourage practitioners to look behind psychological variables such as 'impulsivity' and 'intimacy deficits' in their offender assessments, currently seen as 'personality characteristics' which increase risks of reoffending. Practitioners would be more likely to ask where offenders acquired these tendencies in the first place; if, perhaps, these arose from experience of serious trauma, and if they could be changed.

Some policy implications

If reconnection with the emotional pain of their own victimisation has been found to increase empathy, understanding and a motivation against reoffending among some victim-perpetrators, it is surely worth trialling widely throughout the UK. That work could precede a sex offender programme, or be a very early component in such programmes. The results can be compared with current accredited, cognitive behavioural programmes. Although the latter have been widely considered 'what works', this conclusion did not come from setting hopes very high; and the acid test of known recidivism rates remain a very imperfect indicator of success, since most sexual crime still remains secret and unreported. It is worth remembering that meta-analytic studies (such as Dolan, 2009; Schmucker and Losel, 2008) suggest that a cognitive behavioural/relapse prevention type programme can reduce sexual reoffending by only about ten percentage points. Even then, results from the Prison Service SOTP (The Prison Service Sex Offender Treatment Programme) indicated that high risk offenders need additional intervention.

Detailed exploration of childhood abuse history, along with therapies specifically to address abuse trauma, should be routinely available in work with sexual abuse perpetrators, especially those considered highly dangerous and disturbed, in secure/special and psychiatric hospitals. These may prove more successful in reducing their dangerousness than conventional high-dosage antipsychotic medication, or attempts at behavioural treatments with little connection to their earlier experiences. Such work could better inform the lengthy risk assessments undertaken on such offenders, and the huge unwieldy files which staff accumulate on them in the course of their lives.

Skilled abuse trauma specialists should routinely be available to work with young males in residential schools and secure units who show harmful sexual behaviour. Through this work, some past behaviours in young men may at least become more explicable: rather than shocking stories beyond our understanding, or our humanity.

Feminists need to influence sex offender programmes

What else needs to change about current sex offender programmes? I have argued that feminists need to rethink our approach to victim-perpetrators. But those who design and implement sex offender programmes in turn need to take on board the positive contributions which feminist insights can make. These could make the programmes more effective with male offenders, and more rooted in the 'real world.'

If most conventional sex offender programmes fail to address possible childhood trauma, another problem makes them peculiar and contradictory. Feminist influence and analysis are 'dropped in' at two (admittedly important) points – the content of cognitive distortions about women and children, and acceptance that work with offenders must be challenging and 'distrustful', not collusive or naive. Yet everything else about the programmes seems almost untouched by feminist insights.

Psychological theories continue to dominate theories on the aetiology of sex offending. Offenders are still seen as a minority of *individual* deviants from the rest of society, and their *individual* psychological features and pathology have been the focus, to the neglect of social and cultural influences. There is faith that if we can finally reach a scientific understanding of the causes of child sexual abuse, then recidivism will be reduced.

Yet any basic explanation is lacking about very major points, such as why the vast majority of sex offenders are male, and what the links are with male sexuality and male socialisation. Those drawbacks are recognised by Purvis and Ward (2006) and by Ward and Beech (2006), but these writers miss what sex offender programmes need to integrate from feminist insights. The key questions to resolve are not for example about the precise extent of male power, the dogmatic viewpoints of some radical feminists, nor the relationship of masculinities to sexual prowess. They are about the *interconnection of individual offenders' behaviour and beliefs with those of the wider society.*

I described how feminist writers such as Lancaster and Lumb (1999) and Featherstone and Fawcett (1994) made the important observation that a feminist understanding of the structural nature of sexual violence can inform work with offenders, yet still take humanistic account of their individual situations and needs, in order to bring about personal change. Likewise – to invert this – conventional programmes need to take account of structural features in society, when devising work to challenge sex offenders' beliefs and behaviour towards women and children.

Men of all backgrounds and cultures

Feminists have long been aware, through listening closely to survivors, that sex-crime perpetrators come from every class, religious, educational and ethnic background. Yet sex offender programmes and risk assessments have been heavily based on changing those believed to be a minority of psychologically labelled individual deviants. In fact, they actually reflect the kinds of men who were most likely to be *caught* (for example, those lacking social skills, who were disadvantaged, substance misusers, mentally ill, learning-disabled, care leavers, and so on). But they then have no answer when suddenly, thousands of men are found to be viewing, collecting and exchanging abusive online images of children through developments in technology and detection. Nor when these include many middle class, highly educated, professional men with strong social skills, and *no previous criminal record.*

Nor can they take account of the widespread ambivalence about rape, about consent, and about justifications of sex with under-age girls, shown repeatedly in attitude surveys among the general population, and indeed in public comment online about sex cases in the media (BBC News, 1999; One Poll, 2015; Rape Crisis Scotland, 2014; and see Chapter Four). Nor of the fact that ordinary men appear to desire, and indeed are allowed to marry, prepubertal girls in many countries internationally. Nor of the huge demand for online abuse images of children and the fact that men identified have come from all social classes, many with no past criminal record. They may fail to notice whether the environment in which they are working to change sex offenders is one of gender respect and gender equality or its opposite: as Malcolm Cowburn in his important paper 'A man's world' (2002) has highlighted in relation to working within macho prison subcultures.

This does not mean resorting to some crude parody-feminism that 'all men are as bad as each other'. It does mean closely connecting sex offender programmes to wider work with boys and men in the community, and being informed by that work. It means acknowledging sex offenders' beliefs and behaviours which are, unfortunately, less 'cognitive distortions' than frequent beliefs in our society – which can be challenged by drawing upon wider work being done in the community. The sex offender programmes would then be informed by an honest appraisal and awareness of the links between many offenders, and a much wider range of males in the population.

That will in turn urge more caution about labelling sex offenders with various personality disorders and characteristics which are considered to set them apart. That will also make it easier to identify what remain as more unusual aspects of some sex offenders' beliefs and behaviour, and how these might be worked with. It will mean paying keen attention to the workers' own attitudes and beliefs on gender issues, and to the nature of the learning environment in prisons, probation services and community settings.

Integrating some feminist insights

How might cultural and structural factors be accounted for better in sex offender programmes? Here are some examples:

- By including in all such programmes significant discussion about what it means to be a worthwhile man, partner and father, and about how far 'macho' behaviour is necessary to be a 'real man'.

- By offering some theoretical perspectives on why the vast majority of sex offenders are male, enabling offenders to think about and discuss this too.

- By not shrinking from challenging cultural beliefs which disparage women and girls – or certain women and girls, such as the stigmatised young women who have been heavily involved in child sexual exploitation – with perpetrators from a range of ethnic and cultural backgrounds.

- If they have a generalised hostility to women, by not fearing to explore underlying reasons for this in perpetrators' own lives.

- By taking time and effort to ensure that, as far as possible, the staffing and environment within which people are delivering sex offender programmes give an example of gender equality, non-macho values and a broad understanding of feminism. Cowburn's critique on unintentional yet extensive collusion in prisons (2002) is a valuable resource here. All staff involved on sex offender work need training and awareness-raising about creating appropriate environments for work with sex offenders.

- Joined-up working: sex offender programme designers and staff need to see prevention schemes in the communities to which offenders will return as interconnected with their own work (see Chapter Six). They need to support that community work, and to build links with, for instance, those running respect programmes for young people in schools, and for young men in criminal justice settings beyond prison, and in wider youth settings.

The need to remember

Finally, in any discussion about sex offenders it remains vitally important never to lose sight of two key points.

- If a minority of abused boys do become abusers (if in particular they become the more dangerous, prolific, or sadistic offenders) then this simply gives greater, not less, urgency to implementing programmes for the *primary prevention* of child sexual abuse. If fewer boys are abused in the first place, then an even smaller minority of these will also become abusers. This is not just a practical point but an ethical one, to protect all future victims.

- It must never be forgotten when discussing victim-perpetrators that some major examples of sexual violence both nationally and internationally cannot be explained by reference to prior individual trauma. These include mass sexual violence during wars, against religious or racial minorities, and in political torture. Thus work on victim-perpetrators' own victimisation can only ever be one part of a strategy to combat and reduce CSA; and the central aim for work with victim-perpetrators must *always* be for the greater protection of children and women.

Conclusion

We can never eradicate child sexual abuse. But we can reduce it substantially, along with the numbers of women and men, girls and boys who suffer lifelong pain, distress and stigma as a result. There are already many past and current models of good practice, and this book demonstrates some of them. Harnessed to imaginative use of new technologies, which can meet the considerable and growing challenges in the online world, these can significantly reduce a serious crime which inflicts such costs on the whole of society.

A lack of promising models and initiatives, which can be adapted, are thus are not the problem. Rather it is lack of priority and political will, it is complacency, denial or mere embarrassment, a failure of courage, and continuing prejudice against the most vulnerable young people and those who try to support them. It is the size and power of lobbies which support and protect networks of abusers. Their threadbare theories minimising or denying CSA have been swallowed with relief, in preference to confronting realities which at the extremes excite horror, but which more often are mundane, squalid and distressingly widespread.

This is why those of us who have campaigned for decades against CSA have been pressing many of the same arguments for 20 or 30 years. And why there are so often two steps forward, then two back, in sexual abuse work. Time is overdue now to ask policymakers, managers and practitioners in particular *why* unsustainable things have continued to happen for many decades, and why obvious changes have not.

Pick a few examples from many: why does the criminal justice system still rely so heavily on children disclosing sexual abuse, when we know most children do not? Why have possible indicators of sexual abuse long been written into child protection guidelines if hardly anyone acts on them? Why does the medical model still dominate in mental health when psychiatric wards have always been filled with the victims of child sexual abuse?

The urgency of prevention is one key message of this book, not just from the chapters on children, but at times even more powerfully from the chapters on the consequences for adult survivors. That wide range of mental and physical distress, suicidal feelings, at times addictions and even offending *will* happen to many of today's and tomorrow's children if preventive action is not taken. But it can be.

Instead of repeating the mantra about needing yet more research, or yet more inquiries, why do we not just radically improve policy and practice? I hope this book will hearten campaigners in all professions to put pressure on policymakers and commissioners of services to do that, to implement and evaluate some models here and elsewhere, and to reclaim excellent practice from the past, much of which was apparently considered too dangerously successful to survive. Pressure, too, on national and devolved governments to provide the coherence of at last developing and implanting *an over-arching national strategy* for the prevention of child sexual abuse: as recommended yet again, this time in the Children's Commissioner report (2015).

There are, after all, so many committed people who want change to happen, people who only need consistent, determined leadership and support. With the reopening of many historic inquiries, with the revelations that many figures with power, respectability and celebrity were using children ruthlessly without redress, adult survivors, women and men, are now stronger and more vocal than ever before. That has been the most significant recent development.

There is great strength in alliances with survivors but they need to be made with equality not marginalisation, and without pity or patronisation. Survivors and their support agencies must at last become integral to local safeguarding boards, to child protection committees, policy forums and inquiries at every level. They will not now be silenced again.

Widespread public disgust at the wealth of revelations about powerful and 'celebrity' abusers can also be harnessed to strengthen resolve for change. There are far more of us who want to protect children than those who seek to harm them. We can unite in our collective strength. I hope some of the messages from the chapters in this book have been helpful in that drive for lasting change, and by demonstrating how events throughout survivors' lives are interconnected, those currently painful events can be changed to rewarding ones.

Biggest challenge for the future?

Professor Alexis Jay has warned:

> We need to know why there is an increased demand for sex with children, a demand hugely assisted by the explosion of internet grooming and social networking. I don't know the answer: but there has to be a clear purpose that helps the victims, prevents abuse, and catches the criminals. (in Brown, 2015)

A generational problem?

There is no doubt that contact and communication throughout society will continue shifting increasingly towards the online world. This will become ever more the setting, both for danger to children and young people, and for opportunities to help them build resilience (for instance through creating imaginative means of contact to access help, support and sharing of experiences).

It is valuable to remember research findings that children's offline and online vulnerability is related (see Chapter Four), and that therefore keeping children better protected and valued in the offline world, as early as possible in their lives, remains vitally important. However, in the battles to combat the child sexual abuse and exploitation which feed the huge worldwide trade in abuse images of children, and to combat the influence of freely available sadistic pornography on the way boys and young men in particular see sexual intimacy, there will remain a significant generational problem. It is not only that:

> Now, the most popular and easily accessible forms of pornography contain significant amounts of

violence, degradation and humiliation of women ... many adults, who are beyond the years of sexual development and exploration and who developed their sexual identities prior to the internet, have not encountered the new sexual scripts internet pornography is inscribing on the sexual identities of younger people. Thus, there is a significant gap in how older and younger adults understand what constitutes pornography, which leaves older adults less prepared to help guide sexual choices. (Johnson et al, 2014)

Given this generation gap, even if they are aware of extreme content, most parents and other relatives – indeed many teachers, youth leaders and social workers – lack the technological understanding and know-how even of many ten-year-olds in trying to control access by children to violent, degrading material. That will always be a shortcoming in the frequent, undoubtedly sensible and important, advice that parents must now take more control of their children's internet use. Another shortcoming is that some of the children most vulnerable to damaging internet use will be in families who are either abusive, or less able to control their children's behaviour and contacts. It seems to me essential, first of all, that conscious and serious efforts are now made to recruit the under-35 generation, including young university graduates, with strong expertise and specialism in new technologies. These need to work alongside older generations in keeping children and young people safer from all the dangers posed by online technologies.

Top-level investment and commitment

It also seems to me essential, even in times of spending austerity, that governments nationally and through international collaboration do now commit very substantial investment into combating both the worldwide trade in abuse images, involving exploitation and corruption of children (including very young children) across the world; and into combating the influence on young people of violent and sadistic pornography. And that they make these goals a clearly stated priority, agreeing targets for action both nationally and internationally. We need governments to say clearly that what individual parents try to do will not be nearly as influential as the holding of internet service providers to closer account. Government-led strategies and priorities will not stop these massive trades, but will dent them. They will give publicised, top-level, coherent leadership on issues which leave many people in child protection feeling helpless and horrified at developments which have spiralled out of control; which, although child sexual abuse has probably existed for millennia, constitute a genuinely new and intimidating challenge.

Such effort and investment must include, as Johnson et al (2014) note, concentration on the 'production side of the economic equation' focusing on enhancing protection of those involved in the sex trade, along with regulation and prosecution of the ways in which the pornography industry promotes human trafficking.

Police funding and staffing

Such effort and investment must also include significant increases in funding and staffing for police investigations into those who create, share or download child abuse images, and into the abuse, trafficking and exploitation which feeds the trade. And this work has to be agreed as a police priority. As critics like Mark Williams-Thomas have repeatedly argued,[1] there does not seem much point in identifying and arresting online offenders if most do not get followed up, if hundreds or thousands of seized computers sit waiting years to be investigated and if cutbacks in funding have further reduced the capacity of units like the National Crime Agency to prosecute or even monitor online child sex offenders. As I argue (Chapter One), the risk, when faced with an overwhelming problem, is to be tempted into comforting self-reassurances that these people are probably not as dangerous to children as they may in fact be.

---

[1] www.williams-thomas.co.uk/Online%20Offenders%20-%202014

Schools and youth settings

National effort, planning and funding , informed by the excellent range of research with young people by EU Kids Online (2014a, 2014b) must include ensuring that from primary school onwards all children are taught how to use (online) proactive coping strategies from an early age (d'Haenens et al, 2013). From primary school onwards all children and young people now need sex and relationships education which repeatedly and directly addresses consent, attitudes to women and girls, gender and gender equality, and which critically engages with online pornography, understanding it as fiction rather than a representation of respectful and equal gender relationships. That work also needs to be linked in to government and local authority strategies throughout the UK to combat violence against women and girls. Education work should include all state funded schools, independent and faith schools, and further and higher education colleges.

Too expensive?

Critics will argue: but how do we fund all these developments, and this unrealistic wish list? I believe such national priorities are acutely needed to avert really serious risks to children and young people now and in future, and that everyone who shares this concern needs to argue for urgent action. That would mean much of the funding will have to come from other budgets, which are less urgently needed. Speaking purely personally, I suggest that in the UK, a large slice of the savings – from costs of renewing Trident estimated variously at anything between £15 and £100 billion – could come from non-renewal of Britain's 'independent' nuclear deterrent. Other readers will have their own thoughts.

Courage and political will

Difficult political decisions on priorities for the future always come back to courage, commitment and will, so I could do no better than conclude this book by repeating, with only slight amendments for today, a call I made 15 years ago. That was about the crucial need for professional and political courage (Nelson, 2000). I hope that 15 years from now, there will be no need to keep repeating messages from the past.

Courage can be found from at least three sources: first, from collective will and united action, so that individual agencies, managers and workers are not left isolated and exposed. Second, from the gradual but definite change in public opinion towards more open-minded consideration of the extent of child sexual abuse, and of the facts in publicised cases. Third, from the persisting example of child and adult survivors who have spoken out; and of protective parents – mothers in particular – who have battled for years against abusers, and against unsympathetic child protection systems and courts, to protect their own children.

Surely politicians, policymakers and professionals, with all the advantages they have, can draw on some of that courage and commitment to speak the truth more fearlessly from now on. After all it is not embarrassment, it is not bad publicity, it is not even possible loss of a job that survivors and protective mothers – and at times fathers – have already risked, in their everyday lives and in their decisions to stick their heads above the parapet. It is their physical safety, their bodily integrity, their sanity; it is loss of contact with their children, it is even sometimes risk to their very lives and the lives of their children.

References

Note: Website addresses were correct at time of going to press.

Aaronovitch, D. (2015) 'Ritual abuse: anatomy of a panic', *Analysis*, BBC Radio 4, 25 May and 1 June.

Adams, J. (2003) 'Victim issues are key to effective sex offender treatment', *Sexual Addiction & Compulsivity*, 10(1): 79–87.

Allison, D., Mentore, J., Heo, M., Chandler L., Cappelleri, J., Infante, M. and Weiden, P. (1999) 'Antipsychotic-induced weight gain: a comprehensive research synthesis', *American Journal of Psychiatry*, 156: 1686–96.

Almeida, J., Cohen, A., Subramanian, S. and Molnar, B. (2008) 'Are increased worker caseloads in state child protective service agencies a potential explanation for the decline in child sexual abuse?' *Child Abuse & Neglect*, 32(3): 367–75.

Altemus, M., Cloitre, M. and Dhabhar, F. (2003) 'Enhanced cellular immune response in women with PTSD related to child abuse', *American Journal of Psychiatry*, 160(9): 1705–7.

Amris, K. and. Williams, A. (2007) 'Chronic pain in survivors of torture', *Pain*, 15, 7.

Anda, R., Felitti, V., Douglas-Bremner, J., Walker, J., Whitfield, C., Dube, S. and Giles, W. (2006) 'The enduring effects of abuse and related adverse experiences in childhood: a convergence of evidence from neurobiology and epidemiology', *European Archives of Psychiatry and Clinical Neuroscience*, 256(3): 174–86.

Andrews, B., Morton, J., Bekerian, D., Brewin, C., Davies, G. and Mollon, P. (1995) 'The recovery of memories in clinical practice', *The Psychologist*, 8: 209–14.

Anning, N., Hebditch, D. and Jervis, M. (1997) The JET Report: The Broxtowe Files, republished at www.users.globalnet.co.uk/~dlheb/jetrepor.htm.

Armstrong, L. (1990) 'Making an issue of incest', in D. Leidholdt and J. Raymond (eds) *The sexual liberals and the attack on feminism*, Oxford: Pergamon Press, pp. 43–56.

Armstrong, L. (1994) *Rocking the cradle of sexual politics: What happened when women said incest*, Boston: Addison-Wesley.

Arnold, R., Rogers, D. and Cook, D. (1990) 'Medical problems of adults who were sexually abused in childhood', *British Medical Journal*, 300(6726): 705–8.

Atkar, S., Baldwin, N., Ghataora, R. and Thanki, V. (2000) 'Promoting effective family support and child protection for Asian children', in N. Baldwin (ed) *Protecting children: Promoting their rights*, London. Whiting and Birch, Chapter 21.

Attorney General's (2013) Reference (53 of 2013) EWCA Crim, 2544, para. 20.

Bak, M., Fransen, A., Janssen, J., van Os, J. and Drukker, M. (2014) 'Almost all antipsychotics result in weight gain: a meta-analysis', *PLOS One*, DOI: 10.1371/journal.pone.0094112.

Baldwin, N. and Carruthers, L. (1998) *Developing neighbourhood support and child protection strategies: The Henley Safe Children Project*, Aldershot: Ashgate.

Baldwin, N. and Carruthers, L. (2000) 'Family support strategies: the Henley Project', in N. Baldwin (ed) *Protecting children: Promoting their rights*, London: Whiting and Birch, Chapter 22.

Baldwin, N. and Spencer, N. (2000) 'Strategic planning to prevent harm to children', in N. Baldwin (ed) *Protecting children: Promoting their rights*, London: Whiting and Birch.

Ball, J., Boycott, O. and Rogers, S. (2011) 'Race variation in jail sentences, study suggests', *Guardian*, 26 November.

Balon, R., Coverdale, J., and Roberts, L. (2011) 'Are we heading into a workforce crisis?', *Academic Psychiatry*, 35(1): 1–3.

Banyard, V., Edwards, V. and Kendall-Tackett, K. (2009) *Trauma and physical health: Understanding the effects of extreme stress and of psychological harm*, London: Routledge.

Banyard, V., Plante, E. and Moynihan, M. (2007) 'Sexual violence prevention through bystander education: An experimental evaluation', *Journal of Community Psychology*, 35(4): 463–481.

Barber, K. (2007) 'Enough is enough: Building community capacity to transform child protection', *Journal of Child and Youth Care*, 20(1): 37–44.

Barker, P. and Buchanan-Barker, P. (2004) *The tidal model: A guide for mental health professionals*, Abingdon: Routledge. See also www.tidal-model.com.

Barron, I. and Topping, K. (2010) 'School-based abuse prevention: effect on disclosures', *Journal of Family Violence*, 25(7): 651–9.

Barsky, A., Peekna, H. and Borus, J. (2001) 'Somatic symptom reporting in women and men', *Journal of General Internal Medicine*, 16(4): 266–75.

Barter, C. (2007) 'In the name of love: Partner abuse and violence in teenage relationships', *British Journal of Social Work*, 39: 211–33.

Barter, C., McCarry, M., Berridge, D. and Evans, K. (2009) *Partner exploitation and violence in teenage intimate relationships*, London: NSPCC.

Bartlett, P. (2007) 'Killing Gay Men, 1976–2001', *British Journal of Criminology*, 47(4): 573–95.

Bartley, M. (2007) *Capability and resilience: beating the odds*, Swindon: ESRC.

Bass, E. and Davis, L. (1988) *The courage to heal: A guide for women survivors of child sexual abuse*, New York: Harper Perennial.

Bass, E. and Davis, L. (2008) *The courage to heal: A guide for women survivors of child sexual abuse*, 20th Anniversary Edition, New York: William Morrow.

BBC Drama (1996) 'Flowers of the forest', Director Michael Whyte, 26 October.

BBC News (1999) 'One in two youths "think rape is okay"', 24 September.

BBC News (2003) 'DNA sweep snares sex attacker', 27 January.

BBC News (2006a) 'Boy charged over child pregnancy', 12 May.

BBC News (2006b) 'Sally Clark doctor wins GMC case', 17 February.

BBC News (2006c), 'Orkney abuse children speak out', 22 August.

BBC News (2007)'Care law anomaly to be probed', 14 June.

BBC News (2011) 'School exclusion leads to jail, says prisons inspector', 4 October.

BBC News (2012a) 'Rochdale grooming: "shocking" failure over sex abuse', 29 May.

BBC News (2012b) 'South Yorkshire Police deny hiding girls' sex abuse', 24 September.

BBC News (2013a) 'The woman who could have stopped Orkney satanic abuse scandal,' 5 September.

BBC News (2013b) 'Keir Starmer says new child abuse trial guidelines are 'biggest shift for generation''', 17 October.

BBC News (2013c) 'New sexual abuse prosecution guidelines', 11 June.

BBC News (2014a) 'Rolf Harris jailed for five years and nine months', 4 July.

BBC News (2014b) 'Savile allegations lead to NAPAC demand increase', 26 August.

BBC News (2015a) 'Rotherham abuse scandal: key dates', 26 March.

BBC News (2015b) 'New Zealand judge Lowell Goddard to lead abuse inquiry', 4 February.

BBC News (2015c) 'Lord Janner facers historical sex abuse prosecution', 29 June.

BBC News (2015d) 'Child sexual abuse inquiry "could last until 2020"', 9 July.

BBC News (2015e) 'Child abuse survivors slam 'shambolic' inquiry delays', 1 October.

BBC *Panorama* (2005) 'Crime Wave', 7 February.

Bebbington, P., Jonas, S., Kuipers, E., King, M., Cooper, C., Brugha, T., Meltzer, H., McManus, S. and Jenkins, R. (2011) 'Childhood sexual abuse and psychosis: data from a cross-sectional national psychiatric survey in England', *British Journal of Psychiatry*, 199(1): 29–37.

Beck, J., Elzevier, H., Pelger, R., Putter, H. and Voorham-van der Zalm, P. (2009) 'Multiple pelvic floor complaints are correlated with sexual abuse history', *Journal of Sexual Medicine*, 6(1): 193–8.

Beckett, H. (2011) *Not a world away: The sexual exploitation of children and young people in Northern Ireland*, Belfast: Barnardos.

Beech, A. and Gillespie, S. (2014) 'The understanding and treatment of sexual offenders in the 21st century: a neurobiological perspective', *Monatsschrift für Kriminologie und Strafrechtsreform*, 97(1): 78–84.

Bender, L. and Blau, A. (1937) 'The reaction of children to sexual relations with adults', *American Journal of Orthopsychiatry*, 7: 500–18.

Bentall, R. and Varese, P. (2012) 'A level playing field? Are bio-genetic and psycho-social studies evaluated by the same standards?' *Psychosis*, 4(3): 183–90.

Bentovim, A. (2002) 'Preventing sexually abused young people from becoming abusers, and treating the victimization experiences of young people who offend sexually', *Child Abuse & Neglect*, 26(6): 661–78.

Berelowitz, S., Clifton, J., Firmin, C., Gulyurtlu, S. and Edwards, G. (2013) *"If only someone had listened", Office of the Children's Commissioner's Inquiry into Child Sexual Exploitation in Gangs and Groups Final Report*, London: OCC.

Beresford, P. (2003) 'Listen and Learn', *Community Care*, 31 January.

Berman, G. (2012) Prison population statistics, London, House of Commons.

Berney, L. and Blane, D. (2003) 'The lifegrid method of collecting retrospective information from people at older ages', *Research Policy and Planning*, 21(2): 13–21.

Blast! Films (2006) *The Accused*, BBC2, 22 August.

Bletchly, R. (2008) 'Gymslip mum…revisited', People.co.uk, News-UK & World News, 15 June.

Blewett, J. (2011) 'Review of France A., Munro E., Waring A. 'The evaluation of arrangements for effective operation of the new local safeguarding boards in England, 2010', *Community Care*, 9 September.

Bonomi, A., Anderson, M., Rivara, F., Cannon, E., Fishman, P., Carrell, D., Reid, R. and Thompson, R. (2008) 'Health care utilization and costs associated with childhood abuse', *Journal of General Internal Medicine*, 23(3): 294–9.

Bourke, M. (2012) Rebuttal: Letter to the chair of the United States sentencing commission, the Hon. Patti B. Saris, 17 May, www.ussc. gov/sites/default/files/pdf/amendment-process/public-hearings-and-meetings/20120215/Testimony_15_Bourke.pdf.

Bourke, M. and Hernandez, A. (2009) 'The "Butner Study" redux: a report of the incidence of hands-on child victimization by child pornography offenders', *Journal of Family Violence*, 24(3): 183–91.

Bowcott, O. (2003) 'Thames torso boy was fed toxic bean', *Guardian*, 7 October.

Bowditch, G. (2005) 'A chilling wake-up call to the triumph of evil', *The Times* (Scotland) 11 October

Bowman, E. (1993) 'Etiology and clinical course of pseudoseizures, relationship to trauma dissociation and depression', *Psychosomatics*, 34(4): 333–42.

Boyle, M. (2011) 'Making the world go away, and how psychology and psychiatry benefit', in M. Rapley, J. Moncrieff and J. Dillon (eds) *De-Medicalizing Misery*, New York: Palgrave.

Boyle, M. (2013) 'The persistence of medicalisation', in S. Coles, S. Keenan and B. Diamond (eds) *Madness contested: Power and practice*, Ross on Wye, UK: PCCS Books.

Bracken, P. and Thomas, P. (2005) *Postpsychiatry: Mental health in a postmodern world*, Oxford: Oxford University Press.

Bracken, P., Thomas, P., Timimi, S., Asen, E., Behr, G., Beuster, C., Bhunnoo, S., Browne, I., Chhina, N., Double,D., Downer, S., Evans, C., Fernando, S., Garland, M., Hopkins, W., Huws, R., Johnson, B., Martindale, B., Middleton, H., Moldavsky, D., Moncrieff, J., Mullins, S., Nelki, J., Pizzo, M., Rodger, J., Smyth, M., Summerfield, D., Wallace, J. and Yeomans, D. (2012) 'Psychiatry beyond the current paradigm', *British Journal of Psychiatry*, 201(6): 430–4.

Briere, J. and Zaidi, L. (1989) 'Sexual abuse histories and sequelae in female psychiatric emergency room patients', *American Journal of Psychiatry*, 146(12): 1602–6.

Briggs, F. (2003) 'From victim to perpetrator: factors in the transition process', paper presented to international conference on trauma, attachment and dissociation, www.delphicentre.com.au/conference/2003papers.

Briscoe-Smith, A. and Henshaw, S. (2006) 'Linkages between child abuse and attention-deficit/hyperactivity disorder in girls: behavioral and social correlates', *Child Abuse & Neglect*, 1239–55.

Brock, J. (2015) *Safeguarding Scotland's vulnerable children from child abuse: A review of the Scottish system*, Edinburgh: Children in Scotland.

Brookes, N. (2006) 'Phil Barker: tidal model of mental health recovery' in A. Tomey and M. Alligood (eds) *Nursing theorists and their work* (6th Edition), St Louis, MI: Mosby Elsevier.

Brown, A. (2015) 'Scots sex inquiry expert vows to weed out paedophiles and slates authorities who blanked kids' pleas', *Daily Record*, 24 August.

Brown, J. and L'Engle, K. (2009) 'X-rated: sexual attitudes and behaviors associated with US early adolescents' exposure to sexually explicit media', *Communication Research*, 36: 129–51.

Brown, J., O'Donnell, T. and Erooga, M. (2011) Sexual abuse: a public health challenge, London: NSPCC.

Brown, J., Berenson, K. and Cohen, P. (2005) 'Documented and self reported child abuse and adult pain in a community sample', *Clinical Journal of Pain*, 21(5): 374–7.

Brown, T., Merritt, W. and Evans, D. (1988) 'Psychogenic vocal chord dysfunction masquerading as asthma', *Journal of Nervous and Mental Disease*, 176(5): 308–.

Bullock, R., Little, M. and Mount, K. (1995) *Child protection: messages from research*, London: HMSO.

Burton, C. (2003) 'Beyond somatisation: a review of the understanding and treatment of medically unexplained physical symptoms (MUPS)', *British Journal of General Practice*, 53(488): 231–9.

Busfield, J. (2013) 'The pharmaceutical industry and mental disorder', in S. Coles, S. Keenan and B. Diamond (eds) *Madness contested: Power and practice*, Ross on Wye, UK: PCCS Books.

Butler-Sloss, E. (1988) *Report of the inquiry into child abuse in Cleveland 1987*, Cm 412, London: HMSO.

Bwletin Ystadegol [Statistical Bulletin] (2014) Local authority child protection registers in Wales, 2014, SB 88.

Campbell, B. (1995) 'Moral panic', *Index on Censorship*, 24(2): 57–61.

Campbell, B. (1998) *Unofficial secrets – child sexual abuse: The Cleveland case*, London: Virago.

Campbell, B. (2010) 'Dr David Southall: a cautionary tale of child protection', *Guardian*, 6 May.

Campbell, S. (2003) *Relational remembering: rethinking the memory wars*, Oxford: Rowman and Littlefield.

Carter, H. (2010) 'Derby care agencies "missed chances to help" girls abused by gang of men', *Guardian*, 25 November.

Casey, L. (2015) Report of Inspection of Rotherham Metropolitan Borough Council, Department of Communities & Local Government (DCLG).

CEOP (2012) *A picture of abuse: A thematic assessment of the risk of contact child sexual abuse posed by those who possess indecent images of children*, London: Child Exploitation and Online Protection Centre.

Champion, J., Piper, J., Holden, A., Shain, R., Perdue, S. and Korte, J. (2005) 'Relationship of abuse and pelvic inflammatory disease risk behavior in minority adolescents', *Journal of the American Association of Nurse Practitioners*, 17(6): 234–41.

Channel 4 (1997) *Unspeakable truths: The death of childhood*, produced by Tim Tate, broadcast 27 May.

Charmandari, E., Tsigos, C. and Chrousos, G. (2005) 'Endocrinology of the stress response', *Annual Review of Physiology*, 67: 259–84.

Cheit, R. (2014) *The witch-hunt narrative: Politics, psychology and the sexual abuse of children*, New York: Oxford University Press.

Children 1st (2006) *Confidentiality: Would you keep this to yourself?* Children 1st, Edinburgh.

Children in Scotland (2005) Briefing on SWIA report on Western Isles Child Abuse Case, 12/05 [S], Edinburgh: Children in Scotland.

Children's Commissioner (2015) *Protecting children from harm: A critical assessment of child sexual abuse in the family network in England and priorities for action*, London: Children's Commissioner for England.

Chorley, M. (2014) 'Theresa May announces new paedophile inquiry', *Daily Mail*, 7 July.

Clapton, G. (1993) *The satanic abuse controversy: Social workers and the social work press*, London: University of North London Press.

Clarke, N. (2013) 'A mother of two - aged 15: Thought you couldn't be any more horrified by stories of schoolgirl mums? Then read this jaw-dropping interview', *Daily Mail*, 3 May.

Clarke, R. (2009) 'Situational crime prevention: theoretical background and current practice', *Handbooks of Sociology and Social Research*, 2009: 259–76.

Clouse, R. and Lustman, P. (1983) 'Psychiatric illness and contraction abnormalities of the oesophagus', *The New England Journal of Medicine*, 309: 1337–42.

Clyde, James (1992) *The Report of the Inquiry into the Removal of Children from Orkney in February 1991*, Edinburgh: HMSO.

Coffey, A. (2014) *Real voices: Child sexual exploitation in Greater Manchester*, Manchester: Greater Manchester Safeguarding Partnership.

Cohen, S. (2002) *Folk devils and moral panics: The creation of the mods and rockers*, 3rd edition, New York: Psychology Press.

Cohen, L., McGeoch, P., Gans, S., Nikiforov, K., Cullen, K. and Galynker, I. (2002) 'Childhood sexual history of 20 male pedophiles vs 24 male healthy control subjects', *Journal of Nervous and Mental Disease*, 190(11): 757–66.

Cole, A. and Knowles, J. (2001) *Lives in context: The art of life history research*, Oxford: Altamira Press.

Coleman, J. (1994) 'Presenting features in adult victims of satanist ritual abuse', *Child Abuse Review*, 3(2): 83–92.

Collings, S. (2009) 'See no evil, hear evil: the rise and fall of child sexual abuse in the 20th century', *PINS*, 38: 61–73.

Constance, A. (2014) Education Secretary – Statement on Historical Child Abuse, Scottish Parliament, 17 December, http://news.scotland. gov.uk/Speeches-Briefings/Education-Secretary-Statement-on-historical-child-abuse-13b3.aspx.

Conte, J. (1994) 'Child sexual abuse: awareness and backlash', *Future Child*, 4(2): 224–32.

Corby, B., Doig, A. and Roberts, V. (2001) *Public Inquiries into abuse of children in residential care*, London: Jessica Kingsley.

Cornish, D. and Clarke, R. (1987) 'Understanding crime displacement: An application of rational choice theory', *Criminology*, 25(4): 933–47.

Cowburn, M. (2002) 'A man's world: gender issues in working with male sex offenders in prison', *The Howard Journal of Criminal Justice*, 37(3): 234–51.

Cowburn, M. and Myers, S. (2016) *Social work with sex offenders*, Bristol: Policy Press.

Craine, L., Henson, C., Colliver, J. and MacLean, D. (1988) 'Prevalence of a history of sexual abuse among female psychiatric patients in a state hospital system', *Psychiatric Services*, 39(3): 300–4.

Cramb, A. (2001) 'Fairlie sues over daughter's "false memory" claims', *Telegraph*, 24 March.

Crawley, M., Roberts, P. and Shepherd, W. (2004) *Taking stock: Children and young people at risk of, or involved in abuse through prostitution within Stockton-on-Tees*, London: Barnardos.

Cree, V., Clapton, G. and Smith, M. (2014) 'The presentation of child trafficking in the UK: an old and new moral panic?', *British Journal of Social Work*, 44(2): 418–33.

Creeden, K. (2004) 'The neurodevelopmental impact of early trauma and insecure attachment: rethinking our understanding and treatment of sexual behavior problems', *Sexual Addiction & Compulsivity: The Journal of Treatment & Prevention*, 11(4): 223–47.

Creighton, S. (1993) 'Organised abuse: NSPCC experience', *Child Abuse Review*, 2(4): 232–42.

Crellin, R. and Pona, I. (2015) *On your own now: The risks of unsuitable accommodation for older teenagers*, London: The Children's Society.

Creswell, J.W. (1998) *Qualitative inquiry and research design: Choosing among five traditions*, London, Sage.

Crichton, T. (2001) 'Orkney: 10 years after', *Sunday Herald*, 25 January.

Crisma, M., Bascelli, E., Paci, D., and Romito, P. (2004) 'Adolescents who experienced sexual abuse: fears, needs and impediments to disclosure', *Child Abuse & Neglect*, 28(10): 1035–48.

Cromer, L. and Goldsmith, R. (2010) 'Socio-cultural issues and child sexual abuse: child sexual abuse myths: attitudes, beliefs, and individual differences', *Journal of Child Sexual Abuse*, 19(6): 618–47.

Cronch, L., Viljoen, J. and Hansen, D. (2006) 'Forensic interviewing in child sexual abuse cases: current techniques and future directions', *Aggression and Violent Behavior*, 11: 195–207.

Cross, T., Jones, L., Walsh, W., Simone, M. and Kolko, D. (2007) 'Which sexual abuse victims receive a forensic medical examination? The impact of Children's Advocacy Centers', *Child Abuse & Neglect*, 31: 1053–68.

Daily Mirror (2004) 'McDowell lured a rabbi to his flat for gay sex', 1 October, www.thefreelibrary.com/McDowell+lured+a+rabbi+to+h is+flat+for+gay+sex+..strangled+him,...-a0122685402.

Dale, P. (1999) *Adults abused as children: Experiences of counselling and psychotherapy*, London: Sage.

Dallam, S. (1998) 'Dr. Richard Gardner: a review of his theories and opinions on atypical sexuality, pedophilia, and treatment issues', *Treating Abuse Today*, 8(1): 15–23.

Danese, A. and McEwen, B. (2012) 'Adverse childhood experiences, allostasis, allostatic load, and age-related disease', *Physiology & Behavior*, 106(1): 29–39.

Darves-Bornoz, J., Lempérière, T., Degiovanni, A. and Gaillard, P.(1995) 'Sexual victimization in women with schizophrenia and bipolar disorder', *Social Psychiatry and Psychiatric Epidemiology*, 30(2): 78–84.

Davidson, J., Bilfulco, A., Grove Hills, J. and Chan, J. (2012) *An investigation of Metropolitan Police investigative practices with child victims of sexual abuse*, London: Centre for Abuse & Trauma Studies, Kingston University.

Davies, L. (1997) 'The investigation of organised abuse', in H. Westcott and J. Jones, *Perspectives on the memorandum*, Aldershot: Ashgate.

Davies, L. (2004) 'The difference between child abuse and child protection could be you. Creating a community network of protective adults', *Child Abuse Review*, 13: 426–32.

Davies, L. (2008) 'Reclaiming the language of child protection', in M. Calder (ed) *Contemporary risk assessment in safeguarding children*, Lyme Regis: Russell House.

Davies, L. (2009) *Submission to the protection of children in England: A progress report*, London: London Metropolitan University.

Davies, L. (2010) 'Protecting children – a critical contribution to policy and practice development', a thesis submitted for the degree of Doctor of Philosophy, London: London Metropolitan University, http://lizdavies.net/publications/

Davies, L. (2011) 'Interviewing children – good practice in Sweden', *Community Care*, 4 September.

Davies, L. (2013) 'A&E database is not the answer to child protection failings', *Guardian*, 7 January.

Davies, L. (2014) 'Working positively with the media to protect children', *Journal of Social Welfare and Family Law*, 36(1): 47–58.

Davies, L. and Duckett, N. (2008) *Proactive child protection and social work*, London: Sage.

Davies, L. and Duckett, N. (2016) *Proactive child protection and social work*, 2nd edition, London: Sage.

Davies, L. and Townsend, D. (2008) *Joint investigation in child protection: working together – training together*, Lyme Regis: Russell House.

Davies, M. (2015) 'Churches among first to be investigated by Goddard sex abuse inquiry', *Church Times*, 4 December.

De Bellis, M. and Zisk, A. (2014) 'The biological effects of childhood trauma', *Child and Adolescent Psychiatric Clinics of North America*, 23(2): 185–222.

Dell, P. and O'Neil, J. (2010) *Dissociation and the dissociative disorders: DSM-V and beyond*, Abingdon: Routledge.

Dembo, R., Williams, Li., Wothke, W., Schmeidler, J. Brown, C. and Hendricks, J. (1992) 'The role of family factors, physical abuse, and sexual victimization experiences in high-risk youths' alcohol and other drug use and delinquency: a longitudinal model', *Violence and Victims* 7(3): 245–66

Dempster, H., Henry, M., Houston, A., Matthew, L., McCrae, R., Nelson, S., Rennie, J. and Stark, R. (2013) 'Listening watch', Letters, *Scotsman*, 2 4 January.

Denzin, N. and Lincoln, Y. (2003) *Strategies of qualitative inquiry*, 2nd edition, London: Sage.

Devroede, G. (1999) 'Front and rear: the pelvic floor is an integrated functional structure', *Medical Hypotheses*, 52(2): 147–53.

Department for Education (DfE) (2003) *Every child matters*, London: The Stationery Office.

DfE (2006) *Working together to safeguard children*, London: The Stationery Office.

DfE (2011) Permanent and fixed period exclusions from schools in England 2009/10, www.dcsf.gov.uk/rsgateway/index.shtml

DfE (2014) Characteristics of children in need in England, 2013–14, E Table D4, www.gov.uk/government/statistics/characteristics-of-children-in-need-in-england.

DfE (2015) *Working together to safeguard children. A guide to inter-agency working to safeguard and promote the welfare of children*, March, www.workingtogetheronline.co.uk.

Dhunpath, R. (2000) 'Life history methodology: "narradigm" regained', *International Journal of Qualitative Studies in Education*, 13(5): 543–51.

Dillon, J. (2011) 'The personal is the political', in M. Rapley, J. Moncrieff and J. Dillon (eds), *De-medicalizing misery*, New York: Palgrave.

Dixon, H. (2013) 'The Oxford grooming ring was promoted by imams who encourage followers to think white women deserve to be "punished", an Islamic leader has claimed', *Telegraph*, 16 May.

Dobson, R. (2013) 'North Wales care home abuse: "It was like a world within a world. There was no escape", *Independent*, 29 April.

Dolan, M. (2009) 'Recent advances in therapy for sexual offenders', *F1000 Medicine Reports*, 1: 45.

Donaldson, L. and O'Brien, S. (1995) 'Press coverage of the Cleveland child sexual abuse enquiry: a source of public enlightenment?', *Journal of Public Health Medicine*, 17(1): 70–6.

Dong, M., Giles, W., Felitti, V., Dube, S., Williams, J., Chapman, D. and Anda, R. (2004) 'Insights into causal pathways for ischemic heart disease – the Adverse Childhood Experiences Study', *Circulation*, 110(13): 1761–6.

Donovan, T. (2013) 'Rochdale serious case reviews find dysfunctional multi-agency working and social care failures', *Community Care*, 20 December.

DoH (2000) *Safeguarding children involved in prostitution: Supplementary guidance to Working Together to Safeguard Children*, London: Department of Health publications.

DOH (2002) *Women's mental health: Into the mainstream, strategic development of mental health care for women,* London: Department of Health Publications.

Doward, J. (2004) 'Boys aged 10 for sale in sex scandal', *Observer,* 10 October.

Drainey, N. (2012) 'Teenager who killed gay barman is jailed', *The Times* (Scotland), 7 December.

Drury, I. (2006) 'Girl, 11, will be Britain's youngest mother', *Daily Mail,* 12 May.

Dube, S., Anda, R., Felitti, V., Chapman, D., Williamson, D. and Giles, W. (2001) 'Childhood abuse, household dysfunction and the risk of attempted suicide throughout the life span', *Journal of the American Medical Association, 286(24):* 3089–96.

Dube, S., Felitti, V., Dong, M., Chapman, D., Giles, W. and Anda, R. (2003) 'Childhood abuse, neglect and household dysfunction and the risk of illicit drug use: the adverse childhood experiences study', *Pediatrics,* 111(3): 564–72.

Dube, S., Anda, R., Whitfield, C., Brown, D., Felitti, V., Dong, M. and Giles, W. (2005) 'Long-term consequences of childhood sexual abuse by gender of victim', *American Journal of Preventive Medicine,* 28(5): 430–8.

Dugan, E. (2013) 'Imams to preach against grooming of girls for sex', *Independent,* 17 May.

Duke, N., Pettingell, S., McMorris, B. and Borowsky, I. (2010) 'Adolescent violence perpetration: associations with multiple types of adverse childhood experiences', *Pediatrics,* 125(4): 778–86.

Durbin, B., Golden, S. and Aston, H. (2011) *Devon multi-agency safeguarding hub: Value for money report,* Slough: National Foundation for Educational Research.

Dworkin, A. (1992) 'Prostitution and male supremacy', Symposium on 'Prostitution: From Academia to Activism', Michigan: University of Michigan Law School.

Dyer, (2006) 'Paediatrician in baby death case vindicated after six years', *Guardian* 2 December.

Edmond, T., Rubin, A. and Wambach, K. (1999) 'The effectiveness of EMDR with adult female survivors of childhood sexual abuse', *Social Work Research,* 23(2): 1–24.

Edmond, T., Sloan, L., and McCarty, D. (2004) 'Sexual abuse survivors' perceptions of the effectiveness of EMDR and eclectic therapy: a mixed-methods study', *Research on Social Work Practice,* 14: 259–72.

Edwards, D. and Maddocks, A. (2000) 'All that wheezes is not asthma', *Welsh Paediatric Journal,* 12: 28–30.

Edwards, R., Gillies, V. and Horsley, N. (2015) 'Brain science and early years policy: hopeful ethos or 'cruel optimism'?' *Critical Social Policy*, 35(2): 167–87.

Ehlert, U., Heim, C. and Hellhammer,D. (1999) 'Chronic pelvic pain as a somatoform disorder', *Psychotherapy and Psychosomatics*, 68(2): 87–94.

Eisner, A. (2010) Is social media a new addiction?, 15 March, www.retrevo.com/content/blog/2010/03/social-media-new-addiction%3F

Eley Morris, S., Yates, R. and Wilson, J. (2002) 'Trauma histories of men and women in residential drug treatment: the Scottish evidence', *The Drug and Alcohol Professional*, 2(1): 20–8.

Emery, R., Otto, R. and O'Donohue, W. (2005) 'Child custody evaluations in scientific, legal, and societal context: Improving the science and the system', *Psychological Science in the Public Interest*, 6(1): 1–29.

End Violence against Women (2012) 'Response from the End Violence Against Women Coalition to the Department for Education's consultation on parental internet controls', September, www.endviolenceagainstwomen.org.uk/resources/49/evaw-coalition-submission-to-government-consultation-on-porn-filters-sept-12

Engel, A., Kamm, M. and Bartram, C. (1995) 'Unwanted anal penetration as a physical cause of faecal incontinence', *European Journal of Gastroenterology and Hepatology*, 7(1): 65–7.

Epps, K. and Fisher, D. (2004) 'A review of the research literature on young people who sexually abuse', in G. O'Reilly, W. Marshall, A. Carr and R. Beckett (eds) *The handbook of clinical intervention with young people who sexually abuse*, Hove: Brunner-Routledge, pp. 62–72.

EU Kids Online (2014a) website and research resources, www.lse.ac.uk/media@lse/research/EUKidsOnline/Home.aspx.

EU Kids Online (2014b) *EU Kids online: Findings, methods, recommendations (deliverable D1.6)*, EU Kids Online, London: LSE, http://eprints.lse.ac.uk/60512/

Farestveit, O. (2012) 'Comprehensive services of the Barnahus', www.bvs.is/media/barnahus/childrens-house-brocure.pdf.

Fairweather, E. (2008) '"I have known about Jersey paedophiles for 15 years", says award-winning journalist', *Daily Mail*, 2 March.

Faller, K. (1998) 'The parental alienation syndrome: what is it and what data support it?, *Child Maltreatment*, 3(2): 100–115.

Farley, M. and Barkan, H. (1998) 'Prostitution, violence against women, and posttraumatic stress disorder, *Women & Health*, 27(3): 37–49.

Featherstone, B. and Fawcett, B. (1994) 'Feminism and child abuse: opening up some possibilities?' *Critical Social Policy*, 14(42): 61–80.

Feigenbaum, J. (1997) 'Negative views of the mother after childhood sexual abuse', *Psychiatric Bulletin*, 21: 477–9.

Feinberg, S. and Peterson, L. (1987) 'The use of cricothyroidostomy in oral and maxillofacial surgery', *Journal of Oral and Maxillofacial Surgery*, 45(10): 873–8.

Feinmann, C., Harris, M. and Cawley, R. (1984) 'Psychogenic facial pain: presentation and treatment', *British Medical Journal (Clinical Research Ed.)*, 288(6415): 436–8.

Feiring, C., Miller-Johnson, S. and Cleland, C. (2007) 'Potential pathways from stigmatization and internalizing symptoms to delinquency in sexually abused youth', *Child Maltreatment*, 12(3): 220–32.

Felson, R. and Lane, K. (2009) 'Social learning, sexual and physical abuse, and adult crime', *Aggressive Behaviour*, 35(6): 489–501.

Feldman-Summers, S. and Pope, K. (1994) 'The experience of "forgetting" childhood abuse: A national survey of psychologists', *Journal of Consulting and Clinical Psychology*, 62(3): 636–9.

Feltham, C. (ed) (1999) *Controversies in psychotherapy and counselling*, London: Sage Publications.

Ferenczi, S. (1949) 'Confusion of the tongues between the adults and the child – the language of tenderness and of passion', *International Journal of Psychoanalysis*, 30: 225–30 [first English translation].

Ferguson, E. (1991) 'Orkney reels', *Scotland on Sunday*, 24 March.

Fergusson, D., Boden, J. and Horwood, J. (2008) 'Exposure to childhood sexual and physical abuse and adjustment in early adulthood', *Child Abuse & Neglect*, 32: 607–19.

Fernando, S. (2011) 'Cultural diversity and racism', in M. Rapley, J. Moncrieff and J. Dillon (eds) *Demedicalising misery: Psychiatry, psychology and the human condition*, New York: Palgrave Macmillan.

Fiddler, M., Jackson, J., Kapur, N., Wells, A. and Creed, F.(2004) 'Childhood adversity and frequent medical consultations', *General Hospital Psychiatry*, 26(5): 367–77.

Fillingim, R. and Edwards, R. (2005) 'Is self-reported childhood abuse history associated with pain perception among healthy young women and men?', *Clinical Journal of Pain*, 21(5): 387–97.

Finkelhor, D. (2012) *Characteristics of crimes against juveniles*, Durham, NH: Crimes against Children Research Center.

Finkelhor, D. and Jones, L. (2012) *Have sexual abuse and physical abuse declined since the 1990s?*, Durham, NH: Crimes against Children Research Center.

Finkelhor, D., Ormrod, R. and Chaffin, M. (2009) 'Juveniles who commit sex offenses against minors', *Juvenile Justice Bulletin*, OJDP, Office of Justice Progams.

Finkelhor, D., Turner, H., Ormrod, R. and Hamby, S. (2010) 'Trends in childhood violence and abuse exposure: evidence from two national surveys', *Archives of Pediatric and Adolescent Medicine*, 164(3): 238–42.

Finkelhor, D., Shattuck, M., Turner, H. and Hamby, S. (2014) 'The lifetime prevalence of child sexual abuse and sexual assault assessed in late adolescence', *Journal of Child and Adolescent Health*, 55(3): 329–33.

Firmin, C. (2015) 'Child protection outside of the home: implications for safeguarding practice when young people are abused by their peers', Presentation to BASCPAN Congress, Edinburgh, 12–15 April.

Fish, V., and Scott, C.G. (1999) 'Childhood abuse recollections in a nonclinical population: forgetting and secrecy', *Child Abuse & Neglect*, 23(8): 791–802.

Foley, S. (2012) 'Glaxo Smith Kline pays $3bn for illegally marketing depression drug', *Independent*, 3 July.

Fondacaro, K. and Powell, T. (1999) 'Psychological impact of childhood sexual abuse on male inmates: the importance of perception', *Child Abuse & Neglect*, 23(4): 361–9.

Forrest, D. (1995) 'The physical after-effects of torture', *Forensic Science International*, 76(1): 77–84.

Fowley, D. (2010) *How could she?* London: Arrow Books.

France, A. and Homel, R. (2006) 'Societal access routes and developmental pathways: putting social structure and young people's voice into the analysis of pathways in out and out crime', *The Australian and New Zealand Journal of Criminology*, 39(3): 285–309.

France, A., Munro, E.R. and Waring, A. (2010) *The evaluation of arrangements for effective operation of the new local safeguarding children boards in England: Final report*, Research Report DFE-RR027, Department for Education.

Frankfurter, D. (2001) 'Ritual as accusation and atrocity: satanic ritual abuse, gnostic libertinism, and primal murders', *History of Religions*, 40(4): 352–80.

Frankfurter, D. (2006) *Evil incarnate: Rumors of demonic conspiracy and satanic abuse in history*, Princeton, NJ: Princeton University Press.

Freedman, M., Rosenberg, S. and. Schmaling, K. (1991) 'Childhood sexual abuse in patients with paradoxical vocal chord dysfunction', *Journal of Nervous and Mental Disease*, 179(5): 295–8.

Freeman, S. (2010) 'Woman who became Britain's youngest mother aged 12 is evicted after "throwing wild drug-fuelled parties"', *Mail Online*, 23 September.

French, C. (2014) 'Satanic child abuse claims are almost certainly based on false memories', *Guardian*, 18 November.

Freud, S. (1896) 'The aetiology of hysteria', in J. Masson (1984) *Freud: The assault on truth*, New York: Farrar, Strauss and Giroux.

Freyd, J. (1993) 'Theoretical and personal perspectives on the delayed memory debate: Invited presentation,' Foote Hospital, Continuing Education Conference: Controversies Around Recovered Memories Of Incest And Ritualistic Abuse, Michegan: Ann Arbor.

Freyd, J. (1996) *Betrayal trauma: The logic of forgetting childhood abuse*, Cambridge, MA: Harvard University Press.

Freyd, W. (1995) 'Letter 1, Excerpts: April 17 1995' and 'Second Letter, excerpts: June 7 1995', in 'The Big Lie: FMS Founders Brother Speaks Out', *Accuracy About Abuse*, 8 September, www.accuracyaboutabuse.org.

Frizzell, E. (2009) *Independent Inquiry into abuse at Kerelaw Residential School and Secure Unit*, 11 May, www.scotland.gov.uk/Publications/2009/05/08090356/0.

Fuller-Thomson, E., Stefanyk, M. and Brennenstuhl, S. (2009) 'The robust association between childhood physical abuse and osteoarthritis in adulthood: findings from a representative community sample', *Arthritis Care & Research*, 61(11): 1554–62.

Gaarder, E. (2000) 'Gender politics: the focus on women in the memory debates', *Journal of Child Sexual Abuse*, 9(1): 91–106.

Gall, C. (2011) 'Orkney child sex abuse scandal: 20 years since ordeal that horrified a nation', *Daily Record*, 4 April.

Galley, J. (2010) Derby Safeguarding Children Board: Serious Case Review BD09: Derby, DSCB, www.scie-socialcareonline.org.uk/serious-case-review-bd09-executive-summary/r/a11G000000181nCIAQ.

Garbarino, J. and Sherman, S. (1980) 'High-risk neighbourhoods and high-risk families: the human ecology of child maltreatment', *Child Development*, 51(1): 188–98.

Gardner, M. (1993) 'The false memory syndrome,' *Skeptical Inquirer*, 17: 370–75.

Gardner, R. (1991). Sex abuse hysteria: Salem witch trials revisited , Cresskill, NJ: Creative Therapeutics.

Gardner, R. (1992) *True and false accusations of child sex abuse*, Cresskill, NJ: Creative Therapeutics.

Gardner, R. (1993) 'Revising the Child Abuse Prevention and Treatment Act: our best hope for dealing with sex-abuse hysteria in the United States', *Issues in Child Abuse Accusations*, 5(1): 25–7.

Gardner, R. (2003) *Supporting Families: Child Protection in the Community*, London: Wiley.

Gardner, T. (2012) 'Oxford child sex trafficking probe widens as number of "victims" doubles to 50 girls, some as young as 11', *Daily Mail*, 13 April.

Gill, O. and Jack, G. (2007) *The child and family in context: Developing ecological practice in disadvantaged communities*, Lyme Regis: Russell House/Barnardo's.

Gilligan, P. with Akhtar, S. (2006) 'Cultural barriers to the disclosure of child sexual abuse in Asian communities: listening to what women say', *British Journal of Social Work*, 36, 1361–77.

Glasser, M., Kolvin, I., Campbell, D., Glasser, A., Leitch, I. and Farrelly, S. (2001) 'Cycle of child sexual abuse: links between being a victim and becoming a perpetrator', *British Journal of Psychiatry*, 179: 482–94.

Glennie, A. (2013) 'MI5 and Special Branch "covered up Cyril Smith's abuse of boys"', *Daily Mail*, 12 September.

Goater, G. and Meehan, K. (1998) 'Detection and awareness of child sexual abuse in adult psychiatry', *Psychiatric Bulletin*, 22: 211–13.

Goldsmith, L. and Moncrieff, J. (2011). 'The psychoactive effects of antidepressants and their association with suicidality', *Current Drug Safety*, 6(2): 115–21.

Goodman-Brown, T., Edelstein, R., Goodman, G, Jones, D. and Gordon, D. (2003) 'Why children tell: a model of children's disclosure of sexual abuse', *Child Abuse & Neglect*, 27(5): 525–40.

Goodwin, J. (1993) 'Sadistic abuse: definition, recognition, and treatment', *Dissociation*, 6(2/3): 181–7.

Gornall, J. (2007) 'Undermining the experts', *Guardian*, 27 July.

Gould, C. (1992) 'Diagnosis and treatment of ritually abused children' in D. Sakheim and S. Devine (eds), *Out of darkness: Exploring satanism and ritual abuse*, New York: Lexington Books, pp. 207–48.

Gould, C. (1995) 'Denying ritual abuse of children', *The Journal of Psychohistory*, 22(3): 329–39.

Gray, D. and Watt, P. (2013) *Giving victims a voice: Joint report into sexual allegations made against Jimmy Savile* (Operation Yewtree report), London: Metropolitan Police & NSPCC, January.

Green, L. (2005) 'Theorizing sexuality, sexual abuse and residential children's homes: adding gender to the equation', *British Journal of Social Work*, 35(4): 453–81.

Greig, E. and Betts, T. (1992) 'Epileptic seizures induced by sexual abuse: pathogenic and pathoplastic factors', *Seizure*, 1(4): 269–74.

Grierson, J. (2015) 'Edward Heath child abuse claims investigated by five police forces', *Guardian*, 5 August.

Guasp, A., Gammon, A. and Ellison, G. (2013) *Homophobic hate crime: The gay British crime survey 2013*, London: Stonewall and YouGov, www.report-it.org.uk/files/stonewall_gay_british_crime_survey_2013.pdf.

Guobrandsson, B. (2013) *The CAC/Barnahus response to child sexual abuse and the Council of Europe standard setting*, The Government Agency for Child Protection, Iceland.

Hackett, S. (2002) 'Abused and abusing: work with young people who have a dual abuse experience', in M. Calder (ed) *Young People who Sexually Abuse*, Lyme Regis: Russell House.

Hackett, S., Masson, H., and Phillips, S. (2006) 'Exploring consensus in practice with youth who are sexually abusive: findings from a Delphi study of practitioner views in the United Kingdom and the Republic of Ireland', *Child Maltreatment*, 11(2): 146–56.

Hackett, S., Masson, H., Balfe, M. and Phillips, J. (2013) 'Individual, family and abuse characteristics of 700 British child and adolescent sexual abusers', *Child Abuse Review*, 22(4): 232–45.

Hall, A. (2013) *The Hunt for Britain's Sex Gangs*, True Vision Films, http://truevisiontv.com/films/details/185/the-hunt-for-britains-sex-gangs.

Hall, R. and Hall, R.C. (2007) 'Profile of pedophilia: definition, characteristics of offenders, recidivism, treatment outcomes, and forensic issues', *Mayo Clinic Proceedings*, 82(4): 457–71.

d'Haenens, L., Vandoninck, S. and Donoso, V. (2013) 'How to cope and build online resilience?', EU Kids Online, http://eprints.lse.ac.uk/48115/

Halliday, J. (2014) 'Operation Notarise: a snapshot of child abuse in the UK', *Guardian*, 16 July.

Halliday, J. (2015) 'West Yorkshire Police investigating 180 child sexual exploitation cases', *Guardian*, 12 October.

Hansard (1991) Rochdale Social Services Department, HC Deb 28 March 1991 vol 188 cc1126–35, http://hansard.millbanksystems.com/commons/1991/mar/28/rochdale-social-services-department, 28/3/91.

Hanson, R. and Morton-Bourgon, K. (2013) 'The characteristics of persistent sexual offenders: a meta-analysis of recidivism Studies', *Journal of Consulting and Clinical Psychology*, 73(6): 1154–63.

Haringey Local Children Safeguarding Board (LCSB) (2009) *Serious case review: Baby Peter, 1st review.* London: Haringey LSCB, February.

Haringey Local Children Safeguarding Board (LCSB) (2010) *Serious case review: Baby Peter, 2nd review.* London: Haringey LSCB, October.

Harlow, B. and Stewart, E. (2005) 'Adult-onset vulvodynia in relation to childhood violence victimisation', *American Journal of Epidemiology*, 161(9): 871–80.

Harvey, M. and Herman, J. (1994) 'Amnesia, partial amnesia, and delayed recall among adult survivors of childhood trauma', *Consciousness and Cognition*, 3(3–4): 295–306.

Harvey, M., Herman, J. and Schatzow, E. (1987) 'Recovery and verification of memories of childhood sexual trauma', *Psychoanalytic Psychology*, 4(1): 1–14.

Helweg-Larsen, K., Schütt, N. and Larsen, H. (2011) 'Predictors and protective factors for adolescent internet victimization: Results from a 2008 nationwide Danish youth survey', *Acta Paediatrica*, 101: 533–9.

Henderson, J. (1975) 'Incest', in A.M. Freedman, H.I. Kaplan and B.J. Sadock (eds), *Comprehensive textbook of psychiatry*, 2nd edition, Baltimore, MD: Williams & Wilkins Company, p. 1532.

Herald (1991a) Inquiry told of Orkney boy's 'unusual stories', 21 November.

Herald (1991b) Boy from Orkney 'boasted of killing', 17 December.

Herman, J. and Hirschmann, L. (1981) *Father–daughter incest*, Cambridge, MA: Harvard University Press.

Herman, J., Perry, J., and van der Kolk, B. (1989) 'Childhood trauma in borderline personality disorder', *American Journal of Psychiatry*, 146(4): 490–5.

Herman, J.L. (1992) *Trauma and recovery: The aftermath of violence – from domestic abuse to political terror*, New York: Basic Books.

Herman, J.L. (1995) 'Crime and memory', *Journal of the American Academy of Psychiatry and the Law*, 23(1): 5–17.

Herman, J.L. . and Herman, J.L. (1997) 'Adult memories of childhood trauma: a naturalistic clinical study', *Journal of Traumatic Stress*, 10(4): 557–71.

Hershkowitz, I., Horowitz, D. and Lamb, M. (2005) 'Trends in children's disclosure of abuse in Israel: a national study', *Child Abuse & Neglect*, 29: 1203–14.

Hilton, M. and Mezey, G. (1996) 'Victims and perpetrators of child sexual abuse', *British Journal of Psychiatry*, 169(4): 408–15.

Hindman, J. and Peters, J. (2001) 'Polygraph testing leads to better understanding adult and juvenile sex offenders', *Federal Probation*, 65(3): 8–15.

Hine, K. (2000) 'Retaliation against professionals who report child abuse', www.thelizlibrary.org/liz/retaliation.html.

HM Government (2013) *Working together to safeguard children, A guide to inter-agency working to safeguard and promote the welfare of children*, London: HM Government.

HM Government (2014) *The fifth periodic report to the UN Committee on the Rights of the Child: United Kingdom*, May, www.equalityhumanrights. com/sites/default/files/uploads/Pdfs/The%20UK's%20Fifth%20 Periodic%20Review%20Report%20on%20the%20UNCRC.pdf.

Hobbs, C. and Wynne, J. (1986) 'Buggery in childhood – a common syndrome of child abuse', *The Lancet*, 4(2): 792–6.

Hobbs, C. and Wynne, J. (1994) 'Treating satanist abuse survivors: the Leeds experience' in V. Sinason (ed), *Treating survivors of satanist abuse*, London & New York: Routledge, pp. 214–17.

Holman, R. (1993) *A new deal for social welfare*, Oxford: Lion Books.

Holmes, W. and Slap, G. (1998) 'Sexual abuse of boys: definition, prevalence, correlates, sequelae, and management', *JAMA*, 280: 1855–62.

Holt, A. (2014) 'Rotherham abuse: researcher "faced council hostility"', BBC *Panorama*, September.

Hopper, J. (2008) 'Sexual abuse of males: prevalence, possibly lasting effects and resources', www.jimhopper.com/male-ab/

Hopper, J. (2012) 'Child abuse: statistics, research and resources', www. jimhopper.com/abstats.

Horvath, M., Davidson, J., Grove-Hills, J., Gekoski, A. and Choak, C. (2014) *It's a lonely journey: A rapid evidence assessment on intrafamilial child sexual abuse*, London: Office of the Children's Commissioner.

Horvath, M., Alys, L., Massey, K., Pina, A., Scally, M. and Adler, J. (2012) '"Basically ... porn is everywhere" A rapid evidence assessment on the effect that access and exposure to pornography has on children and young people', University of Middlesex & OCC.

Hoult, J. (2006) 'The evidentiary admissibility of parental alienation syndrome: science, law, and policy', *Children's Legal Rights Journal*, 26(1): 1–61.

House of Commons Education Committee (2012) *Children first: The child protection system in England*, www.publications.parliament.uk/pa/cm201213/cmselect/cmeduc/137/13702.htm.

House of Commons Health Committee (2003) *The Victoria Climbié Inquiry Report: Sixth report of session 2002–03*, London.

Hunter, M. (1995) *Adult survivors of sexual abuse: Treatment innovations*, Sage Publications.

Hunter, S. (1993) 'Prostitution is cruelty and abuse to women and children', *Michigan Journal of Gender and Law*, 1: 1–14.

Hutton, L. (2007) 'Children and young people with harmful, abusive or offending sexual behaviours: a review of the literature', Edinburgh: CJSW Development Centre for Scotland.

Ilyas, S. and Moncrieff, J. (2012). 'Trends in prescriptions and costs of drugs for mental disorders in England, 1998–2010', *British Journal of Psychiatry*, 200(5): 393–98.

Information Services Division (Scotland) (2014) Abortion Statistics 2013, www.isdscotland.org/Health-Topics/Sexual-Health/Publications/index.asp?ID=1252.

Internet Watch Foundation & Microsoft (2015) *Emerging patterns and trends report: Youth-produced sexual content*, Cambridge: Internet Watch Foundation.

Itzin, C. (2000) 'The victim experience of child sexual abuse and its effects: Part 1.2', in C. Itzin (ed), *Home truths about child sexual abuse: Influencing policy and practice*, London and New York: Routledge, pp. 101–23.

Jack, G. (2004) 'Child protection at the community level', *Child Abuse Review*, 13(6): 368–83.

Jack, G. and Gill, O. (2003) *The missing side of the triangle: Assessing the importance of family and environmental factors in the lives of children*, Barkingside: Barnardo's.

Jacobson, A. and Herald, C. (1990) 'The relevance of childhood sexual abuse to adult psychiatric inpatient care', *Hospital Community Psychiatry*, 41(2): 154–8.

Jaffe, R. (1968) 'Dissociative phenomena in former concentration camp inmates', *The International Journal of Psychoanalysis*, 49(2): 310–12.

Jay, A. (2014) *Independent inquiry into child sexual exploitation in Rotherham (1997–2013)*, Rotherham Metropolitan Borough Council.

Jeffreys, S. (1997) *The spinster and her enemies: Feminism and sexuality, 1880–1930*, Melbourne: Spinifex Press.

Jennings, A. (1994) 'On being invisible in the mental health system', *Journal of Mental Health Administration*, 21(4): 374–87.

Jensen, T.K., Gulbrandsen, W., Mossige, S., Reichelt, S. and Tjersland, O.A. (2005). 'Reporting possible sexual abuse: a qualitative study on children's perspectives and the context for disclosure', *Child Abuse & Neglect*, 29(12): 1395–413.

Johnson, J., Sun, C., Bridges, A. and Ezzell, M. (2014) 'Pornography and the male sexual script: an analysis of consumption and sexual relations,' *Archives of Sexual Behavior*, September.

Johnson, R., Ross, M., Taylor, W., Williams, M., Carvajal, R. and Peters, R. (2006) 'Prevalence of childhood sexual abuse among incarcerated males in county jail', *Child Abuse & Neglect*, 30(1): 75–86.

Johnston, J. (2010) 'Revealed: The tragic truth about Britain's youngest mother, a rape and who the father of her child really is', *Daily Mail*, 5 June.

Jonson-Reid, M. (2001) 'Adolescent sexual offenders: incidence of childhood maltreatment, serious emotional disturbance and prior offenses', *American Journal of Orthopsychiatry*, 71(1): 120–130.

Jukes, L. and Duce, R. (1990) 'NSPCC says ritual child abuse rife', *The Times*, 13 March.

Jumper, S. (1995) 'A meta-analysis of the relationship of child sexual abuse to adult psychological adjustment', *Child Abuse & Neglect*, 19(6): 715–28.

Kalathil, J. (2011) *Recovery and resilience: African, African-Caribbean and South Asian women's narratives of recovering from mental distress*, London: Mental Health Foundation.

Kaliray, P. and Drife, J. (2004) 'Childhood sexual abuse and subsequent gynaelogical conditions', *The Obstetrician & Gynaecologist*, 6: 209–14.

Kaufman, K., Hayes, A., and Knox, L. (2010) 'The situational prevention model: creating safer environments for children & adolescents', in K. Kaufman (ed) *The prevention of sexual violence: A practitioner's sourcebook*, Holyoke, MA: NEARI Press.

Kelly, C. (2004) *Report of a serious case review: Ian Huntley, North East Lincolnshire, 1995–2001*, North East Lincolnshire Area Child Protection Committee.

Kelly, L. (1991) 'Unspeakable acts: abuse by and between women,' *Trouble and Strife*, 21: 13–20.

Kelly, L. (1996) 'Weasel words: paedophiles and the cycle of abuse', *Trouble and Strife*, 33: 1–8.

Kendall-Tackett, K. (2007) 'Why trauma makes people sick: inflammation, heart disease and diabetes in trauma survivors', *Trauma Psychology*, Winter: 9–12.

Kessler, R., McLaughlin, K., Green, J., Gruber, M., Sampson,N., Zaslavsky, A., Aguilar-Gaxiola, S., Alhamzawi, A., Alonso, J., Angermeyer, M., Benjet, C., Bromet, E., Chatterji, S., de Girolamo, G., Demyttenaere, K., Fayyad, J., Florescu, S., Gal, G., Gureje, O., Haro, J., Chi-yi Hu, Karam, E., Kawakami, N., Sing Lee, Lépine, J., Ormel, J., Posada-Villa, J., Sagar, R., Tsang, A., Üstün, T., Vassilev, S., Viana, M. and Williams, D. (2010) 'Childhood adversities and adult psychopathology in the WHO World Mental Health Surveys', *British Journal of Psychiatry*, 197(5): 378–85.

Kinderman, P., Read, J., Moncrieff, J. and Bentall, R. (2013) 'Drop the language of disorder', *Evidence Based Mental Health*, 16(1): 2–3.

Kinsey, A., Pomeroy, W. and Martin, C. (1948/1998). *Sexual behavior in the human male*, Philadelphia: W.B. Saunders.

Kinsey, A., Pomeroy, W., Martin, C. and Gebhard, P. (1953) *Sexual behavior in the human female*, Philadelphia: W.B. Saunders.

Kitzinger, J. (2000) 'Media templates: patterns of association and the reconstruction of meaning over time', *Media Culture and Society*, 22(1): 64–84.

Korn, D. (2009) 'EMDR and the treatment of complex PTSD: a review', *Journal of EMDR Practice & Research*, 3(4): 264–78.

Kramer, L. and Berg, E. (2003) 'Survival analysis of timing of entry into prostitution', *Sociological Inquiry*, 73: 511–28.

Krell, R. (1993) 'Child survivors of the Holocaust: strategies of adaptation', *Canadian Journal of Psychiatry*, 38: 384–89.

Kuenssberg, L. (2014) 'Metropolitan Police officer was "moved from child abuse inquiry"', BBC Newsnight, 15 July.

Kuhn, T. (1970) *The structure of scientific revolutions*, 2nd edition, Chicago: University of Chicago Press.

Labbé, J. (2005) 'Ambroise Tardieu: the man and his work on child maltreatment a century before Kempe', *Child Abuse & Neglect*, 29(4): 311–24.

Lafferty, S. and Davidson, R. (2006) 'Person-centred care in practice: an account of the implementation of the tidal model in an adult acute admission ward in Glasgow', *Mental Health Today*, March: 31–4.

La Fontaine, J. (1994) *Extent and nature of organised and ritual abuse: Research findings*, London: HMSO.

La Fontaine, J. (1998) *Speak of the devil: Tales of satanic abuse in contemporary England*, Cambridge: Cambridge University Press.

Laming, Lord (2003) *The Victoria Climbié Inquiry report*, London: The Stationery Office.

Lancaster, E. and Lumb, J. (1999) 'Bridging the gap: feminist theory and practice reality in work with the perpetrators of child sexual abuse', *Child & Family Social Work*, 4(2): 119–29.

Lapane, K., Zierler, S., Lasater, T., Stein., M., Barbour, M. and Hume, A.(1995) 'Is a history of depressive symptoms associated with an increased risk of infertility in women'? *Psychosomatic Medicine*, 57(6): 509–13.

Larson, M., Miller, L., Becker, M., Richardson, E., Kammerer, M., Thom, J., Gampel, J. and Savage, A. (2005) 'Physical health burdens of women with trauma histories and co-occurring substance abuse and mental disorders', *Journal of Behavioral Health Services & Research*, 32(2): 128–40.

Laville, S. (2004) 'Paediatricians shy away from dealing with abuse as backlash from parents grows', *Guardian*, 7 June.

Laville, S. (2013) 'Oxford child sex abuse ring: how police overcame past mistakes to jail gang', *Guardian*, 14 May.

Leclerc, B., Wortley, R. and Smallbone, S. (2011) 'Situational prevention measures: getting into the script of adult child sex offenders', *Journal of Research in Crime and Delinquency*, 48(2): 209–37.

Leeb, R., Barker, L. and Strine, T. (2007) 'The effect of childhood physical and sexual abuse on adolescent weapon carrying', *Journal of Adolescent Health*, 40(6): 551–8.

Leroi, A., Berkelmans, I., Denis, P., Hémond, M. and Devroede, G. (1995) 'Anismus as a marker of sexual abuse: consequences of abuse on anorectal motility', *Digestive Diseases and Sciences*, 40(7): 1411–6.

Leserman, J., Li, Z., Drossman, D., Toomey, T., Nachman, G. and Glogau, L. (1997) 'Impact of sexual and physical abuse dimensions on health status: development of an abuse severity measure', *Psychosomatic Medicine*, 59(2): 152–60.

Levy, A. (2004) *Stigmatised, marginalised and criminalised: An overview of the issues relating to children and young people involved in prostitution*, London: NSPCC.

Liebell, D. (2009) 'The ONE area of the body every fibromyalgia sufferer must have examined', http://necksecret.com/Fibromyalgia__Neck_Cause.html.

Link, C., Lutfey, K., Steers, W. And Mcinlay, J. (2007) 'Is abuse causally related to urologic symptoms? Results from the Boston Area Community Heath (BACH) Survey', *European Urology*, 52(2): 397–406.

Lipowski, Z. (1988) 'Somatisation: the concept and its clinical consequences', *American Journal of Psychiatry*, 145(11): 1358–67.

Lisak, D. (1994) 'The psychological impact of sexual abuse: a content analysis of interviews with male survivors', *Journal of Traumatic Stress*, 7(4): 525–48.

Lisak, D., Hopper, J. and Song, P. (1996) 'Factors in the cycle of violence: gender rigidity and emotional constriction', *Journal of Traumatic Stress*, 9(4): 721–43.

Logan, C., Holcombe, E., Ryan, S., Manlove, J. and Moore, K. (2007) *Childhood sexual abuse and teen pregnancy: A White Paper*, Project of the National Campaign to Prevent Teen and Unplanned Pregnancy, Child Trends, Inc.

Lukianowicz, N. (1972) 'Incest: 1. Paternal incest', *British Journal of Psychiatry*, 120(556): 301–13.

MacKean, L. (2013) 'The paedophile MP: how Cyril Smith got away with it', *Channel 4 Dispatches*, 12 September.

Macpherson, Suzi (2013) SPICe Briefing 13/03 Teenage pregnancy, 22 January, www.scottish.parliament.uk/parliamentarybusiness/58852.aspx.

Mallard, C. (2008) 'Ritual abuse – a personal account' in J. and P. Noblitt (eds) *Ritual abuse in the 21st century: Psychological, forensic, social and political considerations*, Bandon, OR: Robert D. Reed Publishers.

Malone, C. (2014) 'Britain's youngest mum is already on scrapheap at age of just 12', *Sunday Mirror*, 19 April.

Malone, C., Farthing, L. and Marce, L. (1996) *The memory bird: Survivors of sexual abuse*, London: Virago.

Malloy, L., Lindsay, C., Lyon, T. and Quas, J. (2007) 'Filial dependency and recantation of child sexual abuse', *Journal of the American Academy of Child & Adolescent Psychiatry*, 46(2): 162–70.

Malterud, K. (2003) 'It is hard work behaving as a credible patient: encounters between women with chronic pain and their doctors', *Social Science and Medicine*, 57(8): 1409–19.

Maniglio, R. (2009) 'The impact of child sexual abuse on health: a systematic review of reviews', *Clinical Psychology Review*, 29(7): 647–5.

Mann, R. and Barnett, G. (2013) 'Victim empathy intervention with sexual offenders: rehabilitation, punishment, or correctional quackery?' *Sexual Abuse, a Journal of Research & Treatment*, 25(3): 282–301.

Marks, J. (1995) *The hidden children: The secret survivors of the Holocaust*, Toronto: Bantam Books.

Marshall, K. (2014) *Child sexual exploitation in Northern Ireland: Report of the independent inquiry*, Regulation and Quality Improvement Authority (RQIA) for Northern Ireland.

Martin, L. (2005) 'Ruined lives of islanders in child sex fiasco', *Guardian*, 11 December.

Martindale, B. (2012) 'Hope and the ISPS change of name', *Psychosis*, 4: 92–4.

Masson, J. (1984) *The assault on truth: Freud's suppression of the seduction theory*, New York: Farrar, Strauss and Giroux.

Matthew, L. (2002) *Where angels fear: Ritual abuse in Scotland*, Dundee: Young Women's Centre Trading Ltd.

Matthew, L. (2005) *Behind enemy lines*, Dundee: Young Women's Centre Trading Ltd.

Matthews, B., Payne, H., Bonnet, C. and Chadwick, D. (2009) ' A way to restore British paediatricians' engagement with child protection', *Archives Disease in Childhood*, 94:329–32.

McElvaney, R., Greene, S. and Hogan, D. (2012) 'Containing the secret of child sexual abuse', *Journal of Interpersonal Violence*, 27(6): 1155–75.

McElvaney, R. (2013) 'Disclosure of child sexual abuse: delays, nondisclosure and partial disclosure. What the research tells us and implications for practice', *Child Abuse Review*, DOI: 0.1002/car.2280.

McGee, H., Garavan, R., deBarra, M., Byrne, J., and Conroy, R. (2002) *The SAVI Report: Sexual abuse and violence in Ireland*, Dublin: The Liffey Press.

McGregor, K., Glover, M., Gautam, J. and Jülich, S. (2009) 'Working sensitively with child sexual abuse survivors: what female child sexual abuse survivors want from health professionals', *Women Health*, 50(8): 737–55.

McGuire, M. and Dowling, S. (2013) *Cyber crime: A review of the evidence*, Research Report 75, Summary of key findings and implications. London: Home Office.

McInnes, E. (2014) 'Madness in family law: mothers' mental health in the Australian family law system,' Psychiatry, Psychology and Law, 21(1): 78–91.

McKain, B. (1995) 'Sheriff condemns non-appearance of woman key witness', *Herald*, 28 February.

McLellan, B. (1995) *Beyond psych-oppression: A Feminist alternative therapy*, Melbourne: Spinifex Press.

McLeod, S., Hart, R., Jeffes, J. and Wilkin, A. (2010) *The impact of the Baby Peter case on applications for care orders*, Slough: National Foundation for Educational Research.

McMackin, R., Leisen, M., Cusack, J., LaFratta, J. and Litwin, P. (2002) 'The relationship of trauma exposure to sex offending behavior among male juvenile offenders', *Journal of Child Sexual Abuse*, 11(2): 25–40.

McWhinney, I. Epstein, R. and Freeman, T. (1997) 'Rethinking somatisation', *Annals of Internal Medicine*, 126(9): 747–50.

Mehl-Madrona, L. (2010) *Healing the mind through the power of story: The promise of narrative psychiatry*, Rochester, Vermont: Bear & Co.

Meier, J. (2009) *Parental Alienation Syndrome and parental alienation: Research reviews*, Harrisburg, PA: VAWnet, National Resource Center on Domestic Violence/Pennsylvania Coalition Against Domestic Violence.

Mental Health Network (2010) *Delivering same-sex accommodation in mental health and learning disability services,* Issue 195, London: The NHS Confederation.

Middleton, H. and Moncrieff, J. (2011) 'They won't do any harm and might do some good': time to think again on the use of antidepressants?, *Br J Gen Pract*, 61(582): 47 –9.

Middleton, T. and Weitz, K. (2015) *Tressa, the 12 year old mum*, London: John Blake.

Miller, A. (2014) *Becoming yourself: Overcoming mind control and ritual abuse*, London: Karnac Books.

Miller, D. and Brown, J. (2014) *'We have the right to be safe': Protecting disabled children from abuse*, London: NSPCC.

Miller, A. and Rubin, D. (2009) 'The contribution of children's advocacy centers to felony prosecutions of child sexual abuse', *Child Abuse & Neglect*, 33(1): 12–18.

Ministry of Justice (2014) Multi-agency public protection arrangements (MAPPA) annual report 2013–14, www.gov.uk/government/collections/multi-agency-public-protection-arrangements-mappa-annual-reports.

Mollon, P. (1996) *Multiple selves, multiple voices: Working with trauma, violation and dissociation*, Chichester: John Wiley.

Moncrieff, J., Hopker, S. and Thomas, P. (2005) 'Psychiatry and the pharmaceutical industry: who pays the piper?' *BJ PsychBulletin*, 29:84–5.

Morris, A. (2009) 'Gendered dynamics of abuse and violence in families: considering the abusive household gender regime', *Child Abuse Review*, 18(6): 414–27.

Morrison, A., Frame, L. and Larkin, W. (2003) 'Relationships between trauma and psychosis: a review and integration', *British Journal of Clinical Psychology*, 42(4): 331–53.

Morrow, J., Yeager, C. and Lewis, D.(1997) 'Encopresis and sexual abuse in a sample of boys in residential treatment', *Child Abuse & Neglect*, 21(1): 11–8.

Morton, J., Andrews, B., Bekerian, D., Brewin, C., Davies, G. and Mollon, P. (1995) 'Recovered memories: the report of the working party of the British Psychological Society', in K. Pezdek and W. Banks (eds) *The recovered memory/false memory debate*, San Diego, CA: Academic Press, pp.373–92.

Moskowitz, A. (2011) 'Schizophrenia, trauma, dissociation, and scientific revolutions', *Journal of Trauma & Dissociation*, 12(4): 347–57.

Moyes, J. (1997) 'The case of the 12-year-old mother', *Independent*, 9 July.

Munro, E. (2011) *Munro Review of Child Protection: Final report – a child-centred system*, Department for Education, London: The Stationery Office.

Munro, R., Brown,R. and Manful, E. (2011) *Safeguarding children statistics: the availability and comparability of data in the UK*, Loughborough: Childhood Wellbeing Research Centre.

Murphy, E. (2014) 'Children who have been sexually exploited are "blamed for being a victim"', ITV News Report, 29 October.

NAPAC (2014) *NAPAC support line data analysis*, London: NAPAC.

Narang, J. and Quereshi, N. (2015) *Hidden in Silence*, Dawn Films, UK.

Nathan, D. and Snedeker, M. (1995) *Satan's silence: Ritual abuse and the making of a modern American witch hunt*, New York: Basic Books.

National Children's Advocacy Center (2011) *Declining rates of child sexual abuse: A bibliography*, www.nationalcac.org/images/pdfs/CALiO/Bibliographies/declining-rates-bib4.pdf

National Institute for Social Work (1982) *Social workers, their role and tasks*, London: National Institute for Social Work.

Nava, M. (1988) 'Cleveland and the press: outrage and anxiety in the reporting of child sexual abuse', *Feminist Review*, 28: 103–21.

Nelson, S. (1982) *Incest: Fact and myth*, Edinburgh: Stramullion Press.

Nelson, S. (1987) *Incest: Fact and myth*, 2nd edition, Edinburgh: Stramullion Press.

Nelson, S. (1994) 'After the "hype" the myth remains', *Herald*, 27 June.

Nelson, S. (1996) 'Pointing fingers without the facts', *Herald*, 26 October.

Nelson, S. (1997) 'Breaking the silence', *Herald*, 26 May.

Nelson, S. (1998a) 'Time to break professional silences', *Child Abuse Review*, 7(3): 144–53.

Nelson, S. (1998b) 'A test for memories', *Herald*, 25 February.

Nelson, S. (2000) 'Confronting child sexual abuse: challenges for the future', in C. Itzin (ed) *Home truths about sexual abuse*, London: Routledge, pp. 387–403.

Nelson, S. (2001) *Beyond trauma: The mental health care needs of women survivors of sexual abuse*, Edinburgh: Edinburgh Association for Mental Health, www.health-in-mind.org.uk/information-research/reports.html.

Nelson, S. (2002) 'Physical symptoms in sexually abused women: somatisation or undetected injury?' *Child Abuse Review*, 11(1): 51–64.

Nelson, S. (2004a) 'Research with psychiatric patients: knowing their own minds?' in M. Smyth and E. Williamson (eds), *Researchers and their "subjects": Ethics, power, knowledge and consent*, Bristol: Policy Press.

Nelson, S. (2004b) *Neighbourhood mapping for children's safety: A feasibility study in Craigmillar Edinburgh*, Edinburgh: Womanzone Community Health Project.

Nelson, S. (2004c) *Adult male survivors of childhood sexual abuse: Needs assessment*, Lothian, Edinburgh: Edinburgh Association for Mental Health, www.health-in-mind.org.uk/assets/files/Male%20needs%20assessment%20report.pdf.

Nelson, S. (ed) (2008) *See us – hear us! Schools working with sexually abused young people*, Dundee: Violence is Preventable, 18 and Under, www.violenceispreventable.org.uk/see%20us%20hear%20us.pdf.

Nelson, S. (2009) *Care and support needs of men who survived childhood sexual abuse: Report of a qualitative research project*, Centre for Research on Families and Relationships (CRFR), University of Edinburgh, www.health-in-mind.org.uk/information-research/reports.html.

Nelson, S. (2011) 'Are pills making state hospital patients obese?, *Herald*, 8 February.

Nelson, S. (2012a) 'Action needed to end tragedies of "motiveless violence"', *Herald*, 16 November.

Nelson, S. (ed) (2012b) *Surviving well? Good practice for health professionals working with survivors of childhood sexual abuse*, Falkirk: Open Secret.

Nelson, S. (2012c) 'Lynch mob mentality won't make us any safer, *Herald*, 16 July.

Nelson, S. (2012d) 'Preventing tragedy', *Herald*, 3 May.

Nelson, S. (2013) 'Why the Catholic Church is mired in more child sex abuse claims', *Herald*, 1 August.

Nelson, S. and Baldwin, N. (2004) 'The Craigmillar Project: neighbourhood mapping to improve children's safety from sexual crime', *Child Abuse Review*, 13(6): 415–25.

Nelson, S. and Hampson, S. (2008) *Yes you can! Working with survivors of childhood sexual abuse*, 2nd edition, Edinburgh: Scottish Government National Programme for Mental Health & Wellbeing, www.gov.scot/Publications/2008/04/07143029/0.

Nelson, S. and Mackay, K. (2015) *Guidelines on reporting underage pregnancy and underage sex cases*, Edinburgh: University of Edinburgh/NSPCC Child Protection Research Centre.

Nelson, S., Baldwin, N. and Taylor, J. (2012) 'Mental health problems and medically unexplained physical symptoms in adult survivors of childhood sexual abuse: an integrative literature review', *Journal of Psychiatric and Mental Health Nursing*, 19(3): 211–20.

Nelson, S., Lewis, R. and Gulyurtlu, S. (2013). 'Male survivors of childhood sexual abuse: experience of mental health services', in J. Pritchard (ed), *Healing and recovery in sexual abuse*, London: Jessica Kingsley.

Newcomer, J. and Haupt, D. (2006) 'The metabolic effects of antipsychotic medications', *Canadian Journal of Psychiatry*, 51: 480–91.

Newman, D. (2002) *Understanding chronic pelvic pain and vulvodynia*, Seek Wellness LLC, www.seekwellness.com/PDFs/what_is_pelvic_pain.pdf

NHS Confederation (2008) *Briefing 162: Implementing national policy on violence and abuse*, London: Ministry of Health.

Nijenhuis, E. (2001) 'Somatoform dissociation: major symptoms of dissociative disorders', *Journal of Trauma & Dissociation*, 1(4): 1–26.

Nijenhuis, E. (2004) *Somatoform Dissociation: Phenomena, measurement, and theoretical issues*, London: WW Norton.

Nijenhuis, E., van Dyck, R., Ter Kuile, M., Mourits, M. and van der Hart, O. (2003) 'Evidence for associations among somatoform dissociation, psychological dissociation and reported trauma in patients with chronic pelvic pain', *Journal of Psychosomatic Obstetrics & Gynecology*, 24(2): 2, 87–98.

Noblitt, J. and Perskin, P. (eds) (2008) *Ritual abuse in the twenty-first century: Psychological, forensic, social and political considerations*, Bandor, OR: Robert Reed.

Noll, J., Shenk, C. and Putnam, K. (2009a) 'Childhood sexual abuse and adolescent pregnancy: a meta-analytic update', *Journal of Pediatric Psychology*, 34(4): 366–78.

Noll, J., Shenk, C., Barnes, J and Putnam, F. (2009b) 'Childhood abuse, avatar choices and other risk factors associated with internet-initiated victimisation of adolescent girls', *Pediatrics*, 123: 1078–83.

Norfolk, A. (2012) 'Police files reveal vast child protection scandal – confidential papers show a decade of abuse in South Yorkshire', *The Times*, 24 September.

Norfolk, A. (2013) 'Failure to join the dots led to Oxford victims' continued abuse', *The Times*, 15 May.

Norgate, R., Warhurst, A., Osborne, C. and Traill, M. (2012) 'Social workers' perspectives on the placement instability of looked after children', *Adoption & Fostering*, 36(2): 4–18.

Norman, S., Means-Christensen, A., Craske, M., Sherbourne, C., Roy-Byrne, P. and Stein, M. (2006) 'Associations between psychological trauma and physical illness in primary care', *Journal of Traumatic Stress*, 19(4): 461–70.

Nottinghamshire County Council (1990) *Report of Director of Social Services: Child abuse, to Social Services Committee*, Nottingham, 7 November.

NSPCC (2015) *How safe are our children? 2015, Indicator 4*, London: NSPCC.

Oates, R. (2004) 'Sexual abuse and suicidal behaviour', *Child Abuse & Neglect*, 28(5): 487–89.

O'Connor, R. (2015) 'Ched Evans petition over potential Oldham signing becomes one of the fastest-growing ever', *Independent*, 5 January.

Office of the Children's Commissioner (England) (OCC) (2011) *"I thought I was the only one: The only one in the world": Inquiry into child sexual exploitation in gangs and groups*, London: OCC, www. childrenscommissioner.gov.uk/inquiry-child-sexual-exploitation-gangs-and-groups.

Olafson, E., Corwin, D. and Summit, R. (1993) 'Modern history of child sexual abuse awareness: cycles of discovery and suppression', *Child Abuse & Neglect*, 17(1): 7–24.

O'Leary, P. (2009) 'Men who were sexually abused in childhood: coping strategies and comparisons in psychological functioning,' *Child Abuse & Neglect*, 33(7): 471–79..

Olio, K. and Cornell, W. (1994) 'Making meaning not monsters: reflections on the delayed memory controversy', *Journal of Child Sexual Abuse*, 3(3): 77–94.

One Poll Newsletter (2015) 'The language of rape culture', London & New York, *One Poll*, November.

Palmer, E. (2014) 'Medomsley detention centre abuse: officers questioned as 900 alleged victims come forward', *International Business Times*, 13 November.

Pankhurst, C. (1997) 'Controversies in the aetiology of temperomandibular disorders. Part 1. Temperomandibular disorders: all in the mind'?, *Primary Dental Care*, 4(1): 25–30.

Parry, O., Thomson, C. and Fowks, G. (1999) 'Lifecourse data collection: qualitative interviewing using the life grid', *Sociological Research Online*, 4(2), www.socresonline.org.uk/4/2/parry.html.

Peter, J. and Valkenburg, P. (2009) 'Adolescents' exposure to sexually explicit internet material and sexual satisfaction: a longitudinal study', *Human Communication Research*, 35: 171–94.

Peter, J. and Valkenburg, P. (2010) 'Processes underlying the effects of adolescents' use of sexually explicit internet material: the role of perceived realism', *Communication Research*, 37: 375–99.

Peters, K., Carrico, D. and Diokno, A. (2008) 'Characterization of a clinical cohort of 87 women with interstitial cystitis/painful bladder syndrome', *Urology*, 71(4): 634–40.

Pettifor, J. (2013) 'Paedo MP cover-up claim: Top cop removed from sex abuse probe after naming politicians as suspects', *Mirror*, 26 March.

Pidd, H. (2015) 'Alexis Jay on child sex abuse: "Politicians wanted to keep a lid on it"', *Daily Record*, 13 July.

Pilgrim, D. (2014) *Understanding mental health: A critical realist exploration*, London: Routledge.

Pilling, K. (2013) 'Rochdale sex abuse: victims could have been protected', *Independent*, 20 December.

Pipe, M., Lamb, M., Orbach, Y., Stewart, H., Sternberg, K. and Esplin, P. (2007) 'Factors associated with nondisclosure of suspected abuse during forensic interviews', in M. Pipe, M. Lamb, Y. Orbach and A. Cederborg (eds), *Child sexual abuse: Disclosure, delay and denial*, Mahwah, NJ: Lawrence Erlbaum, pp. 77–96.

Police Scotland (2015) 'National Child Abuse Investigation Unit launched', press release, 20 April.

Pope, K. (1997) 'Science as careful questioning: are claims of a false memory syndrome epidemic based on empirical evidence?' *American Psychologist*, 52(9): 997–1006.

Powell, D., Karanfilov, B., Beechler, K., Treole, K., Trudeau, M. and Forrest, L. (2000) 'Paradoxical vocal chord dysfunction in juveniles', *Archives of Otolaryngology–Head Neck Surgery*, 126(1): 29–34.

Power, A. and Willmott, H. (2007) *Social capital within a neighbourhood: CASE Report 38*, Swindon: ESRC.

Priebe, G., and Svedin, C. (2008). 'Child sexual abuse is largely hidden from the adult society: an epidemiological study of adolescents' disclosures', *Child Abuse & Neglect*, 32: 1095–108.

Professional Social Work (2013) 'Mediawatch: Esther W', 6 September.

Purvis, M. and Ward, T. (2006) 'The role of culture in understanding child sexual offending: examining feminist perspectives', *Aggression and Violent Behavior*, 11(3): 298–312.

Radford, L., Corral, S., Bradley, C., Fisher, H., Bassett, C., Howat, N. and Collishaw, S. (2011) *Child abuse and neglect in the UK today*, London: NSPCC.

Rape Crisis Scotland (2014) *Comment on Scottish social attitudes survey, 2014: Attitudes to violence against women in Scotland.* www.rapecrisisscotland.org.uk/news/scottish-social-attitudes-survey/

Rapley, M., Moncrieff, J. and Dillon, J. (2011) *De-medicalizing misery*, New York: Palgrave.

Rasmussen, B. (2011) 'Children's advocacy centers (Barnahus) in Sweden: experiences of children and parents', *Child Indicators Research*, 4(2): 301–21.

Rawlinson, K., Morris, N. and Hall, J. (2013) 'Victims blamed for child sex abuse as Oxford council chief faces calls to quit over exploitation ring', *Independent*, 15 May.

Read, J. (1998) 'Child abuse and severity of disturbance among adult psychiatric inpatients', *Child Abuse & Neglect*, 22(5): 359–68.

Read, J. (2010) 'Can poverty drive you mad? "Schizophrenia", socio-economic status and the case for primary prevention', *New Zealand Journal of Psychology*, 39(2): 7–19.

Read, J. and Bentall, R. (2012) 'Negative childhood experiences and mental health: theoretical, clinical and primary prevention implications', *British Journal of Psychiatry*, 200(2): 89–91.

Read, J. and Dillon, J. (eds) (2013) *Models of madness: psychological, social and biological approaches to psychosis*, London: Routledge.

Read, J., Bentall, R., and Fosse, R. (2009) 'Time to abandon the bio-bio-bio model of psychosis', *Epidemiology and Psychiatric Sciences*, 18(4): 299–310.

Read, J., Dillon, J. and Lampshire, D. (2014) 'How much evidence is required for a paradigm shift in mental health?' *Acta Psychiatrica Scandinavica*, 129(6): 477–8.

Read, J., Agar, K., Argyle, N. and Aderhold, V. (2003) 'Sexual and physical abuse during childhood and adulthood as predictors of hallucinations, delusions and thought disorder', *Psychology and Psychotherapy: Theory, Research and Practice*, 76(1): 1–22.

Read, J., Perry, B., Moskowitz, A. and Connolly, J. (2001) 'The contribution of early traumatic events to schizophrenia in some patients', *Psychiatry*, 64(4): 319–45.

Reder, P. and Duncan, S. (2008) 'Professional dangerousness, causes and contemporary features', in M. Calder (ed) *Contemporary risk assessment in safeguarding children*, Lyme Regis: Russell House, Chapter 6.

Reese-Weber, M. and Smith, D. (2011) 'Outcomes of child sexual abuse as predictors of later sexual victimisation', *Journal of Interpersonal Violence*, 26: 1884–905.

ResPublica/Action for Children (2011) *Children and the Big Society*, London: Action for Children/Res Publica, www.respublica.org.uk/wp-content/uploads/2015/01/Children-and-BS.pdf.

Rheingold, A., Campbell, C., Self-Brown, S., de Arellano, M., Resnick, H. and Kilpatrick, D. (2007) 'Prevention of child sexual abuse: evaluation of a community media campaign', *Child Maltreatment*, 12(4): 352–63.

Richter, J. (2001) 'Do the clinic aspects of the nutcracker oesophagus parallel the features of the irritable bowel syndrome?' in R. Guili, R. McCallum and D. Skinner (eds), *Primary motility disorders of the esophagus*, OESO.

Ristock, J. (2002) *No more secrets: Violence in lesbian relationships*, Abingdon: Taylor & Francis.

Roazen, P. (2001) *The trauma of Freud: Controversies in psychoanalysis*, New Jersey: Transaction Publishers.

Roberts, G., Davenport, S. and Holloway, F. (eds) (2006) *Enabling recovery: The principles and practice of rehabilitation psychiatry*, London: Gaskell.

Robinson, W. (2014) 'Paedophile teacher was allowed to hug his pupils goodbye after his vile acts at international schools around the world were exposed as FBI calls him "one of worst ever"', *Mail Online*, 26 April.

Robinson, B. (2008) 'ABE interviews: is the child's 'best evidence' being achieved in alleged sexual abuse cases? (Part 2)', *Family Law Week* (archive), www.familylawweek.co.uk/site.aspx?i=ed24931.

Roche, A., Fortin, G., Labbé, J., Brown, J. and Chadwick, D. (2005) 'The work of Ambroise Tardieu: the first definitive description of child abuse', *Child Abuse & Neglect*, 29(4): 325–34.

Romans, S., Belaise, C., Martin, J., Morris, E. and Raffi, A. (2002) 'Childhood abuse and later medical disorders in women: an epidemiological study', *Psychotherapy and Psychosomatics*, 71(3): 141–50.

Romme, M. and Escher, S. (1993) *Accepting voices*, London: Mind Publications.

Romme, M. , Escher, S., Dillon, J., Corstens, D. and Morris, M (2009) *Living with voices*, Ross-on-Wye, PCCS.

Rosella Roars Associates (1997) Cleveland: Official Secrets, Conference, Newcastle upon Tyne, 3 November.

Rush, F. (1980) *The best kept secret: Sexual abuse of children*, New Jersey: Prentice Hall.

Sabbagh, D. and Deans, J. (2012) 'BBC to pay Lord McAlpine £185,000 after false child abuse allegations', *Guardian*, 15 November.

Sack, M., Lahmann, C., Jaeger, B. and Henningsen, P. (2007) 'Are there specific somatoform symptoms related to traumatic experiences?', *Journal of Nervous & Mental Disease*, 195(11): 928–33.

Saied-Tissier, A. (2014) *Estimating the cost of child sexual abuse in the UK*, London: NSPCC.

Salter, D., McMillan, D., Richards, M., Talbot, T., Hodges, J., Bentovim, A., Hastings, R., Stevenson J. and Skuse (2003) Development of sexually abusive behaviour in sexually victimised males: a longitudinal study. *Lancet* 361(9356):471-6.

Salter, M. (2013a) *Organised abuse*, London & New York: Routledge.

Salter, M. (2013b), 'Justice and revenge in online counter-publics: emerging responses to sexual violence in the age of social media', *Crime, Media, Culture*, 9(3), pp. 225–42.

Salter, M. and Dagistanli, S. (2015) 'Cultures of abuse: sex grooming, organised abuse and race in Rochdale, UK', *International Journal for Crime, Justice and Social Democracy*, 4(2), www.crimejusticejournal.com/article/view/211.

Say Women (2014) Training day, 3 December, Adelphi Centre, Glasgow, www.say-women.co.uk.

Schachter, C., Stalker, C. and Teram, E. (2009) *Handbook on sensitive practice for healthcare practitioners: Lessons from adult survivors of childhood sexual abuse*, Public Health Agency of Canada, National Clearinghouse on Family Violence.

Scheflin, A. (1999) 'Ground lost: the false memory/recovered memory therapy debate', *Psychiatric Times*, November.

Schreiber, F. (2009) *Sybil*, reissue edition, New York: Grand Central Publishing. Original published in 1973.

Schmucker, M. and Losel, F. (2008) 'Does sexual offender treatment work? A systematic review of outcome evauations', *Psicothema*, 20(1): 10–19.

SCIE (2006) *The participation practice guide 06: The participation of children and young people in developing social care*, London: Social Care Institute for Excellence.

Scott, S. (2001) *The politics and experience of ritual abuse: Beyond disbelief*, Maidenhead: Open University Press.

Scott-Clark, C. and Levy, A. (2009) 'Home to something evil', *Guardian Society*, 14 March.

Scottish Executive (2002) *It's everyone's job to make sure I'm alright: Report of the child protection audit and review*, Edinburgh: The Stationery Office.

Scottish Executive (2004) Children's social work statistics, 2003–04, Edinburgh.

Scottish Executive (2006) *Getting it right for every child* (GIRFEC), Edinburgh: Scottish Government, updated in 2015: www.gov.scot/Topics/People/Young-People/gettingitright.

Scottish Government (2010) *National guidance. Under-age sexual activity: Meeting the needs of children and young people and identifying child protection concerns*, para. 47, www.scotland.gov.uk/Resource/Doc/333495/0108880.pdf.

Scottish Government (2014a) *Children's social work statistics Scotland, 2013–14*, Chart 8.

Scottish Government (2014b) *Child protection key trends: Last update*, March 2014, www.scotland.gov.uk/Topics/Statistics/Browse/Children/TrendChildProtection.

Scottish Government and COSLA (2008) *Early years and early intervention: A joint Scottish Government and COSLA policy statement*, Edinburgh: Scottish Government.

Scottish Parliament (2014) *Inquiry into child sexual exploitation in Scotland: 1st Report*, Public Petitions Committee, www.scottish.parliament.uk/parliamentarybusiness/CurrentCommittees/71818.aspx.

Seebohm, F. (1968) *The Seebohm report*, London: HMSO.

Sellgren, K. (2014) 'Family abuse children "unprotected", Commissioner warns', BBC News, 3 July.

Sereny, G. (1998) *Cries unheard: The story of Mary Bell*, London: Macmillan.

Seto, M. and Eke, A. (2005) 'The criminal histories and later offending of child pornography offenders', *Sexual Abuse: A Journal of Research and Treatment*, 17(2): 201–10.

Seto, M.,Hanson, R. and Babchishin, K.(2011) 'Contact sexual offending by men with online sexual offenses', *Sex Abuse*, 23(1):124-45.

Sharpe, M. and Mayou, R. (2004) 'Somatoform disorders: a help or hindrance to good patient care?', *British Journal of Psychiatry*, 184(6): 465–7.

Shaw, D. (2014) 'Child abuse image investigation leads to 660 arrests', BBC News, 16 July.

Shaw, T. (2007) *Historical abuse systemic review: Residential schools and children's homes in Scotland 1950 to 1995*, www.gov.scot/Publications/2007/11/20104729/0.

Sheaffer, R. (1994) Review of the Courage to Heal, www.debunker.com/texts/courage_to_heal.html.

Shuker, L. (2014) *Evaluation of Barnardo's Safe Accommodation Project for sexually exploited and trafficked young people*, London: Barnardo's.

Simpson, T. and Miller, W. (2002) 'Concomitance between childhood sexual and physical abuse and substance use problems: a review', *Clinical Psychology Review*, 22(1): 27–77.

Sinason, V. (ed) (1994) *Treating survivors of satanist abuse*, New York: Routledge.

Sjöberg, R. and Lindblad, F. (2002) 'Limited disclosure of sexual abuse in children whose experiences were documented by videotape', *American Journal of Psychiatry*, 159(2): 312–4.

Skuse, D., Bentovim, A., Hodges, J., Andreou, C., Lanyado, M., New, M., Williams, B. and McMillan, D. (1998) 'Risk factors for development of sexually abusive behaviour in sexually victimised adolescent boys: cross-sectional study', *British Medical Journal*, 317: 175–9.

Sky News (2015) 'Police record 85 child sex crimes every day', 17 June.

Smahel, D., Helsper, E., Green, L., Kalmus, V., Blinka, L. & Ólafsson, K. (2012) *Excessive internet use among European children*, London: EU Kids Online, LSE, http://eprints.lse.ac.uk/47344/

Smith, M. (2010) 'Victim Narratives of historical abuse in residential child care: do we really know what we think we know?', *Qualitative Social Work*, 9(3): 303–20.

Smith, M. (2014) 'Panicking over the past: researching celebrity historic sexual abuse allegations', *The Justice Gap*, http://thejusticegap.com/2014/08/researching-celebrity-historic-sexual-abuse-allegations/

Smith, M. and Pazder, L. (1989) *Michelle remembers*, New York: Pocket Books.

Snow, B. and Sorensen, T. (1990) 'Ritualistic Child abuse in a neighborhood setting', *Journal of Interpersonal Violence*, 5(4): 474–487.

Social Work Inspection Agency (SWIA) (2005) *An inspection into the care and protection of children in Eilean Siar (Western Isles)*, Edinburgh: Scottish Executive.

Soo, D. and Bodanovskaya, Z. (2012) 'Risk factors of becoming a victim of internet related sexual abuse', in M. Ainsaar, & L. Lööf (eds), *Online behaviour related to child sexual abuse: Literature report*, ROBERT Project, European Union and Council of the Baltic Sea States, www.childcentre.info/robert/

Sorsoli, L., Kia-Keating, M. and Grossman, F. (2008) '"I keep that hush-hush": male survivors of sexual abuse and the challenges of disclosure', *Journal of Counselling Psychology*, 55(3): 333–45.

Speight, N. and Wynne, J. (2000) 'Is the children act failing severely abused and neglected children?', *Archives of Disease in Childhood*, 82: 192–6.

Spencer, N. and Baldwin, N. (2005) 'Economic, social and cultural contexts of neglect', in J. Taylor and B. Danie (eds), *Child neglect: Practice Issues for health and social care*, London, Jessica Kingsley.

Spillett, R. (2014) 'Disgraced broadcaster Stuart Hall jailed for ANOTHER two-and-a-half years for sexually assaulting under-age girl', *Mail Online*, 23 May.

Stacher, G., Wiesnagrotzki, S. and Kiss, A. (1990) 'Symptoms of achalasia in young women mistaken as indicating primary anorexia nervosa', *Dysphagia*, 5(4): 216–9.

Stahl, T., Wismar, M., Ollila, A., Lahtinen, E. and Leppo, K. (2006) *Health in all policies: Prospects and potentials*, Helsinki, Finland: European Observatory on Health Systems and Policies and Ministry of Social Affairs and Health.

Stalker, K., Lister, P., Lerpiniere, J. and McArthur, K. (2010) *Child protection and the needs and rights of disabled children and young people: A scoping study*, Glasgow: University of Strathclyde.

Stanton, M. (1997) 'U-turn on memory lane', *Columbia Journalism Review*, 44–9.

Starkman, M, and Appelblatt, N. (1984) 'Functional upper airway obstruction: a possible somatisation disorder', *Psychosomatics*, 25: 327–33.

Steel, J. and Herlitz, C. (2005) 'The association between childhood and adolescent sexual abuse and proxies for sexual risk behavior: a random sample of the general population of Sweden', *Child Abuse & Neglect*, 29 1141–53.

Stein, A. (2006) *Prologue to violence, dissociation, and Crime*. Routledge.

Stein, M. and Barrett-Connor, E. (2000) 'Sexual assault and physical health: findings from a population-based study of older adults', *Psychosomatic Medicine*, 62(6):838–43.

Stevenson, L. (2014) 'Report warns missing incidents should affect children's home's Ofsted rating after examining over 1,300 cases of missing people', *Community Care*, 31 July.

Stevenson, L. (2015) 'Child sexual exploitation referrals rose 31% last year, reveals Community Care', *Community Care*, 26 June.

Stevenson, S. (2012) *Perceptions of child abuse in scotland's minority ethnic communities*, Glasgow: Roshni Research & Consultancy.

Stewart, K. (2015) 'ADHD Versus PTSD in preschool-aged children: implications for misdiagnosis', *PCOM Psychology Dissertations*. Paper 49.http://digitalcommons.pcom.edu/psychology_dissertations/349.

Stewart, D. and Szymanski, D. (2012). 'Young adult women's reports of their male romantic partner's pornography use as a correlate of their self-esteem, relationship quality, and sexual satisfaction', *Sex Roles*, 67(5): 257–71.

Stoltenborgh, M., van Ijzendoorn, M., Euser, E. and Bakermans-Kranenburg, M. (2011) 'A global perspective on child sexual abuse: meta-analysis of prevalence around the world', *Child Maltreatment*, 16(2): 79–101.

Stoltz, J., Shannon, K., Kerr, T., Zhang, R., Montaner, J. and Wood, E. (2007), 'Associations between childhood maltreatment and sex work in a cohort of drug-using youth', *Social Science & Medicine*, 65, 1214–21.

Stopwatch (2012) *Stop and search factsheet*, London: Stopwatch.

Stuart, M. and Baines, C. (2004) *Progress on safeguards for children living away from home*, York: Joseph Rowntree Foundation.

STV News (2014) 'National inquiry into historic child sex abuse in Scotland announced', 17 December.

Summit, R. (1983) 'The child sexual abuse accommodation syndrome', *Child Abuse & Neglect*, 17: 177–93.

Summit, R. (1988) 'Hidden victims hidden pain: societal avoidance of child sexual abuse', in G. Wyatt and G. Powell (eds) *Lasting effects of child sexual abuse*, Newbury Park, CA: Sage, pp. 39–60.

Sun (2006) 'Pregnant – at 11', 12 May.

Surface, D. (2009) 'Revisiting parental alienation syndrome - scientific questions, real world consequences', *Social Work Today*, 9(5): 26.

Swann, S. (2000) 'Helping girls involved in "prostitution"', in C. Itzin (ed), *Home truths about child sexual abuse: Policy and practice: A reader*, London: Routledge.

Swanston, H., Parkinson, P., O'Toole, B., Plunkett, A., Shrimpton, S. and Oates, K. (2003) 'Juvenile crime, aggression and delinquency after sexual abuse: a longtitudinal study', *British Journal of Criminology*, 43: 729–49.

Talbot, N., Chapman, B., Conwell, Y., McCollum, K., Franus, N., Cotescue, S. and Duberstein,P. (2009) 'Childhood sexual abuse is associated with physical illness burden and functioning in psychiatric patients 50 years of age and older', *Psychosomatic Medicine*, 71(4): 417–22.

Taylor, S.C. (2002) 'Intrafamilial rape and the law in Australia: upholding the lore of the father', paper presented at Townsville International Women's Conference, Victoria.

Taylor, J., Stalker, K., Fry, D. and Stewart, A. (2014) *Disabled children and child protection in Scotland: An investigation into the relationship between professional practice, child protection and disability*, Edinburgh: The Scottish Government.

Teicher, M., Anderson, S., Polcari, A., Anderson, C., Navalta, C. and Kim, D. (2003) 'The neurobiological consequences of early stress and childhood maltreatment', *Neuroscience & Biobehavioral Reviews*, 27(1–2): 33–44.

Telegraph (2014) 'Children as young as four referred for drug and alcohol treatment', 30 April.

Teram, E., Stalker, C., Hovey, A., Schachter, C. and Lasiuk, G.(2006) 'Towards malecentric communication: sensitizing health professionals to the realities of male childhood sexual abuse survivors', *Issues in Mental Health Nursing*, 27(5): 499–517.

Terr, L. (1995) *Unchained memories: True stories of traumatic memories lost and found*, New York: Basic Books.

Thain, E. (2014) 'Peterborough social worker shares learning from child sexual exploitation cases', *Community Care*, 22 January.

Thoennes, N. and Tjaden, P. (1990) 'The extent, nature, and validity of sexual abuse allegations in custody/visitation disputes', *Child Abuse & Neglect*, 4(2):151–63.

Thomson, G. and Khan, K. (2008) *Magic in practice: Introducing medical nlp – the art and science of language in healing and health*, London: Hammersmith Press.

Thornton, P. (2011) 'Youngest mum in cash fight', *Sun*, 30 September.

Toates, F. and Coschug-Toates, O. (2002) *Obsessive compulsive disorder*, 2nd edition, London: Class Publishing.

Trocme, N. and Bala, N. (2005) 'False allegations of abuse and neglect when parents separate', *Child Abuse & Neglect*, 29: 1333–45.

Tunstall, R., Lupton, R., Power, A. and Richardson, L. (2011) *Building the Big Society*, CASE Paper 67. London: ESRC.

Twardosz, S. and Lutzke, J. (2009) 'Child maltreatment and the developing brain: a review of neuroscience perspectives', *Aggression and Violent Behavior*, 15: 59–68.

Tyler, K. (2002) 'Social and emotional outcomes of childhood sexual abuse: A review of recent research', *Aggression and Violent Behavior*, 7: 567–89.

UN (2006) *Millennium Development Goals report*, New York: United Nations.

Ungar, M., Tutty, L., McConnell, S., Barterm, K. and Fairholm, J. (2009) 'What Canadian youth tell us about disclosing abuse', *Child Abuse & Neglect*, 33: 699–708.

Utting, W. (2005) *Progress on safeguards for children living away from home*, York: Joseph Rowntree Trust.

Vachss, A. (1989) 'The child abuse backlash: a time of testing', *Justice for Children*, 2(3).

Valente, S. (2005) 'Sexual abuse of boys', *Journal of Child and Adolescent Psychiatric Nursing*, 18(1): 10–16.

Van der Hart, O. and Horst, R. (1989) 'The dissociation theory of Pierre Janet', *Journal of Traumatic Stress*, 2(4): 1–11.

Van der Hart, O., Witztum, E. and Haim Margalit, H. (2002) 'Combat-induced dissociative amnesia: review and case example of generalized dissociative amnesia', *Journal of Trauma & Dissociation*, 3(2): 35–55.

Van der Hart, O., Nijenhuis, E., Steele, K. and Brown, D. (2004) 'Trauma-related dissociation: conceptual clarity lost and found', *Australian and New Zealand Journal of Psychiatry*, 38(11–12): 906–14.

van der Kolk, B. (2014) *The body keeps the score: Mind, brain and body in the transformation of trauma*, London: Allen Lane.

van der Kolk, B., Pelcovitz, D., Roth, S., Mandel, F. McFarlane, A. and Herman, J. (1996a) 'Dissociation, somatization, and affect dysregulation: the complexity of adaptation of trauma', *The American Journal of Psychiatry*, 153(Suppl): 83–93.

van der Kolk, B., McFarlane, A. and Weisaeth, L. (eds) (1996b) *Traumatic stress: The effects of overwhelming experience on mind, body, and society*. New York: Guilford Press.

van der Kolk, B., Roth, S., Pelcovitz, D., Sunday, S. and Spinazzola, J. (2005) 'Disorders of extreme stress: the empirical foundation of a complex adaptation to trauma', *Journal of Traumatic Stress*, 18(5): 389–99.

van der Kolk, B.A., Hopper, J.W. and Osterman, J.E. (2001) 'Exploring the nature of traumatic memory: combining clinical knowledge with laboratory methods', *Journal of Aggression, Maltreatment, & Trauma*, 4: 9–31.

Van Meeuwen, A., Swann, S., McNeish, D. and Edwards, S. (1998) *Whose daughter next? Children abused through prostitution*, Essex: Barnardo's.

Varese, F., Smeets, F., Drukker, M., Lieverse, R., Lataster, T., Viechtbauer, W., Read, J., van Os, J. and Bentall, R. (2012) 'Childhood adversities increase the risk of psychosis: a meta-analysis of patient-control, prospective and cross-sectional cohort studies', *Schizophrenia Bulletin*, 38(4): 661–71.

W, Esther (2013) *If only I had told*, London: Ebury Press.

Wald, A. (2012) 'Irritable bowel syndrome treatment', www.uptodate.com/contents/irritable-bowel-syndrome-beyond-the-basics.

Waldinger, R., Schulz, M., Barsky, A. and Ahern, D. (2006) 'Mapping the road from childhood trauma to adult somatization: the role of attachment', *Psychosomatic Medicine*, 68(1): 129–35.

Walker, E. (1997) 'Medically unexplained physical symptoms', *Clinical Obstetrics & Gynaecology*, 40(3): 589–600.

Walker, E., Ward, T., Mann, R. and Gannon, T. (2007) 'The good lives model of offender rehabilitation', *Aggression and Violent Behavior*, 12(1): 87–107.

Ward, T. and Beech, A. (2006) 'An integrated theory of sexual offending', *Aggression and Violent Behavior*, 11, 44–63.

Ward, T. and Durran, R. (2013) 'Altruism, empathy, and sex offender treatment', *International Journal of Behavioral Consultation and Therapy*, 8(3–4): 1–6.

Ward, T. and Moreton, G. (2008) 'Moral repair with offenders', *Sexual Abuse: A Journal of Research and Treatment*, 20(3): 305–22.

Warner, S. (2009) *Understanding the effects of child sexual abuse: Feminist revolutions in theory, research and practice*, Abingdon: Routledge.

Warner, S. and Wilkins, T. (2004) 'Between subjugation and survival: women, borderline personality disorder and high security mental hospitals', *Journal of Contemporary Psychotherapy*, 34(3): 265–78.

Warwick, I. (2003) 'Medical examinations and invasion', Paper presented at the National Organisation Against Male Sexual Victimisation conference, University of Minnesota.

Waterhouse, L., Dobash, R. and Carnie, J. (1994) *Child sexual abusers*, Central Research Unit Papers, Edinburgh: Scottish Office.

Waterhouse, R. (1991) 'The secret bungalow of child interrogation', *Independent on Sunday*, 14 April.

Waterhouse, L. (1996) (ed) *Child abuse and child abusers: Protection and prevention*, London: Jessica Kingsley

Watt, N. and Wintour, P. (2014) 'Children's homes were "supply line" for paedophiles, says ex-minister', *Guardian*, 8 July.

Webster, D. (1993) 'Reframing women's health: tension and paradox in framing interstitial cystitis', *Journal of Women's Health*, 2(1): 81–4.

Webster, D. (1996) 'Sex, lies & stereotypes: women and interstitial cystitis', *Journal of Sex Research*, 33(3):197–203.

Weinstein, D. Staffelbach, D. and Biaggio, M. (2000) 'Attention-deficit hyperactivity disorder and posttraumatic stress disorder: Differential diagnosis in childhood sexual abuse' ,*Clin Psychol Review*, 20(3) 359–378.

Welch, J. (2014) 'Peterborough sex gang's 'sophisticated' grooming tactics', BBC News, 15 January.

Weniger, G., Lange, C., Sachsse, U. and IIrl, E. (2008) 'Amygdala and hippocampal volumes and cognition in adult survivors of childhood abuse with dissociative disorders', *Acta Psychiatrica Scandinavica*, 118(4): 281–90.

Westcott, H. and Kynan, S. (2006) 'Interviewer practice in investigative interviews for suspected child sexual abuse', *Psychology, Crime and Law*, 12: 367–82.

White, S., Broadhurst, K., Hall, C. and Wastell, D. (2008) 'Repeating the same mistakes', *Guardian*, 19 November.

Whitfield, C. (1997a) 'Traumatic amnesia: the evolution of our understanding from a clinical and legal prospective', *Sexual Addiction & Compulsivity*, 4(2): 3–34.

Whitfield, C. (2001) 'The "false memory" defense: using disinformation and junk science in and out of court', *Journal of Child Sexual Abuse*, 9(304): 53–78.

Whittle, H., Hamilton-Giachritsis, C., Beech, A. and Collings, G. (2013) 'A review of young people's vulnerabilities to online grooming', *Aggression and Violent Behavior*, 18(1): 135–46.

WHO (2008) *Commission on Social Determinants of Health: Final report*, Geneva: World Health Organization.

Whyte, S., Dyer, M. and Cleaver, L. (2012) Effective thyroid and adrenal testing, diagnosis and treatment, Petition PE0143 to Scottish Parliament, December.

Wiederman, M. Sansone, R. and Sansone, L. (1998) 'History of trauma and attempted suicide among women in a primary care setting', *Violence and Victims*, 13(1): 3–9.

Wiesel, E. (1993) Appearance on 'Oprah', 9 December.

Wilcox, D., Richards, F. and O'Keefe, Z. (2004) 'Resilience and risk factors associated with experiencing childhood sexual abuse', *Child Abuse Review*, 13(5): 338–52.

Williams, A. and Amris, K. (2007) 'Chronic pain in survivors of torture', *Pain*, 15(7).

Williams, L. (1995) 'Recovered memories of abuse in women with documented child sexual victimization histories', *Journal of Traumatic Stress*, 8, 649–673.

Williams, Lord (1997) *Childhood matters: Report of the National Commission of Inquiry into the prevention of child abuse, Vol 1: The report*, London: The Stationery Office.

Williams, R. (2012a) 'Rochdale child abuse case: exploited girls faced "absolute disrespect"', *Guardian*, 20 November.

Williams, R. (2012b) 'Rochdale police and council "repeatedly warned" about sex abuse risk in town', *Guardian*, 27 September.

Williams, R. (2015) 'Young victims of sexual abuse should get help in their local area, not far away', *Guardian,* 9 June.

Williamson, D., Thompson, T., Anda, R., Dietz, W. and Felitti, V. (2002) 'Body weight, obesity, and self-reported abuse in childhood', *International Journal of Obesity*, 26(8): 1075–82.

Wilson, S., Cunningham-Burley, S., Bancroft, A., Backett-Milburn, K. and Masters, H. (2007) 'Young people, biographical narratives and the life grid: young people's accounts of parental substance use', *Qualitative Research*, 7(1): 135–51.

Wolak, J., Finkelhor, D., Mitchell, K. and Ybarra, M. (2008) 'Online "predators" and their victims: myths, realities and implications for prevention and treatment', *American Psychologist*, 63: 111–28.

Wood, C. (1994) 'The parental alienation syndrome: a dangerous aura of reliability', *Loyala of Los Angeles Law Review*, 29: 1367–415.

Woods, J. (2012) 'Jamie is 13 and hasn't even kissed a girl. But he's now on the Sex Offender Register after online porn warped his mind', *Daily Mail*, 26 April.

Wortley, R. and Smallbone, S. (2006) 'Applying situational principles to sexual offences against children', in R. Wortley and S. Smallbone (eds), *Situational prevention of child sexual abuse*, Crime Prevention Studies, vol. 19, Monsey, NY: Criminal Justice Press.

Wosu, A., Gelaye, B. and Williams, M. (2015a) 'Childhood sexual abuse and posttraumatic stress disorder among pregnant and postpartum women: review of the literature', *Archives Women's Mental Health*, February 18(1): 61-72.

Wosu,A., Gelaye, B. and Williams, M. (2015b) 'History of childhood sexual abuse and risk of prenatal and postpartum depression or depressive symptoms: an epidemiologic review,' *Archives Women's Mental Health*, October, 18(5): 659-71.

Wright, L. (1994) 'Child care demons', *New Yorker*, 3 October.

Ybarra, M., Mitchell, K., Hamburger, M., Diener-West, M. and Lea, P. (2011) 'X-rated material and perpetration of sexually aggressive behavior among children and adolescents: is there a link?', *Aggressive Behavior*, 37(1):1-18.

Young, J. (2009) 'Moral panic: its origins in resistance, resentment and the translation of fantasy into reality', *British Journal of Criminology*, 49(1): 4–16.

Young, L. (1992) 'Sexual abuse and the problem of embodiment', *Child Abuse & Neglect*, 16(1): 89–100.

de Young, M. (2000) *'The devil goes abroad': The Export of the Ritual Abuse Moral Panic,* The British Criminology Conference: Selected Proceedings, Volume 3, Papers from the BSC Conference, Liverpool.

de Young, M. (2004) *The day care ritual abuse moral panic,* Jefferson, NC: McFarland & Co.

Youngson, S. (1993) 'Ritual abuse: consequences for professionals', *Child Abuse Review*, 2(4): 251–62.

de Zulueta, F. (2006) *From pain to violence: The traumatic roots of destructiveness,* Chichester: John Wiley.

Index

About the authors

Sarah Nelson

Dr Sarah Nelson, who comes from Aberdeenshire, has been a researcher, writer and campaigner on issues of sexual violence and abuse for more than 30 years. Her book *Incest: Fact and Myth* was influential as the first British book to highlight childhood sexual abuse as a gendered abuse of power.

A graduate of Edinburgh and Strathclyde Universities, she entered professional journalism, where she covered closely the Orkney child abuse case and Inquiry, before returning to academic research. She has since carried out qualitative research at both the Centre for Research on Families and Relationships, University of Edinburgh, and the University of Dundee. This includes studies on mental health and childhood sexual abuse (CSA) in female and male survivors, physical health in CSA survivors and community prevention against sex offending. She has also published on abused young people and schools, on organised abuse and on good practice with survivors in primary care. She contributes regularly to conferences and media discussions. Sarah was an adviser to the Scottish Government's Survivor Scotland team from 2006 to 2011, and adviser to the Scottish Parliament's Inquiry into Child Sexual Exploitation in Scotland (Scottish Parliament, 2014).

Outside of work her enthusiasms are hillwalking, playing music and supporting Aberdeen FC.

Norma Baldwin

Professor Norma Baldwin is Associate of the Social Dimensions of Health Institute (Dundee and St Andrews Universities), Professor of Child Care and Protection [emeritus] at Dundee University, former head of social work at Dundee University and honorary professor at the University of Warwick. She was Chair of the Scottish Executive working group which advised on the development of an Integrated Assessment Framework for all children. Her research, policy and publication interests involve links between disadvantage and harm to children's development, safety and wellbeing, and the assessment of need in families and in communities. She has worked extensively with local authorities and voluntary sector agencies in evaluating services and developing holistic, integrated models of child care and protection, which promote partnership models of family support, preventive services and community safety. Norma is a trustee of the Scottish charity Circle (FSU Scotland), which works with disadvantaged children and families.

Liz Davies

Dr Liz Davies is a Reader in Child Protection (Emeritus) at London Metropolitan University where she has taught on the social work programme since 2002. As a registered social worker, social activist and academic she has written widely on the subject of child protection with a focus on the investigation of organised abuse and investigative interviewing. Her PhD thesis was titled 'Protecting children; a critical contribution to policy and practice'. In the 1990s, she exposed the abuse of children in Islington children's homes and continues to support Islington survivors. She later worked as Child Protection Manager in the London Borough of Harrow where she developed innovative child protection work with the police, closely involving whole-school training and close links with local communities. Liz regularly contributes to the media and political processes and supports the survivor campaign WhiteFlowers (http://whiteflowerscampaign.org).